SOMETHING ABOUT THE AUTHOR®

Something about
the Author *was named
an* ***"Outstanding
Reference Source,"***
*the highest honor given
by the American
Library Association
Reference and Adult
Services Division.*

ISSN 0276-816X

SOMETHING ABOUT THE AUTHOR®

**Facts and Pictures about Authors
and Illustrators of Books for Young People**

volume 125

GALE GROUP

THOMSON LEARNING

*Detroit • New York • San Diego • San Francisco
Boston • New Haven, Conn. • Waterville, Maine
London • Munich*

STAFF

Scot Peacock, *Managing Editor, Literature Product*
Mark W. Scott, *Publisher, Literature Product*

Frank Castronova, Lisa Kumar, *Senior Editors;* Katy Balcer, Sara L. Constantakis, Kristen A. Dorsch, Thomas McMahon, Colleen Laine Tavor, *Editors;* Alana Joli Foster, Motoko Fujishiro Huthwaite, Arlene M. Johnson, Jennifer Kilian, Michelle Poole, Thomas Wiloch, *Associate Editors;* Madeline Harris, Maikue Vang, *Assistant Editors;* Anna Marie Dahn, Judith L. Pyko, *Administrative Support;* Joshua Kondek, Mary Ruby, *Technical Training Specialists*

Alan Hedblad, Joyce Nakamura, *Managing Editors*
Susan M. Trosky, *Literature Content Coordinator*

Victoria B. Cariappa, *Research Manager;* Tracie A. Richardson, *Project Coordinator;* Barbara McNeil, Gary J. Oudersluys, Cheryl L. Warnock, *Research Specialists;* Ron Morelli, Tamara C. Nott, *Research Associates;* Nicodemus Ford, *Research Assistant;* Michelle Campbell, *Administrative Assistant*

Maria L. Franklin, *Permissions Manager;* Shalice Shah-Caldwell, *Permissions Associate*

Mary Beth Trimper, *Manager, Composition and Prepress;* Dorothy Maki, *Manufacturing Manager;* Stacy Melson, *Buyer*

Barbara J. Yarrow, *Manager, Imaging and Multimedia Content;* Randy Bassett, *Imaging Supervisor;* Robert Duncan, Dan Newell, *Imaging Specialists;* Pamela A. Reed, *Imaging Coordinator;* Dean Dauphinais, *Senior Editor;* Robyn V. Young, *Project Manager;* Kelly A. Quin, *Editor*

Library of Congress Catalog Card Number 72-27107

ISBN 0-7876-4713-6
ISSN 0276-816X

Printed in the United States of America

10 9 8 7 6 5 4 3 2 1

Contents

Authors in Forthcoming Volumes

Below are some of the authors and illustrators that will be featured in upcoming volumes of *SATA*. These include new entries on the swiftly rising stars of the field, as well as completely revised and updated entries (indicated with *) on some of the most notable and best-loved creators of books for children.

Marc Aronson: Aronson writes nonfiction titles for young readers that have been praised for the author's engrossing prose style and unique approach to source materials. In addition to his acclaimed 1998 book *Art Attack: A Short Cultural History of the Avant-Garde,* Aronson penned *Sir Walter Raleigh and the Quest for El Dorado,* a work for which he was named the first winner of the Robert F. Sibert Award for the "most distinguished informational book for children published in 2000."

Christopher Bing: Bing is a professional illustrator, contributing editorial and political cartoons to such nationally prominent periodicals as the *New York Times* and the *Washington Post.* In 2000 he produced a new version of Ernest L. Thayer's classic nineteenth-century baseball poem, "Casey at the Bat." In his work, *Casey at the Bat: A Ballad of the Republic Sung in the Year 1888,* Bing uses a pen-and-ink on scratchboard technique to create the look of a century-old scrapbook. *Casey at the Bat* was named a Caldecott Honor Book.

*Anita Desai: Desai focuses her novels upon the personal struggles of her Indian characters to cope with the problems of contemporary life. In this way, she manages to portray the cultural and social changes that her native country has undergone since the departure of the British. Desai has been shortlisted for Britain's prestigious Booker Prize three times: in 1980, for *Clear Light of Day;* in 1984, for *In Custody;* and in 1999, for *Fasting, Feasting.* Her works for children include *The Peacock Garden* and *The Village By the Sea: An Indian Family Story.*

*Sara Fanelli: Fanelli is an award-winning Italian artist whose illustrations combine collage and sketches in crayon to create effects critics find striking and humorous. Many critics have noted that Fanelli's whimsy extends beyond her spectacular illustrations to the presentation of her story and its unusual plot elements. *Button, Wolf!,* and *Dear Diary* are among her works.

Colby Hol: A native of the Dutch city of Leiden, Hol writes and illustrates picture books for young readers that have been published throughout Europe and other parts of the world. An art teacher to young children by profession, Hol creates colorful collages from magazine paper to illustrate charming stories that often feature curious and gentle animals. Many of her works have been translated into English, including *A Visit to the Farm* and *The Birth of the Moon.*

Norma Howe: In her novels for young adults, Howe explores themes ranging from creationism, peer group pressure, and sexuality to questions of free will and gun control. Howe is the author of the critically acclaimed 1999 work *The Adventures of Blue Avenger* and its sequel, *Blue Avenger Cracks the Code.*

*Katherine Kurtz: Kurtz's love of history has helped to shape the medieval worlds of her fantasy novels, as well as her books set in twentieth-century England and Scotland. Her "Deryni" series, composed of four trilogies plus additional novels, focuses on the land of Gwynedd in the Eleven Kingdoms, a world based on medieval Wales.

*Elenore Schmid: The works of Schmid, a prolific illustrator and writer from Switzerland, span a variety of genres, from board books for very young children to elaborately illustrated picture books that present both clever tales and scientific facts. Many of her books have been published in German, and a number of them have appeared in English translation as well. Among her most popular works is *The Living Earth.* In 2000 she published *Hare's Christmas Gift.*

Lemony Snicket: Snicket, aka Daniel Handler, is best known for his droll, mock-Gothic juvenile series "A Series of Unfortunate Events." The books follow siblings Violet, Klaus, and Sunny Baudelaire who not only lose their parents in a fire, but are then set upon by the vile Count Olaf, whose one goal in life is to bilk the children out of their fortune. *The Hostile Hospital,* the eighth title in the projected thirteen-book series, was published in 2001.

Introduction

Something about the Author (*SATA*) is an ongoing reference series that examines the lives and works of authors and illustrators of books for children. *SATA* includes not only well-known writers and artists but also less prominent individuals whose works are just coming to be recognized. This series is often the only readily available information source on emerging authors and illustrators. You'll find *SATA* informative and entertaining, whether you are a student, a librarian, an English teacher, a parent, or simply an adult who enjoys children's literature.

What's Inside SATA

SATA provides detailed information about authors and illustrators who span the full time range of children's literature, from early figures like John Newbery and L. Frank Baum to contemporary figures like Judy Blume and Richard Peck. Authors in the series represent primarily English-speaking countries, particularly the United States, Canada, and the United Kingdom. Also included, however, are authors from around the world whose works are available in English translation. The writings represented in *SATA* include those created intentionally for children and young adults as well as those written for a general audience and known to interest younger readers. These writings cover the entire spectrum of children's literature, including picture books, humor, folk and fairy tales, animal stories, mystery and adventure, science fiction and fantasy, historical fiction, poetry and nonsense verse, drama, biography, and nonfiction.

Obituaries are also included in *SATA* and are intended not only as death notices but also as concise overviews of people's lives and work. Additionally, each edition features newly revised and updated entries for a selection of *SATA* listees who remain of interest to today's readers and who have been active enough to require extensive revisions of their earlier biographies.

New Autobiography Feature

Beginning with Volume 103, *SATA* features three or more specially commissioned autobiographical essays in each volume. These unique essays, averaging about ten thousand words in length and illustrated with an abundance of personal photos, present an entertaining and informative first-person perspective on the lives and careers of prominent authors and illustrators profiled in *SATA*.

Two Convenient Indexes

In response to suggestions from librarians, *SATA* indexes no longer appear in every volume but are included in alternate (odd-numbered) volumes of the series, beginning with Volume 57.

SATA continues to include two indexes that cumulate with each alternate volume: the Illustrations Index, arranged by the name of the illustrator, gives the number of the volume and page where the illustrator's work appears in the current volume as well as all preceding volumes in the series; the Author Index gives the number of the volume in which a person's biographical sketch, autobiographical essay, or obituary appears in the current volume as well as all preceding volumes in the series.

These indexes also include references to authors and illustrators who appear in Gale's *Yesterday's Authors of Books for Children, Children's Literature Review,* and *Something about the Author Autobiography Series.*

Easy-to-Use Entry Format

Whether you're already familiar with the *SATA* series or just getting acquainted, you will want to be aware of the kind of information that an entry provides. In every *SATA* entry the editors attempt to give as complete a picture of the person's life and work as possible. A typical entry in *SATA* includes the following clearly labeled information sections:

• *PERSONAL:* date and place of birth and death, parents' names and occupations, name of spouse, date of marriage, names of children, educational institutions attended, degrees received, religious and political affiliations, hobbies and other interests.

• *ADDRESSES:* complete home, office, electronic mail, and agent addresses, whenever available.

• *CAREER:* name of employer, position, and dates for each career post; art exhibitions; military service; memberships and offices held in professional and civic organizations.

• *AWARDS, HONORS:* literary and professional awards received.

• *WRITINGS:* title-by-title chronological bibliography of books written and/or illustrated, listed by genre when known; lists of other notable publications, such as plays, screenplays, and periodical contributions.

• *ADAPTATIONS:* a list of films, television programs, plays, CD-ROMs, recordings, and other media presentations that have been adapted from the author's work.

• *WORK IN PROGRESS:* description of projects in progress.

• *SIDELIGHTS:* a biographical portrait of the author or illustrator's development, either directly from the biographee—and often written specifically for the *SATA* entry—or gathered from diaries, letters, interviews, or other published sources.

• *BIOGRAPHICAL AND CRITICAL SOURCES:* cites sources quoted in "Sidelights" along with references for further reading.

• *EXTENSIVE ILLUSTRATIONS:* photographs, movie stills, book illustrations, and other interesting visual materials supplement the text.

How a SATA Entry Is Compiled

A *SATA* entry progresses through a series of steps. If the biographee is living, the *SATA* editors try to secure information directly from him or her through a questionnaire. From the information that the biographee supplies, the editors prepare an entry, filling in any essential missing details with research and/or telephone interviews. If possible, the author or illustrator is sent a copy of the entry to check for accuracy and completeness.

If the biographee is deceased or cannot be reached by questionnaire, the *SATA* editors examine a wide variety of published sources to gather information for an entry. Biographical and bibliographic sources are consulted, as are book reviews, feature articles, published interviews, and material sometimes obtained from the biographee's family, publishers, agent, or other associates.

Entries that have not been verified by the biographees or their representatives are marked with an asterisk (*).

Contact the Editor

We encourage our readers to examine the entire *SATA* series. Please write and tell us if we can make *SATA* even more helpful to you. Give your comments and suggestions to the editor:

BY MAIL: Editor, *Something about the Author,* The Gale Group, 27500 Drake Rd., Farmington Hills, MI 48331-3535.

BY TELEPHONE: (800) 877-GALE

BY FAX: (248) 699-8054

Something about the Author Product Advisory Board

The editors of *Something about the Author* are dedicated to maintaining a high standard of excellence by publishing comprehensive, accurate, and highly readable entries on a wide array of writers for children and young adults. In addition to the quality of the content, the editors take pride in the graphic design of the series, which is intended to be orderly yet inviting, allowing readers to utilize the pages of *SATA* easily and with efficiency. Despite the longevity of the *SATA* print series, and the success of its format, we are mindful that the vitality of a literary reference product is dependent on its ability to serve its users over time. As literature, and attitudes about literature, constantly evolve, so do the reference needs of students, teachers, scholars, journalists, researchers, and book club members. To be certain that we continue to keep pace with the expectations of our customers, the editors of *SATA* listen carefully to their comments regarding the value, utility, and quality of the series. Librarians, who have firsthand knowledge of the needs of library users, are a valuable resource for us. The *Something about the Author* Product Advisory Board, made up of school, public, and academic librarians, is a forum to promote focused feedback about *SATA* on a regular basis. The five-member advisory board includes the following individuals, whom the editors wish to thank for sharing their expertise:

- **Eva M. Davis,** Teen Services Librarian, Plymouth District Library, Plymouth, Michigan

- **Joan B. Eisenberg,** Lower School Librarian, Milton Academy, Milton, Massachusetts

- **Francisca Goldsmith,** Teen Services Librarian, Berkeley Public Library, Berkeley, California

- **Monica F. Irlbacher,** Young Adult Librarian, Middletown Thrall Library, Middletown, New York

- **Caryn Sipos,** Librarian--Young Adult Services, King County Library System, Washington

Acknowledgments

Grateful acknowledgment is made to the following publishers, authors, and artists whose works appear in this volume.

ARUEGO, JOSE (ESPIRITU). Aruego, Jose, and Ariane Dewey, illustrators. From an illustration in *Mushroom in the Rain,* by Mirra Ginsburg. Adapted from the Russian of V. Suteyev. Aladdin Paperbacks, 1990. Illustrations copyright © 1974 by Jose Aruego and Ariane Dewey. Reproduced by permission of Simon & Schuster, Inc./ Aruego, Jose, and Ariane Dewey, illustrators. From an illustration in *Antarctic Antics: A Book of Penguin Poems,* by Judy Sierra. Harcourt Brace, 1998. Illustrations copyright © 1998 by Jose Aruego and Ariane Dewey. All rights reserved. Reproduced by permission of the Sheldon Fogelman Agency, Inc. and Harcourt, Inc./ Aruego, Jose, and Ariane Dewey, illustrators. From an illustration in *Safe, Warm, and Snug,* by Stephen R. Swinburne. Harcourt Brace, 1999. Illustrations copyright © 1999 by Jose Aruego and Ariane Dewey. All rights reserved. Reproduced by permission of Sheldon Fogelman Agency, Inc., and Harcourt, Inc./ Aruego, Jose, and Ariane Dewey, illustrators. From an illustration in *Mouse In Love,* by Robert Kraus. Orchard Books, 2000. Illustrations copyright © 2000 by Jose Aruego and Ariane Dewey. Reproduced by permission of the publisher, Orchard Books, New York.

ASHE, GEOFFREY (THOMAS). All photographs reproduced by permission of the author.

BAUER, STEVEN. Sneed, Brad, illustrator. From an illustration in *The Strange and Wonderful Tale of Robert McDoodle: (The Boy Who Wanted to Be a Dog),* by Steven Bauer. Simon & Schuster, 1999. Illustrations copyright © 1999 by Brad Sneed. Reproduced by permission of Simon & Schuster, Inc./ Raglin, Tim, illustrator. From a jacket of *A Cat of a Different Color,* by Steven Bauer. Delacorte Press, 2000. Jacket illustration © 2000 by Tim Raglin. Reproduced by permission of Delacorte Press, an imprint of Random House Children's Books, a division of Random House, Inc.

BEATON, CLARE. Beaton, Clare, illustrator. From an illustration in *Mother Goose Remembers,* by Clare Beaton. Barefoot Books, 2000. Illustrations copyright © 2000 by Clara Barton. Reproduced by permission./ Beaton, Clare, illustrator. From a cover of *Opposites,* by Clare Beaton. Barron's, 1993. Reproduced by permission of Barron's Educational Series, Inc./ Beaton, Clare, photograph. Reproduced by permission.

BLAKE, QUENTIN (SAXBY). Blake, Quentin, illustrator. From an illustration in *The BFG,* by Roald Dahl. Farrar, Straus, and Giroux, 1982. Pictures copyright © 1982 by Quentin Blake. Reproduced by permission of Farrar, Straus and Giroux, LLC and A.P. Watt, Ltd. on behalf of Quentin Blake. www.apwatt.co.uk./ Blake, Quentin, illustrator. From an illustration in *Matilda,* by Roald Dahl. Puffin Books, 1988. Text copyright © Roald Dahl, 1988. Illustrations copyright © Quentin Blake, 1988. All rights reserved. Reproduced by permission./ Blake, Quentin, photograph. Reproduced by permission.

CORCORAN, BARBARA (ASENATH). All photographs reproduced by permission of the author.

CUNNINGHAM, LAWRENCE J. Cunningham, Lawrence J., photograph. Reproduced by permission.

DOUCET, SHARON ARMS. Doucet, Sharon Arms, photograph. Reproduced by permission.

FALCONER, IAN. Falconer, Ian, illustrator. From an illustration in *Olivia,* by Ian Falconer. Atheneum, 2000. Copyright © 2000 Ian Falconer. Reproduced by permission of Atheneum Books for Young Readers, an imprint of Simon & Schuster Children's Publishing Division.

FITZPATRICK, MARIE-LOUISE. Fitzpatrick, Marie-Louise, illustrator. From an illustration in *The Long March: The Choctaw's Gift to Irish Famine Relief,* by Marie-Louise Fitzpatrick. Beyond Words Publishing, Inc., 1998. Text and illustrations copyright © 1998 by Marie-Louise Fitzpatrick./ Fitzpatrick, Marie-Louise, illustrator. From an illustration in *The Sleeping Giant,* by Marie-Louise Fitzpatrick. Wolfhound Press Ltd., 1998. Text and illustration © Marie-Louise Fitzpatrick 1991. Reproduced by permission./ Fitzpatrick, Marie-Louise, illustrator. From an illustration in *Lizzy and Skunk,* by Marie-Louise Fitzpatrick. Dorling Kindersley Publishing, Inc., 2000. Copyright © 2000 by Marie-Louise Fitzpatrick. Reproduced by permission.

FLORIAN, DOUGLAS. Florian, Douglas, illustrator. From an illustration in *Very Scary,* by Tony Johnston. Voyager Books, 1999. Illustrations copyright © 1995 by Douglas Florian. Reproduced by permission of Harcourt, Inc. /Florian, Douglas, illustrator. From an illustration in *Insectlopedia,* by Douglas Florian. Harcourt, Inc., 1998. Copyright © 1998 by Douglas Florian. Reproduced by permission./ Florian, Douglas, illustrator. From an illustration in *Mammalabilia,* by Douglas Florian. Harcourt Brace, 2000. Copyright © 2000 by Douglas Florian. Reproduced by permission of Harcourt, Inc./ Florian, Douglas, illustrator. From an illustration in *Lizards, Frogs, and Polliwogs,* by Douglas Florian. Harcourt, Inc., 2001. Copyright © 2001 by Douglas Florian. Reproduced by permission.

Reproduced bypermission./ Dooling, Michael, illustrator. From a jacket of **Robin Hook: Pirate Hunter!** by Eric A. Kimmel. Scholastic, Inc., 2001. Jacket art © 2001 by Michael Dooling. Reproduced by permission./ Kimmel, Eric, photograph. Reproduced by permission.

KROHN, KATHERINE E(LIZABETH). Princess Diana, photograph. AP/Wide World Photos. From a photograph in **Princess Diana,** by Katherine E. Krohn. First Avenue, 2000. Reproduced by permission of AP/Wide World Photos./ Oakley, Annie, photograph. Ohio Historical Society. From **Women of the Wild West,** by Katherine E. Krohn. Lerner, 2000. Reproduced by permission.

KROLL, STEVEN. Andreasen, Dan, illustrator. From a cover of **The Story of the Star-Spangled Banner: By the Dawn's Early Light,** by Steven Kroll. Scholastic, Inc., 2000. Illustrations copyright © 1994 by Dan Andreasen. Reproduced by permission./ Fiore, Peter, illustrator. From a cover of **The Boston Tea Party,** by Steven Kroll. Holiday House, Inc., 1998. Illustrations copyright © 1998 by Peter Fiore. Reproduced by permission./ Gott, Barry, illustrator. From an illustration in **Patches Lost and Found,** by Steven Kroll. Winslow Press, 2001. Illustration copyright (c) 2001 by Barry Gott. Reproduced by permission.

LAROSE, LINDA. LaRose, Linda, photograph. Reproduced by permission.

LEMIEUX, A(NNE) C(ONNELLY). Bober, Richard, illustrator. From a cover of **The Fairy Lair: A Special Place,** by Anne LeMieux. Aladdin Paperbacks, 1997. Cover illustration copyright © 1997 by Richard Bober. Reproduced by permission of the illustrator./ Beekman, Doug, illustrator. From a cover of **The Fairy Lair: A Hidden Place,** by Anne C. LeMieux. Aladdin Paperbacks, 1998. Cover illustration copyright © 1998 by Doug Beekman. Reproduced by permission of the illustrator./ Beekman, Doug, illustrator. From a cover of**The Fairy Lair: A Magic Place,** by Anne C. LeMieux. Aladdin Paperbacks, 1998. Cover illustration copyright (c) 1998 by Doug Beekman. Reproduced by permission of the illustrator.

MACMILLAN, DIANNE M(ARIE). Nathan, Charlotte, illustrator. From an illustration in **Tet: Vietnamese New Year,** by Dianne M. MacMillan. Enslow Publishers, Inc., 1994. Reproduced by permission./ Eastman, Don, photographer. From a cover of **Missions of the Los Angeles Area,** by Dianne M. MacMillan. Lerner Publications, 1996. Reproduced by permission of The Lerner Group./ Ellis, Gerry, photographer. From a cover of **Cheetahs,** by Dianne M. MacMillan. Carolrhoda Books, 1997. Photographs copyright © 1997 by Gerry Ellis. Reproduced by permission of The Lerner Group./ MacMillan, James R., photographer. From a cover of **Japanese Children's Day and the Obon Festival,** by Dianne M. MacMillan. Enslow Publishers, Inc., 1997. Reproduced by permission.

MAVOR, SALLEY. Mavor, Salley, photograph. Reproduced by permission.

MEDDAUGH, SUSAN. Meddaugh, Susan, illustrator. From an illustration in **Martha Speaks,** by Susan Meddaugh. Houghton Mifflin Company, 1992. Copyright © 1992 by Susan Meddaugh. Reproduced by permission./ Meddaugh, Susan, illustrator. From an illustration in **Cinderella's Rat,** by Susan Meddaugh. Houghton Mifflin Company, 1997. Copyright © 1997 by Susan Meddaugh. Reproduced by permission./ Meddaugh, Susan, illustrator. From an illustration in **The Best Halloween of All,** by Susan Wojciechowski. Candlewick Press, 2000. Illustrations copyright © 1992 by Susan Meddaugh. Reproduced by permission of Walker Books Ltd. Published in the U.S. by Candlewick Press, Inc., Cambridge, MA./ Meddaugh, Susan, photograph by Ruth De Mauro. © 1992 by Ruth De Mauro. Reproduced by permission.

NATTI, SUSANNA. Natti, Susanna, illustrator. From an illustration in **Beany and the Dreaded Wedding,** by Susan Wojciechowski. Candlewick Press, 2000. Illustrations copyright © 2000 by Susanna Natti. Reproduced by permission of Walker Books Ltd. In the U. S. by Candlewick Press, Inc., Cambridge, MA./ Natti, Susanna, illustrator. From an illustration in **Beany (Not Beanhead) and the Magic Crystal,** by Susan Wojciechowski. Candlewick Press, 2001. Illustrations copyright © 1997 by Susanna Natti. Reproduced by permission of Walker Books Ltd. In the U. S. by Candlewick Press, Inc., Cambridge, MA.

NOBLE, MARTY. Noble, Marty, illustrator. From an illustration in **East o' the Sun and West o' the Moon and Other Fairy Tales,** by George Webbe Dasent. Dover Publications, Inc., 1996. Reproduced by permission./ Noble, Marty, photograph. Reproduced by permission.

NUWER, HENRY J. Owens, Jesse, photograph. © Corbis-Bettmann. From a photograph in **The Legend of Jesse Owens,** by Hank Nuwer. Franklin Watts, 1998. Reproduced by permission of Corbis Images./ High school gang, photograph. Liaison Agency, Inc. From a photograph in **High School Hazing: When Rites Become Wrongs,** by Hank Nuwer. Franklin Watts, 2000. Reproduced by permission of GettyImages.

RODRIGUEZ, LUIS J. Vazquez, Carlos, illustrator. From an illustration in **America Is Her Name,** by Luis J. Rodriguez. Curbstone Press, 1996. Illustrations copyright © 1998 Carlos Vazquez. Reproduced by permission./ Kramer, Chuck, illustrator. From a cover of **The Concrete River,** written by Luis J. Rodriguez. Curbstone Press, 1996. Copyright

SOMETHING ABOUT THE AUTHOR

Annie-Jo
  See BLANCHARD, Patricia

*   *   *

ARUEGO, Jose (Espiritu) 1932-

Personal

Born August 9, 1932, in Manila, Philippines; son of Jose M. (a lawyer) and Constancia (Espiritu) Aruego; married Ariane Dewey (an illustrator), January 27, 1961 (divorced, 1973); children: Juan. *Education:* University of the Philippines, B.A., 1953, LL.B., 1955; Parsons School of Design, Certificate in Graphic Arts and Advertising, 1959.

Addresses

Home—New York, NY. *Office*—c/o Author Mail, HarperCollins, 10 E. 53rd St., 20th Fl., New York, NY 10022.

Career

Village Display Co., New York, NY, apprentice, 1959-60; Hayden Publishing Co., New York, NY, designer, 1960-62; Mervin & Jesse Levine (fashion advertising agency), New York, NY, mechanical boardman, 1963-64; Norman Associates (studio), New York, NY, mechanical boardman, 1964-65; Ashton B. Collins, Inc. (advertising agency), New York, NY, assistant art director, 1965-68; freelance cartoonist; writer and illustrator of books for children.

Awards, Honors

Outstanding picture book of the year awards from the *New York Times,* 1970, for *Juan and the Asuangs: A Tale of Philippine Ghosts and Spirits,* 1971, for *The Day They Parachuted Cats on Borneo: A Drama of Ecology,* and 1972, for *Look What I Can Do!; Whose Mouse Are You?,* 1970, *Milton the Early Riser,* 1972, *Mushroom in the Rain,* 1974, and *We Hide, You Seek,* 1979, were American Library Association Notable Book selections; *Look What I Can Do!,* 1972, *The Chick and the Duckling,* 1973, *A Crocodile's Tale,* 1973, and *Owliver,* 1974, were included in Children's Book Council Showcase; *A Crocodile's Tale,* 1972, *Marie Louise and Christophe,* 1974, and *Mushroom in the Rain,* 1974, were included in the American Institute of Graphic Arts' list of children's books of the year; Brooklyn Art Books for Children citations, 1973, for *Leo the Late Bloomer,* and 1974, for *Milton the Early Riser;* honor award, *Horn Book-Boston Globe,* 1974, for *Herman the Helper;* Society of Illustrators citation, 1976, for *Milton the Early Riser;* Outstanding Filipino Abroad in Arts award, Philippine government, 1976; Gold Medal, Internationale Buchkunst-Ausstellung (Leipzig, Germany), 1977, for *Mushroom in the Rain.*

Writings

SELF-ILLUSTRATED; FOR CHILDREN

The King and His Friends, Scribner, 1969.

The award-winning artwork for **Mushroom** in the **Rain** *adapted by Mirra Ginsberg is the result of a collaboration between Jose Aruego and fellow illustrator Ariane Dewey.*

Juan and the Asuangs: A Tale of Philippine Ghosts and Spirits, Scribner, 1970.

Parakeets and Peach Pies, Parents' Magazine Press, 1970.

Symbiosis: A Book of Unusual Friendships, Scribner, 1970.

Pilyo the Piranha, Macmillan, 1971.

(With Ariane Aruego) *Look What I Can Do!,* Scribner, 1971.

(With Ariane Aruego) *A Crocodile's Tale,* Scribner, 1972.

(With Ariane Dewey) *We Hide, You Seek,* Greenwillow, 1979.

(With Ariane Dewey) *Rockabye Crocodile,* Greenwillow, 1988.

ILLUSTRATOR

Robert Kraus, *Whose Mouse Are You?,* Macmillan, 1970.

Kay Smith, *Parakeets and Peach Pies,* Parents' Magazine Press, 1970.

Jack Prelutsky, *Toucans Two, and Other Poems,* Macmillan, 1970.

Charlotte Pomerantz, *The Day They Parachuted Cats on Borneo: A Drama of Ecology* (play), Young Scott Books, 1971.

Christina Rossetti, *What Is Pink?,* Macmillan, 1971.

Robert Kraus, *Leo the Late Bloomer,* Windmill Books, 1971.

(With Ariane Aruego) V. Suteyev, *The Chick and the Duckling,* translated by Mirra Ginsburg, Macmillan, 1972.

(With Ariane Aruego) Robert Kraus, *Milton the Early Riser,* Windmill, 1972.

Elizabeth Coatsworth, *Good Night,* Macmillan, 1972.

Norma Faber, *Never Say Ugh to a Bug,* Greenwillow, 1979.

ILLUSTRATOR; WITH ARIANE DEWEY

Natalie Savage Carlson, *Marie Louise and Christophe,* Scribner, 1974.

V. Suteyev (adapted by Mirra Ginsburg), *Mushroom in the Rain,* Macmillan, 1974.

Robert Kraus, *Herman the Helper,* Windmill Books, 1974.

Robert Kraus, *Owliver,* Windmill Books, 1974.

Doroty O. Van Woerkom (adaptor) *Sea Frog, City Frog* (from a Japanese folktale), Macmillan, 1975.

Mirra Ginsburg, *How the Sun Was Brought Back to the Sky* (adapted from a Slovenian folktale), Macmillan, 1975.

Robert Kraus, *Three Friends,* Windmill Books, 1975.

Natalie Savage Carlson, *Marie Louise's Heyday,* Scribner, 1975.

Robert Kraus, *Boris Bad Enough,* Windmill, 1976.

Mirra Ginsburg, *Two Greedy Bears* (adapted from a Hungarian folktale), Macmillan, 1976.

Mirra Ginsburg, *The Strongest One of All* (adapted from a Caucasian folktale), Greenwillow, 1977.

Natalie Savage Carlson, *Runaway Marie Louise,* Scribner, 1977.

Robert Kraus, *Noel the Coward,* Windmill, 1977.

David Kherdian, editor, *If Dragon Flies Made Honey: Poems,* Morrow, 1977.

Marjorie Weinman Sharmat, *Mitchell Is Moving,* Macmillan, 1978.

Maggie Duff, *Rum Pum Pum: A Folk Tale from India,* Macmillan, 1978.

Robert Kraus, *Musical Max,* Windmill, 1979.

Mitchell Sharmat, *Gregory, the Terrible Eater,* Four Winds Press, 1980.

Robert Kraus, *Mouse Work,* Wanderer, 1980.

Robert Kraus, *Animal Families,* Wanderer, 1980.

Robert Kraus, *Mert the Blurt,* Simon & Schuster, 1980.

Robert Kraus, *Another Mouse to Feed,* Wanderer, 1980.

Mirra Ginsburg, *Where Does the Sun Go at Night?* (adapted from an Armenian song), Greenwillow, 1981.

George Shannon, *Lizard's Song,* Greenwillow, 1981.

George Shannon, *Dance Away,* Greenwillow, 1982.

George Shannon, *The Surprise,* Greenwillow, 1983.

Charlotte Pomerantz, *One Duck, Another Duck,* Greenwillow, 1984.

Robert Kraus, *Where Are You Going, Little Mouse?,* Greenwillow, 1986.

Robert Kraus, *Come Out and Play, Little Mouse,* Greenwillow, 1987.

*Research for the illustrations for Judy Sierra's poetry collection **Antarctic Antics** took Aruego and Dewey on a fact-finding trip to the ends of the Earth ... via the Internet!*

Aruego and Dewey's sensitive pen-and-ink illustrations reveal the universal love of a parent for its young in Stephen R. Swinburne's 1999 book **Safe, Warm, and Snug.**

Crescent Dragonwagon, *Alligator Arrived with Apples: A Potluck Alphabet Feast,* Macmillan, 1987.

Bob Stine, *Pork and Beans: Play Date,* Scholastic, 1989.

Raffi, *Five Little Ducks,* Crown, 1989.

Birthday Rhymes, Special Times, selected by Bobbye S. Goldstein, Delacorte, 1991.

Mirra Ginsburg, *Merry-Go-Round: Four Stories,* Greenwillow, 1992.

Crescent Dragonwagon, *Alligators and Others All Year Long!: A Book of Months,* Macmillan, 1993.

George Shannon, *April Showers,* Greenwillow, 1995.

Craig Kee Strete, *They Thought They Saw Him,* Greenwillow, 1996.

Michael and Mary Beth Sampson, *Star of the Circus,* Holt, 1997.

Robert Kraus, *Little Louie the Baby Bloomer,* HarperCollins, 1998.

Judy Sierra, *Antarctic Antics: A Book of Penguin Poems,* Harcourt, 1998.

George Shannon, *Lizard's Home,* Greenwillow, 1999.

Stephen R. Swinburne, *Safe, Warm, and Snug,* Harcourt Brace, 1999.

Robert Kraus, *Mouse in Love,* Orchard, 2000.

Joseph and James Bruchac, *How Chipmunk Got His Stripes: A Tale of Bragging and Teasing,* Dial, 2001.

Ariane Dewey, *Splash!,* Harcourt, 2001.

Howard Reginald, *The Big, Big Wall,* Harcourt, 2001.

Larry Dane Brimner, *Little One and Big Gray,* HarperCollins, 2002.

OTHER

Illustrator, with Ariane Dewey, of Windmill picture books "Puppet Pal" series, including *Milton the Early Riser Takes a Trip, Owliver the Actor Takes a Bow, Herman the Helper Lends a Hand,* and *Leo the Late Bloomer Bakes a Cake.* Contributor of cartoons to periodicals, including *New Yorker, Look,* and *Saturday Review.*

Sidelights

Author and illustrator Jose Aruego is known for his "imaginative and witty" illustrations, as *Booklist* contributor Emily Melton noted in a review of *Birthday Rhymes, Special Times.* In his nine self-illustrated books, eight works illustrated on his own, and his over forty titles illustrated with his former wife, Ariane Dewey, Aruego has built a body of work noted for its inventiveness, colorful approach, and enduring appeal. Born in the Philippines but a resident of New York City since the mid-1950s, Aruego combines humor and sensitivity in the pen-and-ink drawings of funny animals that have become his hallmark. The award-winning titles *Look What I Can Do!* and *We Hide, You Seek* are representative of his approach of presenting his stories in picture form with little or no accompanying text. *Look What I Can Do!* consists of twenty words, while *We Hide, You Seek* is told in three sentences. Both are coauthored by Ariane Dewey, and both rely on the antics of comical-looking animals to expand and advance the simple text. Besides his own works, Aruego regularly illustrates folktales and original stories for other authors. In all his text and illustrations, his "appeal lies in the universality of his themes, his deep understanding of human nature, and his positive outlook on life," according to Ida J. Appel and Marion P. Turkish in *Language Arts.*

Aruego was born in Manila into a family of lawyers and politicians. His early interests ran not to matters of law, but to comic books and pet animals. At one time, his household included three horses; seven dogs and their puppies; half-a-dozen cats and their kittens; a yard full of chickens, roosters, and pigeons; a pond of frogs, tadpoles, and ducks; and three fat pigs. The happy times Aruego spent in the company of such animals is still apparent in his work. "One thing about my picture books," Aruego explained in the *Fourth Book of Junior Authors and Illustrators,* "they always have funny animals doing funny things.... Most of the characters in my books are animals. It seems no matter how I draw them they look funny." And Appel and Turkish pointed out in *Language Arts* that "Aruego creates unusual animals which have endeared themselves to children as well as adults. With a touch of magic and genius, he manages to change a commonplace theme into an object of irresistible charm."

Despite his lack of interest in legal matters, Aruego followed his father's example and earned a law degree from the University of the Philippines in 1955. Looking back on his career choice, Aruego expresses continued amazement. "I still cannot figure out why I took up law," he wrote in the *Fourth Book of Junior Authors and Illustrators.* "I guess it is because my father is a lawyer, my sister is a lawyer, and all my friends went to law school." It did not take long for Aruego to realize that he was not suited to the legal profession. He practiced law for only three months, handling one case, which he lost.

After abandoning his legal practice, Aruego moved to New York City to pursue his boyhood interest in humorous illustration. He enrolled at the Parsons School of Design, where he studied graphic arts and advertising and developed an interest in line drawing. His first job after graduating in 1959 was at a Greenwich Village studio, where he pasted feathers on angel wings of mannequins. He was laid off shortly after the Christmas season, and for the next six years he worked for advertising agencies, design studios, and magazines. But once he began selling his cartoons to magazines such as the *Saturday Evening Post* and *Look,* he quit the world of advertising for a risky freelance cartooning career. "Every Wednesday I would go to the cartoon editor with fifteen or sixteen drawings in hand, from which he might select one for publication," Aruego said in a biographical portrait released by Greenwillow Books. "The tension was terrible, because selling cartoons was how I made my living. But I learned a lot from the rejected work, so it wasn't wasted. The sink-or-swim experience of drawing cartoons was how I learned to make the most of a small amount of space."

By 1968 Aruego had turned most of his attention to writing and illustrating books for children. His first book, published the following year, was *The King and His Friends.* Illustrated with cartoon-like drawings in red, pink, gray, and tan, *The King and His Friends* is a fantasy about a griffin and two dragons who entertain their friend King Doowah by styling themselves into decorative objects—such as a book stand, a throne, and a bed. *School Library Journal* reviewer Elma Fesler dismissed the tale as "a non-story that serves only to showcase the artistic dexterity of Mr. Aruego," but the book was successful enough to land him illustration work for other authors and to launch his own writing career.

Many of Aruego's most popular books are collaborations with his former wife, with Aruego drawing the outlines and designing the pages and Dewey painting the colors, often using bright school poster paint. After divorcing in 1973, the couple continued their professional partnership, producing *We Hide, You Seek,* one of their enduring favorites, in 1979. Eight years in the making, the twenty-seven-word book uses the game of hide-and-seek to present a lesson in camouflage that both instructs and entertains. A clumsy rhino, joining his East African animal friends in a game of hide-and-seek, bumbles through the jungle, accidentally flushing out the hiders by sneezing, stepping on their tails, or tripping over them. Through careful use of shape and color, Aruego and Dewey hide the animals in their natural settings in such a way that young children can still find them, and then show them clearly jumping out of their cover. "This is done in a series of double-page spreads," explained *New York Times Book Review* contributor William Cole. "First spread a scene full of animals blending with their habitation, second spread with [a] clumsy rhino barging in and sending them fleeing." The story ends playfully with the rhino taking a turn at hiding—cleverly concealing himself in a herd of rhinos. Endpapers identify each species pictured.

The book, which has been continuously in print since 1979, has been widely praised. "It combines an invitation to develop one's powers of observation with the entertainment evolving from antic play," said a *Publishers Weekly* reviewer. "Even in scenes with the wildest

A dreamy-eyed rodent's search for true love is recounted in Robert Kraus's whimsical story **Mouse in Love,** *featuring Aruego and Dewey's humorous pictures.*

unscrambling of creatures ... the chaos is controlled," noted *Wilson Library Journal* critics Donnarae Mac-Cann and Olga Richard, who concluded, "Aruego and Dewey have made an inspired and ingenious book."

Aruego and Dewey do the majority of their collaborative illustration with perennial favorite authors, including Robert Kraus, Mirra Ginsburg, and George Shannon, though they have also worked with a variety of others, including Raffi and Crescent Dragonwagon. With Kraus, the illustrating duo have produced a bevy of humorous and popular picture books: *Leo the Late Bloomer, Herman the Helper, Owliver, Three Friends, Boris Bad Enough, Noel the Coward, Musical Max, Mert the Blurt, Mouse Work,* and several other mouse-related titles.

Kraus's *Musical Max* tells the tale of a musical hippo whose eternal grooving to music drives his neighbors crazy. But when Max decides to put his instruments away, his neighbors complain of the quiet. MacCann and Richard, writing in *Wilson Library Bulletin,* commented that Aruego and Dewey "help Kraus delineate and lampoon Max the Mighty." The two critics praised the "bright, bulbous images" that fit together like a "jigsaw puzzle" and which include "minute mouth and eye details that suggest individuality." Reprising Leo from *Leo the Late Bloomer,* the story of a tiger who finally blooms under the watchful eye of his parents, Kraus presented an older Leo in *Little Louie the Baby Bloomer.* Here Leo the tiger worries about his little brother who cannot do anything right. Leo's parents encourage him to be as patient as they were with him. A reviewer for *Publishers Weekly* drew attention to the "splashy" illustrations that help to make this book "as endearing as Leo's attempts were in the original incarnation." Lisa S. Murphy, writing in *School Library Journal,* observed, "Young readers will appreciate the engaging visual humor as the illustrations show the results of [Leo's] attempts." A mouse is at the center of many of Kraus's rhyming texts, as it is in the 2000 title *Mouse in Love.* "The simple rhyming text is enhanced by Aruego and Dewey's ink-watercolor-and-pastel illustrations," remarked Holly Belli in a *School Library Journal* review. Belli concluded, "This sweetly told tale is sure to be a hit." A contributor for *Publishers Weekly* paid special attention to the "endearingly sketchy mouse" that inhabits "brilliantly blended multicolor backdrops," and further commented that Aruego and Dewey "know how to pack a wide range of experience into a child-size universe."

Working with Ginsburg, Aruego and Dewey have illustrated several books of international folktales, among them *Two Greedy Bears,* which was adapted from a Hungarian tale about two animals with a bad case of sibling rivalry. "Popular illustrators Jose Aruego and Ariane Dewey bring the story to life with their artwork," noted Stephanie G. Miller in a *School Library Journal* review. In *Merry-Go-Round* Ginsburg collects four animal fables. "The simple, spare stories are well served by the bouncy, bright illustrations," noted *Booklist* contributor Annie Ayres, who further commented on the

"amusing" depiction and characterization of the animals by the artists. Virginia Opocensky wrote in *School Library Journal,* "As is typical of the artists' work, bright, incongruous colors prevail in their depiction of expressive, animated creatures."

Collaborating with Shannon, Aruego and Dewey have created lizards and frogs and snakes in a handful of picture book titles. In *Lizard's Song,* a bear tries to copy the very personal song of a lizard, but can only memorize it when he makes its lyrics fit his bear life. Reviewing the Spanish translation of the title, Rose Zertuche, writing in *School Library Journal,* noted the "bright and cheerful" illustrations, whose "colors jump off the pages." Shannon brought Lizard back again in 1999's *Lizard's Home* in which Snake has usurped the protagonist's rock. No amount of pleading will get rid of Snake, so instead Lizard proposes a public contest to decide the true owner of the rock. "Shannon's sprightly, pointed story once again is happily illustrated by Dewey and Aruego's bright watercolors outlined in ink," wrote Donna Beales in a *Booklist* review of *Lizard's Home.* "Aruego and Dewey's characteristic art, favoring high-intensity colors and cartoonlike lines, supports a cast of appealing and expressive characters," noted a reviewer for *Publishers Weekly.* And Patricia Manning, reviewing the same title in *School Library Journal,* praised Aruego and Dewey's "ebullient watercolors of flower-filled landscapes and colorful critters." More such critters abound in Shannon's *April Showers,* which *Horn Book*'s Mary M. Burns described as "bright, splashy, and fun— a spring tonic." Though *Booklist* critic Lauren Peterson felt that Shannon's simple storyline "doesn't quite measure up," she did have appreciative words for Aruego and Dewey's illustrations: "Bright, cheerful watercolors splash across the pages, and although they don't make up for the absence of plot, they do make for lots of fun."

Working with a wide assortment of other authors, Aruego and Dewey have teamed up on picture books from alphabets to birthday rhymes; a collection of the latter are gathered in *Birthday Rhymes, Special Times.* Reviewing that title in *School Library Journal,* Dot Minzer called Aruego's "oversized, whimsical animals that literally leap across each bordered page ... the stars of this anthology." A look at a chameleon's protective coloration is presented in Craig Strete's *They Thought They Saw Him,* with illustrations that "perfectly complement ... [the] witty text," according to Jerry D. Flack in *School Library Journal.* "Children will love the bright and bold colors splashed cheerfully across the double-page watercolor paintings that are both accurate and true to the story, as well as humorous and sly," concluded Flack. *Horn Book* reviewer Hanna B. Zeiger thought that the humor of the chameleon's game and frustration of those trying to find him "are captured perfectly in Aruego and Dewey's striking watercolor-and-ink drawings." A book of months is served up in Dragonwagon's *Alligators and Others All Year Long,* for which Aruego and Dewey provide "fluid, exuberant art," according to a reviewer for *Publishers Weekly.* Reviewing the same title in *School Library Journal*, Judy Constantinides felt that Dewey and Aruego's "pen-and-ink and gouache illustrations are some of the best they've done."

More animals are served up in *Antarctic Antics* by Judy Sierra, *Safe, Warm, and Snug* by Stephen R. Swinburne, and *How Chipmunk Got His Stripes* by Joseph and James Bruchac. A colony of penguins are stage center in the rhyming pages of *Antarctic Antics*. "Whimsical, cartoonlike pen-and-watercolor illustrations of cavorting penguins reinforce the playful mood of the verses," wrote Sally R. Dow in *School Library Journal*. Eleven animal species are portrayed in *Safe, Warm, and Snug*, "an interesting beginning science book," according to Marian Drabkin in *School Library Journal*, which is transformed into a "celebration of the animal world" by Aruego and Dewey's "brightly colored, humorous, and distinctive illustrations." A Native American pourquoi tale is featured in *How Chipmunk Got His Stripes*, for which Aruego and Dewey "create lush landscapes," according to a reviewer for *Publishers Weekly*. "While the story begs to be told, Aruego and Dewey's vibrantly hued trademark watercolors add significantly to the humor," concluded Grace Oliff in a *School Library Journal* review.

Although he has written and illustrated more than sixty children's books, Aruego told his publisher that he is still learning his craft. "Each project teaches me something new and makes me a better artist," he stated in Greenwillow's biographical profile. "Each book brings me closer to children." As Appel and Turkish concluded, "With each succeeding book, Aruego's magic grows, enchanting and delighting both young and old."

Biographical and Critical Sources

BOOKS

Children's Literature Review, Volume 5, Gale (Detroit, MI), 1983, pp. 27-32.
Fourth Book of Junior Authors and Illustrators, H. W. Wilson, 1978, p. 15.

PERIODICALS

Booklist, October 1, 1992, Annie Ayres, review of *Merry-Go-Round*, p. 335; September 15, 1993, Emily Melton, review of *Birthday Rhymes, Special Times*, p. 153; October 15, 1993, p. 445; November 1, 1993, p. 539; April 1, 1995, Lauren Peterson, review of *April Showers*, p. 1428; April 15, 1996, p. 1447; March 15, 1998, p. 1250; May 1, 1998, p. 1520; June 1, 1999, p. 1835; October 1, 1999, Donna Beales, review of *Lizard's Home*, p. 363; July, 2001, Hazel Rochman, review of *Splash!*, p. 2023.
Horn Book, May-June, 1995, Mary M. Burns, review of *April Showers*, pp. 329-330; July-August, 1996, Hanna B. Zeiger, review of *They Thought They Saw Him*, p. 458.
Junior Literary Guild, September, 1979.
Language Arts, May, 1977, Ida J. Appel and Marion P. Turkish, "Profile: The Magic World of Jose Aruego," pp. 585, 590.
New York Times Book Review, October 21, 1979, William Cole, review of *We Hide, You Seek*, p. 52.
Publishers Weekly, September 17, 1979, review of *We Hide, You Seek*, p. 145; August 23, 1993, review of *Alligators and Others All Year Long*, p. 72; March 30, 1998, review of *Little Louie the Baby Bloomer*, pp. 81-82; May 3, 1999, p. 75; September 13, 1999, review of *Lizard's Home*, p. 83; July 24, 2000, review of *Mouse in Love*, p. 93; January 15, 2001, review of *How Chipmunk Got His Stripes*, p. 76.
School Library Journal, May, 1970, Elma Fesler, review of *The King and His Friends*, p. 57; September, 1992, Virginia Opocensky, review of *Merry-Go-Round*, p. 216; June, 1993, Dot Minzer, review of *Birthday Rhymes, Special Times*, p. 97; January, 1994, p. 68; January, 1994, Judy Constantinides, review of *Alligators and Others All Year Long*, p. 106; November, 1994, Rose Zertuche, review of *Lizard's Song*, p. 131; May, 1995, p. 95; March, 1996, p. 192; May, 1996, Jerry D. Flack, review of *They Thought They Saw Him*, p. 100; May, 1998, Sally R. Dow, review of *Antarctic Antics*, p. 137; July, 1998, Lisa S. Murphy, review of *Little Louie the Baby Bloomer*, pp. 77-78; June, 1999, Marian Drabkin, review of *Safe, Warm, and Snug*, p. 122; July, 1999, Stephanie G. Miller, review of *Two Greedy Bears*, p. 54; September, 1999, Patricia Manning, review of *Lizard's Home*, p. 206; August, 2000, Holly Belli, review of *Mouse in Love*, p. 158; February, 2001, Grace Oliff, review of *How Chipmunk Got His Stripes*, p. 109; May, 2001, p. 113.
Wilson Library Bulletin, January, 1980, Donnarae MacCann and Olga Richard, review of *We Hide, You Seek*, p. 325; February, 1988; November, 1991, Donnarae MacCann and Olga Richard, review of *Musical Max*, p. 90.

ON-LINE

Meet Jose Aruego and Ariane Dewey, http://www.eduplace.com/ (June 14, 2001).

OTHER

"Jose Aruego" (biographical profile), Greenwillow Books, c. 1986.*

<hr>

Autobiography Feature

<hr>

Geoffrey (Thomas) Ashe

1923-

I was born in 1923 in a western suburb of London, an only child. My father's people were Protestant Irish, but he was domiciled in England and thoroughly Anglicized. During the part of my childhood that mattered most, he was general manager of a tour agency, a position which meant that he traveled near and far in the British Isles, and in Europe, and my mother and I often traveled with him. My mother came from the large family of an official responsible for lighthouses around Britain's coast, and on her own mother's side was one of the many descendants of "gallant Captain Webb," a naval hero. Their marriage, however, was unfortunate. Their only shared interest that I remember was a fondness for the operas of Gilbert and Sullivan—*The Pirates of Penzance, The Mikado,* and so on. They took me to performances at an early age, and I am very glad they did.

My reading in my school-days was various. It included humorous stories and adventure stories, but, unusually in England then, it was mainly science fiction. I enjoyed classic authors in that field, such as Jules Verne and H. G. Wells, and I also read pioneer magazines that have since become collector's items—Hugo Gernsback's *Amazing Stories,* and *Astounding Stories* and *Wonder Stories.* These were American publications with no British counterparts. You could find them in inexpensive stores, perhaps under a sign saying YANK MAGS. My father solemnly warned me not to take them seriously. However, as we now know, some of the contributors showed more insight into possibilities than almost anyone else in those days.

I tried to retell the stories to other children. Best remembered of them are Ruth and Helen Mitchell, the daughters of a doctor. It was all genuinely among ourselves, with no adult involvement; the only thing I recall about Dr. Mitchell is his teaching us how to prevent car-sickness—by singing. Goodness knows what the children made of the stories, or what I made of them myself, for that matter. But my reading and retelling played a part in juvenile attempts at original writing, the beginning of a lifelong vocation. I passed from the scribbles of infancy to science fiction of my own and planned to be the first person to fly to Mars and reveal its secrets. Mars was regarded then as the most fascinating of the planets, very likely the home of alien beings who dug canals. More recent inspection, alas, has shown that those Martian canals were optical illusions. Still, a paragraph about my flight plans that I sent to a newspaper brought me a prize—a camera—which must count as my first literary payment.

Here is something else from that distant time. When I was eight, we visited Italy. Memories are dim now, but two incidents stand out. In Milan Cathedral, I saw a woman turn and genuflect as she left. In Padua, I saw pilgrims touching the shrine of St. Antony. I had never seen anyone act like that, yet it didn't occur to me to ask what they were doing. If I had, my parents' response would have been unhelpful. Their nominal Church of England affiliations meant, in practice, very little. But—this is the point—I didn't ask. There was no need. Those gestures of devotion were so plainly right.

Geoffrey Ashe

Although, in some inscrutable way, a seed had been planted, no growth from it ensued for a long time. Religion was not much of a concern in my earlier school-days, and my only contact with spirituality in school was through morning prayer and a little Scripture at Ambleside School and at St. Paul's in western London.

At the age of eleven or so, it was sci-fi speculation about the future that inspired the first reading of the Bible that I did of my own accord. The book was the Apocalypse of St. John, Revelation, at the end of the New Testament. The connection was that it made predictions, or was supposed to. I tried to unriddle its cryptic symbolism and, somewhat later, to apply this to people and events that I read about in the papers. Without much success. Among all too many others who have done the same, somebody (I don't know who) once worked out that John's notorious Number of the Beast, 666, could be made by a simple cryptographic trick to mean "Hitler." It was just as well that I didn't hear of this. If I had, it might have lured me on to fantasies better avoided. Many years afterwards, I took up Revelation again and realized how interesting it is, but not as a commentary on modern politics.

An illness when I was twelve restricted my activities for a long time. My literary efforts grew more elaborate: I recall dictating stories and plays to my mother. Looking back on those years, I can see a general attraction to mysteries taking shape. That has remained. It affected my adolescent attempts to write poetry. I began a blank-verse epic on the legend of Atlantis, another mystery, not unfamiliar to sci-fi enthusiasts. Here also, I was saved from going too far. I read the greatest blank-verse epic of all, John Milton's *Paradise Lost.* Milton not only enthralled me, he taught me a valuable lesson: he convinced me that I couldn't do it myself. Project aborted.

Family matters call for attention now. Partly because of the approach of war, partly for his own health reasons, my father had begun to plan emigration. In March 1939 we moved to Vancouver, on Canada's Pacific coast. Was it a wise decision? I don't know. The abandonment of a settled life in England, with its linkages of kin and friendship, was a traumatic break. Moreover, the purpose of the break was not to build a new life in the positive spirit of most emigrants, but simply to be somewhere else. The move was certainly an escape from enemy bombing, but, severe as that was, it was not as devastating as many expected, nor were other wartime ordeals such as food shortage. Maybe I was better off myself because I avoided being swept soon into the British army or a war job; maybe not. As for my mother, she was never reconciled to the move; the continuing alienation of my parents, which would lead to the breakup of their marriage seven years later, and the ongoing turmoil in the household, was a heavy price to pay.

My first uprooted year in Vancouver meant a complete lack of contact with anybody my own age. One result of being solitary, in the new and beautiful Canadian setting, was that I reflected on the Christian religion that I nominally belonged to. Almost by accident, in my late teens, I wandered for a while among churches of the born-again Fundamentalist type. I heard the arch-evangelist Aimee Semple McPherson, once a major celebrity, but, when she preached in Vancouver, an aging woman boasting unashamedly of the lifestyle she owed to the generosity of the faithful. With no one to enlighten me, I imagined that what I heard in such quarters—about "being saved" and so forth—*was* Christianity, and I recoiled from it. For one thing, it was incompatible with the cosmic grandeurs in space and time that my reading of science fiction had opened up. For another, it failed even to tally with the Gospels, as far as I could understand them. I never quite rejected the Christian label, as applied to myself, but I did reject what I thought Christianity to be. Even the more respectable churches, I assumed, merely dressed it up a little.

In due course I attended the University of British Columbia, then a very young foundation on a scenic territory west of the city. A slow process of social adjustment began. Despite mistakes and worse on my part, a few friendships developed and lasted. To this day I exchange Christmas cards with one of my female UBC contemporaries. In the light of later experience, I feel justified in paying tribute to the head of the English department, Dr. Sedgewick, as the best teacher I ever had in my life. A flamboyant personality with a rare understanding of literature, he provided a model worth emulating in my own later teaching experience—far more so than more famous professors I would encounter at Cambridge.

I got through to a B.A. degree in English, but a piece of self-knowledge that emerged on the way was more significant. Outside of curricular requirements, I didn't read what my fellow students read, or feel any pressing need to. One of them, Bill Blissett (afterwards a professor at Toronto), was shocked when he reeled off a list of "correct" modern writers and found that I had read hardly any of them. I caught up with several, but my nonconformity grew, on the whole, more pronounced. Soon after UBC, I read Gibbon's *Decline and Fall of the Roman Empire* from start to finish, with feelings approaching passion. I read most of the enormous Indian epic *Mahabharata*—in translation of course—and eventually reached the end of that too, as, probably, few readers ever have, outside India. While literature did not fade out for me, history and mythology encroached. It was logical that I should find my way into the field of Arthurian legend, where there is so much overlap, and so much mystery. I did, though not at once.

There was a phase when the emigration seemed to have taken effect, and I assumed that my future lay in Canada. However, this attitude changed in the latter part of the war, during a spell of military intelligence work in Ottawa. Exposed to fresh influences in a setting less remote from Europe, I realized that England, after all, was where I belonged.

This may be the right place to touch on a topic which some may think unfashionable, patriotism. When my change of attitude happened, I wouldn't have used that word. Patriotism tended to mean the blind loyalism of my mother's family, bound up with the Crown and the Flag and the still-flourishing British Empire. That never had much appeal for me. Indeed, my first distinct thought about the Empire was that it should be got rid of. Whatever I was learning to value in my country might have little to do with its public image, might even be at odds with its officially revered aspects. But I did grow to value many things about it, to view them with love and pride, and to realize that I couldn't live anywhere else, not permanently. In that sense I can speak of patriotism—an increasingly well-defined patriotism—and say that my return from Canada was a crucial step in affirming it.

All the same, I am profoundly thankful for the trans-Atlantic part of my life, not only because of people and places that I came to know, but because it set me free from what might otherwise have been narrowness. This at least was a clear gain from the emigration, though unintended and unforeseen. Even when planted again in England, I was able to range outside and to do things I would otherwise have been incapable of; able also, when my books were attracting readers in later decades, to take up visiting professorships in the United States and fit in well enough to be invited again.

My first wife was Canadian. We met in the office in Ottawa in 1943. My recollection is that I taught her chess during the lunch hour—adequately, I trust, though I have never been much good at the game. Her name was Dorothy Irene Train. Afterwards, in England, she took to using her second name (with the three-syllable European pronunciation) because "Dorothy" sounded old-fashioned. Her father was a mining engineer in northern Quebec, a tall, rather unhappy man of part-Norwegian descent; her mother's forebears were United Empire Loyalists, people who migrated to Canada from the Thirteen Colonies because they disagreed with American independence. Irene had graduated in history at a Canadian university but had no pretensions to scholarship. Her talents were for music and art, and when the children came, she showed far finer gifts as a mother than I could ever have shown as a father. In the ensuing years we remained together in spite of strains that many marriages would not have survived.

We were married in England in May 1946. During the same month I enrolled at Trinity College, Cambridge, where my Canadian degree allowed me to take the English honours course—the "Tripos"—in a shorter time. That was a pleasant period in some ways, a troubled one in others. My parents had also returned, but separately, and their tormented marriage ended at last, amid disputes and recriminations that continued to involve both Irene and me. It was also becoming increasingly apparent that it was not in me to be wholeheartedly academic. The need grew to write and be published, even if it were only the odd article or book review and even if it interfered with study. Anxiety about the looming exams and the prospects for employment afterwards added to the *angst* of this postwar university experience. At one stage it was hard to go on at all.

But I did go on, for one thing because many compensations existed. Besides membership in interesting societies, I had the privilege of contact with eminent scholars, firsthand or at a moderate distance. I was a guest of G. M. Trevelyan, a leading historian in the interwar period, who had generously awarded me a prize for an essay. I saw, heard, and briefly spoke with Bertrand Russell, the controversial, much-married philosopher and mathematician. Cambridge has a certain distinction in the latter field. (If *Star Trek* is to be believed, its principal Professor of Mathematics a few centuries hence will be the accomplished android Data.) Russell's family spanned an amazing stretch of time. He remembered, as a boy, meeting his grandfather; and his grandfather, incredible as it sounds, had met Napoleon. Towards the close of his own long life, Russell strayed into weird political aberrations, accusing President Kennedy of being worse than Hitler. I prefer to think of him in the days of his wonderful clarity. When dealing with subjects I could understand, he was one of the two best lecturers I ever heard. The other was C. S. Lewis.

Not that I went along with Russell's agnostic beliefs, or nonbeliefs. The most important thing that happened to me at Cambridge was my adherence to the Catholic Church. It was the culmination of influences from my entire life. Technically I am a convert, but I've never felt like that. Converts are usually people who cross over from another affiliation. With me it was not so. Recalling those childhood glimpses of Italian worshippers, I would say I was "there" all along, unconsciously, but realization was slow. Positive, thought-out reasons developed over the years and have grown clearer and stronger. They don't belong here. This is not an argument or a sermon. However, my drift towards the Catholic Church does deserve a few words, because it illustrates a process that has been important to me in other ways as well: the process of shedding misconceptions.

My Vancouver delusion that Christianity always meant emotional, "born-again" Fundamentalism, or something not far from that, was dissolving at UBC and went on doing so. A factor that emerged later was the discovery that Catholicism was really different. Surprisingly, the Church seemed closer to what I thought Christianity ought to be. As one error faded out, however, others arose, notions that were more rampant then than now, but still are not extinct. They were familiar to me already in a vague way, but even the faintest dawning of Catholic sympathy compelled me to face them.

One was that Catholicism meant merely being spellbound and seduced by uplifting music, colorful ritual. That, at least, was easily seen to be absurd, especially in England, where most of the beauty of institutional Christianity was to be found in the churches and cathedrals of the Anglican communion, in sharp contrast with all too much Catholic mediocrity.

A graver accusation was that Catholicism was a body of dogma imposed by priests who allowed no questions, under the authority of a pope who dictated what the faithful must think about everything. The priests, moreover, were supposed to be always "proselytizing," trying to lure more dupes into their clutches. The first part of this accusation had more credibility then than it has today, but—as I grasped, little by little—it was so wildly exaggerated, and Catholics so obviously had their disagreements like other people, that it lost force as a deterrent. As for the charge of proselytizing, my impression was and is that priests, on the whole, are much less zealous in attracting recruits than the evangelists who exhort you to be saved. I know somebody who went to one of them and asked how he could become a Catholic, and the priest said "Don't bother!" and shut the door.

Those are general issues. For myself, there was also a personal issue. My father never practiced his nominal Irish Protestantism, but he had an ancestral family pride that was bound up with it, and he thought Ireland's Catholic majority a second-rate lot. I was taught to believe that all Irish Ashes were Protestants, there simply weren't any Catholic ones. I saw reason to suspect that there were, but plainly they were unmentionable, not "our sort of people." Then, I learned that one of them, Thomas Ashe, had been a hero of the struggle for Irish independence. He played a leading role in the Easter Rising of 1916 and is still warmly remembered. Here was a highly honourable Catholic connection, and I had never been allowed to know of it. Later, at the National Museum in Dublin, when I stood before a whole exhibit devoted to Thomas Ashe, the family barriers began to crack and I came to understand the truth much better.

During the time of my conversion, the removal of such obstacles—of others, of course, as well as these—was helped by reading, especially by reading G. K. Chesterton, a famous English convert whose journalism, essays, novels, and poems were widely influential. For some time, nevertheless, I resisted the crucial step into the Catholic fold. The final push, when it came, was unspectacular. No visions, no voices, no spiritual upheavals. It came from another piece of reading. A recently deceased Cambridge historian, G. G. Coulton, had made it his business to know every iniquity that the Catholic Church ever perpetrated and some that it didn't. During the 1940s he embarked on a controversy about its record with Arnold Lunn, a versatile Catholic who was best known as a promoter of winter sports (he invented the downhill slalom contest that figures in the Winter Olympics), but who was also a professor at Notre Dame.

Their debate appeared in book form. I said to myself, "Let this decide it. If even Coulton can't turn me against the Church, no one can." Both authors, reread today, sound rather old-fashioned, but between them they settled the matter. Arnold Lunn might not be a hundred percent right, but Coulton with his anti-Roman vendetta was wrong. I told Lunn of the decision he had helped me to reach. He replied genially that this gave him an answer to people who said controversy was of no use. We met at the Alpine Club in London. He seemed very absent-minded—it was a kind of humorous pose, I think—but there was nothing absent-minded about his writing.

With the decision taken, I went to Cambridge's Catholic chaplain, Father Alfred Gilbey. His chaplaincy was at Fisher House, up an alley-way where you would hardly have noticed it if you weren't looking. A course of instruction began, theoretically weekly. Some people fancy that you can fling yourself into the Church's arms on a romantic impulse. You couldn't then, and you can't now. It requires months, and with me the process was interrupted so often by Father Gilbey's commitments that it took almost a year to reach the point of reception. I stood fairly low in his priorities.

This chaplain was a remarkable person, part Spanish, a member of the family that made Gilbey's Gin. He was the most impeccably dressed man in Cambridge, even being sighted occasionally in a top hat, though by then hardly anyone else wore them. His ultraconservative outlook didn't appeal to me, and our interests were so far apart that each of us could come up with remarks and questions that were meaningless to the other. His version of the Catholic Faith might now be judged archaic. Yet the thing that was happening overrode all differences. This was the way I was meant to go. I knew then, and know better now, how much that is evil and scandalous the Church contains. I accept that it may need to develop new forms and structures. But I have never felt the least temptation to leave, though England has not been a church-going country in my lifetime, and is less so now than ever.

Geoffrey Ashe, age nine, with the Mitchell children at the London zoo

Father Gilbey's most memorable saying was this: "You can't be received into the Church if you just think it's a good thing. You must believe that its teachings are true." The issue had never been put to me quite like that. Ever since, I have tried to put the truth first, and not in this respect only. Moreover, although the Church's "truth" can be taken various ways, it is never in irreconcilable conflict with other truths. In many years of research into controversial topics, I have never encountered a single case where Catholic doctrine was an obstacle to accepting what I found to be true. With its firm basis, Catholicism proved to be a source of strength, focus and community ties that helped Irene and me through many tribulations.

I can't resist adding a final word about Father Gilbey-Monsignor, as he became after my time. He retired from the chaplaincy and spent his last years as a resident in a London club. He lived to be ninety-six. Once, the near-centenarian Queen Mother visited the club and they happened to meet. The Monsignor didn't recognize her. She, however, knew who he was and remarked, "I'm even older than you." "Nonsense," he replied, "no woman is older than me, except the Queen Mother."

Irene, from a Methodist background, converted and was received into the Catholic Church separately. That step had nothing to do with influences at Cambridge. Nor was she merely following me; she would never have done so— at least, I hope not. The decision was made for her by an event that she saw as miraculous. This was a strictly personal matter, and it would not be right for me to describe it. It was associated, however, with a certain place, and it contributed to the life-shaping importance which that place acquired for me. I am speaking of Glastonbury, in the southwest English county of Somerset.

Glastonbury is sometimes called the Isle of Avalon because of its links with the Arthurian legend. Early in the Christian era, it actually was an island, or nearly so; the low-lying farmland round about is the result of centuries of drainage and reclamation. The present town is cradled in a small cluster of hills, the highest being the famous Tor, an odd whaleback formation with a tower on top. The Isle has been a holy place from time immemorial, and was once very likely a pagan sanctuary—some think a sanctuary of goddess worship. Christian legend makes it the "holiest earth of England," the home of the country's first Christian settlers, headed by Joseph of Arimathea, the rich man who obtained Christ's body after the Crucifixion and laid it in the tomb. As a Christian place, Glastonbury is certainly old, and the belief in its extreme antiquity grew around a

tangible fact, a church so ancient that no one knew who had built it. In more or less historical times, this church was the first in western Europe to be dedicated to the Virgin Mary.

A great abbey arose here during the Middle Ages, claiming, among much else, to have the grave of Arthur within its precinct. Its legends played a part in the mysterious theme of the Holy Grail and the quest for it by his knights. King Henry VIII dissolved the abbey in 1539, but impressive ruins remain, including the Lady Chapel on the site of the old church, perpetuating Glastonbury's status as the senior British shrine of Mary. In modern times, Glastonbury has woven a unique spell, reviving as a religious and cultural centre, and—for better or worse— becoming a haven for the "alternative" spirituality that is sometimes given the label "New Age."

I first took an interest in it because of my reading of Chesterton, whom I already mentioned. One of his many books is *A Short History of England.* I read this while I was still in Ottawa. My intelligence work gave me access to Canada's parliamentary library, which housed many volumes not often taken out by parliamentarians, and there I found Chesterton's *Short History.* He begins with a chapter on "The Age of Legends," in which he has a good deal about Glastonbury. After my return to England, I visited the place with Irene. Or, to be precise, we shot through it in a bus and had a fleeting but indelible glimpse. Even this brief contact had its effect—in her case, it was crucial for

Ashe at Stonehenge

her conversion. The delayed sequel had a far more potent effect, as I shall explain in a moment.

Our first children were arriving within a couple of years of that fleeting glimpse. Others followed; eventually we had five—four boys and a girl. But with the first two, and the consequent obligations, problems were piling up already. I was holding a precarious job in an improvised postwar institution, the Polish University College. War service and other factors had brought many Poles to Britain, who had no wish to go back to a Communist homeland. The college was set up in London to prepare them for resettlement. Staff and students were Polish; classes in English were part of the preparation.

Maybe I helped some of them on their way, but it was not a very rewarding job, it was indifferently paid, and the college would presumably come to an end. I was making a little progress with my writing, but persistent postwar shortages included a shortage of paper, and space in publications was limited. We also had housing problems. A temporary retreat to Canada was virtually forced upon us. We went to the little town in northern Quebec where Irene's parents lived. The only employment there was in the gold mine where her father was chief engineer. For several months I was digging ditches underground and assisting in the machine shop. There were those—my mother, for instance—who saw this as a disaster and a terrible waste. In reality, I rather enjoyed it. Perhaps because it showed my ability to adapt, I found my way to a better post in manufacturing industry.

The Ford Motor Company of Canada, then located at Windsor, Ontario, happened to include a department with an unusual head, Ken Philp. He wanted someone who could write instruction manuals and kindred material, and accordingly hired me, with a cheerful and doubtless true assurance that no one else in the company would have done so. In his office I rose to be an "administrative assistant." I probably wasn't much good at it, and I wouldn't have chosen to work in industry forever, but I am thankful for that further enlargement of scope and for the escape from an academic groove that it made possible when I was finally back in England, armed with the new qualifications that Ford had given me. These enabled me to find a position in a London technical college that provided us with income while the writing built up further.

But shortly before the final return, that second installment of Canadian life brought a second impulse from a Canadian library, immensely reinforcing the first. In Toronto, something reminded me of Glastonbury, and I looked in at the Public Library there, curious to see what it had on the subject. It turned out to have a considerable amount. One item was *Glastonbury and England,* an early book by Christopher Hollis, later noted as a publisher and politician. He had plenty to say about Glastonbury's historic greatness as well as its legends, and he quoted a prophecy attributed to an old man named Austin Ringwode, who was the last survivor of its dissolved community: "The Abbey will one day be repaired and rebuilt for the like worship which has ceased, and then peace and plenty will for a long time abound."

That gave me a new purpose. It didn't matter whether Austin Ringwode really had a prophetic gift. It didn't even matter whether the story, as recorded, was true. It rang true for me. Glastonbury was no mere heap of ruins, it was alive, or potentially so; and I had to do whatever was in my power to further its reawakening.

The conviction that something special had happened was reinforced. Back in England, an obvious thing for me to do was to write a book on Glastonbury, drawing attention to it and shedding any fresh light I could. During my researches, I read the plentiful material that already existed, yet I never found anything else that mentioned the prophecy. Christopher Hollis seemed to have been alone in doing so. I asked him where he had read it, and he referred me to an old guidebook, but his memory was at fault; it wasn't there. Furthermore, his book was now rare itself, and I never found it in any other place, except of course in the British Museum, which had everything.

Not only had inspiration struck in Toronto Public Library, it would almost certainly not have struck in any other library that I might have visited, because none would have had Hollis's unique book with the prophecy—and he himself couldn't quote any source for it. However explained, this was a kind of "leading" that has happened to me very rarely indeed, and cannot be ignored when it does. Ever since, I have spoken of the rebirth of "Glastonbury with all it implies" as a ruling aim in my life, whether that means Ringwode's literal restoration of the abbey, or a rebirth of some other kind which he could not have conceived.

Our return to England was accompanied at first by new difficulties which I need not go into. This time they passed, but we were dependent for a while on the hospitality of a religious foundation, the Carmelite priory at Aylesford in Kent, the only place in England where a Catholic order recovered the house which the Reformation took away. During our time there, the restored community was still dominated by the charisma of its restorer, Father Malachy Lynch. He was a large Irishman, deeply and happily devoted to the Blessed Virgin; a Protestant might have called him a Mariolater, and so, indeed, might some Catholics. At Aylesford I finished my Glastonbury book. Father Malachy's devotion, and the surrounding artwork and atmosphere reflecting it, harmonized with my awareness of Glastonbury's own Marian tradition. The book was entitled *King Arthur's Avalon.* I dedicated it to Father Malachy, perhaps giving him a shade too much credit for help and guidance, but better to err on that side than on the other; and he had found a house for us in neighbouring Maidstone.

Published in 1957, *King Arthur's Avalon* was well received. In various editions, with updating prefaces, it went on appearing and selling for forty years. At its original debut, such attacks as there were came mostly from opposite directions and were prompted by my treatment of Glastonbury's legends. Romantics said I was too critical and believed too little. Academics (it might be better to call them academically conditioned grumblers) said I wasn't critical enough and believed too much. Both sides made their points, but both were astray. I would suggest, now, that while parts of the book are sketchy and speculative, it is far more right than wrong. As a communication of vision, it survives.

A word here about a general principle. Over the years, it has been my experience that you can start from a story or belief that is not literally true and arrive, by careful probing, at an underlying reality that is: a reality that scholars miss because they merely reject the story or belief as false and explain it away, or try to, without examining it or following it up. I offer a guiding maxim here: "There is a wrongness that can lead to rightness more effectively than rightness itself." And a related maxim: "It is important to take legends seriously without taking them literally." The romantic who believes them literally is mistaken. But the ultraskeptic who simply dismisses them, often with ridicule, is also mistaken. There is a third way, a wiser way.

The success of *King Arthur's Avalon* led me to further studies, reaching out into other fields of tradition. I am still fond of *Land to the West* (1962), which explores the Irish legend of St. Brendan's Voyage and the theory that the Irish knew of America before the Norse. The travelling that this book required, in Ireland (accompanied by my son Tom) and in the Americas, was financed partly by writing newspaper articles. The same source of funding helped me to travel widely in other directions.

In the intervals of various activities, I have returned several times to the topic of King Arthur himself. This was not an early interest of mine, but writing on Glastonbury opened it up for me, because I had to discuss not only his legendary links with the place but the question of who he was—if he was anybody. And I must speak here of a project that presently involved me, partly because of the publicity that it had, partly because it illustrated my point about taking legends seriously.

The saga of King Arthur is almost entirely romance and legend, dating from the Middle Ages, when it was the best-loved theme of imaginative literature in most of Europe. If there was a real Arthur at the beginning of it all, he lived much earlier, in the fifth or sixth century A.D. Opinions have wavered back and forth. I think there was such a person, though not quite as even pro-Arthur historians have pictured him. Certainly the documentation is frail. It is worth asking, however, what light can be shed by archaeology: not on the hypothetical king in person— that would be too much to hope for—but on the facts in which the king's saga may be rooted.

For instance, I wondered long ago, could excavation show whether Camelot was real? In *King Arthur's Avalon* and the book that came next (*From Caesar to Arthur*), I touched on that question, briefly. The key to its proper investigation is an aspect of Camelot that is seldom stressed. It isn't portrayed as the capital of Britain. It is Arthur's personal headquarters. The splendid Camelot of romance and film is a medieval fantasy, but it might have a prototype; it might echo a tradition about the real headquarters of a real Arthur. This could have been one of Britain's ancient hill-forts—hills with an inhabited enclosure on top and earthwork ramparts encircling and defending it. They date from pre-Roman times but were not all entirely deserted later. Some are called "castles," though not because there ever was a castle on the site, in a medieval sense. The fortified hill itself was the castle.

One such hill-fort is Cadbury Castle, a few miles from Glastonbury. Most of it is now covered with woods, colourful in springtime with bluebells and primroses, but part of its earthwork fortification system is in the open, and very formidable it is. John Leland, in the time of Henry VIII, wrote quite simply that this was Camelot. No buildings or even ruins were visible in the eighteen-acre enclosure within the ramparts, but other antiquarian writers were willing to repeat Leland's assertion. Local folklore includes ghost stories about the king and his knights, and one legend tells of a hidden cave where he lies asleep. When some archaeologists visited Cadbury many years ago, an old man from the nearby village asked if they intended to dig him up.

In the 1950s, renewed attention began to focus on this hill. The summit enclosure was regularly ploughed for crops, and a local amateur archaeologist, Mary Harfield, climbed up every so often to walk her dog, and poked about in the furrows with the ferrule of her umbrella—a very elementary form of archaeology. She turned up fragments of pottery and showed them to Ralegh Radford, the doyen of research into the obscure post-Roman period. He recognized that some were of a type that pointed to the presence of a wealthy household, at about the right time for Arthur ... well, more or less. In a report on Mrs. Harfield's finds, he remarked on the Camelot connection.

In 1959 I ventured to write to Dr. Radford suggesting that Cadbury Castle should be excavated, and I repeated the suggestion in print soon afterwards. No archaeologist would have undertaken it merely on the strength of an alleged link with Arthur, but analogy with other hill-forts showed that Cadbury must have had occupants over many centuries and would repay excavation with or without him. Dr. Radford's response was that the summit enclosure was too big. He wouldn't know where to start and preferred, for the moment, to concentrate on sites with a limited area, such as the enclosures surrounding churches and monasteries. He had already done some digging at Glastonbury Abbey, and now he returned for a couple of seasons and located what the monks had claimed in 1191 was the grave of Arthur. The view that is normally taken by historians is that this was a hoax, a sort of publicity stunt. Radford, however, proved that the monks did dig where they said and did find a very early burial, though the coffin holding the remains had been removed.

I saw the place myself. While the story certainly raises queries, it seems to me that it can't simply be brushed aside. Arthur's grave may have been a fake, but it wasn't an obvious fake. Occasionally I guide groups of visitors around the abbey and encourage them to be photographed on the spot; some even like to be photographed lying down on it.

I had my first practical experience of archaeology in 1964, when Philip Rahtz excavated the top of Glastonbury Tor and found traces of what might have been a small fort or a chapel, taking Glastonbury's history back at least to the sixth century A.D. My own part in the dig was confined to unskilled activity with a trowel and a wheelbarrow. From the top of the Tor you can see Cadbury. While Rahtz's excavation was still going on, the first steps were taken towards the much larger Cadbury project that an increasing number of people were hoping for.

A Camelot Research Committee was finally launched in 1965. Dr. Radford was in the chair, and I was secretary. Most of the members represented learned societies, which, between them, raised enough money for an exploratory dig. Sir Mortimer Wheeler, England's most famous archaeologist and an effective popularizer, accepted the presidency. Leslie Alcock of University College, Cardiff, was appointed Director of Excavations. He carried out a tentative programme in the following year, which unearthed enough

Ashe with first wife, Irene, and all five of their children, 1958

material to justify a public appeal for funds. Fullscale seasons of work during the next four summers were financed by individual and corporate donations. Hundreds of volunteers took part, and thousands of visitors climbed the hill to see what was going on, so many that they necessitated a guide service.

Guiding, here as at Glastonbury, was something I could do without getting in anybody's way. More actual archaeology was done by my son Michael and my daughter Sheila, who both took part. Another junior member of the team (aged thirteen at the time) was Richard Tabor, who has returned to Cadbury in recent years and found interesting remains at the foot of the hill, including a burial that seems to be aligned toward Glastonbury Tor in the distance.

At the time of Leslie Alcock's dig, in 1966-70, removal of the topsoil in the summit enclosure disclosed the house foundations and artifacts of a thriving pre-Roman settlement. When the Roman army arrived in this part of Britain, Cadbury had evidently become a centre of resistance. The invaders stormed it and evicted the inhabitants. For a long time the enclosure was empty or nearly so. That, however, was not the end. In the fifth century A.D., after Britain broke away from the Roman Empire, Cadbury was reoccupied and refortified. On top of the early ramparts around the enclosure, resurgent Britons built a new wall of stone and timber, sixteen feet thick and nearly three-quarters of a mile long, with a gatehouse where an ascending trackway entered the enclosure. Cadbury had been taken over by someone with great resources of

manpower, whose people were responsible for the pottery fragments that Mary Harfield disturbed with her umbrella fifteen hundred years later. That "someone" was not identifiably Arthur, but, as one member of the team observed, he was an Arthur-type figure.

Furthermore, subsequent work on other sites never revealed a parallel case. Some hill-forts were reoccupied, but they were smaller and had no similar new walls or gatehouses. So far as the evidence went, Cadbury was unique, the only hill-fort in post-Roman Britain that underwent such a reconstruction, with such implications about its overlord. When John Leland claimed it as Camelot in 1542, he somehow picked the only credible Camelot in the only credible sense. How did he do it? Even a modern archaeologist could not have detected that refortification by merely looking at the hill, without digging. I don't see how Leland could have singled out the best candidate in all Britain, unless he heard a long-standing, deep-rooted tradition of this place's importance during the right period—an importance now proved.

Under Leslie Alcock's direction, the project had been ably run, widely publicized, and richly productive. You might suppose that other British archaeologists would have applauded such a fine advertisement for their science. Not so. The more vocal ones did their best to discredit it. They attacked Alcock for talking about Camelot and Arthur at all. The truth, I suspect, is that they resented a rival's ability to finance an excavation by invoking those names, when they had no similar names to invoke. They accused him—wrongly—of deceiving the public by pretending to search for the Camelot of romance, which never existed, and predicted that when the Camelot of romance failed to emerge, people would feel cheated and it would henceforth be harder to raise money for other projects. Actually, my experience on the site was that most of the visitors didn't expect anything romantic. They were quite prepared for the unspectacular traces that came to light—the bits of pottery, the rough foundations, the tumbled walls—and few were disappointed. One hard fact refuted the dismal forecasts: the public fundraising appeal brought in more money each year.

But I was struck and saddened by some of the venomous reactions, and not only from archaeologists but even from disgruntled amateurs on the Committee whose desire for control nearly wrecked the excavation. The Arthurian legend could stir up passion, pro and con, and it still can. On the surface, it doesn't seem to mean much in present-day Britain. Most people, if asked, would probably have nothing to say about it, or would dismiss it as just a story, maybe even a story for children. And yet ... yes, it can stir up passion. It lurks deeper in the national psyche than might be thought.

This was borne in upon me by the reception of a book called *The Quest for Arthur's Britain* (1968), which I edited and partly wrote, with contributions from other members of the Committee. Its sales ran into hundreds of thousands. It is out of date now in various ways, yet nothing has altogether taken its place. There used to be objectors who

With Mark Vecchio's American college students at site of King Arthur's grave in Glastonbury Abbey, 2000 (student in foreground is simulating the dead king)

said: "We have the immortal literature—Arthur, Guinevere, Merlin, the Round Table, and all the rest. What's the point of rummaging for alleged facts behind it?" Well, facts are worth discovering for their own sake. Moreover, it enriches the legend itself to show it in depth, to trace how it started and how it evolved. But a more decisive answer came from the new writing which the quest inspired. Novelists and poets began producing work going behind the medieval romance and imagining Arthur's Britain as it might have been, or weaving new myths about it. I think of the prize-winning poet John Heath-Stubbs and the novelists Rosemary Sutcliff, Marion Zimmer Bradley, Persia Woolley, Bernard Cornwell, and several more. Over the past decades, the quest has enlarged the literature itself. It has not been irrelevant or disillusioning.

The fictional flowering was encouraged by a vogue for mythology in general, even invented mythology. The most powerful single factor was the success of J. R. R. Tolkien's trilogy *The Lord of the Rings*. In a recent sampling of public opinion in Britain, where respondents gave their choice for the greatest book of the twentieth century, *The Lord of the Rings* came top. I don't know what that implies about the general literary awareness of the respondents; it's the fact.

Tolkien probably never read anything of mine, but we met once at a gathering where he was being given an award. I came prepared with a question that didn't seem to be answered in the appendices at the end of his book: Why was the Ring destroyed on March 25? It happened to be a presidential election year. Finding myself face to face with him, I remarked: "Americans are going around with buttons saying GANDALF FOR PRESIDENT"—Gandalf being one of his chief characters. Tolkien replied: "I don't approve. I would only approve if they said TOLKIEN FOR PRESIDENT." Then I fired off my question about March 25. His answer was immediate: "Because the world was created on that day." I have found since that this idea goes back to an astrological calculation that Dante mentions, but at the time it was startling.

I never met Tolkien's friend and fellow-bestseller C. S. Lewis, but I heard him lecture—superbly—and I value his story *The Great Divorce* as going farther than anything else I've read towards making Christian ideas of the hereafter intelligible. It was an honour to find him citing my own *Land to the West* in one of his later works. I gathered that he read *King Arthur's Avalon* also, but it was *Land to the West* that he referred to in print. This was especially gratifying, because I have always wanted to avoid being typecast as an Arthurian author.

When interviewed, I tend to begin by telling the interviewer that I'm not an Arthur monomaniac. Certainly I have returned to him from time to time, sometimes because a publisher has invited me to write (for example) a guidebook to Arthurian places. But I have often explored other fields, and seldom more actively than during the Cadbury excavation itself. During the first phases of it, I was busy with a biography of Gandhi, the Indian leader popularly styled the Mahatma, whose campaign against British rule between the two World Wars was the main driving force towards independence.

Oddly, Gandhi was the first political figure I was ever aware of, owing to the publicity he had during a visit to England in 1931. I doubt if I could have named the British

Prime Minister. Later, learning more about Gandhi, I came to have a profound admiration for his nonviolent strategy, his grounding of it in religious conviction, and his courage in pursuing it. I have already mentioned my interest in matters Indian. This lay dormant for years but finally welled up again and impelled me to attempt a book about Gandhi, the only biography I've ever written. The theme was not really so remote from Arthur. Here too was a patriotic leader, mythified, almost deified; here too was a sort of collective mystique surrounding him, as a mystique surrounded Arthur, only in this case it was well document- ed and its growth could be studied.

My proposal for this book was not instantly welcome. My publishers almost threw me out of the office. Nobody would read a book about Gandhi! How many copies did I think would be sold? I suggested ten thousand, and was ridiculed. Accepted by another publisher, *Gandhi* (1968) sold about thirteen thousand. A reissue in 2000 has been adding to the total.

When it was first under way, I had never been to India. Obviously I had to go there, talk with some of Gandhi's associates, and follow the record of his career across the subcontinent. Two visits were financed, as other journeys of mine had been, by writing newspaper articles. These were to be illustrated, and my editor teamed me with Marilyn Silverstone, an outstanding American photojour- nalist who lived in India and knew the right people. Without her help and guidance, I doubt if I could have done the job. India was so vast, so overpowering. Someone has told me since that Marilyn became a Buddhist nun.

The book attracted notice partly because of the radical restlessness that marked the later sixties. Many saw Gandhi as an inspiration for activists in the West. This had a divisive effect on events at the centenary of his birth, in 1969. Britain's centenary committee was headed by Earl Mountbatten, who had been India's last viceroy and worked with Gandhi on the transfer of power. He saw the occasion as an exercise in British-Indian goodwill, and invited the Prime Minister and other dignitaries to the main meeting in London. The committee, however, included the actress Vanessa Redgrave, whose outlook was left-wing and who wanted a display of interracial amity among the immigrant population in Birmingham. My own role in the committee, as Gandhi's biographer, provided me with a rare privilege—and I have to add, a rather amusing one: that of watching two such famous and powerful personali- ties colliding across the table. Both achieved something of what they wanted.

The sixties saw radical talk of another kind and attempts at violent action for social change. Demonstrations were held in London—as an eyewitness I am bound to say, very feeble ones. Supporters waved the "little red book" of the Thoughts of Chairman Mao, the Chinese Communist leader, and poured scorn on Gandhian nonviolence. One of my more hostile *Gandhi* reviewers insisted that violence was the only way of getting results: that was why so many young activists were turning to it. How antiquated that reviewer sounds today! In practice, of course, violence failed to get any results whatever; whereas the later twentieth-century revolutions that restored democracy in Russia and eastern Europe, though not explicitly Gandhian, were largely nonviolent and, on the whole, a vindication.

That ferment in the sixties had a lasting impact on Glastonbury itself. Austin Ringwode's prophecy of rebirth began to be fulfilled, if in unexpected ways. Several developments that were already stirring were traditional. Church pilgrimages, Catholic and Anglican, were bringing thousands to the abbey each summer, and these have remained annual events. The abbey also became a venue for outdoor drama and music. More surprising—far more— was the discovery of Glastonbury about 1970 by what was then called the hippie culture. The place's unique spell inspired an exuberant festival, a sort of pop-mystical Woodstock, held on farmland a few miles off but within sight of the Tor.

A book I wrote during that hectic period reflected current events in an unexpected way and has since had an even more unexpected revival. The would-be liberation of the sixties had, as is well known, a dark side, exemplified at its worst by the dreadful "Family" of Charles Manson in California. In such contexts, liberation meant simply lawlessness, a total subversion of morality. California even produced a Church of Satan; one of its members joined Manson's Family and took part in its most notorious crime, the murder of the actress Sharon Tate.

In England and Ireland, something of the same kind, though generally not so evil, had happened before. The eighteenth century saw the rise of a number of "Hell-Fire Clubs," devoted to blasphemy, debauchery, and, according to hostile rumours, satanism. The most famous met at Medmenham, beside the River Thames, where the motto over the doorway was "Do what you will." I never took any notice of these scandalous fellowships till a publisher remarked to me over lunch that there was no good account of them, and suggested that I might write one, however remote the topic seemed from anything I had written till then.

A little research revealed a sort of "Do what you will" tradition in France as well as England. This became interesting to me, and I wrote the book, making the connection with Manson's activities and other recent phenomena, while stressing that the Hell-Fire Clubs were apparently much less sinister and much more amusing. It was great fun to write—and it didn't sell. Someone has kindly suggested that it showed a perception of what people were doing at the time, or had been doing recently, which didn't register yet with the people concerned. *Do What You Will* (1974) remained one of my favourites among my own productions but, I thought, a defunct favourite. As it turned out long afterward, I was wrong. I save the end of that account for later. For now, I revert to the Glastonbury Festival in its early years.

Shocked local citizens violently opposed it. In the main shopping street, you could see notices saying "No hippies served." After a few years of cooling down, however, another was held, and from then onward the Glastonbury Festival grew into a major event, with international fame. It still takes place at the summer solstice, with well-known groups performing for audiences of more than a hundred thousand. Profits from ticket sales go to causes such as Greenpeace and local charities. Today, owing to its sheer size (it is the largest contemporary music festival in Europe) and the difficulty of keeping the crowds under control, some doubt has arisen over its future. But the record is one of success and gradual acceptance.

Ashe with wife, Patricia, at Buckfast Abbey, Devon, 2000

Other developments that I have seen in Glastonbury since the sixties have been the restoration of the Assembly Rooms, a fine community centre that almost perished of neglect, and the creation of a unique Library of Avalon, with a collection of books on historical, mythological, religious, and philosophical topics. A donation of books from my personal library formed the nucleus of the Library of Avalon, and I serve as its patron. Both these civic achievements—accessible to all sectors of the public—are largely due to the kind of enthusiasts who were denounced for supporting the Festival, an interesting comment on certain local attitudes.

However, it is true that Glastonbury's magic nurtures a medley of neo-pagan and New Age activities. It has become, as some put it, the "alternative" spiritual capital of England. Many of these things would have startled Austin Ringwode. In 1587, when he is said to have uttered his prophecy, he could only have pictured a rebirth in the way he did, as the repair of his battered and plundered abbey for "the like worship which has ceased." To some extent, even

that has happened. The ruins have been repaired as far as feasible and are now carefully preserved by the Church of England. The pilgrimages have brought "the like worship" back. Other modern growths are certainly very different. Yet in a more complex society, Glastonbury's rebirth or reactivation must transcend the specific image under which Ringwode had to imagine it. For decades now, it has been taking place; the fulfilment of the prophecy has been under way, in forms appropriate to the time.

Personally, I welcome some of this. Not all. But my commitment remains, and I have aided several of the developments without ever wanting to take charge. My role in the rebirth has been to catalyze, not control. Participation became easier from 1974 onward, because, by then, Irene and I were living in Glastonbury ourselves. I had always assumed that the move would happen, perhaps after the sons and daughter left home, but I had never seriously tried to bring it about. The step came sooner than expected, through a multiple coincidence, one of those "leadings" that simply have to be followed, like my discovery in the

Toronto Public Library. I am habitually cautious about detecting supernatural guidance or intervention, but there have been a few moments when something occurred so extraordinary that it made the claim excusable. The result in each case was a radical change for the better, and twice it was more than that, salvation from disaster. The event that brought us to Glastonbury was less than salvation, but it was crucial enough.

I had written *The Finger and the Moon,* a novel of sorts, published in 1973. Its locale was a fictitious house with a view of Glastonbury Tor, run as a school of magic and occult philosophy. Keep that in mind. A well-known figure in Glastonbury—that is, the real Glastonbury—was John Shelly, who made pottery on the wheel and taught classes how to make it. He lived and worked at Chalice Orchard, a house on the lower slope of the Tor. I had met him when visiting the town but had never gone to his house and knew nothing about it. Soon after *The Finger and the Moon* appeared, when we were staying in Blandford, Dorset, I heard that he was selling his house and already had a buyer.

The following January, a Dutch TV producer came to me in Blandford and explained that he was making a topical programme which would include references to King Arthur and present-day attitudes to the legend. I told him that he should go to Glastonbury and that for current information he should talk to Patrick Benham, a teacher. I was right to think of Patrick: he has since written *The Avalonians,* the best account of Glastonbury during the twentieth century. At the time of the Dutch visit, it was hard to find him during the day. However, I accompanied the TV crew, and we stopped at the foot of the Tor. It was raining. I got out of the car to look for any sign of a break in the weather. A few yards behind us was Patrick Benham himself, in conversation with John Shelly, the owner of Chalice Orchard.

I introduced Patrick to the producer and went back to ask John about the sale of his house. He replied gloomily that after months of negotiation the deal had fallen through and he had reduced the price. The reduction put it within my own reach, and I asked if he could consider me; he could. The rain stopped, having lasted just long enough to produce a most improbable meeting. You might think that this was remarkable enough, but there was more to come. When I visited Chalice Orchard to look it over, John told me something I had been quite unaware of, that it had once belonged to Dion Fortune, a novelist and exponent of esoteric matters. She had in fact run the place as a school of magic and occult philosophy, like the fictitious house in *The Finger and the Moon,* which I had invented two years before, with no knowledge of Chalice Orchard and almost no knowledge of Dion Fortune.

The purchase followed. It had to. I am still there.

I mentioned before that *Gandhi* reflected a revival of interests that had long lain dormant or, at least, unproductive. The seventies brought another such revival. Twenty years before, we had lived for a while in the Aylesford Carmelite community, with its ardent and tasteful devotion to the Virgin Mary. During that time I tried to extract the meaning of *The White Goddess,* by the poet and novelist Robert Graves. This book was not as famous then as it became later, and that perhaps was understandable. I've been told that when Graves submitted it to his usual

publisher, the publisher's reader reported that Graves had "gone round the bend," and turned it down. It is a highly imaginative study of mythology. Graves argues with immense ingenuity that all the goddess figures of ancient religion were aspects or manifestations of The Goddess, the ultimate female Power or Energy and, as Muse, the source of all genuine inspiration. Male gods such as Jupiter supplanted her, but she is still a reality.

Without embracing all Graves's theories (or, for that matter, understanding them) I eventually began to perceive the gracious, prayer-hearing, miracle-working Virgin of Catholic belief as meeting a deeper need than the Church liked to acknowledge—a need that had expressed itself, for thousands of years before Mary's earthly life, in the worship of female divinity under myriad images. Pagan goddess-worshippers, converted to Christianity, found in the Mother of Christ a being who could be raised as near to divinity as Christian doctrine would allow. To see her thus in her celestial nature was not to explain her away as a Christian outgrowth of paganism. She did not merely imitate what had gone before, she fulfilled it and went beyond it. But I realized that a great deal *had* gone before and that the glorified Mother was better understood and not in the least reduced by recognizing it.

Nothing more came of these reflections for a long time, though the status of Glastonbury itself as a Marian shrine kept me from forgetting them. And then one day I was contacted by Richard Cavendish, the editor of *Man, Myth and Magic,* a reference book to which I had contributed. He was now acting as an adviser to the publishers Routledge and Kegan Paul. Would I be interested, he asked, in writing a history of the Catholic devotion to Mary? I would. I submitted an outline, and the book was contracted for.

It soon became clear that the subject raised problems I had not been fully aware of. Among much else, it involved considering the background of female divinity that Graves had set me thinking of, which was certainly real despite the far-fetched theology he had built on it; and I had to spell out its continued presence in a new form. I did my best. *The Virgin,* which appeared in 1976, was not what either the publishers or myself had expected at the outset. Nor would I write it quite like that today. In a paperback edition published twelve years later, I added a preface intended to put parts of it in a truer light. But I think it is far more right than wrong ... like *King Arthur's Avalon.* It was approved not only by reviewers, but by two scholars whose judgment carried weight, and it led to an unforeseen convergence.

I was only marginally aware of people who, at that time, were promoting interest in goddess mythology and female divinity, often from a feminist point of view. Terms such as "Women's Spirituality" and "Goddess Consciousness" were coming into currency, with support from Robert Graves's book, which was being belatedly discovered. One day a visitor appeared on my doorstep at Chalice Orchard, Carolyn Shaefer, from Santa Cruz in California. She began by talking about familiar legendary matters, but when she asked politely what I'd been doing lately, I mentioned *The Virgin* and she brightened. She said University of California Extension should sponsor a seminar on it.

Carolyn meant this. Back in Santa Cruz, she made her proposal in the proper quarter. It started something much bigger. Several women historians and anthropologists were working along related lines. The artist Merlin Stone, author of *When God Was a Woman,* was making her voice heard, and so were Anne Kent Rush, Charlene Spretnak, and others. When these developments were taken into account, the result was more than a seminar, it was a conference entitled "The Great Goddess Re-Emerging," held in 1978. About five hundred attended, the vast majority being women, though fifty or so slightly bewildered men could be observed among them.

I just survived, myself, as the solitary male speaker. To get a visa, I went to the U.S. Embassy in London with a form giving details. My dialogue with the official behind the counter went like this:

Official: What sort of a conference is this, Mr. Ashe?

Me: I suppose you could call it an anthropological conference.

Him (having read further): "The Great Goddess Re-Emerging." What's that?

Me: Well, some people think God is moving into the background a bit, and the Goddess is coming forward.

Him: You don't mean to say we're getting Women's Lib in religion?

Me: Yes, especially on the West Coast.

Him: I suppose if it's going to happen anywhere, it'll be on the West Coast. I hope you're going to tell them God is a man.

I didn't, and it would not have been well received. The programme included not only lectures but rituals and meditations and dances, acts of worship, in fact. The goddess movement that still goes on, here and there, may be said to have started at that conference.

So far as it found a haven in England, it was at Glastonbury. Glastonbury again! A speculation of my own, that the place's primary sacredness might have been due to its being a goddess sanctuary, was picked up and improved upon by a local women's group. A leading member, Kathy Jones, wrote plays with mythological themes, some of them suggested by Graves's theory that the myths we know—Greek ones especially—are versions rewritten in the interests of male gods and a male-ruled society, and the authentic underlying myths would have been different. Kathy's plays, intended to reconstruct those myths, were staged in the Assembly Rooms with success. She also wrote a small book on Glastonbury as a goddess sanctuary and made a film that reached American television.

While I had given an early impulse to this movement, it soon left me behind, and quite properly. Still, I did acquire a later goddess connection. By way of preface I should explain that in the eighties, I began going to the United States on visiting professorships. The first was at the University of Southern Mississippi, in Hattiesburg. The invitation came from the Arthurian scholar Charles Moorman, a most generous academic. Others followed. I was lucky in their distribution: they were spread widely around the country, so that I saw many parts of it. None were long

in duration—a few weeks, a semester at the longest—and on most, arrangements were made for Irene to accompany me. A visiting professorship has much to be said for it. You are an honoured guest, everybody is hospitable, and you don't have to worry about tenure or get drawn into campus politics. I have always liked American students and, on the whole, American academia.

Portland State University, Oregon, had a policy of appointing staff from overseas for the summer session, and I was teaching there during several summers in the 1990s. During the initial discussion of possible courses, my sponsor, Professor Charles White, made the startling suggestion that we should offer a goddess course, dealing with the mythology and literature to which the goddess exponents had been drawing attention. I agreed to try. Attendance was good, and this course may have been the first of its kind to be given anywhere.

During one summer, we brought Kathy Jones from England. She staged one of her plays, recruiting a cast from the students and presenting the Sumerian myth of the goddess Inanna. Since then, she has organized a series of goddess conferences in Glastonbury. They attract numerous devotees, who parade through the town carrying a noncommittal image of female deity. I am less sympathetic than I was. It seemed to me once that the goddess movement was discovering a lost layer of spirituality and might be a factor in a genuine advance in religion, a "next step" as I ventured to call it. My impression today is that in so far as it continues, it has become too much a women's sect, too much a reaction against a Christianity reviled as "patriarchal."

That, however, is enough about it for now.

Irene died in 1991. In spite of our having had to surmount daunting obstacles, we had stayed together for forty-five years. She had seen her children grow up, two of them becoming successful teachers, one a nurse, another a probation officer, another a musician and composer, and all of them fully capable of making their way in the world. With her passing, my feelings were mixed. There was the immediate sorrow, yet there was no feeling that all was over. Rather, we had done all we could together, and a fresh start would not in any way be disloyal. In the next few disoriented years, there were several fresh starts, including a second marriage that didn't work, and a tentative approach to joining a religious order. Equilibrium gradually returned. My present wife, Patricia, is a retired professor of English from an American university. The Arthurian scholar Charles Moorman was her academic mentor, and Glastonbury was an important part of her intellectual life even far away in the deep South. We were married in 1998 and still live in the house at the foot of Glastonbury Tor. It is a deeply happy, harmonious partnership.

How much is left to say? I could mention other books, one about Atlantis, for instance. I never wrote the Atlantis epic unwisely attempted in my youth, but I approached the vanished continent from a different angle, placing it in the context of perennial myths which I now knew more about—myths of a lost Golden Age, a lost Ancient Wisdom. What else? I have put forward a new idea about the original Arthur, which has made its way into one or two of the standard works and may be found in my own *Mythology of the British Isles* (1990). This book is modelled on Robert Graves's *Greek Myths.* Taking each topic in succession, I tell the story and then discuss the background. Let me repeat a guiding principle that I stated before: when confronting such topics, you must take them seriously without taking them literally.

People have asked me for advice on "how to write a book." It depends a lot on what kind of book it is. However, one all-purpose rule is to try, as far as you can, to write something every day. That doesn't mean keeping regular hours, or setting yourself a daily target. The "something" can be written in the morning, the afternoon, the evening; it may be long or short; but when one "something" keeps following another, they pile up. Another point worth making is that when writing my own books, I have sometimes found that they change as I go along and insist on being different from what was planned first. It was thus with my one attempt at a novel, *The Finger and the Moon,* which wasn't even fiction when it started out; and it was thus with *The Virgin.* A writer who finds this change happening very likely has no need to worry. It may be a sign of vitality.

For anyone who has been published but with disappointing results, a source of encouragement is the fact that a book isn't necessarily dead because it seems to be. Various motives can prompt a publisher to reissue it, even after decades of silence. The theme may have acquired a new topicality. Or the book may have gained fresh interest because of others by the same author that have appeared in the interval. I speak from experience. Within the past few years, several of my own books have been resurrected, and they include the one originally called *Do What You Will,* which failed completely when it was published, but which, under the new title *The Hell-Fire Clubs: A History of Anti-Morality* (2000), has been noticed and read. I'm not sure why: perhaps, in part, because my remarks on things that had just been happening when it came out have now matured (so to speak) in a longer perspective.

Meanwhile, recent years have brought me to another rebirth of earlier interests, which I can do no more than indicate by way of conclusion. This time the theme is prophecy, which, you may remember, entered my junior consciousness from science fiction about the future and involved me with the Apocalypse of St. John. Austin Ringwode's Glastonbury pronouncement prevented the subject from being entirely shelved, and so did my acquaintance with Merlin, who foretells what is to come in the legendary Britain of Arthur. But the reawakening of interest has been due to less apparent causes.

Somebody asked me once if there was a constant motif running through my work. Well, through much of it—through the evocation of Arthur and Camelot, for instance—the motif might be described as "making the past live in the present." It could be said that all writers on history and mythology do the same. Yet I feel that some of my work has had an aspect that is rather different. In the conventional use of source materials I have done my conscientious best, and done it well enough, once or twice, to be published in scholarly journals. But I have a sense of something beyond, an awareness of things past that sometimes comes through in other ways. People claim to have recollections of previous lives or to receive messages from the dead. I am very doubtful of both claims. Yet sometimes it is *as if* consciousness of the past can enter the

mind through a transcendence of time which I don't pretend to understand. Robert Graves (here he is again) spoke of it in connection with his historical novels, such as *I, Claudius.* He coined the term "analepsis." Don't ask me how it works, if it does.

But if, through some undefined process, the past can be manifested in the present, is it possible that the future too can be manifested in the present? Are there different ways of transcending time? To sweep the notion aside as impossible is unscientific. The proper course is to establish the facts. Does foreknowledge ever actually happen? The approach of the year 2000 produced a crop of injudicious writing about such famous prognosticators as Nostradamus. My own contribution—I hope, a more judicious one—was *The Book of Prophecy,* published just ahead of the century's close. I surveyed various cases where prevision appears to be well attested, and I considered how it might have happened. It seems to me that the mind can, occasionally, escape the limitations of here-and-now bodily existence; and in doing so it can, occasionally, absorb knowledge from the future as well as the past. If so, we must seek a new understanding of consciousness in relation to time and maybe reassess ideas about survival or otherwise after physical death.

These, however, are deep waters. At the moment, let me end my story by assuring you that it isn't ending. It's going on.

Writings

The Tale of the Tub: A Survey of the Art of Bathing through the Ages, Newman Neame (London, England), 1950.

King Arthur's Avalon: The Story of Glastonbury, Collins (London, England), 1957.

From Caesar to Arthur, Collins (London, England), 1960.

Land to the West: St. Brendan's Voyage to America, Collins (London, England), 1962.

The Glass Island (play), 1964.

The Land and the Book: Israel, the Perennial Nation, Collins (London, England), 1965.

The Carmelite Order, Carmelite Press, 1965.

Gandhi: A Study in Revolution, Heinemann (London, England), 1968, Cooper Square Press (New York, NY), 2000.

(Editor and contributor) *The Quest for Arthur's Britain,* Pall Mall (London, England), 1968, Academy Chicago Publishers (Chicago, IL), 1987.

All about King Arthur (for children), W. H. Allen (London, England), 1969, published as *King Arthur in Fact and Legend,* T. Nelson (Nashville, TN), 1971.

Camelot and the Vision of Albion, Heinemann (London, England), 1971.

(With others) *The Quest for America,* Pall Mall (London, England), 1971.

The Art of Writing Made Simple, W. H. Allen (London, England), 1972.

The Finger and the Moon (novel), Heinemann (London, England), 1973.

Do What You Will: A History of Anti-Morality, W. H. Allen (London, England), 1974, reprinted as *The Hell-Fire Clubs,* 2000.

The Virgin, Routledge & Kegan Paul (London, England), 1976, Penguin (New York, NY), 1991.

The Ancient Wisdom, Macmillan (New York, NY), 1977.

Miracles, Routledge & Kegan Paul (London, England), 1978.

A Guidebook to Arthurian Britain, Longman (London, England), 1980.

Kings and Queens of Early Britain, Methuen (London, England), 1982, reprinted, 2000.

Avalonian Quest, Methuen (London, England), 1982.

The Discovery of King Arthur, Doubleday (New York, NY), 1985.

(Associate editor) *The Arthurian Encyclopedia,* Garland (New York, NY), 1986.

The Landscape of King Arthur, Henry Holt (New York, NY), 1988.

(With Norris J. Lacy) *The Arthurian Handbook,* Garland (New York, NY), 1988, revised edition, 1998.

Mythology of the British Isles, Methuen (London, England), 1990.

King Arthur: The Dream of a Golden Age, Thames & Hudson (London, England), 1990.

Atlantis: Lost Lands, Ancient Wisdom, Thames & Hudson (London, England), 1992.

Dawn behind the Dawn: A Search for an Earthly Paradise, Henry Holt (New York, NY), 1992.

(Associate editor) *The New Arthurian Encyclopedia,* St. James Press (Chicago, IL), 1991.

The Book of Prophecy: From Ancient Greece to the Millennium, Blandford (London, England), 1999.

Encyclopedia of Prophecy, ABC-CLIO (Santa Barbara, CA), 2001.

Merlin, Wessex Books (Salisbury, England), 2001.

OTHER

Columnist in *Resurgence* magazine, 1973-78. Contributor to numerous periodicals, including *Speculum.*

B

BACH, Mary 1960-

Personal

Born December 23, 1960, in Grafton, WI; daughter of John R. (an engineer and metallurgist) and Helen L. (a secretary) Bach; married Tom Filla (a veterinarian), August 16, 1983; children: Michael R., Kathryn L. *Education:* University of Wisconsin—River Falls, B.S., 1983; University of Wisconsin—La Crosse, M.E.P.D., 1995. *Politics:* Independent. *Religion:* Roman Catholic.

Addresses

Home—N2396 Highway 162, Bangor, WI 54614.

Career

Writer. Also works as a teacher of religion. Friends of the Library, Bangor, WI, president.

Writings

Termites, illustrated by Tammi Lyon, Richard C. Owen Publishers (Katonah, NY), 1998.

*   *   *

BAUER, Steven 1948-

Personal

Born September 10, 1948, in Newark, NJ; son of Albert H. and Alice Marian (Horrocks) Bauer; married second wife Elizabeth Arthur (a writer), June 19, 1982. *Education:* Trinity College (Hartford, CT), B.A. (with honors), 1970; University of Massachusetts at Amherst, M.F.A., 1975.

Addresses

Home—14100 Harmony Rd., Bath, IN 47010. *Office*—Department of English, Miami University, Oxford, OH 45056.

Career

University of Massachusetts at Amherst, head resident at Orchard Hill Residential College, 1977-78; Colby College, Waterville, ME, instructor, 1979-81, assistant professor of English, 1981-82; Miami University, Oxford, OH, assistant professor, 1982-86, associate professor, professor of English, 1996—, director of creative writing, 1986-2001. *Member:* Associated Writing Programs, Poets and Writers.

Awards, Honors

Grant from Massachusetts Arts and Humanities Foundation, 1978; writing fellow at Fine Arts Work Center, Provincetown, MA, 1978-79; Allan Collins fellow at Bread Loaf Writers' Conference, 1981; Poets and Writers reading grant, 1981; Strousse Award for Poetry, *Prairie Schooner,* 1982, for "This Silence" and "Daylight Savings"; fellow of Ossabaw Island Project, 1982; master fellowship from Indiana Arts Council, 1988; Peregrine Smith Poetry Prize, 1989, for *Daylight Savings;* Miami University, outstanding teacher award, 1991, distinguished educator award, 1995, and E. Phillips Knox Teaching Award, 1997; Fiction Recommended Winner citation, Parent's Choice Foundation, for *A Cat of a Different Color,* 2000; outstanding teacher award, 2001.

Writings

Satyrday (novel), Putnam (New York, NY), 1980.
The River (novel based on screenplay of the same title by Robert Dillon and Julian Barry), Berkley Books (New York, NY), 1985.
Steven Spielberg's Amazing Stories (short stories based on the teleplays for the television series *Amazing Stories*), two volumes, Charter Books (New York, NY), 1986.

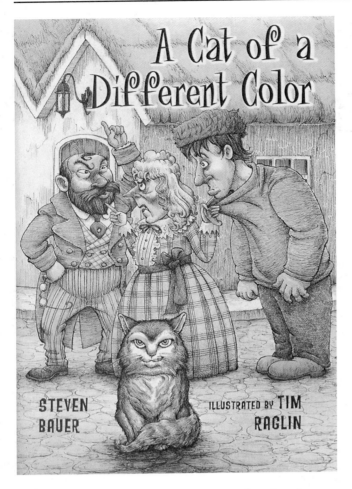

Ulwazzer, a feline with fur of ever-changing hues, teams up with a young girl and a flock of birds to rid his town of a human menace in Steven Bauer's fanciful middle-grade novel.

Daylight Savings (poetry), Gibbs Smith (Layton, UT), 1989.

The Strange and Wonderful Tale of Robert McDoodle (The Boy Who Wanted to Be a Dog) (for children), illustrated by Brad Sneed, Simon & Schuster (New York, NY), 1999.

A Cat of a Different Color (for children), illustrated by Tim Raglin, Delacorte (New York, NY), 2000.

Work represented in anthologies, including *The Gritloaf Anthology,* Palaemon Press, 1978, and *Anthology of Magazine Verse and Yearbook of American Poetry,* 1980. Contributor of numerous poems, articles, and reviews to magazines, including *Ascent, Massachusetts Review, Denver Quarterly, Poetry Now, Glamour, Mississippi Review, Indiana Review, Prairie Schooner, Missouri Review, Southwest Review, Nation,* and *Chariton Review.*

Work in Progress

The Seven Months of Winter and *Country Club,* novels.

Sidelights

Steven Bauer has written several fantasies featuring animals and young adults. Born in Newark, New Jersey, in 1948, he attended public schools in Florham Park, New Jersey, and went on to university at Trinity College, graduating in 1970. Thereafter, the young Bauer moved to the West Coast, living in the foothills of California's Sierra Nevadas for a couple of years. In 1972, he entered the master's program in writing at the University of Massachusetts at Amherst. After graduation in 1975, he wrote and taught, and then in 1978, he attended the renowned Bread Loaf Writer's Conference in Vermont; he returned in 1979 and 1980 as the headwaiter of the Conference's dining room. In 1981, he was awarded a fellowship for *Satyrday,* and was a staff associate in 1984 and 1987.

While on a fellowship to the Fine Arts Work Center in Provincetown, Massachusetts, Bauer completed his first novel, *Satyrday,* the story of an owl who wants to bring eternal darkness to the Earth by stealing the moon and causing the sun to go out. A young boy, a satyr, and a raven are called upon to free the moon from her imprisonment. A reviewer for *Library Journal* found the story to be "far more than a mere fantasy-genre piece; it is an unusual, beguiling work that will attract discerning readers." The critic for *Publishers Weekly* judged it a "sweet and gentle fable" and "a delicately written adult tale, full of haunting images and righteous magic."

Following publication of *Satyrday,* Bauer was offered a tenure-track position at Ohio's Miami University, where he moved with his second wife, novelist Elizabeth Ann Arthur. Bauer has been at Miami University since 1982. Continuing with his writing career, he also penned a novelization of the movie *The River* as well as adapted teleplays of *Steven Spielberg's Amazing Stories.* A poet of note, Bauer's 1989 collection, *Daylight Savings,* won the Peregrine Smith Poetry Prize. Then in 1999, his writing career took a different turn with his first publication for children.

In *The Strange and Wonderful Tale of Robert McDoodle,* Bauer tells a story in verse about a little boy who, to avoid going to kindergarten, enrolls at the Jellicoe School for Dogs in hopes of learning how to become a dog instead. After taking the course in digging, sniffing, panting, and snapping, he decides that the life of a dog is not an easy one. "Bauer's poetic flair is undeniable," Jody McCoy noted in the *School Library Journal,* while *Booklist* critic Shelley Townsend-Hudson called the book "an immensely appealing farce, impeccably childlike in its logic." "Few children have not wished for a dog's life," admitted a critic for *Kirkus Reviews,* "and Bauer's ballad delivers that wish fulfilled, with all its disadvantages exposed for comic effect."

With *A Cat of a Different Color,* Bauer produced a fantasy novel for middle-grade readers. Felicity-by-the-Lake is the mythical setting for the novel and that town is transformed when the swindler Jeremiah Hoytie is elected mayor. Together with his tight-fisted wife,

Hoytie conspires to steal all that is valuable and wonderful. He proclaims that all villagers must remain indoors after dark and that the beautiful lake is off limits to all but himself. His dim-witted son becomes a self-appointed policeman who carts off any offending villager to his father. All is going swimmingly for the Hoytie clan, in fact, until the arrival of clever Ulwazzer the cat who teams up with Hoytie's neglected step-daughter, Daria, to push the townspeople into action and reclaim their village and lake. Judith Everitt, writing in *School Library Journal,* dubbed Bauer's tale a "droll story," noting that "the cat is cleverer than the humans and he is unwilling to abdicate his ability to think and act for himself." Reviewing this offering in *Horn Book,* Anne St. John noted that the "plot and characters are drawn with broad comedic strokes." St. John also felt that though the message about the dangers of compla-cency was "a bit heavy-handed," Bauer's "light treat-ment of the subject prevents the moral from over-shadowing the story." *Booklist*'s Shelle Rosenfeld had unconditional praise for *A Cat of a Different Color:* "This creative, whimsical tale is also a thought-provok-

A six-year-old boy is determined to "go to the dogs" in Bauer's quirky 1999 novel The Strange and Wonderful Tale of Robert McDoodle. *(Illustration by Brad Sneed.)*

ing fable about democracy versus dictatorship and appearances versus reality." Rosenfeld concluded, "Bauer's witty prose has a read-aloud quality."

Biographical and Critical Sources

PERIODICALS

Booklist, September 1, 1999, Shelley Townsend-Hudson, review of *The Strange and Wonderful Tale of Robert McDoodle,* p. 137; June 1, 2000, Shelle Rosenfeld, review of *A Cat of a Different Color,* p. 1890.

Contemporary Review, January, 1982, review of *Satyrday,* p. 48.

Horn Book, July-August, 2000, Anne St. John, review of *A Cat of a Different Color,* p. 450.

Kirkus Reviews, September 1, 1999, review of *The Strange and Wonderful Tale of Robert McDoodle,* p. 1424.

Kliatt, fall, 1982, review of *Satyrday,* p. 18.

Library Journal, December 15, 1980, review of *Satyrday,* p. 2591.

Publishers Weekly, October 31, 1980, review of *Satyrday,* p. 78; September 13, 1999, review of *The Strange and Wonderful Tale of Robert McDoodle,* p. 82; July 3, 2000, p. 71.

School Library Journal, October, 1999, Jody McCoy, review of *The Strange and Wonderful Tale of Robert McDoodle,* p. 102; August, 2000, Judith Everitt, review of *A Cat of a Different Color,* p. 177.

Science Fiction Chronicle, February, 1987, review of *Steven Spielberg's Amazing Stories,* p. 47.

Times Literary Supplement, November 20, 1981, Richard Brown, review of *Satyrday,* p. 1375.

Voice of Youth Advocates, December, 1985, review of *Satyrday,* p. 345.

*   *   *

BEATON, Clare 1947-

Personal

Born April 20, 1947, in Stanmore, Middlesex, England; daughter of Charles F. (a physician) and Barbara (a homemaker) Beaton; married Robert A. Simpson (marriage ended, 1988); partner of Gavin A. Weightman since 1988; children: Jack Simpson, Kate Simpson, Tom Weightman. *Education:* Hornsey College of Art, diploma first (with honors). *Politics:* Labour.

Addresses

Home and office—15 Kelross Rd., London N5 2QS, England.

Career

Children's TV Programmes, BBC-TV, London, England, worked as an illustrator for children's programs *Playschool, Playaway, Jackanory, Fingermouse,* and others, 1970-78; freelance illustrator, 1978—; conducts workshops with children based on books and teaches art in schools on a volunteer basis. *Member:* Society of Authors.

Awards, Honors

Best Book Award (Gold Seal), Oppenheim Toy Portfolio, 2000, for *Mother Goose Remembers.*

Writings

SELF-ILLUSTRATED

Cards, Warwick Press (New York, NY), 1990.
Costumes, Warwick Press (New York, NY), 1990.
Face Painting, Warwick Press (New York, NY), 1990.
Hats, Warwick Press (New York, NY), 1990.
Masks, Warwick Press (New York, NY), 1990.
T-Shirt Painting, Warwick Press (New York, NY), 1990.
The Complete Book of Children's Parties, Kingfisher Books (New York, NY), 1992.
Monster Party Kit, Running Press, 1993.
The Felt Book: Easy to Make Projects for All Ages, Sterling (New York, NY), 1994.
Summer Activity Book, Barron's (Hauppauge, NY), 1994.
Beads, Badges, and Bangles, Fitzgerald Books (Bethany, MD), 1995.
Animals (in French, Spanish, and English), Barron's (Hauppauge, NY), 1996.
Clothes (in French, Spanish, and English), Barron's (Hauppauge, NY), 1996.
Numbers (in French, Spanish, and English), Barron's (Hauppauge, NY), 1996.
Colors (in French, Spanish, and English), Barron's (Hauppauge, NY), 1996.
Opposites (in French, Spanish, and English), Barron's (Hauppauge, NY), 1996.

Clare Beaton

Family (in French, Spanish, and English), Barron's (Hauppauge, NY), 1996.

Easter Activity Book, Barron's (Hauppauge, NY), 1996.

Halloween Activity Book, Barron's (Hauppauge, NY), 1996.

The Box Book, Traflagar Square (North Pomfret, VT), 1996.

Let's Pretend: Fun Ideas for Make Believe, Barron's (Hauppauge, NY), 1997.

The Clown Activity Box, Trans-Atlantic Publications, 1997.

My First Books, World Book, 1997.

Felt Pictures, photographs by Steven Shott, Contemporary Books (Lincolnwood, IL), 1998.

Mother Goose Remembers, Barefoot Books, 2000.

One Moose, Twenty Mice, Barefoot Books, 2000.

Zoë and Her Zebra, Barefoot Books, 2000.

Are We There Yet?, B Small, 2000.

A Book of Cat Postcards, B Small, 2000.

A Book of Teddy Postcards, B Small, 2000.

Playtime Rhymes for Little People, 2001.

Weather (in French and English), Barron's (Hauppauge, NY), 2001.

At Home (in French and English), Barron's (Hauppauge, NY), 2001.

ILLUSTRATOR

Marjorie Newman, *Wilkins, the Armchair Cat,* A. & C. Black (London, England), 1978.

At the Lord's Table: A Communion Book, Collins (San Francisco, CA), 1987.

Catherine Bruzzone, *Early World of English: Libro para los niños,* World Book (Chicago, IL), 1993.

Catherine Bruzzone, *Activity Book,* Barron's (Hauppauge, NY), 1993.

Catherine Bruzzone, *Spanish for Children,* Passport Books (Lincolnwood, IL), 1993.

Catherine Bruzzone, *Action French! A Lively Activity Starter Pack for Adults and Children,* Passport Books (Chicago, IL), 2000.

Catherine Bruzzone, *Action Spanish! Activity Starter Pack,* Passport Books (Chicago, IL), 2000.

Stella Blackstone, *How Big Is a Pig?,* Barefoot Books, 2000.

Stella Blackstone, *There's a Cow in the Cabbage Patch,* Barefoot Books, 2001.

Work in Progress

Working on picture books illustrated with sewn pictures using felt, antique fabrics, buttons, braids, beads, and other textile arts; working on activity books, illustrated in pen and ink.

Sidelights

London-based artist and author Clare Beaton spent several years illustrating and model making for children's television shows at the British Broadcasting Corporation before venturing into children's book publishing in 1978. Her works for young readers have won praise from reviewers for their elaborately detailed pages that incorporate fabric, beads, buttons, and even feathers. These tactile books offer holiday-themed craft activities

Basic concepts and objects are clearly illustrated by Beaton—with the help of two loveable teddy bears—in her English-Spanish picture book that includes a pronunciation key.

or three-dimensional images of animals and children that help preschoolers learn the alphabet and numbers. "Beaton's work evokes the cozy domesticity and unhurried days of a bygone era," declared a *Publishers Weekly* critic.

Beaton's first project was illustrating Marjorie Newman's *Wilkins, the Armchair Cat,* which appeared in 1978. By 1990, Beaton and her publisher had launched a series of activity books for youngsters that provided directions for various craft projects. The half-dozen titles include such books as *Costumes, Masks, Face Painting,* and *T-Shirt Painting.* She created more how-to works, including *Monster Party Kit* and *The Complete Book of Children's Parties,* and a series of bilingual works (in French, Spanish, and English) for preschoolers in 1996 that include the titles *Numbers, Colors, Opposites,* and *Family. The Felt Book: Easy to Make Projects for All Ages* provides directions for some forty projects. Simple instructions and an appendix of templates allow children to create hair accessories, a puppet, and even a pair of slippers. In 1999, she created another counting book featuring animals and an elusive orange cat in the well-received *One Moose, Twenty Mice.* Various animals are featured in this work, some of whom are stalked by the cat, some of whom seem to frighten the feline off the page. A mouse hunt at the finale, naturally, delights the cat. Beaton used various fabrics to flesh out each species, and the work won praise from reviewers for its unusual presentation. "Beaton's felt-art pictures are brightly colored and feature cheery animals," declared Susan Marie Pitard in *School Library Journal. Bulletin of the Center for Children's Books* reviewer Deborah Stevenson praised Beaton's "clever effects" and predicted that "young readers will ... find the fuzzy menagerie endearing."

Beaton used a similar tactic for her 2000 work *Zoë and Her Zebra.* Beads and fabric help create textured children and animals for the spreads, each of which features a child, his name, and the animal whose first letter matches that name. The animals, however, are not named, and readers must guess their identity. A guide at the end helps them discover some of the more unusual creatures, such as the xoona moth. The names of the children were also unique, ranging from Ben and Luke to Farooq and Sita. *School Library Journal* reviewer Jody McCoy called it "a visually tactile phantasmagoria" full of "illustrations [that] beg to be touched."

Mother Goose Remembers presents nearly fifty traditional nursery rhymes, but the pages invite young readers to search for clues from the verse inside. They can collect a feather from each page from among the vintage fabrics and trimmings. *School Library Journal* reviewer Janet M. Bair called it "an exquisite collection" of images from Beaton's fabric archives and "a delight to pore over." Beaton also won praise for *How Big Is a*

Beaton trades in pen and paper for needle and thread in creating the imaginative artwork for **Mother Goose Remembers,** *a vivid, highly textured patchwork of antique fabrics, finishings, and stitchery.*

Pig?, winner of a best book award from the Oppenheim Toy Portfolio. Several different farm animals are introduced in rhyme, but the narrator wonders how each stacks up against a mysterious pig. In the end, after meeting geese, a cow, and various other creatures, the narrator emerges as a little piglet contentedly nestled up against its mother, whom it terms "biggest of us all!" A *Publishers Weekly* reviewer termed the book "a sassy, unexpected wrap-up; Beaton will have her audience's attention all sewn up." Anne Parker, writing in *School Library Journal,* called it "another successful concept book" from Beaton and commended its "brightly colored appliquéd felt artwork," while *Booklist* critic Ellen Mandel declared it "wonderfully entertaining." According to the author, these books are an ongoing partnership with Barefoot Books, with Beaton working on her eighth book for the publisher.

Beaton told *SATA,* "Throughout my career from making puppets and other props for BBC children's programs and through the activity and craft books I illustrate and write, up to the picture books I illustrate using fabrics and buttons, I have always loved collecting a huge amount of braids, stamps, sweet wrappers, raffia, wire, wool, ribbons, postcards, threads, shells, and so on, and recycling these things into my work. I work in a large studio in my house surrounded by all these items stored on shelves and on the floor in tins, boxes and baskets. Most are discarded items bought in thrift shops and the idea of giving them new life through my work appeals to me. I hope to inspire people with my 'sewn illustrations'; children and adults alike can give it a go themselves."

Biographical and Critical Sources

PERIODICALS

Booklist, October 15, 1992, Stephanie Zvirin, review of *The Complete Book of Children's Parties,* p. 392; August, 1994, Barbara Jacobs, review of *The Felt Book,* p. 2014; May 15, 1999, Carolyn Phelan, review of *One Moose, Twenty Mice,* p. 1701; October 15, 1999, Marta Segal, review of *Zoë and Her Zebra,* p. 450; October 1, 2000, Ellen Mandel, review of *How Big Is a Pig?,* p. 344.
Bulletin of the Center for Children's Books, July-August, 1999, Deborah Stevenson, review of *One Moose, Twenty Mice,* p. 380.
Kirkus Reviews, August 1, 1999, review of *Zoë and Her Zebra,* p. 1223.
Publishers Weekly, June 6, 1994, review of *Summer Activity Book,* p. 66; July 24, 2000, review of *Mother Goose Remembers;* July 24, 2000, review of *How Big Is a Pig?,* p. 93.
Reading Today, December, 2000, Lynne T. Burke, review of *Mother Goose Remembers,* p. 35.
School Library Journal, February, 1991, Denise Krell, review of *Masks, Costumes, Face Painting,* and *T-Shirt Painting,* pp. 84-85; June, 1999, Susan Marie Pitard, review of *One Moose, Twenty Mice,* p. 91; December, 1999, Jody McCoy, review of *Zoë and Her Zebra,* p. 87; September, 2000, Janet M. Bair, review

of *Mother Goose Remembers,* p. 213; December, 2000, Anne Parker, review of *How Big Is a Pig?,* p. 96.

*   *   *

BLAKE, Quentin (Saxby) 1932-

Personal

Born December 16, 1932, in Sidcup, Kent, England; son of William (a civil servant) and Evelyn Blake. *Education:* Downing College, Cambridge, England, M.A., 1956; University of London Institute of Education, P.G.C.E., 1956-57; attended Chelsea School of Art, 1958-59.

Addresses

Home—Flat 8, 30 Bramham Gardens, London SW5 0HF, England. *Agent*—(International) A. P. Watt Ltd., 20 John St., London WCIN 2DR, England.

Career

Author, artist, editor, and educator. Primarily an illustrator, drawing for *Punch,* beginning 1948, and other British magazines, including *Spectator,* and illustrating children's and educational books; freelance illustrator, 1957—; Royal College of Art, London, England, tutor in School of Graphic Design, 1965-78, head of Illustration Department, 1978-86, visiting tutor, 1986-89, visiting professor, 1989—, senior fellow, 1988. Has also worked as an English teacher at French Lycee in London, 1962-65. *Exhibitions:* Work has been exhibited at Workshop Gallery, 1972, 1973, 1974, 1976; at the National Theatre, 1984; at the Royal Academy, 1984, 1986, 1987; and at the London Group, England, 1987. *Military service:* Served in the Army Education Corps, 1951-53.

Awards, Honors

Several of Blake's books were named to the Child Study Association of America's Children's Books of the Year list, including *Put on Your Thinking Cap,* 1969, *Arabel's Raven,* 1974, *Custard and Company,* 1985, and *The Giraffe and the Pelly and Me,* 1986; *Guardian* Award, second prize, 1969, for *Patrick;* Hans Christian Andersen Award for illustration, International Board on Books for Young People (IBBY), 1976, for *How Tom Beat Captain Najork and His Hired Sportsmen,* 1982, for *Mister Magnolia,* and 1997, for *Clown; A Near Thing for Captain Najork* was selected one of the *New York Times* Best Illustrated Books of the Year, 1976, as was *Clown* in 1997; Kate Greenaway Medal high commendation, British Library Association, 1980, for *The Wild Washerwomen: A New Folktale;* Kate Greenaway Medal, British Library Association, and Children's Book Award, Federation of Children's Book Groups, both 1981, both for *Mister Magnolia;* Children's Book Award, Federation of Children's Book Groups, 1982, for *The BFG;* Kurt Maschler Award runner-up, National Book League (London, England), 1982, for *Rumbelow's*

Quentin Blake

Dance, 1984, for *The Story of the Dancing Frog,* 1985, for *The Giraffe and the Pelly and Me,* and 1986, for *The Rain Door; The Rain Door* and *Cyril Bonhamy and Operation Ping* were exhibited at the Bologna International Children's Book Fair, 1985; Reading Magic Award, 1989, for *Quentin Blake's ABC;* Kurt Maschler Award, National Book League, 1990, for *All Join In;* Smarties Prize (ages six to eight), 1990, for *Esio Trot;* British Book Award (illustrated runner-up), 1990, for *Alphabeasts;* Ragazzi Award, Bologna Children's Book Fair, and Blue Ribbon citation, *Bulletin of the Center for Children's Books,* both 1996, both for *Clown; How Tom Beat Captain Najork and His Hired Sportsmen* and *The Witches* were named Notable Books by the American Library Association; *How Tom Beat Captain Najork and His Hired Sportsmen* and *The Wild Washerwomen: A New Folktale* were named to the *Boston Globe/Horn Book* Award honor list.

Blake was elected a Royal Designer for Industry in 1981, awarded the Silver Pencil (Holland) in 1985, named an officer of the Order of the British Empire in 1988, and made Children's Laureate of the United Kingdom in 1999. In 1993, he received the University of Southern Mississippi Medallion for his body of work. Blake has also been the recipient of several child-selected awards.

Writings

SELF-ILLUSTRATED; FOR CHILDREN

Patrick, Cape, 1968, Walck, 1969.

Jack and Nancy, Cape, 1969.

Angelo, Cape, 1970.

Snuff, Cape, 1973, Lippincott, 1973.

Lester at the Seaside, Collins Picture Lions, 1975.

(Compiler, with John Yeoman) *The Puffin Book of Improbable Records,* Puffin, 1975, published as *The Improbable Book of Records,* Atheneum, 1976.

The Adventures of Lester, British Broadcasting Corporation (BBC), 1978.

(Compiler) *Custard and Company: Poems by Ogden Nash,* Kestrel, 1979, Little, Brown, 1980.

Mister Magnolia, Merrimack, 1980, Random Century (London, England), 1991.

Quentin Blake's Nursery Rhyme Book, Cape, 1983, Harper, 1984.

The Story of the Dancing Frog, Cape, 1984, Knopf, 1985.

Mrs. Armitage on Wheels, Cape, 1987, Knopf, 1988.

Quentin Blake's ABC, Knopf, 1989, Cape, 1989.

All Join In, Cape, 1990, Little, Brown, 1991.

Quentin Blake's Nursery Collection, Cape, 1991.

Cockatoos, Little, Brown, 1992, Cape, 1992.

Simpkin, Cape, 1993, Viking (New York, NY), 1994.

(Compiler) *The Quentin Blake Book of Nonsense Verse,* Viking (New York, NY), 1994, Viking Penguin (New York, NY), 1997.

(Compiler) *The Penguin Book of Nonsense Verse,* Penguin (New York, NY), 1995.

Clown, Cape, 1995, Holt, 1996.

The Quentin Blake Book of Nonsense Stories, Viking (New York, NY), 1996.

Mrs. Armitage and the Big Wave, Harcourt (San Diego, CA), 1997.

Ten Frogs, Pavilion, 1997, Michael di Capua Books/HarperCollins (New York, NY), 2000.

The Green Ship, Cape, 1998.

Zagazoo, Orchard Books (New York, NY), 1998.

(With John Cassidy) *Drawing for the Artistically Undiscovered,* Klutz Press, 1998.

Fantastic Daisy Artichoke, Rand, 2001.

ILLUSTRATOR

Evan Hunter, *The Wonderful Button,* Abelard, 1961.

Frances Gray Patton, *Good Morning, Miss Dove,* Penguin, 1961.

John Moore, editor, *The Boys' Country Book,* Collins, 1961.

Rosemary Weir, *Albert the Dragon,* Abelard, 1961.

Edward Korel, *Listen and I'll Tell You,* Blackie, 1962, Lippincott, 1964.

John Moreton, *Punky: Mouse for a Day,* Faber, 1962.

Ezo, *My Son-in-Law the Hippopotamus,* Abelard, 1962.

Rupert Croft-Cooke, *Tales of a Wicked Uncle,* Cape, 1963.

Richard Schickel, *The Gentle Knight,* Abelard, 1964.

Joan Tate, *The Next-Doors,* Heinemann, 1964.

Rosemary Weir, *Albert the Dragon and the Centaur,* Abelard, 1964.

Rosemary Weir, *The Further Adventures of Albert the Dragon,* Abelard, 1964.

Fred Loads, Alan Gemmell, and Bil Sowerbutts, *Gardeners' Question Time,* BBC Publications, 1964, second series, 1966.

Ennis Rees, *Riddles, Riddles Everywhere,* Abelard, 1964.

James Britton, editor, *The Oxford Books of Stories for Juniors,* three volumes, Oxford University Press, 1964-66.

Ennis Rees, *Pun Fun,* Abelard, 1965.

Bill Hartley, *Motoring and the Motorist,* BBC, 1965.

Charles Connell, *Aphrodisiacs in Your Garden,* Mayflower, 1965.

Barry Ruth, *Home Economics,* Heinemann Educational, 1966.

Jules Verne, *Around the World in Eighty Days,* Chatto, 1966.

Thomas L. Hirsch, *Puzzles for Pleasure and Leisure,* Abelard, 1966.

Robert Tibber, *Aristide,* Hutchinson, 1966, Dial, 1967.

Marjorie Bilbow and Antony Bilbow, *Give a Dog a Good Name,* Hutchinson, 1967.

Joan Tate, *Bits and Pieces,* Heinemann, 1967.

Ennis Rees, *Tiny Tall Tales,* Abelard, 1967.

Joan Tate, *Luke's Garden,* Heinemann, 1967.

Helen J. Fletcher, *Put on Your Thinking Cap,* Abelard, 1968.

G. Broughton, *Listen and Read with Peter and Molly,* BBC, 1968.

Gordon Fraser, editor, *Your Animal Book,* Gordon Fraser, 1969.

H. P. Rickman, *Living with Technology,* Zenith Books, 1969.

G. Broughton, *Success with English: The Penguin Course,* Penguin, 1969.

Nathan Zimelman, *The First Elephant Comes to Ireland,* Follett, 1969.

James Reeves, *Mr. Horrox and the Gratch,* Abelard, 1969.

Ennis Rees, *Gillygaloos and the Gollywhoppers: Tall Tales about Mythical Monsters,* Abelard, 1969.

Gillian Edwards, *Hogmanay and Tiffany: The Names of Feasts and Fasts,* Geoffrey Bles, 1970.

D. Mackay, B. Thompson, and P. Schaub, *The Birthday Party,* Longman, 1970.

Elizabeth Bowen, *The Good Tiger,* Cape, 1970.

Helen J. Fletcher, *Puzzles and Quizzles,* Platt, 1970.

Thomas Corddry, *Kibby's Big Feat,* Follett, 1970.

H. Thomson, *The Witch's Cat,* Addison-Wesley, 1971.

J. B. S. Haldane, *My Friend Mr. Leakey,* Puffin, 1971.

Ruth Craft, *Play School Play Ideas,* Penguin, 1971.

Aristophanes, *The Birds,* translated by Dudley Fitts, Royal College of Art, 1971.

Marcus Cunliffe, *The Ages of Man: From Sav-age to Sew-age,* American Heritage, 1971.

G. Broughton, *Peter and Molly,* BBC, 1972.

Natalie Savage Carlson, *Pigeon of Paris,* Blackie, 1972, Scholastic, 1975.

Norman Hunter, *Wizards Are a Nuisance,* BBC, 1973.

Julia Watson, editor, *The Armada Lion Book of Young Verse,* Collins, 1973.

R. C. Scriven, *The Thingummy-jig,* BBC, 1973.

F. Knowles and B. Thompson, *Eating,* Longman, 1973.

Clement Freud, *Grimble,* Penguin, 1974.

Dr. Seuss (pseudonym of Theodor Seuss Geisel), *Great Day for Up!,* Random House, 1974.

Bronnie Cunningham, editor, *The Puffin Joke Book,* Penguin, 1974.

Willis Hall, *The Incredible Kidnapping,* Heinemann, 1975.

Willis Hall, *Kidnapped at Christmas,* Heinemann Educational, 1975.

G. Broughton, *Peter and Molly's Revision Book,* BBC, 1975.

Lewis Carroll, *The Hunting of the Snark,* Folio Society, 1976.

Sylvia Plath, *The Bed Book,* Faber, 1976.

Adele De Leeuw, *Horseshoe Harry and the Whale,* Parents Magazine Press, 1976.

Ellen Blance and Ann Cook, *Monster Books,* twenty-four volumes, Longman, 1976-1978.

Margaret Mahy, *The Nonstop Nonsense Book,* Dent (London, England), 1977, Margaret K. McElderry Books (New York, NY), 1989.

Sara Brewton, John E. Brewton, and John B. Blackburn, editors, *Of Quarks, Quasars, and Other Quirks: Quizzical Poems for the Supersonic Age,* Harper, 1977.

Ted Allan, *Willie the Squowse,* McClelland & Stewart, 1977, Hastings House, 1978.

Carole Ward, *Play School Ideas 2,* BBC, 1977.

Stella Gibbons, *Cold Comfort Farm,* Folio Society, 1977.

Bronnie Cunningham, editor, *Funny Business,* Penguin, 1978.

Helen Young, *What Difference Does It Make, Danny?,* Deutsch, 1980.

Evelyn Waugh, *Black Mischief,* Folio Society, 1981.

Jonathan Gathorne-Hardy, *Cyril Bonhamy v. Madam Big,* Cape, 1981.

Tony Lacey, editor, *Up with Skool!,* Kestrel, 1981.

Tim Rice and Andrew Lloyd Webber, *Joseph and the Amazing Technicolor Dreamcoat,* Holt, 1982.

Jonathan Gathorne-Hardy, *Cyril Bonhamy and the Great Drain Robbery,* Cape, 1983.

Evelyn Waugh, *Scoop,* Folio Society, 1983.

George Orwell, *Animal Farm,* Folio Society, 1984.

Rudyard Kipling, *How the Camel Got His Hump,* Macmillan (London, England), 1984, Bedrick Books, 1985.

Jonathan Gathorne-Hardy, *Cyril Bonhamy and Operation Ping,* Cape, 1984.

Jeff Brown, *A Lamp for the Lambchops,* Methuen, 1985.

Margaret Mahy, *The Great Piratical Rumbustification and the Librarian and the Robbers,* Godine, 1986, Morrow, 1993.

Jan Mark, *Frankie's Hat,* Kestrel, 1986.

Dr. Pete Rowan, *Can You Get Warts from Touching Toads?: Ask Dr. Pete,* Messner, 1986.

Jeff Brown, *Stanley and the Magic Lamp,* Methuen, 1990.

Dick King-Smith, *Alphabeasts,* Gollancz, 1990, Simon & Schuster, 1992.

John Masefield, *The Midnight Folk,* Heinemann, 1991.

Hilaire Belloc, *Algernon and Other Cautionary Tales,* Cape, 1991.

John Masefield, *The Box of Delights,* Heinemann, 1992.

Hilaire Belloc, *The Winter Sleepwalker,* Cape, 1994.

Hilaire Belloc, *Cautionary Verses,* Red Fox, 1995.

Carol Ann Duffy, *Meeting Midnight,* Cape, 1995.

Charles Dickens, *A Christmas Carol,* Simon & Schuster, 1995, Pavilion (London, England), 1995.

Sylvia Sherry, *Elephants Have Right of Way,* Cape, 1995.

Catherine Anholt and Emma Quentin, editors, *The Candlewick Book of First Rhymes,* Candlewick Press, 1996.

John Hedgecoe, *Breakfast with Dolly,* Collins, 1997.

John Julius Norwich, *The Twelve Days of Christmas,* St. Martin's Press, 1998.

William Steig, *Wizzil,* Farrar Straus (New York, NY), 2000.

ILLUSTRATOR; ALL BY JOAN AIKEN

The Escaped Black Mamba, BBC Publications, 1973, published as *Arabel and the Escaped Black Mamba,* BBC Books, 1990.

Tales of Arabel's Raven, Cape, 1974, published as *Arabel's Raven,* Doubleday, 1974.

The Bread Bin, BBC Publications, 1974.

Mortimer's Tie (also see below), BBC Publications, 1976.

Mortimer and the Sword Excalibur (also see below), BBC Publications, 1979.

The Spiral Stair (also see below), BBC Publications, 1979.

Arabel and Mortimer (includes *Mortimer's Tie, The Spiral Stair,* and *Mortimer and the Sword Excalibur*), Cape/BBC Publications, 1979, Doubleday, 1981.

Mortimer's Portrait on Glass, BBC Publications, 1980.

The Mystery of Mr. Jones's Disappearing Taxi, BBC Publications, 1980.

Mortimer's Cross, Cape, 1983, Harper, 1984.

Mortimer Says Nothing, Harper, 1987.

(With Lizza Aiken) *Mortimer and Arabel,* BBC Children's Books, 1992.

The Winter Sleepwalker and Other Stories, Cape, 1994.

Handful of Gold, Cape, 1995.

ILLUSTRATOR; ALL BY PATRICK CAMPBELL

Come Here Till I Tell You, Hutchinson, 1960.

Constantly in Pursuit, Hutchinson, 1962.

Brewing Up in the Basement, Hutchinson, 1963.

How to Become a Scratch Golfer, Blond, 1963.

The P-P-Penguin Patrick Campbell, Penguin, 1965.

Rough Husbandry, Hutchinson, 1965.

A Feast of True Fandangles, W. H. Allen, 1979.

ILLUSTRATOR; ALL BY ROALD DAHL

Danny: The Champion of the World, Cape, 1975.

The Enormous Crocodile, Knopf, 1978.

The Twits, Knopf, 1980.

George's Marvellous Medicine, Cape, 1981, published in the United States as *George's Marvelous Medicine,* Knopf, 1982.

The BFG, Farrar, Straus, 1982.

Roald Dahl's Revolting Rhymes, Cape, 1982, Knopf, 1983.

The Witches, Farrar, Straus, 1983, Random House (London, England), 1995.

Roald Dahl's Dirty Beasts, Cape, 1983, Penguin, 1986.

The Giraffe and the Pelly and Me, Farrar, Straus, 1985, Cape, 1985.

Matilda, Cape, 1988, Random House (London, England), 1994.

Rhyme Stew, Cape, 1989, Viking, 1990.

Esio Trot, Viking, 1990.

The Dahl Diary, Puffin, 1991.

Roald Dahl's Guide to Railway Safety, British Railways Board, 1991.

The Vicar of Nibbleswicke, Random Century, 1991, Viking, 1992.

My Year, Viking, 1994.

Blake's illustrations for Dahl's **Matilda** *reflect the wicked humor underlying this offbeat story of a young girl with extraordinary powers.*

Roald Dahl's Revolting Recipes (compiled by Josie Fison and Felicity Dahl), photographs by Jan Baldwin, Viking, 1994.

The Complete Adventures of Charlie and Mr. Willy Wonka (includes *Charlie and the Chocolate Factory* and *Charlie and the Great Glass Elevator*), Viking, 1995.

James and the Giant Peach, Viking, 1995.

The Magic Finger, Viking, 1995.

The Roald Dahl Quiz Book 2 (compiled by Sylvia Bond and Richard Maher), Puffin, 1996.

Fantastic Mr. Fox, Viking, 1996.

Charlie and the Great Glass Elevator, Puffin, 1998.

The Wonderful Story of Henry Sugar and Six More, Puffin, 2000.

Even More Revolting Recipes (compiled by Felicity Dahl), Viking, 2001.

ILLUSTRATOR; ALL BY SID FLEISCHMAN

McBroom's Wonderful One-Acre Farm, Chatto & Windus, 1972, Greenwillow, 1992.

Here Comes McBroom!, Chatto & Windus, 1976, Greenwillow, 1992.

McBroom and the Great Race, Chatto & Windus, 1981.

ILLUSTRATOR; ALL BY NILS-OLOF FRANZEN

Agaton Sax and the Diamond Thieves, Deutsch, 1965, translated by Evelyn Ramsden, Delacorte, 1967.

Agaton Sax and the Scotland Yard Mystery, Delacorte, 1969.

Agaton Sax and the Incredible Max Brothers, Delacorte, 1970.

Agaton Sax and the Criminal Doubles, Deutsch, 1971.

Agaton Sax and the Colossus of Rhodes, Deutsch, 1972.

Agaton Sax and the London Computer Plot, Deutsch, 1973.

Agaton Sax and the League of Silent Exploders, Deutsch, 1974.

Agaton Sax and the Haunted House, Deutsch, 1975.

Agaton Sax and the Big Rig, Deutsch, 1976.

Agaton Sax and Lispington's Grandfather Clock, Deutsch, 1978.

ILLUSTRATOR; ALL BY RUSSELL HOBAN

How Tom Beat Captain Najork and His Hired Sportsmen, Atheneum, 1974.

A Near Thing for Captain Najork, Cape, 1975, Atheneum, 1976.

The Twenty Elephant Restaurant, Cape, 1980.

Ace Dragon Ltd., Cape, 1980, Merrimack, 1981.

The Marzipan Pig, Farrar, Straus, 1986.

The Rain Door, Gollancz, 1986, Crowell, 1987.

Monsters, Scholastic, 1990.

Trouble on Thunder Mountain, Orchard Books (New York, NY), 2000.

ILLUSTRATOR; ALL BY J. P. MARTIN

Uncle, Cape, 1964, Coward, 1966.

Uncle Cleans Up, Cape, 1965, Coward, 1967.

Uncle and His Detective, Cape, 1966.

Uncle and the Treacle Trouble, Cape, 1967.

Uncle and Claudius the Camel, Cape, 1969.

Uncle and the Battle for Badgertown, Cape, 1973.

ILLUSTRATOR; ALL BY MICHAEL ROSEN

Mind Your Own Business, S. G. Phillips, 1974.

Wouldn't You Like to Know?, Deutsch, 1977.

The Bakerloo Flea, Longman, 1979.

You Can't Catch Me!, Deutsch, 1981.

Quick, Let's Get Out of Here, Deutsch, 1984.

Don't Put Mustard in the Custard, Deutsch, 1986.

Under the Bed, Prentice-Hall, 1986.

Smelly Jelly Smelly Fish, Prentice-Hall, 1986.

Hard-Boiled Legs: The Breakfast Book, Prentice-Hall, 1987.

Spollyollydiddlytiddlyitis: The Doctor Book, Walker, 1987.

Down at the Doctor's: The Sick Book, Simon & Schuster, 1988.

The Best of Michael Rosen: Poetry for Kids, RDR Books, 1995.

ILLUSTRATOR; ALL BY JOHN YEOMAN

A Drink of Water and Other Stories, Faber, 1960.

The Boy Who Sprouted Antlers, Faber, 1961, revised edition, Collins, 1977.

The Bear's Winter House, World, 1969.

Alphabet Soup (poem), Faber, 1969, Follett, 1970.

The Bear's Water Picnic, Blackie, 1970, Macmillan, 1971.

Sixes and Sevens, Blackie, 1971, Macmillan, 1972.

Mouse Trouble, Hamish Hamilton, 1972, Macmillan, 1973.

Beatrice and Vanessa, Hamish Hamilton, 1974, Macmillan, 1975.

The Young Performing Horse, Hamish Hamilton, 1977, Parents Magazine Press, 1978.

The Wild Washerwomen: A New Folktale, Greenwillow, 1979.

Rumbelow's Dance, Hamish Hamilton, 1982.

The Hermit and the Bear, Deutsch, 1984.

Our Village (Poems), Atheneum, 1988, Walker Books, 1988.

Old Mother Hubbard's Dog Dresses Up, Walker Books, 1989, Houghton, 1990.

Old Mother Hubbard's Dog Learns to Play, Walker Books, 1989, Houghton, 1990.

Old Mother Hubbard's Dog Needs a Doctor, Walker Books, 1989, Houghton, 1990.

Old Mother Hubbard's Dog Takes up Sport, Walker Books, 1989, Houghton, 1990.

The World's Laziest Duck and Other Amazing Records, Macmillan (London, England), 1991.

The Family Album, Hamish Hamilton, 1993.

Featherbrains, Hamish Hamilton, 1993.

The Singing Tortoise and Other Animal Folktales, Gollancz, 1993, Morrow, 1994.

Mr. Nodd's Ark, Hamish Hamilton, 1995.

The Do-It-Yourself House That Jack Built, Atheneum Books for Young Readers (New York, NY), 1995.

Sinbad the Sailor (retelling), Pavilion, 1996.

The Princes' Gifts: Magic Folktales from Around the World, Pavilion, 2000.

OTHER

(And illustrator) *A Band of Angels* (picture book for adults), Gordon Fraser, 1969.

Illustrator for "Jackanory," BBC-TV. Contributor of illustrations to periodicals, including *Punch* and *Spectator.*

Adaptations

Patrick (filmstrip), Weston Woods, 1973; *Snuff* (filmstrip with record or cassette), Weston Woods, 1975; *Great Day for Up!* (filmstrip), Random House.

Sidelights

Three-time winner of the Hans Christian Andersen Award for illustration, the "Nobel" of such prizes, British author-illustrator Quentin Blake is regarded by many critics as a master artist whose line drawings and watercolors are touched with genius. Dubbed a "wizard with a scribbly line and a color wash," by *Booklist*'s Michael Cart, Blake has written and illustrated numerous well-received books for children and has provided the pictures for over two hundred titles by other authors for children and adults. Considered an especially inventive and adaptable illustrator, he has created a highly recognizable style—called "calligraphic" by Brian Alderson in *Horn Book*—that ranges from the childlike to the highly sophisticated. Blake generally uses squiggly black lines heightened with color to express a variety of characteristics and expressions with a minimum of strokes. Full of life and fluid movement, the humor, drama, and spirit of his illustrations are thought to make them most inviting to viewers, especially children. Although these pictures may appear casual, they are acknowledged for the artistry and technical skill that the artist brings to them; in addition, Blake is praised for his keen observation of human nature as well as for the depth and pathos with which he underscores many of his works.

As the creator of his own picture books and concept books and the editor of collections of stories and poems, Blake uses familiar motifs—the folktale, the cumulative tale, the alphabet book, the counting book, and the nursery rhyme—to provide his young audience with works that are considered both original and delightful.

Lauded as a gifted humorist and storyteller, he invests his works with a strong theatricality and includes elements of fantasy in many of his books, which he writes in both prose and verse. Blake often uses historical settings such as the Middle Ages and the eighteenth and nineteenth centuries to introduce elements of social history along with his broadly comic yet incisive characterizations. He is often celebrated by critics as both creator and collaborator. Writing in the *Times Literary Supplement,* John Mole asserted, "[Blake's] instantly recognizable combination of sprightly pen and watery brush is a guarantee of frequent delight. He is our street-wise Ardizzone." *Signal* critic Elaine Moss called him "the genius who turns a difficult manuscript into a thoroughly acceptable and beckoning book," while *Times Educational Supplement* reviewer Naomi Lewis added, "Any book which has Quentin Blake as an illustrator is in luck, for who can match his zany wit and euphoria, his engaging charm, his wild assurance of line?" Alderson named him "the laureate of happiness," and added that "thought and graphic wizardry ... underline almost the whole of Quentin Blake's oeuvre."

The son of a civil servant and a homemaker, Blake grew up in Sidcup, Kent, a suburb of London, England. He once told *SATA,* "I can remember drawing on the back of my exercise books as far back as primary school. I wasn't especially encouraged by anyone. Aside from children's comics, there wasn't a great deal of illustrated material available when I was a young boy. If you were growing up in a wealthy family, you would perhaps be conscious of Arthur Rackham. But in general, children had no notion of 'an illustrator.' Once I got past children's books, I became an omnivorous reader. I read anything and everything."

Blake began submitting prose and pictures to the *Chronicle,* the school magazine of Chiselhurst Grammar School. He told *SATA,* "My most significant experience at Chiselhurst was meeting Alfred Jackson, a cartoonist for *Punch* and other magazines. His wife, my Latin teacher, took an interest in my drawings, and arranged a meeting between us. I was fifteen at the time, and had no idea how one went about submitting drawings to magazines. After my informative meeting with Jackson, however, I began to send my work to *Punch.* ... [Eventually,] they accepted a few small drawings. I was drawn to the work of Ronald Searle and Andre Francois. I was influenced by them, not in terms of style, but because each in his own way seemed to be absolutely unrestricted by the conventions of illustration." When asked by Moss in *Signal* if his early success helped his parents to support Blake's leanings toward a career in humorous art, he responded that they wanted security for him, "something like banking or teaching."

After graduating from Chiselhurst, Blake served in the Army Education Corps for two years, teaching English at Aldershot and illustrating a reader for illiterate soldiers. After completing his national service, Blake went to Downing College at Cambridge University to read English. "I had decided against art school," he told

Roald Dahl and Blake collaborated on **The BFG,** ***in which a Big Friendly Giant and orphaned Sophie thwart the efforts of less pleasant giants to add "human beans" to their dinner menu.***

SATA, "because I wanted an education in literature. Had I enrolled in art school I knew that I would lose the opportunity to study literature. I could still continue to draw." Blake studied for three years at Cambridge, where he drew for their undergraduate magazines as well as for *Punch.* In 1956, he went to the University of London for a year of teacher's training. "On the verge of becoming a teacher," Blake said, "I completed the training program and took the qualifications, but took no full-time job and went back to what I had always intended for myself—art and illustration."

Becoming a freelance artist, Blake was hired to do a drawing a week for *Punch* and also began working for the literary magazine *Spectator.* In addition, he became a part-time student at Chelsea College of Art, "because," he said, "I wanted to learn more about life drawing and painting." Blake enrolled at Chelsea in order to study with Brian Robb, a noted painter, illustrator, and cartoonist who taught at the school. Blake's early cartoons, he said, "were funny, which was their main objective. I was not at all interested in political satire, which is probably why my career developed more in the direction of book illustration than cartooning. I was drawn to the drama of illustration and the theatricality of it. Books offered a continuity of narrative, which was very important to me. I was interested in storytelling and in showing how people react, how they move, and how they're placed in a scene. I was fascinated with the way one could tell a story by visually portraying the action of the characters. Of course, I didn't identify this as a motive at the time, but it certainly had a lot to do with my development in the direction of book illustration."

"For *Punch* I had to think up funny things and invent visual jokes. Whereas for the *Spectator* I was briefed once a week when I went to the office and expected to come up with something by the next day. One week it was Kruschev, the next it was French cooking. I liken this kind of work, and the versatility it demands, to repertory acting: one week you're Ophelia and the next Macbeth."

At the age of thirty-six, Blake created his first children's book, *Patrick,* a picture book fantasy about a young man who fiddles his way through Ireland on a magical violin. Years earlier, he had begun illustrating books for other authors. Throughout his career, Blake has provided the pictures for writers such as Lewis Carroll, Sylvia Plath, Rudyard Kipling, Dr. Seuss, Jules Verne, Margaret Mahy, George Orwell, John Masefield, Joan Tate, Evelyn Waugh, and Aristophanes. He is especially well known for his illustrations for the children's books of Joan Aiken, Michael Rosen, Sid Fleischman, J. P. Martin, and Nils-Olof Franzen. However, some of Blake's greatest successes as an illustrator have been for the works of Roald Dahl, Russell Hoban, and John Yeoman, the latter a friend with whom Blake attended Cambridge and with whom he has cowritten some texts. Blake sees his work as an illustrator as a collaboration with text and author: "The first collaboration is with the story. If you're the right illustrator for the text, you get a rush of ideas and feelings from the story itself. Then you

can go to the author and confer. If you're not the right illustrator, I don't believe the collaboration will ever be fruitful."

Reviewing Blake's illustrations for Hoban's *How Tom Beat Captain Najork and His Hired Sportsmen,* Moss declared that Blake was "perhaps the only illustrator who could have given visual form to [Hoban's] text without underplaying or overplaying the absurdity." Mary Nickerson, reviewing the same title in *School Library Journal,* called attention to Blake's "loony, pop-eyed characters" who "enliven some of the best current English books." Writing of his illustrations for Yeoman's *The Wild Washerwoman, Horn Book* reviewer Paul Heins noted, "The preposterous, joyful narrative and the expressive caricaturing of the slapdash line drawings washed with color are perfectly balanced." "The team of John Yeoman and Quentin Blake is way out on its own, far ahead of the field," declared Marcus Crouch in a *Junior Bookshelf* review of *The Wild Washerwoman.* "This is genuine, all-pervading humor, untouched with satire but firmly based in real values." And some of Blake's most endearing and signature work can be found in his classic illustrations for Dahl's sardonic tales, such as *The Enormous Crocodile, The Twits, George's Marvelous Medicine, Matilda,* and *Charlie and the Chocolate Factory.* Reviewing Blake's artwork for Dahl's *The Giraffe and the Pelly and Me, Horn Book* critic Ann A. Flowers felt his illustrations "are an integral part of the story; it is hard to imagine it without his choleric Duke, cheerful pelican, and scruffy little boy."

Beginning in the late 1960s, Blake began to intersperse his original picture books, comic fantasies, concept books, and compilations with the books for which he provided illustrations. One of his most acclaimed works is *Mister Magnolia,* the story of how the cheerful, dashing title character searches for and is presented with a boot to match the one he is wearing. Called "Blake's masterpiece" by Alderson, *Mister Magnolia* is the author's own favorite among his books; he told *SATA,* "It's not autobiographical, but reflects the things I like in *pictures.*" Blake tells a rhyming nonsense tale in which flute, newt, hoot, rooty-toot and other words guide the story. *Growing Point* reviewer Margery Fisher added that his "typically active line and emphatic colour and his comic detail" were never better. Writing in *Book Window,* Margaret Walker claimed that Blake "has excelled himself" and urged all: "Do buy it."

One book that demonstrates Blake's sensitivity and understanding of the human condition particularly well is *The Story of the Dancing Frog.* Recounted as family history by a mother to her small daughter, the tale describes how Great Aunt Gertrude, who has recently been widowed, is prevented from drowning herself by the sight of a frog dancing on a lily pad. Gertrude and the frog, which she names George, become increasingly successful on the strength of George's talent; they travel the world before retiring to the south of France. At the end of the story, the daughter asks, "Are they dead now, then?" Her mother, whom Blake implies is herself widowed, replies, "That was a long time ago, so I suppose they must be." Writing in *The Signal Selection of Children's Books,* Jane Doonan noted, "The light touch with pen and paint catches the humor and hints at the sadness." She concluded, "It is Blake at his best." In his book *The Telling Line: Essays on Fifteen Contemporary Book Illustrators,* Douglas Martin called *The Story of the Dancing Frog* "storytelling and illustrative book designing at its most accomplished."

Blake continues to write and illustrate books of his own while compiling collections of prose and verse and providing pictures for the works of other authors. His 1993 work *Simpkin* is a picture book with a rhyming text that is noted for expressing the duality of a small boy's nature while explaining the concept of opposites; in his review in *Junior Bookshelf,* Crouch asserted, "This artist grows more assured with every book." *The Singing Tortoise and Other Animal Folktales* is a collection of international cautionary tales from the nineteenth and early twentieth centuries collected by John Yeoman which Blake decorates with, according to a *Publishers Weekly* reviewer, "[his] inimitably puckish art." With 1995's *Clown,* Blake has created a story that is considered to have the panache of such works as *The Story of the Dancing Frog.* In his wordless picture book, the artist outlines how a discarded toy clown searches for a home for himself and his stuffed animal friends, all of whom have been discarded in a trash can in a tough urban neighborhood. Thrown through the window of a run-down apartment where a crying baby is being cared for by her older sister, the clown cheers up the girl and the infant with juggling tricks, helps with the dishes, sweeps, and even changes the baby. After rescuing the other toys, he goes back to the apartment, where the children's tired mother returns to find a clean house and smiling offspring. *Horn Book* reviewer Flowers maintained, "Only Quentin Blake's remarkable skill as an artist could produce such a touching, endearing story." Writing in *School Library Journal,* Carol Ann Wilson commented, "Blake succeeds admirably in presenting a multilayered and thought-provoking tale that will capture readers' imaginations." Jim Gladstone of the *New York Times Book Review* noted the "pitch-perfect details and often unsettling undertones" of the story. Blake, Gladstone continued, "draws up serious underlying questions that go on to follow Clown.... Is it really better to be owned or on one's own?" He concluded that the author "delivers a Dickensian happy ending that can easily be read as very unhappy, uniting the city's underclass: the children, the poor, and the wide-eyed toys." Blake, in fact, has illustrated a book by Charles Dickens, an edition of *A Christmas Carol* that was, like *Clown,* published in 1995. *Horn Book* reviewer Flowers wrote that "everything is handsome about this edition.... It would be hard to think of a more quintessentially Dickensian illustrator."

Blake has also written two comic adventures about the unflappable Mrs. Armitage. In 1997's *Mrs. Armitage and the Big Wave,* the gray-haired heroine is off to catch a big wave with her surfboard, accompanied by her faithful dog, Breakspear. However, on the way out from shore she always thinks of some absurd thing she most desperately needs and then paddles back to the beach. "Awash with droll particulars, Blake's winsome cartoon art ensures that this tale will have even young landlubbers dipping eagerly," wrote a contributor for *Publishers Weekly.* In another original title, *Zagazoo,* the postman brings George and Bella a delightful pink creature that suddenly and quite frighteningly turns into a variety of repellent creatures: a warthog, a dragon, a hairy monster. "Blake's devotees ... will most appreciate this quirky tale," noted a writer for *Publishers Weekly.* Abbott Combes, writing in the *New York Times Book Review,* praised Blake's "dead-on illustrations and 574 well-suited words [that] capture perfectly the joy of bringing someone new into the world." In *The Green Ship,* two youngsters come upon a topiary ship and explore its leafy treetop only to lose their perch over the years as nature returns the carefully pruned domain to a tree. "An aura of melancholy pervades this imaginative tale," commented a reviewer for *Publishers Weekly.*

No melancholy intrudes, however, in Blake's 2000 collaboration with William Steig, *Wizzil,* which is about a bored witch who causes trouble when she decides to take revenge on an old man. Her actions ultimately backfire, though, providing a happy ending. "*Wizzil* is literary ambrosia," declared a contributor to *Horn Book.* "Blake's pen-and-ink and watercolor illustrations, full of energy and humor and movement ... are sublime." A reviewer for *Publishers Weekly* concluded, "Steig and Blake start with unrefined nastiness, then blindside their characters (and readers) with a comical but sincere look at love." "Blake's lively watercolor cartoons, filled with humorous detail, are a delightful companion to this ultimately good-natured tale of transformation and rebirth," observed Rosalyn Pierini in a *School Library Journal* review. Collaborating with Hoban again on the 2000 title *Trouble on Thunder Mountain,* Blake served up illustrations in the service of environmentalism. The O'Saurus family, threatened by the transformation of their mountain into a hi-tech theme park, resort to faith and glue to rectify matters. In *School Library Journal,* Lauralyn Persson called the book a "quirky story full of humor and drama," and praised Blake's "effortless" watercolors, which manage to capture "so much emotion with just a few sketchy lines."

Writing in *Horn Book,* Blake commented, "I embrace the simplicity of both the story and the pictures, in which there may not seem to be, for the grownup, much to talk about. To ease that frustration, it would be quite possible for me to invoke a range of stylistic references—I have extensive knowledge of my drawing's genealogy—but at the present moment I would rather invite the spectator of whatever age to believe that I have never spoken in any other language and that these pictures are simply happening.

"I don't have children," Blake concluded in *Horn Book,* "but am still in touch with the child in me, and this has been immensely important to me as an artist. Part of keeping one's child-self alive is not being embarrassed to admit it exists."

Biographical and Critical Sources

BOOKS

Children's Literature Review, Volume 31, Gale (Detroit, MI), 1994.

Holtze, Sally Holmes, editor, *Fifth Book of Junior Authors and Illustrators,* H. W. Wilson, 1983.

Kingman, Lee, and others, compilers, *Illustrators of Children's Books: 1967-1976,* Horn Book, 1968.

Martin, Douglas, *The Telling Line: Essays on Fifteen Contemporary Book Illustrators,* Julia MacRae Books, 1989.

Peppin, Brigid, and Lucy Micklethwait, *Book Illustrators of the Twentieth Century,* Arco, 1984.

Silvey, Anita, editor, *Children's Books and Their Creators,* Houghton, 1995.

PERIODICALS

Artist's and Illustrator's Magazine, April, 1987, pp. 14-17.

Booklist, January 15, 1995, p. 916; October 15, 1995, p. 401; April 15, 1996, p. 1445; January 1, 1998, pp. 808-809; October 1, 2000, Michael Cart, review of *Wizzil,* p. 337.

Book Window, spring, 1980, Margaret Walker, review of *Mister Magnolia,* p. 12.

Christian Science Monitor, December 22, 2000, p. 14.

Folio, autumn, 1976.

Graphis (children's book edition), September, 1975.

Growing Point, May, 1980, Margery Fisher, review of *Mister Magnolia,* p. 3708.

Guardian, June 29, 1999, p. EG2.

Horn Book, January-February, 1980, Paul Heins, review of *The Wild Washerwoman,* pp. 50-51; September-October, 1981, Quentin Blake, "Wild Washerwomen, Hired Sportsmen, and Enormous Crocodiles," pp. 505-513; January-February, 1986, Ann A. Flowers, review of *The Giraffe and the Pelly and Me,* pp. 46-47; September-October, 1995, Brian Alderson, "All Join In: The Generous Art of Quentin Blake," pp. 562-571; January-February, 1996, Ann A. Flowers, review of *A Christmas Carol,* p. 73; July-August, 1996, Ann A. Flowers, review of *Clown,* p. 444; March-April, 1998, p. 228; May-June, 2000, review of *Wizzil,* p. 466.

Junior Bookshelf, February, 1980, Marcus Crouch, review of *The Wild Washerwoman,* p. 19; February, 1994, Marcus Crouch, review of *Simpkin,* pp. 12-13.

New Statesman, October 31, 1969; November 9, 1973; November 21, 1980.

New York Times Book Review, November 3, 1974; January 15, 1989. September 22, 1996, Jim Gladstone, review of *Clown,* p. 28; November 16, 1997, p. 38; September 20, 1998, p. 33; December 5, 1999, Abbott Combes, review of *Zagazoo,* p. 95.

Observer, April 15, 1990.

Publishers Weekly, May 16, 1994, review of *The Singing Tortoise and Other Animal Folktales,* p. 64; May 15, 1995, p. 31; December 18, 1995, pp. 54-55; March 25, 1996, p. 83; March 16, 1998, review of *Mrs. Armitage and the Big Wave,* pp. 62-63; January 4, 1999, p. 92; July 26, 1999, review of *Zagazoo,* p. 89; July 3, 2000, review of *Wizzil,* p. 70; November 27, 2000, review of *The Green Ship,* p. 76.

Punch, December 15, 1965.

School Library Journal, October, 1980, Mary Nickerson, review of *How Tom Beat Captain Najork and His*

Hired Sportsmen, p. 119; May, 1996, Carol Ann Wilson, review of *Clown,* p. 84; December, 1997, p. 150; May, 1998, p. 106; July, 1999, p. 16; July, 2000, Lauralyn Persson, review of *Trouble on Thunder Mountain,* p. 80; August, 2000, Rosalyn Pierini, review of *Wizzil,* p. 165.

Sewanee Review, winter, 1998, pp. 112-117.

Signal, January, 1975, Elaine Moss, "Quentin Blake," pp. 33-39.

The Signal Selection of Children's Books, 1984, Jane Doonan, review of *The Story of the Dancing Frog,* p. 8.

Spectator, December 5, 1970; April 16, 1977.

Times Educational Supplement, March 28, 1980; October 31, 1980; November 19, 1982, Naomi Lewis, "Once Upon a Line," p. 32; June 9, 1989, p. B9; June 2, 1995, p. 16A; March 19, 1999, p. 23.

Times Literary Supplement, November 26, 1982, p. 1303; November 9, 1984, John Mole, "Space to Dance," p. 1294; May 6, 1988, p. 513; July 7, 1989, p. 757.

Wilson Library Bulletin, June, 1995, p. 125.

ON-LINE

Young Writer Magazine Online, http://www.mystworld.com/youngwriter/ (September 3, 2001), interview with Quentin Blake.*

*   *   *

BLANCHARD, Patricia
(Annie-Jo, a joint pseudonym)

Personal

Born in Lockport, NY; daughter of George (a construction worker) and Olive (an educator; maiden name, Sherman) Bane; married Pete Arthur Blanchard (in trucking business); children: Bruce, Michelle. *Education:* State University of New York College at Brockport, earned degrees in education.

Addresses

Home—62 Lake Ave., Lyndonville, NY 14098.

Career

Lyndonville Central School, Lyndonville, NY, elementary teacher.

Writings

WITH JOANNE SUHR

There Was a Mouse, illustrated by Valeri Gorbachev, Richard C. Owen Publishers (Katonah, NY), 1997.

My Bug Box, Richard C. Owen Publishers (Katonah, NY), 1999.

Old Bumpy Alligator, Richard C. Owen Publishers (Katonah, NY), 2000.

WITH JOANNE SUHR; UNDER JOINT PSEUDONYM ANNIE-JO

In the Woods, Mondo Publishing, 1998.

Itch, Itch, Mondo Publishing, 1998.*

C

CALDER, Charlotte 1952-

Personal

Born September 4, 1952, in Adelaide, South Australia; daughter of Richard Arthur (a supreme court judge) and Bryony Helen (a pilot and malacologist; maiden name, Dutton) Blackburn; married Alistair Guy Calder, February 14, 1976; children: Emily, Angus, Alexander. *Education:* Flinders University, B.A., 1973. *Hobbies and other interests:* Reading, gardening, tennis.

Addresses

Home—P.O. Box 2070, Orange, New South Wales 2800, Australia. *Agent*—Curtis Brown, P.O. Box 19, Paddington, New South Wales 2021, Australia. *E-mail*—sugarlf@ix.net.au.

Career

Writer. Conducts writing workshops. Children's Book Council of Australia, committee member at Central West Branch; Central West Writers' Centre, committee member. Also worked as an actor and photographer.

Writings

Settling Storms (young adult novel), Lothian (Port Melbourne, Australia), 2000.

Contributor to periodicals, including *Sydney Morning Herald* and *Australian.*

Work in Progress

A young adult novel, tentatively titled *Cupid Painted Blind,* "incorporating Shakespeare's *A Midsummer Night's Dream,* the Internet, and a teenage romance"; a children's novel.

Sidelights

Charlotte Calder told *SATA:* "For me writing is an extension of my earlier work as an actor; each occupation requires a very similar process of searching for the truth, in character and situation.

"I try very hard to reflect the day-to-day lives of young people as they really are; young adult literature (in Australia anyway) often seems to focus too relentlessly on scenarios of gloom and doom. Certainly issues as social isolation, suicide, anorexia, and drug abuse are of major concern, but the everyday lives of most teenagers also contain friends, laughter, horsing about, junk television, and just plain 'veging out'! In particular I'm fascinated by the energy of adolescence and the constant switching back and forth between childish and adult personas.

"It's always amusing (and somewhat reassuring!) to find that the preoccupations of my teenage daughter and her friends seem to have changed very little from my own of more than thirty years ago!"

Biographical and Critical Sources

PERIODICALS

Booktalkers, July, 2000, Agnes Nieuwenhuizen, review of *Settling Storms,* p. 6.
Lollipops, September-October, 2000, review of *Settling Storms,* p. 7.
Magpies, September, 2000, Moira Robinson, review of *Settling Storms,* pp. 37-38.
Viewpoint, summer, 2000, review of *Settling Storms,* pp. 42-43.

CAMPBELL, Carole R. 1939-

Personal

Born 1939, in Philadelphia, PA; daughter of George N., Sr. (in corporate sales) and Jeanne (a logistics engineer; maiden name, Bieber; later surname, Bechtel) Redington; married R. Thomas Campbell (a health systems consultant and writer), June 25, 1960; children: Stephen S., Caren J. *Education:* West Chester University, B.S.Ed. and M.Ed; also attended St. Joseph's University, Philadelphia, PA. *Hobbies and other interests:* Golf, tennis, watercolor painting.

Addresses

Home and office—1415 Allan Lane, West Chester, PA 19380.

Career

Classroom teacher in and around West Chester, PA, 1961-65, substitute teacher, 1968-70; Exton Baptist Nursery School, Exton, PA, teacher, 1970-72; Coatesville Area School District, Coatesville, PA, educator and reading specialist, 1972-97. Immaculata College, teacher, 1978-79. Operator of a framing business for computer cartoons, 2000—. Volunteer reader at local library. *Member:* International Reading Association, National Education Association, Pennsylvania Education Association, Chester County Historical Society, Friends of Chester County Library, Beta Sigma Phi (served variously as president, vice president, and treasurer, 1965-75).

Awards, Honors

Outstanding Teacher Award, Coatesville Area School District, 1988 and 1995.

Writings

Teacher's Guide for Window of Time, White Mane (Shippensburg, PA), 1997.
Powder Monkey (historical fiction for children), White Mane (Shippensburg, PA), 1999.

Contributor of children's poems to newsletters.

Work in Progress

Author of a juvenile historical novel based on the story of the CSS *Hunley,* "a submarine built and used successfully during the Civil War, as seen through the eyes and experiences of a young boy."

CAPPETTA, Cynthia 1949-

Personal

Born January 18, 1949, in Waterbury, CT; daughter of William J. and Mildred (Ziello) Teuber; married John A. Cappetta (a teacher), November 17, 1973; children: Katherine, Daniel, Sarah. *Education:* Western Connecticut State College, B.S.; Southern Connecticut State College, M.A. *Religion:* Roman Catholic.

Addresses

Home—39 Morgan St., Middletown, CT 06457.

Career

Teacher of second grade at public schools in North Haven, CT, 1970-76; Middletown Adult Education Program, Middletown, CT, teacher in "Even Start" family literacy program, 1997—. Literacy Volunteers of Greater Middletown, volunteer, 1997-99. *Member:* National Association for the Education of Young Children.

Awards, Honors

EdPress Awards for *Weekly Reader.*

Writings

Chairs, Chairs, Chairs!, illustrated by Rick Stromoski, Children's Press (Danbury, CT), 1999.

Past editor of "Pre-K" edition, *Weekly Reader.*

Work in Progress

Books for young children.

Biographical and Critical Sources

PERIODICALS

School Library Journal, August, 1999, Christina Dorr, review of *Chairs, Chairs, Chairs!,* p. 125.*

*   *   *

CHASE, Samantha
See GLICK, Ruth (Burtnick)

*   *   *

COGAN, Karen 1954-

Personal

Born September 24, 1954, in Houston, TX; daughter of Hugh (an accountant) and Kathryn (a homemaker; maiden name, DeGaugh) Smith; married John Cogan (an artist), May 15, 1976; children: Jennifer, Tiffany, Kimberly, Courtney. *Education:* University of Houston, degree, 1976. *Hobbies and other interests:* Reading, gardening.

Addresses

Home—5102 Lee Lane, Farmington, NM 87402. *E-mail*—KeCogan@infoway.lib.nm.us.

Career

Kindergarten teacher in Houston, TX, 1976-79; freelance writer in Farmington, NM, 1980—. Kindergarten teacher in Farmington, 1999-2000. *Member:* Society of Children's Book Writers and Illustrators.

Writings

My Little Brother Ben, Richard C. Owen (Katonah, NY), 1999.
When Animals Sleep, Seedling, 1999.

Contributor of nearly 200 articles and stories to magazines.

Work in Progress

An adult inspirational novel, *Desert Flower;* a juvenile adventure, *Do Not Disturb;* research on the Regency period, with adult fiction expected to result.

Sidelights

Karen Cogan told *SATA:* "I began making up stories before I knew how to print. I conned my older sister into writing them down for me. I wrote little during my busy high school and college years and pursued a degree in elementary education. After three years of teaching I 'retired' to care for my firstborn and to pursue the dream of completing and publishing a book. I am still captivated by the writing process. I have two early readers in print and have sold nearly 200 articles and short stories, many for the inspirational market.

"I enjoy my family, my children's pets, and my hobbies of reading and gardening, and, of course, my life as a writer."

CONLEY-WEAVER, Robyn 1963- (Robyn Weaver; Robyn M. Weaver)

Personal

Born February 8, 1963, in Billings, MT; children: Andrew, Samantha.

Addresses

Office—P.O. Box 506, TX 79510. *E-mail*—bookdr@flash.net.

Career

Writer and book editor. Texas Christian University, teacher of writing classes; public speaker; gives readings from her works. *Member:* Society of Southwestern Authors, Oklahoma Writers Federation.

Writings

(Under name Robyn M. Weaver) *Depression,* Lucent Books (San Diego, CA), 1999.
(Under name Robyn Weaver) *Meerkats,* Bridgestone Books (Mankato, MN), 1999.
(Under name Robyn M. Weaver) *John Grisham,* Lucent Books (San Diego, CA), 1999.
(Under name Robyn M. Weaver; with Bradley Steffens) *Cartoonists,* Lucent Books (San Diego, CA), 2000.
(Under name Robyn M. Weaver) *Alexander Graham Bell,* Lucent Books (San Diego, CA), 2000.
What Really Matters to Me: A Guided Journal, Walking Stick Press (Cincinnati, OH), 2000.

Author of "The Country Common-tater," a column in *Country Coupons;* columnist for various Internet Web sites, including Delphic Moments. Contributor to magazines, including *Personal Journaling, ByLine, Victory, Positive Parenting,* and *Youth Update.*

Biographical and Critical Sources

ON-LINE

Robyn Weaver Web site, http://www.robynconleyweaver.com/ (June 22, 2001).

Autobiography Feature

Barbara (Asenath) Corcoran

1911-

Twenty thousand feet in the air somewhere between Dallas and Austin I begin to consider my life. It was a good moment for it; American had sold seat 7-F twice, so I was moved to First Class. I told the flight attendant I wasn't entitled to the free drink she offered because I was a stowaway, but she said, "Oh, have one. And sit by the window. We want you to be happy." As they say, way to go.

First Class. Do we, I wondered, make our own first class or is it as random as two boarding passes that say 7-F? But never mind the philosophy; enjoy first class when it's there.

According to my mother, my arrival, in Hamilton, Massachusetts, on April 12, 1911, was not first class. I broke her pelvis, and she never quite forgave me. I justify myself by noting that her life was a series of broken bones. She didn't drink milk when she was young.

Her name was Anna Tuck, and the Tucks and Dodges and Buxtons of her background had been around Hamilton and vicinity for about 250 years, give or take.

My grandfather Walter E. Tuck had owned a small shoe manufacturing plant in Beverly until "those Democrats" forced him into bankruptcy in the 1890s. He spent the rest of his life farming in a small way, and somehow managed to pay off his creditors. His crotchety disposition was not improved by adversity, but he had a certain gritty integrity. He used to regale me with stories of the Civil War, which he got from books and newspapers. He was too young even to be a drummer boy. It was the great frustration of his life. Unlike his father Rufus, who twice made the long trek to California to be a gold miner (and twice came home broke), my grandfather lived out his life in Hamilton.

My grandmother was a Buxton of Peabody, and she was a sweetheart. My best friend and greatest sharer of secrets and jokes. When she died, I had my first real sorrow.

We are in a touring car, and it is 1915. I am sitting between my grandparents on the back seat. My mother is in front, and my father, an Essex boy who worked his way through Tufts Medical and is now practicing medicine, is driving. Before he went to college, he learned to be an auto mechanic, a rare thing in those days. We are in Swampscott, and out from a blind side road comes probably the only other car within twenty miles. A big, black chauffeur-driven limousine. It plows into us. I am thrown to the floor, and I see my grandparents flying out of the car, one on one side, one on the other, in what looks like slow motion. It strikes me as an odd thing for them to be doing.

The woman who owns the limousine is holding me. She is dressed in black and seems enormously tall. Blood gushes from my mother's broken nose. My grandmother's ribs are broken, and she will develop heart problems and eventually die of this accident. My grandfather is bruised and his temper is fractured. He never did trust "machines"; if God had meant for man to have wheels, he'd have been born with them.

Automobiles. On weekends I ride around with my father on his calls. We have a game of counting mailboxes in Essex. (Hamilton had none.) And we count horses in Beverly Farms. My father is a good doctor, and his practice has grown to include most of the surrounding towns. His patients include the George Pattons, (then Major Patton), the Henry Cabot Lodges, the Saltonstalls, and the Gildarts and Mullinses and Maiones, the Laskis and Katzes and Joneses.

In winter he makes his calls in a sleigh. He gets chilblains and runs barefoot in the backyard snow to cure them. I like it when we go to Essex to see my Corcoran grandparents. My tall, quiet grandfather is Irish, a runaway when he was twelve, a sailor in the Civil War, on Admiral Farragut's flagship. My grandmother is a Haskell, a sweet lady.

My father takes me to concerts, has me take piano lessons from the age of six. In my first recital I played from memory and wowed the audience by that feat rather than by my talent, which turned out in six years of lessons to be fairly inconspicuous.

He takes me to Bunker Hill Monument and the Peabody Museum and he lets me hitch my toboggan to the back of his car, and he lets me "hook pungs" while my mother wrings her hands, expecting me to kill myself. He takes me out on the porch during thunderstorms and teaches me to like them.

I skip the second grade. Later I am supposed to skip the sixth but my father objects. Instead I spend most of that sixth grade year having surgery for double mastoids,

Barbara Corcoran

finding out about pain, having the experience of temporary deafness which I will use nearly half a century later in a book called *A Dance to Still Music*.

In the years before I was twelve I spent a lot of time on skis and sleds and skates. I had the only toboggan on the hill, and my cousin Ernest brought me real racing skis from Canada. We built jumps on the side of the hill and collected bruises and sprained ankles. When I was ten, I fell in love with Herbert Pope, who came to visit family at Christmas. We caused a sensation by climbing the hill holding hands. I usually forgot about him after Christmas. There were other boys at dancing school to think about.

After the mastoid year, I changed to Tower School in Salem, and commuted by train. I got a lot of encouragement to write. Since the first grade I had been writing "stories" on my father's prescription pads or whatever was handy. At twelve I wrote real stories on real paper for a real magazine, *The Turret*. One was about a garter snake who was afraid of little girls. I had begun my six happy summers at Camp Allegro in New Hampshire, where little girls tended to be afraid of garter snakes. Now I have written a series of mysteries for children set in Camp Allegro. Art trots dutifully in Life's footsteps.

I was an avid reader, everything from the *Bobbsey Twins on a Houseboat* to *David Copperfield*. I startled my

father when I was thirteen by asking for Darwin's *Origin of Species* for Christmas. I still have it.

Thirteen was a traumatic age. My parents separated. I was an only child, and my foundation was the three of us. Now there were two of us. My mother and I moved out of the house that I had thought of as the only conceivable place to live. My father, who had his office there, stayed alone with a housekeeper, and we moved to a house in North Beverly. We stayed five years, and to this day I shudder when I pass it, although it's a perfectly good house. Five years later, when I was a freshman in college, my father remarried, and we moved back to the Hamilton house.

I left Tower School for Beverly High. One of my friends at Tower School had been Jane Kelsey. We lost track of each other, but fifty years later I encountered her in Tbilisi, in the USSR, by the purest chance. We almost missed discovering each other's identity, during our casual touristy chat in the hotel coffee shop. When we realized, we fell into each other's arms in astonishment and delight.

Automobiles. My father taught me to steer a car when I was too small to reach the pedals. As soon as I could touch the accelerator, I drove, alone, long before I was old enough to get a license. I spent weekends with him, and Vi Mason and I would put down the top of his old Buick roadster and drive to Plum Island, where Vi would dance with the gallants, and I, having plunged into adolescent shyness, would lurk in the coatroom.

Bob Robertson and I and sometimes another couple would chase the big bands all over the area. Ella Fitzgerald with Chick Webb's band, Benny Goodman, Gene Krupa, Fletcher Henderson. On the night before the Fourth of July we always drove to Hampton Beach, in New Hampshire, where some name band would play in the huge ballroom, with the colored chandeliers twirling over our heads. We would dance till dawn, and on the way home we would ride on the Salisbury Beach roller coaster, all but passing out with vertigo.

I made the National Honor Society in spite of never understanding what algebra was all about. And I was the class poet. My Camp Allegro friend, Frankie Jones, had introduced me to poetry, and I wallowed in Amy Lowell, Rupert Brooke, Edna Millay, Sara Teasdale, Keats, Shelley, Frost. I wrote an impressionistic poem for graduation, but somehow Miss Winship guided my pen into a more Whitmanesque version. I think of it as Miss Winship's poem. But she and Helena Cronin taught me well, and I went through my English college board like a breeze. Latin and French were okay, but I blew chemistry, and had to take a postgraduate year at Beverly.

My father, who had graduated cum laude from Tufts, had enrolled me at Wellesley the year I was born. I finally made it in 1929. Having always been the fair-haired student in English, I expected to be exempted from freshman comp, and to make the news staff. I did neither. My ego was badly dented.

The campus was beautiful, and most of the professors were excellent, but it took me a while to adjust. There were highlights: like reading Wordsworth's *Prefaces* and being suddenly struck all of a heap by the wonder of abstract thought; like step-singing; like Ella Keats Whiting (grand-niece of John Keats) aglow over Chaucer; like Miss Manwaring reading poetry in her extraordinary voice; like sundaes at the Dainty Shoppe.

Too many tea dances and Harvard events nearly flunked me out my second year, but I pulled myself together (with a little help from my indignant father) and did all right the last two years. No cum laude, but I made it. My best friend won the John Masefield Prize for excellence in writing, and never wrote another word.

Nineteen thirty-three. I graduated and FDR was elected. I came into the Real World, which was still in the throes of the Depression. I job-hunted, lived at home, started writing plays. I got a job with the WPA Writers Project and wrote town histories for schools. I got a summer job as assistant stage manager and prop girl with the Oceanside Theatre, in the huge Oceanside Hotel in Magnolia. Five dollars a week and lunch in the formal, be-chandeliered dining room. It was the kind of hotel where people sat on the porch and rocked. I worked fifteen-hour days and loved it. Ann Andrews was our star, and she became a good friend. Later in New York she would introduce me to dazzling folks like Judith Anderson, Louis Bromfield, and such. I was stage-struck.

Two of my father's patients were writers, George Brewer, who wrote *Dark Victory*, and Judith Kelly, author

of *Marriage Is a Private Affair* and other novels. They had me to lunch and gave me encouragement. Mrs. George Patton called me with kind words, as did Mrs. C. C. Williams, daughter of the elder Henry Cabot Lodge. But on the whole, my fellow-townsmen thought I was wasting my time, throwing away that expensive college education. They felt sorry for my father.

I wanted to go to Yale Drama School, but my father balked at the expense. He did stake me to a few months in New York. I went to play after play after play, and it was the heyday of Broadway theatre. I talked to Katharine Cornell (or listened; when I actually met her, I was tongue-tied). She read a couple of my plays and gave me good, constructive criticism. So did Bette Davis.

Elmer Rice and Sam Jaffe interviewed me for a workshop they were planning. I was accepted, but the plans fell through.

I sold a one-act play about the Spanish Revolution to the Theatre Workshop, and it was produced by labor theatres in Philadelphia and Montreal and several other places.

I spent a few months with my college friend Cappy Lambeth in Chapel Hill, North Carolina. She had a job distributing flour and corn meal for President Roosevelt's CWA, and we spent many hours bouncing across roadless fields and down country roads visiting the poor. I had never seen that kind of poverty, and I was appalled. A heavy smell of frying pork fat saturated the air. Women worked in

Barbara with her mother, Anna Tuck Corcoran, about 1914

the fields wearing bonnets, like the ones my great-grand-mother wore. They were old, many of these women, and so frail one wondered how they survived. An old, blind black man lived alone in a deserted school house, as sweet and cheerful as if he had never a problem. A young woman whose husband was on the chain-gang was angry at having to accept government handouts. Cappy's mother said, "They ask for bread and you give them a stone." My consciousness was being raised.

Part of that time I worked in the University of North Carolina Press offices, stuffing envelopes for twenty-five cents an hour. Stuffing envelopes all day is hard on the hands, and the exposure to a university press that I had looked forward to was conspicuous by its absence.

A young man I had thought I was in love with came down to drive me home. Lacking money, we drove nonstop, and fought all the way. I learned a lesson: if you want to test a love affair, take a trip with him, without cash.

I was beginning to sell a few pieces to magazines. The first one was a humorous essay about summer theatre, sold to *Cue* for fifteen dollars. They accepted it with a telegram, and I assumed that would be the first of many such happy telegrams, but I never got that kind of acceptance again.

I worked at the Oceanside again, as stage manager. We had a new set of players, Muriel Kirkland, Whit Bissell, Staats Cotsworth, and a young man who would make a difference in my life, Shepperd Strudwick, fresh from success in *Both Your Houses.* He read some of my plays and invited me to join the Surry Players in Maine the following summer. The Surry Players were backed by Dwight Deere Wiman, and they were planning a permanent company. Anne Revere and Katherine Emery, stars of *The Children's Hour,* were board members, and Anne's brilliant husband, Sam Rosen, was the director. They were to be my close lifelong friends.

At Surry I did props again, but I was treated like a playwright. There were other playwrights, Janet Marshall, doing costumes, Phil Stevenson, publicity, among them. Janet and Phil later married. Tambi Larsen, later to become a highly successful Hollywood scene designer, was doing sets. I stayed with the Surry Theatre for three happy summers, and I learned a great deal about playwriting from Sam, and from watching rehearsals.

I continued to go to New York in the winter, grabbing whatever odd job I could find. I was secretary to Carlos Chavez, the Mexican composer-conductor, a sweet man, although neither of us ever quite understood what the other was saying. For a while I was receptionist at the Authors League, saying brilliant lines like "Just a moment please, I'll ring Miss Sillcox," to writers like Paul Green and Rita Weiman and Marc Connelly. I got $18 a week. My career was plunging upward.

And I was writing and writing. Short pieces for *Glamour* magazine, *Charm* magazine, a mystery in four installments for the Catholic monthly, *Extension.* The mystery was called "Fancy That, Hedda!" Everything I wrote was theatre-related.

I was writing play and movie reviews and theatre news for an ItalianAmerican newspaper under the name of Angela Barracini. I didn't get paid, but it was fun. My dear friend Albert Pezzati had arranged it. He was responsible for many good things in my life. He was a CIO organizer, and when I was at home and he happened to be organizing in that area, he took me to hear John L. Lewis speak, one of his rivetting, Shakespeare-sprinkled rousers; and Albert took me with him sometimes when he visited mill workers in Lawrence and Lowell, trying to persuade them that the CIO was not going to leave them shafted, as they had been in earlier AFL experiences. I sat in the kitchens of these people while they listened to Albert's quiet, persuasive talk. I was learning a lot.

When we were both in New York, we cruised Fifty-second Street whenever he had the free time, listening to the small, wonderful bands, like Joe Marsala at the Hickory House, and people like Billie Holliday at Tony's. We heard Benny Goodman and Glenn Miller at the hotels, and Cab Calloway at the Cotton Club. It was a jazz-lover's dream time.

We went to rallies at Madison Square Garden, and belted out the "Internationale" with the best of them. And we went to endless fundraising cocktail parties where people stood jammed together trying to find the room to hoist an elbow, everybody talking full volume in order to be heard. At such a party for *Il Popolo d'Italia,* Albert introduced me as Angela Barracini, and I was instantly inundated with floods of Italian. My one year of Italian at Wellesley did me no good at all; I managed a "grazie" and a "ciao," and fled.

In 1940 I had two plays produced. A group called the Peabody Players in Boston did an anti-Nazi play of mine called *From the Drawn Sword.* It was a terrible play, but they did it well and it got kind reviews from everyone except John Hutchens at the *Transcript,* who roasted it thoroughly.

At Bard College, on the Hudson River, a Surry friend, Jack Lydman, got a production for me of a play about Shays' Rebellion called *Yankee Pine.* Katherine Emery and Frank Overton starred, with a student cast. The MGM story editor covered it, and the whole experience was very heady. Audrey Wood, the play agent who I think was the best in the business, tried to sell it on Broadway, but there was another more immediate war in the offing, and plays about historic wars were not marketable.

America was at war, and suddenly, like Rosie the Riveter, I was useful. I got a job as a Navy inspector at the Sylvania factory in Ipswich, where the Navy was first experimenting with and then mass-producing the proximity fuse, which ultimately saved England from the V-2 rockets.

I had won $2000 and a lot of publicity from a script for the "Dr. Christian" radio show. At last my fellow-townspeople noticed that I was a writer. Magazine pieces and two plays went for nothing, but a radio play—that was something they could relate to. But writing would now be out, for the duration. I was working a forty-eight-hour week at Sylvania.

It was a new world for me. I got to know women who had been working on the line all their lives. They were tough, funny, wary women, to whom I had to prove that I was okay in spite of being a college graduate. I made some good friends. Rosalie Gosbee, an Essex girl who knew my Corcoran relatives, became one of the best friends I would ever have. Mary Conley, a fellow-inspector, also was to be a lifelong friend.

It was a stressful job. An inspector who failed to notice a defect could be responsible for deaths. Of course if we did our job well, we were also responsible for deaths, German deaths. It was a difficult spot for a pacifist to be in, but like many others, it seemed to me that the number-one priority then was to check fascism before it swallowed up the world.

After a year at Sylvania I got sick and had to resign. I worked for a while at an advertising job in Boston, and then Rosalie and I went to see an Army recruiting officer, and signed up for a Civil Service job with the Signal Corps, in Arlington, Virginia. We decoded Japanese military telegrams, but each section did only one small part of each telegram. My section did the date and the point of origin. We were constantly cautioned to "button our lip" but actually any one of us didn't know much that would have been useful to the enemy camp. It made us feel important and Mata Hari-ish, however.

We worked swing shift, and explored Washington by day. Compared to the Navy job, it was like a month in the country.

A few years ago I used some of the Navy experience in *Axe-Time, Sword-Time,* but so far I haven't used the Signal Corps experience in a book.

When I went back home, I worked for a while as advertising manager for a small department store chain. I wrote copy and learned about layout and type sizes and such arcane matters.

During the Boston advertising job, I had to clip ads from the *Los Angeles Times,* and I was intrigued by the "Farmers Market" column by Fred Beck, and the sound of Los Angeles in general. It stayed in my mind as New England winter howled and drifted around me. And finally I set out in a blizzard in a prewar Ford with worn recap tires (new ones were not available, even though the war was over), with my mother, my cousin Helen, and Rosalie. We headed south and southwest, shedding our winter underwear and heavy socks and sweaters as we went. It took us a month to get to California. Provincial New Englanders that we were, we were fascinated by everything, from cotton fields to cactus. We encountered a flood in Mississippi, and Coolidge Dam, and an Indian reservation, desert, and Joshua trees. America in one long gulp.

Many of my Surry friends were already in California, and I joined Anne Revere and Sam Rosen at the Phoenix Theatre in Westwood. The group was backed by Paramount, and they used young Paramount contract players. I was prop girl again.

The housing situation in Los Angeles was a mess. Every GI who had passed that way seemed to have come back. I had read about Anne Lehr, who ran the Hollywood Guild Canteen, and before we left, I had written her because she sounded like a woman who would know if it was really impossible to find a place to live or whether it was newspaper talk. Her secretary wrote me that it was true, all right, but that if we wanted to rent the third floor in Anne's own house, we would be welcome, $25 a month apiece.

We lived there happily for several years, and Anne became a close friend. As thousands of GI's will remember, she was a remarkable woman, all heart and humor and generous acceptance of other people. Her husband, Abe Lehr, had been president of Samuel Goldwyn's company until a stroke incapacitated him. Anne knew everyone in Hollywood, it seemed, and through her we met some interesting people. Mary Pickford was president of the Guild, and each year she opened Pickfair for a fund-raising party. She herself never showed up, but it was a great party, with combos, and booths with food and drinks, scattered around the Japanese-lantern-lit grounds of Pickfair.

We bought a house eventually, in the Valley, but Anne remained a beloved friend whom we saw often. She had been to dinner at our house a few days before she died.

Both Rosalie and I were working for Earl Blackwell, running the west coast branch of Celebrity Service. I stayed there eight years, longer than I ever stayed in any other job in my life. It was an interesting job, keeping track of celebrities for the entertainment industry, and issuing a daily bulletin about who was in town and where they were staying. The service was on a subscriptions basis, for studios, TV people, agents, and anyone who had a legitimate reason for wanting information of that kind. We were constantly checking with any source we could think of who would help us keep our information current. I made a lot of telephone friends who were famous, but who I usually never saw. Hedda Hopper called now and then, and some of our more frequent callers were Diana Barrymore, Joseph Schildkraut, and Queenie Smith, a favorite of mine, who was running the coast office of the Theatre Guild.

I was taking a UCLA extension course one evening a week, in Writing for Television, hoping to get in on this new medium. I was still selling "Dr. Christian" scripts occasionally to that radio program. I was also trying to sell movie originals, working often with my agent and friend, Lou Schor, and getting encouragement but little else. Mostly I learned what not to do, like not tying to hit a trend, because by the time a script was finished, the trend was over. I find that still to be true, even in children's books, which are on the whole far less trend-influenced than adult books.

I was selling a piece to the magazines now and then, but it was not adding up to anything resembling a career.

Rosalie had gotten married, and Lynn Bowers, who was on Louella Parsons' staff, joined Celebrity Service. She knew everyone in the business, and she was wonderful at finding out whatever we needed to know. We became good friends, and we co-wrote four "Medal of Honor" scripts for a producer. The series as such never materialized, but the four scripts were produced and one of them, "Rodriguez," about a hero of the Korean War, got a splashy star-strewn preview in Pasadena and eventually was a nominee for a documentary Oscar.

Los Angeles was growing at a stupefying rate, and traffic and smog were becoming problems. In 1953 I visited a friend who had moved to Missoula, Montana, and I was enchanted with the place. After a certain amount of correspondence I managed to get a job at radio station KGVO in Missoula, writing copy.

A year later I enrolled in the university graduate program as a teaching assistant. Walter Van Tilburg Clark was teaching there, and Leslie Fiedler was department chairman. I lived on my thousand-dollar-a-year stipend, and got a little thinner, but I had a very happy year, and I wrote part of a novel, a medium I hadn't paid much attention to before. Walter taught me how to make the switch from dramatic scene and dialogue to narration. I remember his saying, "Detail! Detail! Detail!" I say the same thing now to the writing class I teach at the same university.

I wrote a play for my thesis, however, because I could do it in the limited time that I had. It won a Samuel French award, but it never was produced.

At the end of the year, my M.A. in hand, my Montana friend Jeanne and I set forth for Mexico, with about $150 between us. I can't remember too clearly why we went to Mexico; I had mono, and I wasn't registering anything very clearly.

Travelling without money is the way to have adventures. It may be hell at the time, but it makes for good reminiscing long afterward. We went to Hermosillo, thinking it would be non-touristy. It was non-touristy all right, and it was almost impossible to find a room. Jeanne tried out her Spanish on some friendly workmen, asking, she thought, if they knew of a good cheap hotel. She got the word for "cheap" wrong, and what she said was, "Do you know of a good drunken hotel?" They enjoyed the joke and directed us to a good cheap hotel with bars on the windows and a toilet seat that fell on the floor when you tried to sit on it. The crickets had already taken over the room, but we pushed our way in.

We learned the hard way not to drink the water or eat the salads. I added amoebic dysentery to my mono. I have never remembered how long we stayed. A lot seemed to happen, a lot of friendly people tried to help us find a place to live. We ended up at another hotel where three Mexican gentlemen somewhat the worse for tequila spent the night trying to climb in through the transom.

In the end we went back to Los Angeles. The next couple of years were an exercise in survival. I also had anemia by this time, and I lost my first decent job, at the Board of Education, when I kept passing out on top of the typewriter.

I worked at the Old Age Assistance office for quite a while, typing and filing and living in fear of being fired for being overqualified. Finally I was offered a chance to be a case worker, but I turned it down for another radio copywriting job in Santa Barbara.

Along with that full-time job, I taught three classes a week in my lunch hour at the University of California at Goleta, and two nights a week I drove to Los Angeles and taught at Los Angeles State. I was going to get out of debt if it killed me, and it nearly did.

A teaching offer came from the University of Kentucky Northern Center, and I grabbed it. The Center was in Covington, just across the river from Cincinnati, and at that time the classes were held in a public school, after the kids had gone home. The day before the semester began I broke my ankle. Classes were on the third floor of the school. It was interesting, especially since they kept having fire drills. Fortunately there was never a real fire; a soft-hearted department secretary had taken to hiding me in the closet

when the alarm went off, to save me from negotiating those stairs in my cast.

Somehow a year of northern Kentucky was enough for me. After a few false starts I got a job in the story department at CBS-TV in Hollywood. It was pretty much routine, but the ambience was nice. Bud Kay, who had been story editor at Warner Brothers, was head of the department. He knew me from the old days as an aspiring screenwriter who never quite made it.

This time around I was an aspiring TV writer, but I never quite made that either. Once a script of mine was accepted by "Studio One," but before they got to the point of writing a check, the series was cancelled.

Eventually I had to give up my job to a returning vet, but I was shifted to the department where shows were shipped out to affiliate stations. This was the day of the kinoscope. It was a boring job, but I liked the people.

After a couple of years at CBS, I was offered, out of the blue, a teaching job at Marlborough School, an elegant day-school for rich Los Angeles girls whose parents passed scrutiny. It was one of the most exhausting years of my life, but I made at least one permanent friend, a student named Chris Miller who is going great guns now as a New York advertising executive, and I also accumulated enough material to provide for a lot of books later on. The girls were thirteen or fourteen, and somehow I got to know a lot more about them than I really wanted to know, but it's all turned into grist for the mill.

Corcoran, about 1924

One of the universities where I had been trying every year to get a job was Colorado. In 1960 they came through. I spent five satisfying years in Boulder, teaching English, and probably would have stayed forever if there had not been a requirement of a Ph.D. after five years.

I had been selling quite a few magazine stories, and during that first year at Boulder I sold a novel to *Redbook* for their back-of-the-book piece. I sold it "over the transom" for $5000. It was a heady experience. I went out and paid cash for an Austin Healey Sprite, baby blue. From then on I sold short stories fairly regularly to *Redbook,* and to *Woman's Day* and some of the other women's magazines. The long *Redbook* story, which they called "The Runaways," was rewritten after I started doing children's books. I went back to my original title, *A Row of Tigers,* and the only change I made was in viewpoint. I changed from the adult character's point of view to the child's. The adult was a dwarf, a young man named Gene Locke, whom I had first invented when I was trying to write a novel for Walter Van Tilburg Clark. Writers should never throw away their failures; one never knows when they will suddenly become useful.

Boulder, in the days before IBM and the other growth industries, was a beautiful city. The most beautiful city in America, Lyndon Johnson is alleged to have said. In some ways it was like Missoula.

In those days creative writers were *persona non grata.* My chairman told me that if he had known I wrote an original play for my thesis, he wouldn't have been able to hire me. We were not considered scholarly enough. In the five years I was there I never got a raise. I began at $5000 and ended at $5000.

In the seventies, after I had come back to Montana, I heard that Richard Hugo was paid $20,000 to spend a year at Colorado setting up a creative writing program. My timing was never good.

But Colorado had many rewards other than financial. The English department was a good one, barring a few old-timers who had grown crotchety with age. I enjoyed the students. It was a laid-back university in many ways. It had the reputation of being the playground of western campuses, but that was not necessarily true. Anyone who wanted to could get an excellent education there. A lot of fascinating people came to lecture. I heard Margaret Mead three days in a row, quite spellbound by her. And Buckminster Fuller was there for several days, dazzling us with his views of the world. It was a good five years.

One of the highlights of that time was the birth of my friend Jeanne's daughter, my godchild. Her name is Andrea, but within the family she has always been Gigi. I held her when she was fifteen minutes old, and her look of outrage made me laugh. She has been making me laugh with delight ever since. She is a rare person.

I had given up my Sprite, rather reluctantly, for a Volvo wagon. The Sprite had been fun, but it held only one other person, and it tended to get blown off the road when I made my summer trips to California to see my mother. The Volvo was sturdy. In fact, I still see it going efficiently around town here in Missoula, Montana, twenty-one years after I bought it.

My mother died during that last year that I was in Boulder. She had been living in Vista, California, and coincidentally when I started applying for teaching jobs, the one I got was at Palomar College in San Marcos, the town adjacent to Vista.

I packed up once more and took off for San Marcos, leaving Boulder sorrowfully but looking forward to a salary that would be more than double what I had been getting.

During the summer I taught full time and I was also writing a novel called *Sam.* It took me a long time to finish *Sam* because of the teaching schedule, but when it was finally done, I made an interesting discovery. My agent said I had written a good children's book. I told her that was not possible because I had no idea how to write children's books. *Sam* was about a fifteen-year-old girl, but I thought it was an adult novel, and I pointed out to her that *The Heart Is a Lonely Hunter* and *The Catcher in the Rye* are about children but they are adult books. Wisely, she ignored me and sent the book to Jean Karl at Atheneum, who astonished me by buying it. I had to do some cutting and make some minor changes, but apparently I really had written a children's book. It came out in 1967 and it's still selling.

I had based Sam's story on the early life of one of my students at the University of Montana, who had grown up in a cabin in the forest that her father had built. The children of the family were taught at home, and seldom left their isolation. When she had to go out into the world to a public high school, the shock was severe. Her story had fascinated me, and after I wrote the book, I returned several times to the theme of a young person abruptly encountering a place or situation that is totally unfamiliar. *Sasha, My Friend,* my third book, and *The Long Journey,* my fourth, both deal with this idea. In *Sasha* a sophisticated Los Angeles teenager finds herself living on a Christmas tree farm in an isolated part of Montana. And in *The Long Journey* the situation is reversed: the girl who has been brought up in a deserted mining camp by her grandfather has to venture out into the so-called civilized world on her own when he becomes ill.

In *Sasha* I was reaching back to my experience with the girls at Marlborough. I used one of those girls as a model again in *This Is a Recording.*

I talk to school children around the country quite a lot, and they always want to know where I "get my ideas." I try to explain that ideas are all over the place. The trick is simply in being always on the lookout for them. It's a habit, a way of looking at the world, that writers have. Even one's own most traumatic experiences are grist to the mill. Part of every writer, I think, stands aside watching himself react and taking mental notes.

I had been working too hard. After summer school, I was teaching evening classes as well as a full-time daily schedule. In the autumn of my first year at Palomar, I had what used to be called a nervous breakdown. When I was able to get myself together enough to travel, I packed a few things and my Basenji dog and drove back to Colorado, to Denver this time.

For a while I did very little except sleep and try to straighten myself out without benefit of counselling, which was stupid, but I was broke, with no salary coming in, and psychiatry seemed like a luxury that I couldn't afford.

In time I began to write again, and during the last half of the year I started working on a doctorate at the University of Denver. I was enjoying that and feeling better, but Palomar tempted me back for the 1966-67 year. To this day I remain about a fifth of a Ph.D.

Palomar was a good place to be. At that time it was rather small and rural. Time and progress have changed that, but it was right for me then. I made good friends, especially my big Italian chum, Angelo Carli, who is now dean of Continuing Education. I stayed there four years, and during that time I began writing more books for children.

In 1969 I turned down tenure and decided that if I was ever going to write full time, this was the year to begin. It was a risk. My doctor helped me to make up my mind; I was having a problem with angina, and he made it clear that I couldn't keep on both writing and teaching. I chose to write, the choice I had always made when the chips were down.

I moved back to Missoula. By this time I had an enchanting godson, Gigi's brother Jamie, who later grew up to be Jim. They were in Missoula, and I had all the delights of watching children develop, without having any of the problems. Both of them have provided me with much love and story material.

I sometimes write under the name of Paige Dixon as well as the name of Gail Hamilton, and why I use pen names is always the first question anyone asks. It was a simple matter of marketing. With all my time free to write, I began to do more than two books a year. Most publishers don't like to have a writer competing with himself on their list of new books, so my editor suggested that I find a pen name for the book *A Lion on the Mountain.* Since it had a boy protagonist, I chose a male identity. Later I used that name for all the wild animal books I have done, and for some others as well, whenever there was an overlap.

A few times I wrote five books in a year, which meant finding another name for the fifth book. Gail Hamilton was the pen name of a popular nineteenth-century writer in my home town (her real name was Abigail Dodge) who was a cousin of my grandfather's. She died before I was born, but I had always been intrigued by her books. The house she had lived in stood empty during my childhood; in fact, on Hallowe'en it was usually on our route because it qualified as a haunted house. By the time I was a teenager it had burned down, but I used to go and sit on the stones of the foundation, where some of the rose bushes she and her sister had planted still bloomed, and I would think about being a writer like Gail Hamilton. She was quite a remarkable woman, especially for her time; an ardent feminist with a wonderfully satirical way with overbearing males.

She is a heroine in our town, and I think some of the locals thought it was presumptuous of me to borrow her name. I think that she would have been amused. At least I hope so. I wrote only a few books under that name, since I seldom wrote more than four books a year. *Titania's Lodestone* is the one I like best; it's about a very conventional teenager's disapproval of her hippie parents.

The statistic for writers in this country who write full time and survive is, I believe, somewhere around one percent. I have been able to do it because of my volume. I write fast and I write all the time. And until this last recession, when the public libraries were shorn of their budgets and the warehousing bill discouraged publishers from keeping up an inventory of past books, I was doing a little better every year.

It was good to be living in a university town again. I took a poetry course with Madeline DeFrees, just for the joy of hearing and thinking about poetry again. There were plays and concerts to go to. Montana has an outstanding music school and the drama department was getting better all the time. I wrote another play, just for the fun of it.

My father died. He was in his late eighties, but still it was a grievous blow. I went back to Hamilton, Massachusetts, for the funeral, and stayed a while with Bob Robertson, renewing acquaintance with my home town, which had changed remarkably little. I saw my cousin Ethel Towne for the first time in many years, and that led eventually to knowing her son Arthur and his wife Jean, and their four children, a whole wonderful branch of "family" that I had not known before. Since my father's death I have returned to Hamilton for a visit every two or three years. In the summer of 1983 I was there for several months, seeing a lot of the Townes and getting to know a quintet of cousins on the Tuck side, ranging in age from five to fifteen. For an only child who had only one first cousin left, it was a bonanza.

In Missoula one of my best friends was English professor Vedder Gilbert, whose children I had babysat when I was in graduate school. The Gilberts had a big Victorian house and they gave marvelous parties, often. I spent holidays and birthdays, mine and theirs, enjoying their hospitality.

One Christmas in the mid-seventies Jeanne and the children and I went to Key West for Christmas. We loved the place, and later on I set *A Dance to Still Music* in and around Key West. It is a book about a girl who loses her hearing when she is about thirteen. I used my memory of the mastoid days to recreate what it feels like suddenly to be deaf. It was a subject I had thought a lot about, not only because of my own experience but because my cousin Ralph's mother was deaf, and I had had a friend in the 1930s who was also deaf. It seemed to me that the deaf got a lot less sympathy than, for instance, the blind. People got tired of repeating, of having to raise their voices, of being misunderstood, and they were often impatient, or, worse, behaved as if the deaf person were not there. *A Dance to Still Music* remains my favorite of my own books.

When we got back from Key West, I realized that Vedder Gilbert was not well. He had lost weight, his hands trembled, and he moved stiffly. A short time later he went to the Mayo Clinic and was diagnosed as having amyotropic lateral sclerosis, "Lou Gehrig's disease." I remembered the old newsreel in which Lou Gehrig made his farewell appearance in Yankee Stadium in 1941; I remembered how gaunt and sad he had looked.

Vedder's condition deteriorated quickly, although he kept on teaching until nearly the end, his voice nearly gone. He was a genial, cheerful, generous man and a treasured friend. I still miss him.

That summer I fulfilled a lifelong dream: I went to Europe. Except for Bermuda and Mexico and Canada, I had never been out of the country. I spent a long time

Corcoran, 1971

poring over travel books and maps, planning the trip, which was to last fourteen months.

Jeanne and the children went with me. Travelling with young children is something I recommend. You see many things and have many experiences that you would not otherwise encounter. Gigi was approaching eight, Jamie was six. Good ages.

We spent the summer in Finland, most of it in a holiday village at Hilloma, on one of Finland's many lakes. Jamie and I shared one cabin, Gigi and Jeanne the other. There are many highlights from that happy summer: the day Jamie worked all day long building a raft, which sank like iron when he finally launched it; the fantastic dinner given by the management, that Gigi and I went to, featuring crayfish and "ox," which turned out to be the best steak I ever had; the day Gigi's hand got mashed by a rock, and she was rushed to Kouvala, an hour's drive away, where an efficient young doctor took the necessary stitches and gave her antibiotics, on a Sunday afternoon, and the bill came to two dollars fifty cents; the time Jamie told me that "work was his hobby."

In September Jeanne and the children spent a week in Lapland, with a Lapp family, and I stayed in Rovaniemi, a lovely little city on the edge of the Arctic Circle.

At the end of September our visas for the USSR finally arrived, and we took off from Helsinki, toward the Finland Station in Leningrad. In my youth I had been a sympathizer of the Soviet Union's great experiment, but time had tarnished that idealistic image, and I really had no idea what to expect.

At the border there was a long wait, during which we had to trudge what seemed like miles back to the baggage car to stand by while the customs man went through our

things. It was an odd experience to see one's personal mail being read, even letters that Jeanne had written home and sealed but had not had time to send. She had brought along school books for the couple of months that we would not be able to send the children to school; these fascinated the customs man, especially the arithmetic book, which I suspect he thought was a code book. He spent a long time poring over it. Surprisingly he was not interested in my multiband radio, which I had expected he might confiscate.

There seemed to be a whole cadre of inspectors peering at everything, when we went back to the passenger car. They quite thoroughly examined the space under our seats, and I wondered what or whom they expected to find. Our money, which was Finnish, was carefully counted and noted on the customs slip. Later that Finnish money was to be a problem.

Leningrad is a beautiful city. Our hotel was on the Neva, across the river from the famous boat in which the Communists attacked the city during the revolutionary years. We spent a day at the Hermitage, and I was interested to find that their great collection of French impressionists was hung rather haphazardly on the top floor, where few people went.

Our Intourist woman was a beautiful blue-eyed witch who went to really imaginative lengths to frustrate us, and whose contempt for Americans approached what might be called state-of-the-art. Throughout our month in Russia the Intourist people we had to deal with ranged from the maddeningly rude and unhelpful to the beyond-the-call-of-duty kind and sympathetic. The further we got from Moscow and Leningrad, the more likely they were to be friendly.

Moscow was a surprise. I had expected a drab city, and parts of it are drab, but the startling Oriental beauty of St. Basil's, and the pastel-colored chapels that Ivan the Terrible is said to have built every time he wanted to atone for a particularly gruesome sin, are a delight. We were not allowed inside the Kremlin wall because we were not connected with any tour, but even the view we got was impressive.

I went alone one night to see *Il Trovatore* at the elegant Czarist-built opera house, and I felt as if I had stepped back into an earlier Russia. Although their version of the opera was purely Soviet-inspired, the gilt and red velvet ambience was of another world, and even the people seemed different. They were smiling and helpful and friendly.

During the time we were in Moscow Richard Nixon was making truculent noises, and the Arab-Israeli war was going on, but we knew nothing about any of this. There was no word in the press or on the radio. Jeanne spoke fluent Russian, so we would have known if these things were in the news. I overheard an Intourist woman speak of the war to an Arab tourist, and that was our first indication. Jeanne went to the U.S. embassy to find out what was going on, but they were as close-mouthed as the Russians.

I had contracted with Atheneum to do a book set in Samarkand, so I flew down there in an Aeroflot plane that I was convinced was going to fly into a million pieces before we arrived, and Jeanne and the children went by train to Tbilisi, where we would meet five days later.

Samarkand was another world, an Arabic ancient world, where old men with long white beards dressed in long white robes and, looking like Old Testament prophets, went around the quiet desert city in two-wheeled carts pulled by goats. My Intourist guide was a university student, and since I was her only customer, I got the grand tour of all the beautiful blue and white tiled tombs, the City of the Dead, Tamerlane's Tomb, and the rest. Eventually I would write a sort of suspense story called *Meet Me at Tamerlane's Tomb,* and another Russian-set book called *The Clown,* based loosely on a clown we had seen in the circus in Moscow and on my own experiences in getting out of Moscow.

I had to change planes in the pitch dark in Tashkent, and I tripped over something on the airfield, fell flat, and sprained an ankle and a knee rather painfully. But I was determined to get to Tbilisi and to avoid Soviet medical attention, so I bit my lip and kept going. Unfortunately most of my stay in Tbilisi was spent in bed. Georgia is a fascinating place, and the Georgians, who make no secret of disliking Russians, were delightful. It was here, in the hotel coffee shop, that I had my encounter with my old Tower School friend, Jane Kelsey.

We spent a few days in Kiev, and then took off for Budapest by train. At the border we ran into trouble about money. Almost all we had was in rubles by this time, and one cannot take rubles out. The problem was that since we had come in with Finnish money, we had to go out with Finnish money, and at that particular station they had no Finnish money. The Intourist guide did her best for us, even gave us a handful of kopeks so we could get the children something to eat on the train, but we left Russia with a receipt for about a hundred dollars, two English pounds, and the kopeks. About six months later, after I had complained to the U.S. travel agency, we got our money back.

Fortunately our rooms in Budapest were prepaid. We found that the Duma hotel would take Diners Club, so we went there and spent a lot of time eating sumptuous meals. We couldn't afford taxis, and I was still lame from my fall, so our activities were limited, but we did get to the Budapest Zoo. I had wanted to see that ever since I went four times to the Gene Raymond movie. It is not one of the world's great zoos, but it is a pleasant place.

I had been given ten dollars by the U.S. consulate, and I had arranged with the state bank to wire my bank at home for funds. Every day I went back to that damned bank only to be told that there was no news. On the very last day of our stay, the beautiful smiling young woman (all Hungarians are beautiful and smiling) said that they had received authorization from my bank, but it was not worded correctly so they would not honor it.

Airlines take credit cards, thank God. We were booked for London. When we arrived, we didn't have enough money to get to our hotel, so I left Jeanne and the children at Heathrow and took a bus to the Savoy Hotel where there was an American Express office. As Karl Malden says, Don't leave home without it. I got some money with such beautiful ease I could hardly believe it.

We stayed in London a few days, and arranged to rent an apartment in, of all places, Tintagel, in Cornwall. Why not, after all, go all the way in romance?

We rented a flat on the grounds of a great stone nineteenth-century hotel called King Arthur's Castle—what else? In the eight months that we lived in the flat, we never saw any guests at the hotel, although the owners lived there in a kind of subterranean collection of rooms resembling torture chambers.

We were on a cliff right on the Atlantic, and the typical weather was cold and very windy. Across a small inlet, on even more forbidding rocks was the castle where Arthur was allegedly born. Actually, according to more reliable sources, it was a very old monastery.

Cornwall in winter is buttoned up tight, but we did a good deal of exploring nevertheless. We got to know not only Tintagel but Camelford and Boscastle and Bude and St. Ives and all the villages where there were ancient churches. The children went to school in Tintagel while we prowled the National Trust paths and boned up on local history. It was a good year.

When school was out, Jeanne and the children went to an island between Sweden and Finland, and I divided my time between a rented room at the University of Kent, and another room at the University of Edinburgh. At Kent I did some research on epilepsy, which I used nearly ten years later in a book about a girl with epilepsy, *Child of the Morning.* The subject had been on my mind since my last year in Boulder, when I had spent an evening with the daughter of an old friend. She was a beautiful girl, and she was having problems because of *petit mal* seizures. Her fiancé's parents had talked him into breaking the engagement, on the grounds that it was hereditary (it isn't), and she was going through the humiliation of falling down frequently and being treated like a drunk. Since then, effective drugs have been discovered for the treatment of epilepsy, but it is still of course a difficult problem.

We came home in time for the new school year. Jeanne was selling science fiction stories, and in a year or two she would begin science fiction books for children. I was finishing a book about a boy who died of amyotropic lateral

Corcoran with her cat, 1980

sclerosis. I called it *May I Cross Your Golden River?* I was afraid it might be too sad to sell, but it has done very well.

One result of that book was a correspondence with a young man dying of ALS, who wrote me a long letter after he read the book. His name was Jacob Adler, and in time I discovered that he was one of the theatrical Adler family, son of Luther Adler and Sylvia Sidney, grandson of the Jacob Adler whose Yiddish theatre was popular in New York when I had lived there. Jacob was a brilliant young man, and it was hard to see his letters giving evidence of physical decline. Like Vedder, he never underwent any mental impairment. I never met Jacob but I cherish his memory.

A couple of years after Europe, we decided to spend a year in Hawaii. We chose the Big Island. Hilo seemed like a good place for the children. It was a happy milk-and-honey kind of year, punctuated by a seven-point-three earthquake and predawn evacuation from our bayside apartment house. None of us will forget parking in a schoolyard part way up a hill, where the Red Cross provided coffee and milk and doughnuts, as we watched the bay, waiting for the tsunami that never hit that end of the island. On a beach outing near Kona some Boy Scouts were drowned. From where we watched, the bay looked like flat pewter. Nothing moved, no birds sang, even people's voices were hushed.

I wrote two books out of the Hawaiian experience, *Make No Sound* and *Love Comes to Eunice K. O'Herlihy.*

I coauthored two books with the outdoor writer Bradford Angier, an old high school friend: *A Star to the North,* set in the Canadian wilderness that he was familiar with, and *Ask for Love and They Give You Rice Pudding.* Nearly all my books have been published by Atheneum, but *Rice Pudding* was a Houghton Mifflin book. I enjoyed working with Melanie Kroupa, an editor who is both sympathetic and tough, and when she moved to the Atlantic Monthly Press, she published my *Making It.*

I have been unusually lucky in having Jean Karl as my editor at Atheneum ever since my first book. In a business where people seem to move around in a frantic game of musical chairs, she has stayed with that house for many years, and I hope she never leaves. I owe her a great deal, as indeed any writer owes a good editor.

Scholastic had reprinted quite a few of my books, and they did one as an original publication, *The Mustang and Other Stories,* three rather long short stories. Thomas Nelson also published a few of my early books, including *A Star to the North.*

Some of my books were appearing in European editions. I have some German and Swiss versions of *A Trick of Light,* and *The Lifestyle of Robie Tuckerman,* and *Don't Slam the Door When You Go.* I don't read German at all, so these books look very mysterious to me.

Sasha, My Friend won the William Allen White Award in 1972, and I made the first of many trips to talk to schools. I was in Kansas for a week, because of the award, and I discovered how much fun it was to talk to the kids who were reading my books. I suppose most writers have the feeling that no one reads their books, that it is a secret process that goes on between themselves and their typewriters, but here were all these kids asking me about my

characters and how I happened to do this or that. Since then I have made many similar trips. Shawnee Mission in Kansas and the Richardson school district in Dallas are two of my favorite places to go. Beverly White and Jo Ann Bell are supreme experts in organizing an author's visit and making the author feel at home. The experience can be a real ego trip for a writer, and most writers need that now and then.

In Cody, Wyoming, recently, I had a slightly different kind of encounter. Although I answered questions, as usual, the focus was on helping kids to begin stories of their own. I spent two days talking to the first through the sixth grades. It was exciting and fun to watch their imaginations begin to spin. It was the first author-visit for that school but librarian Claire Macha and the PTA women ran it like veterans.

In the spring of 1978 Jeanne and the children and I made another journey to the British Isles, this time renting a house from an agency in New York. First we spent several weeks in Ireland and two weeks in Wales, then on to the oasthouse in Sussex that sounded so picturesque. It was picturesque with a vengeance. It really was a former oasthouse on an ancient estate, and every insect who had every snuggled in there with the barley was there still, with all its descendants. And—the usual complaint of Americans in England—it was cold. In Cornwall we had had an electric heater in the fireplace that was nourished with shillings. Here we had something that was laughingly defined as central heating. Sussex was delightful, but in the end we came home to get warm and to comb the earwigs out of our belongings.

On my way home I stopped in Germany long enough to buy a Mercedes 240-D. One does save, buying a car abroad, but by the time it is shipped to the States and delivered, the savings have pretty well faded out. Nevertheless my Mercedes, now five years old, is the joy of my life. I'd rather lose the roof over my head than lose my Mercedes. I've gone through a lot of cars since I first drove my father's Buick roadster, many of them secondhand disaster wagons. Except for the Volvo I've never had a really dependable one. Now I have it, and anybody that wants my Mercedes will have to fight me for it. Including the bank.

Toward the end of the seventies I began to write an adult historical novel called *Abigail.* It was to be long, and it would cover three generations, from the start of the Civil War up to the First World War. I had a wonderful time doing my research. In fact I got so carried away I also wrote a much shorter Civil War novel called *Beloved Enemy,* about a young woman who disguises herself as a man and takes a message through the lines. It was based on a newspaper clipping that I found in my grandfather's papers, about a generally unknown and unrecorded secret group of couriers called the "Silent Seven."

Ballantine bought *Abigail* and *Beloved Enemy* and four other historical romances, all within a year or so. Unfortunately they broke up *Abigail* into three separate books, and cut the first one a good deal. The perils of publishing. I still yearn for a chance to publish *Abigail* some time as a whole. The other romances were fun, but *Abigail* I take seriously.

Ballantine bought three other books written around sustaining characters, but the romance market had begun to change and they were never published.

Now I stay with children's books, where I belong. The adult market is too fickle to keep up with.

In 1983 I went back to a touch of teaching, after all those years away from it. I spent six months in Austin, Texas, where I have good friends and some favorite relatives, and I taught something called Expressive Writing at Austin Community College. I enjoyed it, and now that I am back in Missoula I am teaching a Women's Center course at the university, in Writing for Children. I have a small but excellent group of older students.

I'm also cautiously testing the waters in the field of computer software. It is too soon to tell how that is going to go, but a group called Panda Productions is working on a script I gave them, a story with multiple choices.

I have sold fifty-four books, and I'm in the middle of number fifty-five. I just had my seventy-third birthday. I'm not sure I'll have time for fifty-five more books, but I'm going to give it a try.

POSTSCRIPT, 2001

My cat sits at the top of the stairs patiently waiting for me. In her voice that sounds like a cracked violin she scolds me for being late. This is the time of day when we have games for fifteen or twenty minutes, before she curls up in the tattered Kinko box that she uses for a bed.

Order, she is telling me, is essential to a well-planned life.

She is right, and if anyone should have learned that, it is a writer. And when the gods disrupt the order of one's life, it is more necessary than ever that one keep control as much as possible.

From the late sixties to the early eighties I had been enjoying the life that I had spent years aiming for, the life of a full-time writer, keeping to a schedule, four and sometimes five books a year for older children and young adults. Most of the time I had the same publisher and the same editor, Jean Karl, who was a writer's dream of an editor. And the small but highly respected publishing house of Atheneum was also all that a writer could ask for.

Then with what seemed like incredible swiftness, things changed, and I learned what any writer should have known, that the writing life is by its very nature subject to change.

Big publishing houses began to buy up small independent houses, editors moved from one house to another, or, like mine, went into semi-retirement. Jean Karl no longer had the last word about the purchase of manuscripts. And, a special blow for children's authors who depended so much on library sales, the generous money that President Johnson had allotted to the public libraries disappeared entirely in the Reagan administration.

My income, which had been increasing every year for fifteen years, plummeted. At the same time the major (for me) investment in real estate that I had thought was so smart, also collapsed. I lost my house and eventually went into bankruptcy, a most humiliating experience.

Instead of doing as my cat would have done, rearranging my order of living to fit the circumstances, I panicked.

I told myself I needed a change of scene. I did not use the word "panic" but that was what it was. I spent time in Texas, still writing but on a disrupted schedule; I spent more time in Massachusetts where I did not write at all.

It took personal tragedy to bring me back to myself.

My godson, who was very dear to me, died at the age of seventeen, in tragic circumstances.

Although I did not spell things out to myself at the time, my life changed. Losing my money, my house, my beloved Mercedes no longer were of prime importance. Adjusting to a smaller income no longer seemed so terrible. The sense of what was important in my life was emphasized again when my lifelong friend, Bob, who had been like a brother to me, suddenly died while he was sitting in his favorite chair watching television.

Back in Missoula I moved into a duplex outside of town, with mountains all around me, pleasant neighbors, and in the meadow next to us, four llamas loping around in their awkward gait that looks as if they will fall on their faces at any moment.

I reactivated the small group of writers with whom I had worked off and on for many years. We were down to four now: myself, Kimberly Dowling, Sharon Barrett, and the popular puppeteer, Peggy Meinholtz. Originally they had come to me to learn, but we had long since reached the point where we learned from each other. They will be heard from.

Although I was not aware of it at the time, there was a change in my work. At my editor's request I wrote a short mystery for younger children. I had fun with that. I called it *Which Witch Is Which?* But then I turned to a somewhat more serious tone in *A Horse Named Sky,* in which a girl, unwillingly transported to an unfamiliar place, Montana, because of family disruption, finds herself dealing with the problems of another displaced creature, a little mustang captured in the wilds and confined in a domestic situation. The little horse, unable to submit to tameness, tries to escape and is killed. The girl must learn to adapt to the circumstances that life has dealt her.

In *Annie's Monster,* there is a minor theme concerning the obligations of a church, an Episcopal church in this case; does the church itself come first, with its services, its traditions, its history? Or is the first duty to the needs of the parishioners? The question goes unanswered, but Annie's vision of the church and society is widened.

In the early years at Atheneum the woman who took care of our contacts with libraries and schools, Suzanne Glazer, gave me some good advice. Referring to one of my books, she said, "It's too messagey." Once a writer lets her characters become her mouthpiece, the credibility of the story is lost. Characters develop in their own way. Often they change and surprise me in ways I least expected. The answer, I suppose, is to trust one's unconscious, and to be alert to the behavior of other human beings.

While I was not noticing, Old Age had begun to give me small nudges. I had no more imagined myself old than a six-year-old might imagine herself twenty-one.

Soon after my eightieth birthday I flew three thousand miles to attend the wedding of a young man I had known since he was born. I was able to combine it with a short visit to cousins whom I had used in my book, *I Am the*

Author with friend Kara-Lynn on the patio, 1994

Universe. I had a wonderful time; I even danced at the wedding. But by the time I got home I realized that I was no longer quite up to such delights. It took me many days to get over the fatigue.

When I got my annual invitation to the children's book festival at the University of Missouri at Warrensburg, I accepted. Then I began to remember not only how much I had loved those festivals, with their eight thousand children, many writers, some new to me, some old friends, but also how exhausting that week was, even for the younger writers. Reluctantly I took back my acceptance. From then on I accepted no more invitations to such pleasant affairs unless they were within five or six miles.

Another disappointment was the reception of my book set at the time of World War One, *The Private War of Lillian Adams.* I had set it in my home town in 1918, making Lillian a few years older than my six years. I loved writing it, and I used more autobiographical detail than I ever had. Many small things I remembered, especially my cousin's service as a sailor among the crew of a mystery ship, so-called, that prowled enemy waters, sinking German ships. I wanted to write a book about that time, because it seems to me it was a very important moment in our history. We were not yet a world power; life in the United States was slow, quiet, isolated. Radio was in its infancy, there was no TV, no computers, nothing "electronic," relatively few automobiles, no passenger planes. It would seem like another planet to today's children, and yet it was the age of their great-grandfathers, even grandfathers.

The war, with so little news, seemed to Americans almost like some great competition. Our "doughboys" sailed off to cheerful songs by Irving Berlin: *Over There,* or *Oh, How I Hate to Get up in the Morning.* We had no conception of the incredible death and suffering on the other side of the Atlantic.

To Lillian Adams, in elementary school in a small village, the war was personal. The enemy was the local bootmaker, a taciturn man with a foreign accent. The glorious hero was her sailor cousin. Her role in the war effort was to collect peach pits for the government, though she had no idea what they were for.

Well, writing the book evoked many memories, and I enjoyed it, but no one else did. *Lillian* bombed.

I dove into *The Potato Kid* and enjoyed it all the way.

Old age kept giving me little reminders. Deafness was catching up with me, and I had to get a hearing aid. Aside from the realization that you are getting on other people's nerves by asking them to repeat much of what they have said, it is also a loss for a writer, who depends so much on hearing and using the rhythm and cadences of voices of different kinds of people. Especially among young people, the slang and the colloquialisms that change so often have rhythms of their own.

Perhaps because I realized that I had been in my home territory for the last time, I set both of my new books in small New England towns, usually with my father's home town of Essex in my mind. I have always had strong sentimental ties to Essex because of the childhood visits with my grandparents, who lived across the road from one of the town's famous shipyards. Shipbuilding and clams were the things Essex was famous for in the days of my childhood. However, in *Annie's Monster* and *Family Secrets* I used a modern village.

At about the time that *Family Secrets* was published, I received an award that I especially treasured. The University of Montana Friends of the Library gave me the H. G. Merriam award "for distinguished contribution to Montana literature." It is always a special pleasure to be recognized in the place where one lives. Also, I had had the delightful experience of meeting and talking to Dr. Merriam when I first came to Montana. He was an exceptional man who did much for western literature.

There was a banquet on the occasion of the award, and again it was fun to give a speech to an audience that included many of my friends.

I started a new book, set in Montana this time, making use of an experience that had meant a lot to me. I had spent part of an afternoon in the forest near Flathead Lake where a young couple had taken in wild animals that they had found who were hurt or sick or abandoned. The animals had multiplied, and when I was there, there were four beautiful foxes, some coyotes, and a pack of wolves. I have always been intrigued by wolves and have used them several times in my books. It was very exciting to find myself in a forest setting with these magnificent animals coming out silently and cautiously to see who this new human being was. In a short time they accepted me, and some of the younger ones were chewing at my shoestrings and sniffing the back of my neck. They were gentle and playful. The young woman who lived there warned me that with any encouragement they would delight in removing my socks and shoes and whatever else intrigued them. But they confined their explorations to my sneakers.

I was eager to start a book using some of this wonderful experience. The title is *Wolf at the Door*. I used a story of two sisters who are at odds with each other, and I combined their story with a story of some rescued wolves. I enjoyed it more than I had enjoyed any book for a long time, and happily it did well. Western Writers of America gave me an award, it was on the "Best" lists of three states, and it was published in Norway. At the moment it is in its eighth printing.

At about this time I was having trouble with my vision. Macular degeneration meant a loss of close vision, for reading and so on, in my left eye. There was the possibility of a similar problem with the right eye.

I had been thinking about writing a memoir, and now seemed to be the time, while I could still see well enough. At that time I could not manage the typewriter at all, so I wrote in longhand, as much as I could manage every day, not really seeing clearly what I was writing, but hoping it would be legible to my friend Linda who had often done such a good job of typing my manuscripts. I loved writing this kind of autobiography, in spite of the physical difficulties. I wrote at full speed, not stopping to reread. It was fascinating to come upon experiences and people in my life that I had virtually forgotten, and to find myself giving a different perspective to past events.

A day or so after I finished it, I had to go to the doctor with a fearful pain in my arm and shoulder. Work too steady, too long, for aging muscles? Old Author's syndrome? Anyway the memoir was done, and Linda miraculously translated it into readable prose without typos. Some critical friends and a few pros such as the late Jean Karl liked it. Now it is out in the cold world looking for a publisher.

There was an interim that required readjustments. Several sessions with the ophthalmologist. No more driving a car. That was a blow. I have driven since I was twelve, and my car was always my private refuge as well as the chariot that took me to unknown places.

The last book I was able to read, at a page or two a day, was one that all writers for children would find both fascinating and instructive, in my belief. It was *Dear Genius*, the collected letters of Ursula Nordstrom, Harper's editor for children's books from the thirties till the eighties. Her humor and charm make them delightful reading, but much more than that, they are full of keen insights that can help a writer. She was one of the handful of women editors and librarians who brought new life to children's books.

I began to practice on the typewriter. Even though I could not see what was appearing on the page until I could take it out of the machine and puzzle over it, it seemed to me that after some sixty or so years of typing, I should be able to work from memory at a reasonable speed. It was hopeless at first, but gradually it got better.

I had a book in mind. It was inspired by a recent arrival in our household, a dog named Indigo. She is the sweetest and most loving dog I have ever known, provided you pass her standards. Her devotion to her owner was almost instantaneous, but she needed a few weeks of reserve before she decided that I would do. She looks like a glossy black Rottweiler, except that she is about half the size. I thought a lot about what I wanted to do with Indigo, with all that love and intelligence and good manners.

Recently Kurt Vonnegut said on the radio that there are two kinds of writers: one starts with page one and stops with the last page; the other writes page one, rewrites it, discards it, starts again, and so on. I have always belonged to the first group, but now I found myself in the second. I made many false starts, thought of and discarded characters, threw out story lines. Finally, at last, I came up with a story about two loners, a boy with asthma and a dog whose puppies have been taken from her. Slowly and with many interruptions it became the tale of a boy and a dog finding in each other the love they need. I call the book *Ebony*. My agent likes it, and it is now out there looking for an editor. A writer's life is a waiting game.

My cat is waiting for me at the foot of the stairs. It is time for a game or two and a nap. I lean my cane on the bottom step and look up. Fifteen steps. Today they could be a hundred.

The cat switches her long tail impatiently. What am I waiting for?

I tell her, "We are getting old. In April I will be ninety, and you will be seven."

She makes the trill in her throat that I love to hear. Then in three feather-light leaps she is at the top of the stairs.

I make it to the bedroom and we have a few games. Then she curls up, cradles her head in my hand and goes to sleep.

I may have to try for one more book. About a cat.

Writings

NOVELS; FOR CHILDREN AND YOUNG ADULTS

Sam, illustrated by Barbara McGee, Atheneum (New York, NY), 1967.

(With Jeanne Dixon and Bradford Angier) *The Ghost of Spirit River,* Atheneum (New York, NY), 1968.

A Row of Tigers, illustrated by Allan Eitzen, Atheneum (New York, NY), 1969.

Sasha, My Friend, illustrated by Richard L. Shell, Atheneum (New York, NY), 1969, published as *My Wolf, My Friend,* Scholastic (New York, NY), 1975.

The Long Journey, illustrated by Charles Robinson, Atheneum (New York, NY), 1970.

(With Bradford Angier) *A Star to the North,* Thomas Nelson (Nashville, TN), 1970.

The Lifestyle of Robie Tuckerman, Thomas Nelson (Nashville, TN), 1971.

This Is a Recording, illustrated by Richard Cuffari, Atheneum (New York, NY), 1971.

A Trick of Light, illustrated by Lydia Dabcovich, Atheneum (New York, NY), 1972.

Don't Slam the Door When You Go, Atheneum (New York, NY), 1972.

All the Summer Voices (historical), illustrated by Charles Robinson, Atheneum (New York, NY), 1973.

The Winds of Time, illustrated by Gail Owens, Atheneum (New York, NY), 1974, published as *The Watching Eyes,* Scholastic (New York, NY), 1975.

A Dance to Still Music, illustrated by Charles Robinson, Atheneum (New York, NY), 1974.

The Clown, Atheneum, 1975, published as *I Wish You Love,* Scholastic (New York, NY), 1977.

Axe-Time, Sword-Time (historical), Atheneum (New York, NY), 1976.

Cabin in the Sky (historical), Atheneum (New York, NY), 1976.

The Faraway Island, Atheneum (New York, NY), 1977.

Make No Sound, Atheneum (New York, NY), 1977.

(With Bradford Angier) *Ask for Love and They Give You Rice Pudding,* Houghton (Boston, MA), 1977.

Hey, That's My Soul You're Stomping On, Atheneum (New York, NY), 1978.

Me and You and a Dog Named Blue, Atheneum (New York, NY), 1979.

Rising Damp, Atheneum (New York, NY), 1980.

Making It, Atlantic-Little, Brown (Boston, MA), 1980.

Child of the Morning, Atheneum (New York, NY), 1982.

Strike!, Atheneum (New York, NY), 1983.

The Woman in Your Life, Atheneum (New York, NY), 1984.

Face the Music, Atheneum (New York, NY), 1985.

A Horse Named Sky, Atheneum (New York, NY), 1986.

I Am the Universe, Atheneum (New York, NY), 1986.

You Put Up with Me, I'll Put Up with You, Atheneum (New York, NY), 1987.

The Hideaway, Atheneum (New York, NY), 1987.

The Sky Is Falling, Atheneum (New York, NY), 1988.

The Private War of Lillian Adams, Atheneum (New York, NY), 1989.

The Potato Kid, Atheneum (New York, NY), 1989.

Annie's Monster, Macmillan (New York, NY), 1990.

Stay Tuned, Atheneum (New York, NY), 1991.

Family Secrets, Atheneum (New York, NY), 1992.

Wolf at the Door, Atheneum (New York, NY), 1993.

Some of Corcoran's novels have been translated into German, Swedish, and Spanish.

MYSTERY NOVELS; FOR YOUNG ADULTS

Meet Me at Tamerlane's Tomb, illustrated by Robinson, Atheneum (New York, NY), 1975.

The Person in the Potting Shed, Atheneum (New York, NY), 1980.

You're Allegro Dead, Atheneum (New York, NY), 1981.

A Watery Grave, Atheneum (New York, NY), 1982.

Which Witch Is Which?, Atheneum (New York, NY), 1983.

August, Die She Must, Atheneum (New York, NY), 1984.

Mystery on Ice, Atheneum (New York, NY), 1985.

The Shadowed Path (part of "Moonstone Mystery Romance" series), Archway (New York, NY), 1985.

When Darkness Falls (part of "Moonstone Mystery Romance" series), Archway (New York, NY), 1986.

NOVELS; FOR YOUNG ADULTS; UNDER PSEUDONYM PAIGE DIXON

A Lion on the Mountain, illustrated by J. H. Breslow, Atheneum (New York, NY), 1972.

Silver Wolf, illustrated by Ann Brewster, Atheneum (New York, NY), 1973.

The Young Grizzly, illustrated by Grambs Miller, Atheneum (New York, NY), 1974.

Promises to Keep, Atheneum (New York, NY), 1974.

May I Cross Your Golden River?, Atheneum (New York, NY), 1975, published as *A Time to Love, a Time to Mourn,* Scholastic (New York, NY), 1982.

The Search for Charlie, Atheneum (New York, NY), 1976.

Pimm's Cup for Everybody, Atheneum (New York, NY), 1976.

Summer of the White Goat, Atheneum (New York, NY), 1977.

The Loner: A Story of the Wolverine, illustrated by Grambs Miller, Atheneum (New York, NY), 1978.

Skipper (sequel to *May I Cross Your Golden River?*), Atheneum (New York, NY), 1979.

Walk My Way, Atheneum (New York, NY), 1980.

NOVELS; FOR YOUNG ADULTS; UNDER PSEUDONYM GAIL HAMILTON

Titania's Lodestone, Atheneum (New York, NY), 1975.

A Candle to the Devil (mystery), illustrated by Joanne Scribner, Atheneum (New York, NY), 1975.

Love Comes to Eunice K. O'Herlihy, Atheneum (New York, NY), 1977.

HISTORICAL ROMANCE NOVELS

Abigail, Ballantine (New York, NY), 1981.
Abbie in Love (continuation of *Abigail*), Ballantine (New York, NY), 1981.
A Husband for Gail (conclusion of *Abigail*), Ballantine (New York, NY), 1981.
Beloved Enemy, Ballantine (New York, NY), 1981.
Call of the Heart, Ballantine (New York, NY), 1981.
Love Is Not Enough, Ballantine (New York, NY), 1981.
Song for Two Voices, Ballantine (New York, NY), 1981.
By the Silvery Moon, Ballantine (New York, NY), 1982.

OTHER

From the Drawn Sword (play), produced in Boston, MA, 1940.
Yankee Pine (play), produced at Bard College, Annandale-on-Hudson, NY, 1940.
The Mustang and Other Stories, Scholastic (New York, NY), 1978.

Also coauthor, with Louella Parsons, of four *Medal of Honor* scripts, including "Rodriguez." Contributor of radio scripts to *Dr. Christian* program; also contributor of short stories and other pieces to *Glamour, Charm, Woman's Day, Redbook, American Girl,* and *Good Housekeeping.*

CRONIN, Doreen
See CRONIN, Doreen A.

*   *   *

CRONIN, Doreen A.
(Doreen Cronin)

Personal

Born in Queens, NY; daughter of a police officer. *Education:* Pennsylvania State University, B.A., 1988; St. John's Law School, J.D., 1998. *Hobbies and other interests:* Writing, collecting antique typewriters, baseball.

Addresses

Office—c/o Simon & Schuster Books for Young Readers, 1230 Avenue of the Americas, New York, NY, 10020.

Career

Writer and attorney. Mound, Cotton, Wollan & Greengrass, New York, NY, associate attorney. Admitted to the Bar of New York State. Also worked as an editor and rights/permissions manager.

Writings

AS DOREEN CRONIN

Click, Clack, Moo: Cows That Type, illustrated by Betsy Lewin, Simon & Schuster Books for Young Readers (New York, NY), 2000.
Giggle, Giggle, Quack, illustrated by Betsy Lewin, Simon & Schuster Books for Young Readers (New York, NY), 2002.

Sidelights

Doreen A. Cronin's path to the field of children's literature is a unique one. Working first as editor in the publishing industry, Cronin left that field after earning a degree from St. John's Law School. Still a practicing attorney, Cronin produced her first book, *Click, Clack, Moo: Cows That Type,* in 2000, featuring illustrations by Betsy Lewin. Farmer Brown's cows are tired of living in a cold barn and decide to go on strike, refusing to produce any milk. The discontented bovines find an old manual typewriter in the barn and list their demands to Farmer Brown. Soon the chickens join in on the work stoppage, and a neutral party, the ducks, begin negotiations between the feuding animals and farmer. *School Library Journal* contributor Maura Bresnahan called *Click, Clack, Moo* "a terrific picture-book debut," going on to describe the work as "a laugh-out-loud look at life on a very funny farm." Several reviewers noted that though young preschoolers may have little, if any, experience with old typewriters, they will nevertheless enjoy the story. A *Horn Book* critic predicted that children "may have never heard the racket of a real typewriter, but they will certainly be familiar with the art of negotiation, and will soon be chanting" along with the story. Writing in *Booklist,* Hazel Rochman suggested that readers will "love the slapstick of the domesticated animals who get the farmer to toe the line."

Biographical and Critical Sources

PERIODICALS

Booklist, April 1, 2000, Hazel Rochman, review of *Click, Clack, Moo: Cows That Type,* p. 1468.
Horn Book, March, 2000, review of *Click, Clack, Moo,* p. 183.
Publishers Weekly, February 21, 2000, review of *Click, Clack, Moo,* p. 86.
School Library Journal, December, 2000, Maura Bresnahan, review of *Click, Clack, Moo,* p. 52.

Sesame Street, June, 2000, Hazel Rochman, review of
   Click, Clack, Moo, p. 2S37.*

*   *   *

CUNNINGHAM, Lawrence J. 1943-

Personal

Born February 27, 1943, in Pittsburgh, PA; son of Clyde
Franklin (an electrical engineer) and Estella (a home-
maker; maiden name, Craft) Cunningham; married
Cheryl Faith Napier (a homemaker), June 13, 1964;
children: Kim Thai. *Education:* University of Cincinnati,
B.S.Ed., 1965, M.Ed., 1967; University of Oregon,
Ed.D., 1987. *Politics:* Democrat. *Religion:* Protestant.
Hobbies and other interests: Hiking, aikido (shodan,
first-degree black belt), sea kayaking, traditional outrig-
ger canoe sailing.

Addresses

Home—326 South Santa Cruz, Agat, GU 96928; and
P.O. Box 7187, Agat, GU 96928-0187. *Office*—University of Guam, MARC UOG Station, Mangilao, GU
96923. *E-mail*—Lcunning@uog9.uog.edu.

Career

Mathematics teacher at a junior high school in Covington, KY, 1967-68; teacher of science and social studies
at schools in Guam, 1968-93, coach of Guam's Mock
Trial Team, 1984-98; University of Guam, Mangilao,
research associate, 1994—. Worked as L. Joseph, the

Lawrence J. Cunningham

Woodcarver, 1974-91. Agat Municipal Council, member, 1981-84. *Member:* American Federation of Teachers, Association for Supervision and Curriculum Development, Guam Federation of Teachers, Guam Library
Association, University of Oregon Alumni Association
(vice-president of Guam chapter, 1988-94), University
of Guam Seafarers, Phi Delta Kappa.

Awards, Honors

Onran I/Espiriton Hurao Award for Chamorro Culture
Publications, governor of Guam, 1978; six commenda-
tions from Guam Legislature, between 1990 and 1998,
for coaching Guam's Mock Trial Team in U.S. National
Mock Trial Championships; Governor's Literary Arts
Award, 1992, for *Ancient Chamorro Society;* member,
Ancient Order of the Chamorri, 1993; added to Guam
Museum Wall of Fame, 1996.

Writings

Ancient Chamorro Society, Bess Press (Honolulu, HI),
   1992.
*Rare Illustrations in the Collection of the Nieves M. Flores
   Memorial Library and Guam Museum, Agaña, Guam,*
   Kayon Publications (Agat, GU), 1994.
(With Janice J. Beaty and Remedios L. G. Perez) *A History
   of Guam,* Bess Press (Honolulu, HI), in press.
(With Janice J. Beaty) *Guam: A Natural History,* Bess
   Press (Honolulu, HI), in press.

Contributor to books, including *Unfaithing U.S. Colo-
nialism,* Pacific and Asian American Center for Theology and Strategies (Berkeley, CA), 1999. Contributor to
periodicals, including *Journal of the Pacific Society* and
Journal of Experimental Education.

Work in Progress

Ethnography of the Mariana Islands: Spanish Period,
completion expected c. 2005; research on Carolinian
traditional outrigger sailing canoes and navigation.

Sidelights

Lawrence J. Cunningham told *SATA:* "A knowledge of
one's history, culture, and language is essential. I am
one of many teachers who pioneered courses in local
studies for the Mariana Islands and the Chamorro
people. I became an author by necessity, because we
lacked appropriate books. Every culture has wisdom and
ways of being that should be shared with the world.

"I am very proud of my students, their many accom-
plishments, and the lives they are living. I've always told
them: 'We are stuck with the gifts God gave us, but we
can work as hard as we want.' In 1998, the mock trial
team that I coached at Guam's Southern High School
played for the U.S. National Mock Trial Championship
in the final round. It was a thrill to see my students
compete against the best and the brightest in the United
States and see them succeed!"*

D

DEXTER, Alison 1966-

Personal

Born September 2, 1966, in Derby, England. *Education:* Attended Derby College of Further Education, 1986-87; Bath College of Art, B.A. (with honors), 1990. *Hobbies and other interests:* Travel, photography, hill walking, cycling, reading, films, making three-dimensional works from driftwood and rusty iron.

Addresses

Home—1 Caechwarel, Rachub, Bangor, Gwynedd LL57 3HN, Wales. *E-mail*—alison@alisondexter.co.uk.

Career

Illustrator. Sheffield College, Sheffield, England, lecturer in illustration and graphic design, 1994-95. Creator of greeting cards and gift wrapping materials; designer of logos, letterheads, and book covers; illustrator for calendars, clothing, and gift items, including a mug for Amnesty International. *Exhibitions:* Work has appeared in the Llanberis Art Exhibition, Electric Mountain (Llanberis, Wales), 1998, and the Illustrators' Exhibition, Mary Kleinman Gallery (London, England), 1998. *Member:* Association of Illustrators.

Writings

(Self-illustrated) *Grandma,* HarperCollins (New York City), 1993.

ILLUSTRATOR

Jane Sebba, *Ring-A-Ding-Ding: Simple Ideas for Tuned Percussion in the Classroom,* A & C Black (London, England), 1997.
Jane Sebba, *Glock around the Clock: Simple Ideas for Tuned Percussion in the Classroom,* A & C Black (London, England), 1998.

Jane Sebba, *Agogo Bells to Xylophone: A Friendly Guide to Classroom Percussion Instruments,* A & C Black (London, England), 1998.
Caitlin Matthews, *The Blessing Seed: A Creation Myth for the New Millennium,* Barefoot Books, 1998.
Laura Berkeley, *The Seeds of Peace,* Barefoot Books (New York, NY), 1999.
Jane Sebba, *Piano Magic,* two volumes, A & C Black (London, England), 1999.
Sandra McCabe, *Monstergrams: Twelve Spooky Pop-Up Greeting Cards to Make Yourself,* Dial (New York, NY), 1999.
Laura Berkeley, *The Keeper of Wisdom,* Barefoot Books (New York, NY), 2000.

Illustrator of numerous educational books for A & C Black. Contributor of illustrations to magazines, including *Playdays, Child Education, Nursery World, Health Guardian, Green,* and *BBC Vegetarian.*

Biographical and Critical Sources

PERIODICALS

Booklist, October 15, 1998, review of *The Blessing Seed: A Creation Myth for a New Millennium.*
Publishers Weekly, December 28, 1992, review of *Grandma;* August 31, 1998, review of *The Blessing Seed;* July 26, 1999, review of *The Seeds of Peace.*
School Library Journal, June 1, 2000, review of *The Keeper of Wisdom.*

ON-LINE

Axis, http://www.axisartists.org.uk/ (February 14, 2001), biography of Alison Dexter.
Alison Dexter Home Page, http://runningman.co.uk/adexter/ (August 25, 2001).

DISHER, Garry 1949-

Personal

Born August 15, 1949, in Burra, South Australia; son of Donald Frederick (a farmer) and Lettie (Tiver) Disher; married; children: Hannah. *Education:* University of Adelaide, B.A., 1971; Monash University, M.A. (history), 1978; attended Stanford University, 1978-79; La Trobe University, Dip.Ed., 1981. *Hobbies and other interests:* Reading, walking, cinema.

Addresses

Home—Merricks North, Australia. *Office*—c/o Jenny Darling and Associates, P.O. Box 235, Richmond, Victoria 3121, Australia. *Agent*—Australian Literary Management, 2A Armstrong St., Middle Park, Victoria 3206, Australia.

Career

Writer. Holmesglen Tafe College, Victoria, Australia, lecturer in creative writing, 1979-88; University of Northumbria, Newcastle, England, writer in residence, 1998. Member of Spoleto Writers Festival Committee, 1990, 1991. *Member:* Australian Society of Authors, Fellowship of Australian Writers, Victorian Writers' Centre.

Awards, Honors

Stegner writing fellowship, 1978-79; National Short Story Award (Australia), 1986; Book of the Year for Older Readers, Australian Children's Book Council (ACBC), and New South Wales Premier Award shortlist, New South Wales Ministry for the Arts (NSWMA), both 1993, both for *The Bamboo Flute;* Australian nomination for International Board on Books for Young People honour list, 1994; National Book Council shortlist, and South Australian Festival Award for fiction shortlist, both 1996, and National Festival Award for Literature (Fiction) shortlist, 1998, all for *The Sunken Road;* Book of the Year for Older Readers, ACBC, New South Wales Premier Award shortlist, NSWMA, Ethnic Affairs Commission Award shortlist, NSWMA, and Ethel Turner Prize, all 1999, all for *The Divine Wind. The Difference to Me* and *Flamingo Gate* were shortlisted for the Steele Rudd Award.

Writings

FOR CHILDREN

Wretches and Rebels: The Australian Bushrangers ("Inquiring into Australian History" series), Oxford University Press (Melbourne, Australia), 1981.

Bushrangers (part of "Australia File" series), illustrated by Rolf Heimann and others, Nelson (Melbourne, Australia), 1984.

The Bamboo Flute (novel), Angus & Robertson (North Ryde, Australia), 1991, Ticknor & Fields (New York, NY), 1993.

Ratface (novel), Angus & Robertson (Pymble, Australia), 1993, Ticknor & Fields (New York, NY), 1994.

Switch Cat (picture book), Ashton Scholastic (Pymble, Australia), 1994, Ticknor & Fields (New York, NY), 1995.

Restless: Stories of Flight and Fear, Angus & Robertson (Pymble, Australia), 1995.

Ermyntrude Takes Charge, illustrated by Craig Smith, Angus & Robertson (Pymble, Australia), 1995.

Blame the Wind, illustrated by Melanie Feddersen, Angus & Robertson (Pymble, Australia), 1995.

Walk Twenty, Run Twenty (part of "Bluegum" series), Angus & Robertson (Pymble, Australia), 1996.

The Half Dead (part of "After Dark" series), illustrated by Shaun Tan, Lothian (Port Melbourne, Australia), 1997.

The Apostle Bird, Hodder Headline (Sydney, Australia), 1997.

The Divine Wind (novel), Hodder Headline (Sydney, Australia), 1998.

From Your Friend, Louis Deane, Hodder Headline (Rydalmere, Australia), 2000.

FICTION; FOR ADULTS

Approaches: Short Stories, Neptune Press (Newtown, Australia), 1981.

Steal Away (novel), Angus & Robertson (North Ryde, Australia), 1987.

The Difference to Me (stories), Angus & Robertson (North Ryde, Australia), 1988.

The Stencil Man (novel), HarperCollins (Sydney, Australia), 1988.

Flamingo Gate (short stories), Angus & Robertson (North Ryde, Australia), 1991, HarperCollins, 1992.

Kickback, Allen & Unwin (North Sydney, Australia), 1991.

Paydirt, Allen & Unwin (North Sydney, Australia), 1992.

Deathdeal, Allen & Unwin (St. Leonards, Australia), 1993.

Crosskill, Allen & Unwin (St. Leonards, Australia), 1994.

Port Vila Blues, Allen & Unwin (St. Leonards, Australia), 1995.

The Sunken Road, Allen & Unwin (St. Leonards, Australia), 1996.

The Fallout, Allen & Unwin (St. Leonards, Australia), 1997.

Straight, Bent and Barbara Vine: Short Stories, Allen & Unwin (St. Leonards, Australia), 1997.

(Editor) *Below the Waterline: 31 Australian Writers Choose Their Best Short Stories,* HarperCollins (Pymble, Australia), 1999.

The Dragonman, Allen & Unwin (St. Leonards, Australia), 1999.

Past the Headlands (Crow's Nest, Australia), Allen & Unwin, 2001.

OTHER

Total War: The Home Front, 1939-1945, Oxford University Press (Melbourne, Australia), 1983.

Writing Fiction: An Introduction to the Craft, Penguin Australia, 1983, second edition, 1989.

Australia Then and Now, Oxford University Press, 1987.

(Editor) *The Man Who Played Spoons* (anthology), Penguin Australia, 1988.

(Editor) *Personal Best* (anthology), Collins, 1989.

Writing Professionally: The Freelancer's Guide to Writing and Marketing (originally published, 1989), Allen & Unwin, 1991.

(Editor) *Personal Best 2: Stories and Statements by Australian Writers,* Angus & Robertson, 1991.

Contributor to *How to Write Crime,* edited by Marele Day, 1996.

Sidelights

Garry Disher is an Australian author of fiction and nonfiction for children and adults. Writing on topics as diverse as early Australian history, the impact of World War II on Australians, and the craft of writing, Disher has also written popular crime novels for adults featuring the hard-boiled detective Wyatt. Praised by critics for his award-winning juvenile fiction, Disher's young adult novels frequently feature teenage protagonists, often alienated from family and friends, who begin the transition to adulthood by overcoming obstacles such as war, economic depression, and death. "He's a fine writer," claimed *Australian Book Review* contributor Peter Nicholls, "no question about it, and his work has certainly been critically undervalued."

Disher has impressed many readers and reviewers with his first novel for children. Set in Depression-era Australia, *The Bamboo Flute* tells of twelve-year-old Paul's longing to bring back the music and happiness that have been missing from his family's life since money troubles forced them to sell his mother's piano. When Paul meets Eric the Red, a drifter he finds camping on the family's ranch, the man's musical talent leads Paul to befriend him even though his parents have warned him to stay away from "swagmen." Eric teaches the boy how to carve and play his own bamboo flute, and Paul's music allows him to make connections with classmates and his parents, particularly his father, who shares with his son his own artistic expressions.

"From its exquisite opening line ... to the moving finale, this elegantly delineated tale never strikes a false note," wrote a contributor to *Publishers Weekly.* Disher is "a gifted writer," the critic continued, and his novel "is symphonic in its composition and layering of tones." A *Kirkus Reviews* writer also had praise for Disher's "spare, lyrical prose," which captures "a mood or the nuances of his character's perceptions with wonderful subtlety." Similarly remarking on the characterization of the book, Gerry Larson noted in *School Library Journal* that "Paul's artistic sensitivity is underscored by the vivid, sensory details of his first-person narrative." As Nancy Vasilakis concluded in her *Horn Book* review: "The spare, subdued language in this introspective novel and the subtle development of character create an aura that lingers long after the last page."

The Bamboo Flute, Disher once revealed to *SATA,* "grew out of a heartache in my father's childhood. How do I account for the book's power to move readers? I wrote it from the heart. I am reminded of Colette's classic advice: 'Look long and hard at the things that please you, even longer and harder at what causes you pain.'"

Set a few years after *The Bamboo Flute,* Disher's 1998 novel, *The Divine Wind,* tells the story of two teenagers whose lives are altered by the Second World War. Born to an owner of a fleet of pearl-fishing ships, Hartley Penrose finds his relationship with Mitsy Sennosuke, a Japanese-Australian, difficult after the outbreak of the war. With reports of Japanese atrocities in the Pacific, Hartley's feelings for Mitsy change, particularly after his sister, who enlisted in the military, is reported missing in action. Mitsy herself is no stranger to tragedy as she loses her father, Zeke, who drowned while successfully rescuing Hartley from the same fate. Plagued by the guilt over Zeke's death and his unjustified ill-treatment of Mitsy, Hartley learns to separate his true feelings from the anti-Japanese sentiment of the townspeople and helps Mitsy and her family find refuge. Hartley "is an exceptionally well-drawn character, real in flaws," wrote *Magpies* reviewer Helen Purdie. Purdie went on to call *The Divine Wind* "a mature and exciting piece of work that is highly recommended." Adèle Geras, writing in the *Times Literary Supplement,* had high praise for the "wonderfully moving, exact and economical retelling of an unusual love story," going on to claim that "this is one of the best books I read in 1999, and Disher is someone to watch out for."

In *Ratface,* Disher tackles the theme of white supremacy as young Max and Christina realize that they were never orphaned by their biological parents but rather kidnaped by members of a racist cult. Raised by kind but rather clueless parents, Max and Christina begin wondering about their true origins after a newspaper reporter begins poking around their remote mountain farm, asking questions about their leader. After another obviously abducted child, Stefan, joins the White League compound, Max and Christina realize that they must try to escape, hoping to reunite the new boy with his original family and perhaps find their own as well. Pursued by a cult member the children have nicknamed Ratface, the trio manage in the end not to escape but instead convince their adoptive parents of the White League's evils. While reviewers were not as enthusiastic with this novel as others by Disher, *School Library Journal* reviewer Joel Shoemaker suggested that young adult readers might be willing to overlook the book's flaws in favor of its "generally dark mood and quick moving, if unrealistic, action." Describing the book as a "thrilling, chilling ride," a contributor to *Kirkus Reviews* found *Ratface* "a fast and exciting book that also raises some serious questions, although it provides no answers."

In addition to his novels for young adults, Disher has also written several children's picture books, including *Switch Cat.* The young narrator of the story, a tomboy, owns a sleek, black cat named Evangelina who would much rather spend time with the dainty and proper next-door neighbor, Cecilia. Fortunately, Cecilia's cat, Ms. Whiz, would much rather spend her days with *Switch Cat*'s rough and tumble narrator. The arrangement works well until Cecilia's family packs up and moves away, leaving all four creatures at a loss. However, the scruffy Ms. Whiz takes matters into her own paws, working out a solution to fit both girls. "A sure-fire selection for anyone who has ever been owned by a cat," suggested Joy Fleishhacker in *School Library Journal.* "Disher's verse ... has a natty, asymmetrical allure," remarked a critic in *Publishers Weekly,* "... that makes for a jaunty read aloud."

Disher once told *SATA,* "I grew up on my father's farm in Australia. Isolation from other children—and a love of books and family storytelling—encouraged in me a strong desire to become a writer. I first sought commercial publication (of literary magazine stories) whilst a student, but I did not fully understand or appreciate the craft of writing until I was awarded a creative writing fellowship to Stanford University in the United States in 1978. For the next decade I taught creative writing part-time in order to support my writing career, producing novels, story collections, writers' handbooks, anthologies, and history textbooks. I have been a full-time writer for several years now, writing 'literary' fiction and crime novels (both influenced by my love of contemporary North American and Canadian fiction), together with a range of books for children. I write to express, not impress; I write to entertain, please myself, and make the best thing I can make, not instruct or change the world."

Biographical and Critical Sources

PERIODICALS

Australian Book Review, September, 1988; May, 2000, Peter Nicholls, "A Well-Made Cake," p. 56.

Booklist, April 15, 1993, p. 1496; September 1, 1993, p. 60; November 1, 1994, Anne O'Malley, review of *Ratface,* p. 491; March 15, 1995, Hazel Rochman, review of *Switch Cat,* p. 1334.

Bulletin of the Center for Children's Books, December, 1994, p. 126.

Horn Book, January-February, 1994, Nancy Vasilakis, review of *The Bamboo Flute,* p. 69.

Kirkus Reviews, July 15, 1993, review of *The Bamboo Flute,* p. 932; November 15, 1994, review of *Ratface,* p. 1527.

Magpies, September, 1995, Michael Gregg, review of *Blame the Wind,* p. 35; September, 1996, Jo Goodman, review of *Walk Twenty, Run Twenty,* p. 31; September, 1998, Helen Purdie, review of *The Divine Wind,* p. 36.

Publishers Weekly, June 28, 1993, review of *The Bamboo Flute,* p. 79; September 19, 1994, review of *Ratface,* p. 72; January 23, 1995, review of *Switch Cat,* p. 69.

School Librarian, spring, 1999, Tony O'Sullivan, review of *The Apostle Bird,* p. 44.

School Library Journal, September, 1993, Gerry Larson, review of *The Bamboo Flute,* p. 229; December, 1994, Joel Shoemaker, review of *Ratface,* p. 108; March, 1995, Joy Fleishhacker, review of *Switch Cat,* p. 179.

Times Literary Supplement, January 22, 1988, p. 81; January 21, 2000, Adèle Geras, review of *The Divine Wind,* p. 23.*

DOUCET, Sharon Arms 1951-

Personal

Born January 15, 1951, in Champagne, IL; daughter of H. Windle (a geologist) and Miriam C. (a teacher and sales executive) Arms; married Michael L. Doucet (a musician), August 26, 1983; children: Melissa Louise Maher, Ezra Amédí, Matthew. *Education:* University of Louisiana at Lafayette, B.A., 1974, M.A., 1977; University of Nice (France), Études Supérieures, 1973. *Hobbies and other interests:* Violin, guitar, Shambhala Buddhism, herbal and energy healing, gardening, yoga, swimming.

Addresses

Agent—Frances M. Kuffel, Maria Carvainis Literary Agency, 235 West End Ave., New York, NY 10023. *E-mail*—sadosay@aol.com.

Career

University of Louisiana, Lafayette, LA, instructor of English as a second language (ESL), 1981-88; Northeast Louisiana University, Monroe, LA, instructor of ESL and French, 1982-83; Ascension Day School, Lafayette, LA, instructor of French, 1984-89. Meditation teacher, participant in Labyrinth Project, St. Gabriel Women's

Sharon Arms Doucet

Prison. Author. *Member:* Society of Children's Book Writers and Illustrators, Writer's Guild of Acadiana.

Writings

Le Hoogie Boogie Songbook: Louisiana French Music for Children, Mel Bay (Pacific, MO), 1994.

Why Lapin's Ears Are Long: And Other Tales from the Louisiana Bayou (picture book), Orchard Books (Danbury, CT), 1997.

Fiddle Fever (middle grade novel), Clarion Books (New York, NY), 2000.

Lapin Plays Possum (picture book), Farrar, Strauss (New York, NY), 2002.

Articles published in *Fiddler Magazine, Children's Digest,* and *Journal of Popular Culture.*

Work in Progress

Alligator Sue, a picture story book for Farrar, Strauss, to be published in 2003; *On Earth as It Is,* a novel completed in 2000; *Kay Cee and the Thunderation Mule,* a comic chapter book set on a Colorado homestead. Research on the civil war, and herbal healing.

Sidelights

Sharon Arms Doucet told *SATA:* "They say that at age eleven or twelve, we know what we're meant to be when we grow up. As a young girl, I changed my name to Jo after Louisa May Alcott's character in *Little Women,* and dreamed of writing in a romantic garret and receiving word that my first work was to be published. I wrote poems and Nancy Drew-type mysteries. But somewhere along the way, I lost that youthful confidence in having something to say that anyone would want to hear. After many years of teaching French and English as a second language, the birth of my last child gave me the excuse to stay home and begin to realize that youthful dream. At long last I can say, 'I'm a writer.'

"After a very brief stay in my birthplace, Champagne, Illinois, my formative years were spent in Casper, Wyoming, where my father worked as a geologist. The many weekends we spent camping in the gorgeous Rocky Mountains taught me a love of nature and the outdoors. My family later moved to Denver, Colorado, and then to Lafayette, Louisiana, where I still live. I must have heard the echoes of my French ancestors when I found a warm place among the French-speaking Cajuns of southwest Louisiana. My husband Michael is a fiddle player in a Cajun band, BeauSoleil, and I have two children, Melissa and Ezra, and a stepson, Matthew. We often play music at home and have occasionally performed as the Doucet Family Band. I play guitar and am learning the fiddle.

"My love of history, folklore and language was nurtured by good teachers and the rich stories of the places I've lived. Since my parents moved far from their family homes at early ages, and since I married into such a close-knit, traditional culture, my works tend to reflect a search for belonging, for a realization of a destiny. Children, I think, need to be encouraged to find and follow their passions in order to truly fulfill themselves. In my recent middle-grade novel, *Fiddle Fever,* Félix must defy his parents and his circumstances to find a way to let the music out of his heart. In the upcoming *Alligator Sue,* Sue, blown away by a hurricane and raised by a mama alligator, must reconcile the two halves of herself to 'be who she is, half Gator and half Girl.' In my recently-finished adult novel, *On Earth as It Is,* the death of Frannie's father leads her on a search for the right place and true purpose in her life, which she feels she lost touch with along the way. And in my adaptions of Cajun and Creole folktales, the incorrigible trickster Compère Lapin (the Louisiana version of Br'er Rabbit) constantly turns everything upside down and makes everyone question reality.

"I have been fortunate enough to study with such Louisiana-based writers as Ernest Gaines, Robert Olen Butler, and Luis Urrea. I believe good writing, whether for children or adults, must come from a place deep inside where we face our most private issues and fears. My own search for truth has led me on an ever-broadening spiritual path that includes yoga, Tibetan Buddhism, Native American wisdom, and herbal and energy healing. I wake up every morning and say, 'What do I get to write today?'"

Doucet has been praised for seamlessly incorporating the colorful south Louisiana dialect and penchant for unusual similes into her stories for children. In *Why Lapin's Ears Are Long: And Other Tales from the Louisiana Bayou,* Doucet retells three traditional Cajun Creole stories featuring Compère Lapin, the Louisiana version of Br'er Rabbit. The stories follow the traditional folktale in form, as one story tells why Lapin's ears are long, another tells why his tail is short, and the third tells what happens when he falls in love. Doucet's introduction traces these stories and the character of the trickster rabbit back to narratives brought by West Africans to the United States as slaves in earlier centuries. However, critics praised her ability to capture the nuances of the Cajun culture that nurtured the stories on this continent. "This book offers a slice of folklore from a unique culture," observed Judith Constantinides in *School Library Journal.* Other reviewers had similar praise, including a contributor to *Publishers Weekly,* who remarked that Doucet "clearly relishes her flavorful region, slinging about humorous colloquialisms with great joy." Doucet's colorful prose makes the stories in *Why Lapin's Ears Are Long* especially useful for story hours and for storytelling, reviewers noted. "The extravagant descriptive prose, preposterous characterizations, and hilarious use of the vernacular join to create a totally satisfying literary experience," concluded a reviewer in the *Horn Book.*

An effective incorporation of Cajun dialect and culture is the hallmark of Doucet's middle-grade novel, *Fiddle Fever,* as well. In this coming-of-age story, young Félix comes alive in a way he never has before when he first hears his uncle, 'Nonc Adolphe, an itinerant musician in the turn-of-the-twentieth-century American South, play the fiddle. Unfortunately, Félix's no-nonsense parents forbid him to take up the instrument, though he seems to have inherited a natural love of its music from his uncle and grandfather. The boy rebels and teaches himself to play a violin he constructs out of a cigar box, and then participates in the revelries of Mardi Gras in a mask. Though he is punished when his deception is revealed, Félix's rebellion ultimately leads to a compromise both he and his parents can accept. "Doucet ably portrays both a youngster's all-consuming passion for a forbidden act and his determination to find his own way," remarked a reviewer in *Horn Book. School Library Journal* contributor Judith Constantinides was even more enthusiastic in her praise for *Fiddle Fever,* highlighting the book's accomplished depiction of Cajun culture early in the last century, as well as its portrait of the power of music. "A book not to be missed," Constantinides concluded.

Biographical and Critical Sources

PERIODICALS

Horn Book, September-October, 1997, review of *Why Lapin's Ears Are Long;* October, 2000, review of *Fiddle Fever.*

Publishers Weekly, October 20, 1997, review of *Why Lapin's Ears Are Long.*

School Library Journal, September, 1997, Judith Constantinides, review of *Why Lapin's Ears Are Long,* p. 201; October, 2000, Judith Constantinides, review of *Fiddle Fever.*

ON-LINE

Sharon Arms Doucet Web site, http://www.sharonarmsdoucet.com/ (August 31, 2001).

E

EDWARDS, Becky Jane 1966-
(Becky Edwards)

Personal

Born April 27, 1966; daughter of Victor (a lawyer) and Lisa (a field officer; maiden name, Schenk) Gersten; married Ninesh Edwards (an engineering manager), May 25, 1995; children: Mia, Joss. *Education:* University of Liverpool, B.A., 1989; Thames Polytechnic, post-graduate certificate in education, 1990. *Politics:* Socialist.

Addresses

Home—42 Cambrai Ave., Chichester, West Sussex PO19 2JY, England. *E-mail*—nineshandbecky@compuserve.com.

Career

Special education teacher at a primary school, 1992-94; home therapist for autistic children, 1995-97; writer and homemaker, 1997—.

Awards, Honors

Citation for "Key Stage 1 picture fiction book" from English Association.

Writings

AS BECKY EDWARDS

My Brother Sammy, illustrated by Paul Armitage, Millbrook Press (Brookfield, CT), 1999.
My Cat Charlie, illustrated by Paul Armitage, Bloomsbury, 2000.

Work in Progress

My First Day at Nursery, publication expected in 2003.

Sidelights

Becky Jane Edwards told *SATA:* "My work with children and adults with special needs over the years has made me realise that the best way to prevent prejudice and create acceptance is for children of all abilities to be together and to learn to accept and understand each other's differences. I hope with *My Brother Sammy* to show that the world of an autistic child is just as appealing, stimulating, and 'shareable' as any other and that love between siblings knows no boundaries.

"Writing for children gives me a great deal of pleasure, and I hope to be lucky enough to continue doing so for many years."

Biographical and Critical Sources

PERIODICALS

Children's Book Review Service, spring, 1999, Barbara Baker, review of *My Brother Sammy,* p. 134.
School Librarian, autumn, 1999, Deepa Earnshaw, review of *My Brother Sammy,* p. 130.
School Library Journal, July, 1999, Sally R. Dow, review of *My Brother Sammy,* p. 70.*

*　　*　　*

EDWARDS, Becky
See EDWARDS, Becky Jane

*　　*　　*

EIKEN, J. Melia 1967-

Personal

Born November 27, 1967; married Matthew Eiken (a chiropractor), April 26, 1996; children: Lindsey, Zoe. *Education:* Earned Doctor of Chiropractic degree, 1997. *Religion:* "Christ seeker, no denomination."

Addresses

Home—300 Thelma Dr., Mauldin, SC 29662. *E-mail*—mmlz@bellsouth.net.

Career

Doctor of chiropractic in Greenville, SC, 1997—.

Writings

Cheese Flavored Candy, Press-Tige Publishing (Catskill, NY), 2000.

Work in Progress

The Everywhere Secret, about "a journey to the secret part of a cloud."

Sidelights

J. Melia Eiken told *SATA:* " 'Unplug the cable and open a book' is the motto in our house. My husband, Matthew, and I plunge head-first with our kids into waves of belly laughs, ear-piercing squeals, and mystical 'ooohs.'

"We love reading to our children, Lindsey, age eleven, and Zoe, age three. Heroic escapades, imagination, and fantasy blaze across the pages of their favorite books. We know we've found a great one when Zoe starts wiggling her toes in anticipation of the next page—when the excitement is simply too great to contain. That's the reaction I'm going for in the stories I write. I believe children who experience great books—the ones that really tap their imaginations—develop a lifetime passion for reading. What a gift!

"With two kids, four dogs, career stress, and the world in general, there are precious few quiet moments in my day. There is, however, a special book reserved for those enchanted times of solitude—my Bible. It touches my heart and stirs my soul with each page I turn. It is simple enough for a child to understand, yet too complex for any adult ever to comprehend. As a born-again Christian, the themes of all my future works will be sharing the glorious celebration of life through Jesus Christ."*

F

FALCONER, Ian

Personal

Male. *Education:* Attended New York University and Parsons School of Design.

Career

Author, illustrator, painter, and set designer. Paintings have been published on the cover of the *New Yorker* magazine.

Awards, Honors

Parents' Choice Gold Award, 2000, and Caldecott Honor Book, American Library Association, 2001, both for *Olivia*.

Writings

SELF-ILLUSTRATED; FOR CHILDREN

Olivia, Atheneum (New York, NY), 2000.
Olivia Saves the Circus, Atheneum (New York, NY), 2001.

Work in Progress

Two more titles in the "Olivia" series.

Sidelights

Ian Falconer's award-winning premier children's book, *Olivia,* has been widely hailed as an important debut for both author-artist and his creation, a memorable child heroine who has garnered comparisons to Kay Thompson's Eloise and Kevin Henkes's Lilly. "Olivia, a delightful little pig, is Everychild," proclaimed Ilene Cooper in *Booklist*. Olivia is exuberant, intelligent, and unstoppable. "One could argue that Olivia's precociousness grows out of a three-year-old's relentless curiosity and unself-conscious belief that she can accomplish whatever she sets her mind to," remarked Jennifer M. Brown in *Publishers Weekly*. Coupled with

Falconer's laconic text and his bold, black-and-white-and-red illustrations, Olivia's spirit quickly captured the hearts of reviewers and readers.

Falconer's story begins on the end pages of the book, where Olivia's red clothes are strewn hither and thither, with her choice, a red sailor dress with black-and-white striped tights, revealed on the title page. The narrator introduces Olivia as someone who does many things well—first and foremost of these many things is to wear

Artist and theatrical designer Ian Falconer captures the imaginative world-without-limits of a young pig in his award-winning picture-book Olivia.

out everyone around her, and then herself. The illustrations accompanying this statement, drawn in charcoal on a white background with dashes of bright red as the only color, show Olivia in thirteen small vignettes engaged in a variety of frenetic activities until she is found in the last one, utterly spent. Critics noted that the design and layout used in these spreads in particular, with charcoal drawings on a white background dotted with splotches of bright red, effectively convey Olivia's boundless energy. Subsequent pages show Olivia at her favorite hang-out, in an art museum; dreaming of being a prima ballerina, bowing before her adoring public; building a stupendous sand castle; painting her wall at home to resemble a Jackson Pollack creation; trying on every outfit in her closet, all seventeen of them, all in her favorite color of red, before choosing the perfect one. As this list demonstrates, "there's no real plot here," as Cooper put it, but "the strong, clever art," the design of the book, and its humor make up for this lack, Cooper concluded. Indeed, "the text is brief, funny, and sometimes ironic in relation to the highly amusing illustrations," commented Marianne Saccardi in *School Library Journal.*

The book *Olivia* began with some doodles Falconer made for his niece as a Christmas present. The set designer and *New Yorker* artist was so inspired by the real-life Olivia's energy and can-do attitude that he continued to work on the piece until it was complete, story and art, and eventually showed the whole project to an agent, who suggested the illustrations be given over to an established author who would write the story. Instead, Falconer put the project away for several years until he was approached by Anne Schwartz, leader of an imprint for Atheneum books. Falconer chose the challenge of working in only black, white, and red, the same palette used by traditional Russian political posters, for a variety of reasons. He told *Publishers Weekly*'s Brown, "I think black-and-white can be just as arresting as color. It can also be much less information going into your eye, your brain, so that you pay attention to subtler detail in, say, facial expressions." Reviewers praised the results of this reasoning. "Falconer's choice to suggest Olivia with a minimum of details and a masterful black line allows readers to readily identify with her—no doubt, they will," predicted a reviewer in *Publishers Weekly.* "There's a little bit of Olivia in everyone," the critic concluded.

A sequel, *Olivia Saves the Circus,* in which the fearless pig gets the chance to play the role of every performer in the circus, was published in 2001.

Biographical and Critical Sources

PERIODICALS

Booklist, August, 2000, Ilene Cooper, review of *Olivia,* p. 2134.

BP Report, July 16, 2001, "Olivia Takes Over the World."

California, October, 1988, Donna Keene, "Ian Falconer: Work in Progress," p. 13.

Entertainment Weekly, December 8, 2000, Clarissa Cruz, "Bound for Glory: "A Bevy of Books Suitable for Gift Giving Speaks Volumes about the Eclectic Pitch to Readers," p. 85.

Interview, August, 1987, "Art and Comedy," p. 38; September, 1988, Greg Gorman, "Ian Falconer," p. 44.

New York, June 21, 1999, Tobi Tobias, "School of American Ballet," p. 66.

New York Times Book Review, November 19, 2000, M. P. Dunleavy, "Renaissance Pig: Meet Olivia, Who Dreams of Becoming a Dancer, or a Diva, or a Painter, or . . . ," p. 66.

Publishers Weekly, July 17, 2000, review of *Olivia,* p. 193; November 20, 2000, "The Little Pig That Could," p. 19; December 18, 2000, Jennifer M. Brown, "Ian Falconer," p. 26.

School Library Journal, September, 2000, Marianne Saccardi, review of *Olivia,* p. 196; December, 2000, review of *Olivia,* p. 53.*

*   *   *

FAVOLE, Robert J(ames) 1950-

Personal

Surname is pronounced "Fa-*vo*-lee"; born September 27, 1950, in New York, NY; son of Patrick A. (a hair stylist) and Bernadine (a nurse; maiden name, Martin) Favole; married Cynthia L. Remmers (an attorney), January, 1985; children: Miesje Remmers, Bjorn Remmers, Patrick R., Kristian M. *Education:* State University of New York at Buffalo, B.A., 1972; University of Arizona, J.D., 1980.

Addresses

Home—Auburn, CA. *Agent*—c/o Flywheel Publishing, 1223 High St., Auburn, CA 95603. *E-mail*—rfavole@ wizwire.com.

Career

Arizona Training Program, Tucson, habilitation worker and supervisor, 1973-77; U.S. Court of Appeals, 9th Circuit, San Francisco, CA, law clerk, 1980-82; Orrick Herrington & Sutcliffe, San Francisco, attorney in San Francisco and Sacramento, CA, 1982-90; Law Offices of Robert J. Favole, Sacramento, attorney, 1990-2000; full-time writer, 2000—. Miles Exploratory Learning Center, staff member, 1976; Alta Vista School Site Council, member, 1998-2000.

Awards, Honors

Charles L. Strous Prize, *Arizona Law Review,* 1980, for the article "Artificial Gestation: New Meaning for Right to Terminate Pregnancy"; first place award in young adult category, "Persie" Awards, Writers International Network/Writers Interage Network, 2000, for *Through the Wormhole.*

Writings

Through the Wormhole (novel), Flywheel Publishing (Auburn, CA), 2001.

Contributor to law journals.

Work in Progress

A Day Redux (tentative title), a young adult novel about a high school student who tries to prevent violence; research on African-American lawyers before the Civil War.

Sidelights

Robert J. Favole told *SATA:* "I grew up in Roosevelt, New York, a small, integrated town, intimate and tight-knit. Among my strongest influences remain friends and teachers, black and white, from Roosevelt.

"I have pursued three careers: education, law, and writing. After receiving my B.A. from the University of Buffalo, I taught developmentally delayed children at the Arizona Training Program at Tucson. There, and at the Graduate School of Education at the University of Arizona, I received extensive training in theories of learning, child development, and the principles of reading. I worked also at the Miles Exploratory Learning Center, an open-classroom, public, magnet elementary school. Most recently I have served on the Alta Vista School Site Council in Auburn, California.

"In 1977 I enrolled in the University of Arizona College of Law. While a law student, I assisted a professor in his analysis of bio-ethics and the law, conducted tutorials in constitutional law, and served as student member of the Curriculum Committee. In 1980 I began a clerkship with the U.S. Court of Appeals, serving as law clerk to the Honorable James R. Browning, then Chief Judge of the Ninth Circuit. In 1982 I entered private practice, including the representation of individuals in civil rights cases.

"In 2000 I gave up the law to write fiction full-time. *Through the Wormhole,* a novel for young adults, expresses my conviction that our youth view history as a dead letter. But it can be enlivened by the use of 'story.' To foster a sense of connection to the past, I employed the vehicle of time travel. Nothing else allows a protagonist to come face to face with his own distant ancestor. In *Through the Wormhole,* Michael, an African-American high school student, meets his great, great, etc. grandfather, John Banks, a Continental cavalryman. John was a real person, whose actual history is woven into the story. John and Michael share an overriding interest in horses, and they each have a certain twinkle in the eye. These serve as metaphors for their familial connection and for the vestige of John's contributions to liberty and our national past.

"Those who forget the past, it is said, are condemned to relive it. That tells only the half of it. They are condemned, too, to lose sight of that which is most noble. My goal is to bring history to life through story."

Biographical and Critical Sources

PERIODICALS

Booklist, March, 2001, review of *Through the Wormhole,* p. 1278.
Kliatt, January, 2001, Claire Rosser, review of *Through the Wormhole,* p. 7.
School Library Journal, April, 2000, review of *Through the Wormhole.*

*   *   *

FITZPATRICK, Marie-Louise 1962-

Personal

Born March 2, 1962, in Dublin, Ireland; daughter of Bernard (an engineer) and Deborah (a secretary and homemaker; maiden name, O'Neill) Fitzpatrick. *Education:* College of Marketing and Design, Dublin, Ireland, diploma, 1983. *Hobbies and other interests:* Travel, culture, literature, film, history, photography, gardening.

Addresses

Home—6 St. Brigid's Rd., Clondalkin, Dublin 22, Ireland. *Office*—The Mill Studios, 32 North Brunswick St., Dublin 7, Ireland. *Agent*—Eunice McMullen, 38 Clewer Hill Rd., Windsor, Berkshire SL4 4BW, England. *E-mail*—marielouisef@hotmail.com.

Career

Freelance writer and illustrator for children. Part-time art teacher; McPartlin Design, graphic assistant trainee, 1983-84. *Member:* Green Partridge Club.

Awards, Honors

Book of the Year, Consumer Choice, 1988, Children's Book Award, Reading Association of Ireland, 1989, Design Medal from Irish Book Awards, 1989, and Bisto Book of the Decade Award, Irish language category, 1990, all for *An Chanáil;* Bisto Book of the Year Award, picture book category, 1992, for *The Sleeping Giant;* special merit award, Reading Association of Ireland, Bisto Merit Award, and nomination to Honours List, International Board on Books for Young People, all 1999, all for *The Long March;* Bistro Merit Award shortlist, 2001, for *Lizzy and Skunk.*

Writings

FOR CHILDREN; SELF-ILLUSTRATED

An Chanáil (title means "The Canal"; translated into Irish by Bernadine Nic Ghiolla Phádraig), An Gúm (Dublin, Ireland), 1988.
The Sleeping Giant, Brandon (Dingle, Ireland), 1991.

The Long March: The Choctaw's Gift to the Irish Famine Relief, edited by Gary WhiteDeer, Beyond Words, 1998.

Lizzy and Skunk, David & Charles (London, England), 1999, Dorling Kindersley (New York, NY), 2000.

I'm a Tiger, Too, Gullane (London, England), 2001, Roaring Brook (Brookfield, CT), 2002.

FOR CHILDREN; ILLUSTRATOR

Margrit Cruickshank, *Anna's Six Wishes,* Poolbeg (Dublin, Ireland), 1995.

Aislinn O'Loughlin, *Cinderella's Fella,* Wolfhound (Dublin, Ireland), 1995.

Aislinn O'Loughlin, *A Right Royal Pain Rumpelstiltskin—The True Story,* Wolfhound (Dublin, Ireland), 1996.

Aislinn O'Loughlin, *The Emperor's Birthday Suit,* Wolfhound (Dublin, Ireland), 1997.

Aislinn O'Loughlin, *Shak and the Beanstalk,* Wolfhound (Dublin, Ireland), 1997.

Peadar Ó Laoghaire, *Séanna,* Cois Life Teoranta (Dublin, Ireland), 1998.

OTHER

(Illustrator) *Rusty Nails and Astronauts: A Wolfhound Poetry Anthology,* edited by Robert Dunbar and Gabriel Fitzmaurice, Wolfhound (Dublin, Ireland), 1999.

Work in Progress

Mother, Aunt Alice, and Me Go to Sea, a children's picture book for Gullane.

Sidelights

Marie-Louise Fitzpatrick told *SATA:* "I was four when I decided I wanted to be an artist. Much to my mother's horror, I never grew out of the idea! My father worked in a paper mill, and I always had plentiful supplies of rough paper to draw on. Just as well, as I could go through a dozen sheets a day.

"After art college, I did some part-time teaching and a lot of illustration work for schoolbooks while trying to break into publishing as an author. After my first two books were published, I hit a shaky patch. Over twelve months during 1997-1998, not one, but three publishers collapsed or ran into business problems, and I held on to dear life wondering if it was time to consider a change of career. I found an agent who got me back on track, and

With gentle watercolor illustrations, Irish author and artist Marie-Louise Fitzpatrick portrays the bond between a girl and her stuffed toy in Lizzy *and* Skunk.

Fitzpatrick's **The Sleeping Giant** *was inspired by an island off the Irish coast that is shaped like a giant lying at rest on top of the ocean.*

ideas which have been around for a while are finally getting to see the light of day."

Regarding her inspiration for the stories she writes, Fitzpatrick once said, "Something simple may inspire an idea. I always recognize the spark but usually have to wait a long time while it grows in my mind and finally becomes clear enough for me to work with. I work the books up layer by layer, story and pictures together, until they seem right.

"*The Long March* was a story I felt I had to write after hearing about the Choctaw gift to Ireland's famine victims in 1847. I intended to write it more from an Irish point of view, but as I researched it, it became the story of the Choctaws and their long march. I traveled to Oklahoma to research the story and pictures, and met Gary WhiteDeer, who became the book's Choctaw editor.

"*The Long March* presented me with a writing challenge, quite unlike my other books. It forced me to explore the writer in me and see what I was made of! Perhaps I will eventually get around to attempting the two ideas for novels that are floating in my head."

Reviewers found Fitzpatrick's rendition of the story she calls *The Long March* affecting. Drawing on the little-known fact that the impoverished Choctaw nation sent

money in 1847 to help relieve the Irish people starving during the great potato famine, Fitzpatrick created a story about a young Choctaw who wonders why his people should help Europeans when, not so long before, the Europeans stole the Choctaw land and made them walk the Trail of Tears. The boy's great-grandmother remembers the Long March and proclaims that the Choctaw should help those in need even as they could not help themselves in their own hour of need. "This deeply moving work quietly and effectively underscores the drama and pathos of a little-known historical episode," remarked a reviewer for *Publishers Weekly*. Other reviewers similarly praised the power of Fitzpatrick's words and pictures. "Fitzpatrick's strong, detailed pencil illustrations are as direct and beautiful as the words," stated Hazel Rochman in *Booklist*. Calling *The Long March* a "sophisticated picture book," *School Library Journal* reviewer Darcy Schild concluded: "The words and illustrations work together extremely well, presenting the story in a clear and compelling manner."

Fitzpatrick took a completely different approach in *Lizzy and Skunk,* a picture book story about a little girl whose puppet helps her deal with her fears. With Skunk in hand, Lizzy can brave skating down the sidewalk and performing in the school play, but when Skunk gets lost,

Fitzpatrick links two continents in **The Long March,** *which recounts the true story of a compassionate Choctaw settlement and its efforts to help those starving in Ireland during the potato famine of the mid-1800s.*

Lizzy must visit such frightening places as the space underneath her bed (where it's dark) and the attic (where there are spiders) in her search for her beloved companion. But this calamity also offers Lizzy a chance to bravely rescue Skunk and to give back some of the reassurance she's always gotten from her friend. A *Publishers Weekly* critic described *Lizzy and Skunk* as "a reassuring story with an upbeat message about overcoming fears," while *School Library Journal* reviewer Sue Sherif found the book "a cozy, well-executed choice for sharing with a special friend."

Biographical and Critical Sources

PERIODICALS

Booklist, July, 1998, Hazel Rochman, review of *The Long March*, p. 1875.

Publishers Weekly, June 1, 1998, review of *The Long March*, p. 48; May 1, 2000, review of *Lizzy and Skunk*, p. 69.

School Library Journal, June, 1998, Darcy Schild, review of *The Long March*, p. 98; July, 2000, Sue Sherif, review of *Lizzy and Skunk*, p. 72.

*   *   *

FLORIAN, Douglas 1950-

Personal

Born March 18, 1950, in New York, NY; son of Harold (an artist) and Edith Florian; married Marie (a chef), November 3, 1985; children: five. *Education:* Queens College of the City University of New York, B.A., 1973; also attended the School of Visual Arts in New York in 1976.

Addresses

Home—New York, NY. *Office*—c/o Harcourt Brace & Co., 6277 Sea Harbor Dr., Orlando, FL 32887.

Career

Author and illustrator, 1971—. Has held lectures and book signings at various elementary schools. *Exhibitions:* Illustrations from *Monster Motel* were displayed at "The Original Art 1993" show and the "36th Annual Exhibition," sponsored by the Society of Illustrators.

Awards, Honors

Outstanding Science Trade Book for Children, National Science Teachers Association/Children's Book Council, 1987, for *A Winter Day,* and 1992, for *Vegetable Garden;* Parents' Choice Award for story book, 1991, for *An Auto Mechanic;* Gold Medal for poetry, National Parenting Publications Awards, 1994, Lee Bennett Hopkins Award for poetry, 1995, and American Library Association Notable Book citation, all for *Beast Feast;* Reading Magic Award, *Parenting,* 1994, for *Bing Bang Boing; Discovering Seashells* was on the International Board on Books for Young People honor list.

Writings

SELF-ILLUSTRATED

A Bird Can Fly, Greenwillow (New York, NY), 1980.
The City, Crowell (New York, NY), 1982.
People Working, Crowell (New York, NY), 1983.
Airplane Ride, Crowell (New York, NY), 1984.
Discovering Butterflies, Scribner (New York, NY), 1986.
Discovering Trees, Scribner (New York, NY), 1986.
Discovering Frogs, Scribner (New York, NY), 1986.
Discovering Seashells, Scribner (New York, NY), 1986.
A Winter Day, Greenwillow (New York, NY), 1987.
A Summer Day, Greenwillow (New York, NY), 1988.
Nature Walk, Greenwillow (New York, NY), 1989.
Turtle Day, Crowell (New York, NY), 1989.
A Year in the Country, Greenwillow (New York, NY), 1989.
A Beach Day, Greenwillow (New York, NY), 1990.
City Street, Greenwillow (New York, NY), 1990.
Vegetable Garden, Harcourt (San Diego, CA), 1991.
At the Zoo, Greenwillow (New York, NY), 1992.
Monster Motel: Poems and Paintings, Harcourt (San Diego, CA), 1993.
Bing Bang Boing: Poems and Drawings, Harcourt (San Diego, CA), 1994.
Beast Feast (poems), Harcourt (San Diego, CA), 1994.
On the Wing: Bird Poems and Paintings, Harcourt (San Diego, CA), 1996.
In the Swim: Poems and Paintings, Harcourt (San Diego, CA), 1997.

Triangle eyes that stared. Raggedy eyebrows that glared.

Tony Johnston's 1995 picture book **Very Scary** *features Douglas Florian's engaging watercolors.*

Florian's illustration of a plague of locusts highlights the award-winning Insectlopedia, *wherein inchworms and even the despised termite become fitting subjects for poetry.*

Insectlopedia: Poems and Paintings, Harcourt (San Diego, CA), 1998.

Laugh-eteria: Poems and Drawings, Harcourt (San Diego, CA), 1999.

Winter Eyes: Poems and Paintings, Greenwillow (New York, NY), 1999.

Lizards, Frogs, and Polliwogs: Poems and Paintings, Harcourt (San Diego, CA), 2000.

Mammalabilia: Poems and Paintings, Harcourt (San Diego, CA), 2000.

A Pig Is Big, Greenwillow (New York, NY), 2000.

Summersaults: Poems and Paintings, Greenwillow (New York, NY), 2002.

"HOW WE WORK" SERIES

An Auto Mechanic, Greenwillow (New York, NY), 1991.

A Carpenter, Greenwillow (New York, NY), 1991.

A Potter, Greenwillow (New York, NY), 1991.

A Chef, Greenwillow (New York, NY), 1992.

A Painter, Greenwillow (New York, NY), 1993.

A Fisher, Greenwillow (New York, NY), 1994.

ILLUSTRATOR

(With Kristin Linklater) *Freeing the Natural Voice*, Drama Books, 1976.

Dorothy O. Van Woerkom, *Tit for Tat*, Greenwillow (New York, NY), 1977.

Thomas M. Cook and Robert A. Russell, *Introduction to Management Science*, Prentice-Hall, 1977.

Mirra Ginsburg, adaptor, *The Night It Rained Pancakes*, Greenwillow (New York, NY), 1980.

Bill Adler, *What Is a Cat?: For Everyone Who Has Ever Loved a Cat*, Morrow (New York, NY), 1987.

Mary Lyn Ray, *A Rumbly Tumbly Glittery Gritty Place*, Harcourt (San Diego, CA), 1993.

Tony Johnston, *Very Scary*, Harcourt (San Diego, CA), 1995.

Contributor of illustrations to periodicals, including the *New Yorker, New York Times, The Nation, Travel and Leisure,* and *Across the Board.*

Sidelights

Although he has been writing and illustrating children's books for years, Douglas Florian did not receive special attention until switching from nonfiction books to writing and illustrating collections of nonsense verse. The silly poems and imaginative artwork in books such as *Beast Feast, Mammalabilia,* and *Insectlopedia* have caused some reviewers to compare Florian to the famous writer of free verse Ogden Nash as well as other well-known poet/illustrators, including Jack Prelutsky, Shel Silverstein, and John Ciardi.

The son of artist Hal Florian, Douglas Florian first got the idea to follow in his father's footsteps when he was ten years old. "The walls of our house were always covered with paintings, mostly landscapes done by my father," Florian stated in *Sixth Book of Junior Authors and Illustrators*. Reflecting upon his educational experience in art, Florian once said on the *Embracing the Child* Web site, "I studied drawing with many teachers, but my first was my father. He taught me to love nature in all of its forms." When he turned fifteen, Florian had the opportunity to attend a summer painting course at New York's School of Visual Arts. He enjoyed the experience so much that he decided to make art his career. "When I walked into the school's large studio filled with paint-encrusted easels, vivid palettes, and the smell of linseed oil," Florian stated in his Harcourt Brace publicity release, "I knew then and there I was going to be an artist." Later, the budding artist attended Queens College, studying under the Caldecott award-winning illustrator Marvin Bileck. "He taught me to treat a drawing like a person: with love and affection," wrote Florian in *Embracing the Child.*

Florian soon discovered that desire alone was not enough to make it as an artist. The hard work of honing his skills did not pay off until he was twenty-one years old when he had his first drawings published in the *New York Times*. He continued to successfully publish work in a variety of magazines, yet became tired of the rush to meet deadlines. After a few years, Florian finally received the good news that his illustrations for Mirra Ginsburg's *The Night It Rained Pancakes*, which received a starred review in the *School Library Journal*, had been praised by critics. Then Florian decided that he wanted to write as well as illustrate, and so he began working on a series of nonfiction books for children, many of which teach children about nature—such as in his "Discovering" series—or different adult occupations, such as what it is like to be a chef or an auto mechanic.

However, it is for his poetry and their accompanying illustrations that reviewers began to take serious notice of Florian as a major player in the children's book market. When asked how he made the transition to verse, Florian replied on the *Embrace the Child* Web site, "One day at a flea market, I bought a book of poems called *Oh, That's Ridiculous,* edited by William Cole. The poems in that book were so funny that I was inspired to write some of my own. A few early poems wound up in my book *Monster Motel*, and others in *Bing Bang Boing.*"

Florian received praise for his early nonsense verse collections *Monster Motel* and *Bing Bang Boing.* With *Monster Motel*, the author created fourteen poems about remarkable creatures, including the "Gazzygoo" and the "Fabled Feerz," accompanying each with pen-and-ink and watercolor illustrations. "Similar in style to the works of Jack Prelutsky," Kay Weisman remarked in *Booklist*, "this will make an excellent choice for youngsters." *School Library Journal* contributor Laura-lyn Persson concluded in her review of *Monster Motel* that "Florian's seemingly simple watercolors grow more intriguing with each new book." In a *School Library Journal* review of *Bing Bang Boing*, Kathleen Whalin complimented Florian's "control of the medium," comparing his work to that of John Ciardi.

Discussing his initial attraction to verse forms, Florian said in a response to *Booklist* interviewer Gillian Engberg, "I didn't want to be tied down to the literal." He went on to say, "I just felt that I wanted to be able to flex my imagination a little bit more—to use my so-called poetic license (I get it renewed every six months by the way)." Asked how he handles children's questions about breaking the rules of grammar, spelling, and writing, Florian replied, "I tell them that they should do whatever they have to do to make their poems better, even if it means putting words upside down, or backwards, or spelling words wrong, or using bad grammar.... The only rule in poetry is that it has to work."

Following his own instructions for writing children's verse, the poet and illustrator began an award-winning series of books about creatures big and small in *Beast Feast*. A collection of lighthearted poems about animals, *Beast Feast* took a great deal of effort on Florian's part to complete. "I actually wrote eighty poems and painted more than fifty watercolors for the book," the author/illustrator said in his publicity release, "and then my editor and I picked the ones we like the best. We wanted *Beast Feast* to be absolutely first-rate."

Recipient of the National Parenting Publications Gold Medal award for poetry along with the Lee Bennett Hopkins Award for poetry in 1995, *Beast Feast,* which includes twenty-one carefully selected poems and illustrations, has been praised by critics. One *Kirkus Reviews* contributor described the work as "subtle, sophisticated, and quite charming." The poems in the collection rely on alliteration and puns on animal names that invite the verses to be read aloud to children. "Florian's distinctive, full-page watercolors are as playful as his verse," a *Publishers Weekly* reviewer added, calling the book an "ideal read-aloud." Also noting the useful factual information about animals that Florian has included in

the poems, Lee Bock commented in *School Library Journal* that Florian "knows what children find funny.... Clearly a wonderful book."

Florian followed *Beast Feast* with *On the Wing, In the Swim, Insectlopedia, Lizards, Frogs, and Polliwogs,* and *Mammalabilia. On the Wing* offers readers twenty-one poems about various birds, while *In the Swim* presents children with the same number of poems about water-loving creatures. Writing in *Booklist,* reviewer Carolyn Phelan claimed that *On the Wing*'s "appeal lies in its fluent wordplay and generous use of humor in both the poetry and the paintings." Commenting on *In the Swim,*

Florian injects humor into **Mammalabilia,** *which takes a playful and often wacky view of the animal kingdom.*

Horn Book contributor Roger Sutton reported that "these clipped verses splash with mischief and wit." In a review of the same book, *School Library Journal* critic Ellen D. Warwick observed, "What's unusual here is the sheer, unforced playfulness, the ease and fluidity informing both verse and pictures."

Keeping up with the nature theme, *Insectlopedia* again uses twenty-one short poems, this time to entertain children about the uniqueness of bugs. Covering worms, beetles, termites, and mayflies, Florian's poems received high praise from reviewers, particularly regarding his efforts to capture the spirit of the verse in his accompanying watercolor illustrations. "Readers may not be able to stop looking at the inventive watercolor-and-collage illustrations," predicted a *Publishers Weekly* reviewer, who went on to say, "But the silly, imaginative verses . . . (almost) match the exquisite pictures in playfulness and wit." Carolyn Phelan, writing in *Booklist,* stated, "The clever artwork, deftly constructed, and the entertaining collection of insect and arachnid verse it illustrates will delight readers." "There are other books of poetry about insects and lots of collections of humorous verses about animals," noted *School Library Journal* critic Carolyn Angus, "but none match *Insectlopedia.*"

Similar high marks were given to *Mammalabilia* and *Lizards, Frogs, and Polliwogs.* Through twenty-one poems, Florian covers a wide-range of animals, both familiar and exotic, in *Mammalabilia,* including an aardvark, a fox, and a tapir. Offering compliments for Florian's unique gouache artwork, *New York Times* book reviewer Cynthia Zarin remarked, "The combination of his winsome pictures and often inspired text transforms the animals he scrutinizes into boarders at his own personal bestiary: they're Florianized." Describing the book as an "irresistible homage to mammal memorabilia," a *Publishers Weekly* critic noticed that "Florian's humor is eccentric, but just right for his target audience." Comparing *Mammalabilia* to Florian's earlier successes *Insectlopedia* and *On the Wing, Booklist* contributor John Peters found the book "ideal for reading aloud, to one listener or to a crowd."

This time taking up the cause of reptiles and amphibians, Florian again combines short, playful verse with watercolor illustrations in his book *Lizards, Frogs, and Polliwogs.* Constructing poems and pictures for geckoes, Gila monsters, and skinks, the author/illustrator continued to earn warm words from critics. "This one stands up to the rest," remarked *School Library Journal* reviewer Nina Lindsay, who went on to say: "Beautifully designed, this title is as irresistible as Florian's others." A contributor to *Publishers Weekly* pointed out that in addition to the "mischievous reptile lore that will make young readers laugh," Florian has added a new dimension to his artwork. "These frogs and friends don't necessarily jump out at readers," according to the critic, "but continually take them by surprise."

In *Winter Eyes,* Florian displays his talents with other subjects, treating readers to forty-eight short poems about the bright and dark sides to the last season of the year. *Winter Eyes* discusses the joys of cold-weather activities, such as sledding, skating, and ice fishing, while echoing the complaints of many individuals that winter is too cold and lasts too long. Commenting on Florian's "appealing" artwork, *New York Times* contributor Tiana Norgren said, "The beautiful washes of watercolor that make the snow, ice, thawed earth, and pink sunset sky so convincing are punctuated by cheerful penciled patches of bright orange, blue, and hot pink." Writing in *School Library Journal,* Shawn Brommer predicted that "this book will be as welcome as a warm cup of cocoa after a long day of making snowmen and turning figure eights." *Horn Book* reviewer Roger Sutton found "the rhymes are just predictable enough—without being boring—to make the book a good choice for newly independent readers."

Children attracted to the rhymes of "Shel Silverstein and Jack Prelutsky and other purveyors of nonsense" are bound to enjoy *Laugh-eteria,* according to *School Library Reviewer* Barbara Chatton. In this collection of short verse, Florian takes on topics familiar to children, including school, dinosaurs, and eating strange foods. "Kids won't have to force their laughter while reading Florian's . . . pithy verses," observed a *Publishers Weekly* critic. Writing in *Booklist,* Carolyn Phelan remarked, "Often clever, occasionally gross, the short rhymes appeal to an elementary-school child's sense of humor."

In *A Pig Is Big,* a picture book designed for younger readers, Florian explores the concept of size as a pig is compared to larger and larger objects. On each page, a pig shows his relative size next to other things, beginning with a hat before moving on to other animals and concluding with the entire universe. While admitting that the later pages feature vocabulary that might be out of a preschooler's grasp, a *Publishers Weekly* contributor nonetheless felt the book's "presentation is clever and humorous, well suited for elementary school children prepared to grasp the size of [the] universe." "Florian's illustrations, watercolors with colored pencils, expand the text to make this a satisfying book," claimed Carolyn Phelan in another *Booklist* review.

Called "one of the most remarkable contemporary versers for young readers" by *Bulletin of the Center for Children's Books* contributor Deborah Stevenson, Florian continues to build upon his well-established reputation as a poet who understands how to delight children and present poetry in a way that appeals to them. Appreciated for his illustrations as well as his verse, Florian persists, according to critics, in taking his art work and poetry to new levels. "While it's never possible to have too much good poetry, children's literature is particularly blessed with a fullness in this area," continued Stevenson. "Douglas Florian is one of those blessings."

In typical Florian fashion, every watercolor illustration in **Lizards, Frogs, and Polliwogs** *tells a whimsical story of its own.*

Biographical and Critical Sources

BOOKS

Sixth Book of Junior Authors and Illustrators, H. W. Wilson, 1989.

PERIODICALS

Booklist, March 15, 1993, Kay Weisman, review of *Monster Motel,* p. 1351; September 15, 1993, Carolyn Phelan, review of *A Painter;* February 15, 1994; August, 1994; March 15, 1996, Carolyn Phelan, review of *On the Wing,* p. 1258; March 15, 1998, Carolyn Phelan, review of *Insectlopedia,* p. 1240; March 15, 1999, Carolyn Phelan, review of *Laugh-eteria,* p. 1340; March 15, 2000, Gillian Engberg, "The *Booklist* Interview: Douglas Florian," p. 1382; March 15, 2000, John Peters, review of *Mammalabilia: Poems and Paintings,* p. 1380; September 15, 2000, Carolyn Phelan, review of *A Pig Is Big,* p. 247.

Bulletin of the Center for Children's Books, December, 1992, p. 110; July-August, 1994, p. 355; November, 1994, p. 77.

Horn Book, December, 1980, p. 632; July, 1997, Roger Sutton, review of *In the Swim,* p. 470; November, 1999, Roger Sutton, review of *Winter Eyes,* p. 752;

March, 2000, review of *Mammalabilia: Poems and Paintings,* p. 204.

Kirkus Reviews, March 1, 1983, review of *People Working;* April 15, 1994, review of *Beast Feast.*

New York Times, November 21, 1999, Tiana Norgren, review of *Winter Eyes,* p. 41; November 19, 2000, Cynthia Zarin, review of *Mammalabilia: Poems and Paintings,* p. 46.

Publishers Weekly, April 1, 1983, review of *People Working,* p. 60; March 7, 1994, review of *Beast Feast;* March 9, 1998, review of *Insectlopedia,* pp. 69-70; April 19, 1999, review of *Laugh-eteria,* p. 73; March 13, 2000, review of *Mammalabilia: Poems and Paintings,* p. 84; October 9, 2000, review of *A Pig Is Big,* p. 87; March 12, 2001, review of *Lizards, Frogs, and Polliwogs,* p. 90.

School Library Journal, August, 1982, Mary B. Nickerson, review of *The City,* p. 96; June, 1993, Lauralyn Persson, review of *Monster Motel;* May, 1994; Lee Bock, review of *Beast Feast;* September, 1994, Tom S. Hurlburt, review of *A Fisher,* p. 207; November, 1994, Kathleen Whalin, review of *Bing Bang Boing;* May, 1997, Ellen D. Warwick, review of *In the Swim,* p. 119; April, 1998, Carolyn Angus, review of *Insectlopedia,* pp. 115-116; June, 1999, Barbara Chatton, review of *Laugh-eteria,* p. 114; September, 1999, Shawn Brommer, review of *Winter Eyes,* p. 212; April, 2000, Barbara Chatton, review of *Mammalabilia: Poems and Paintings,* p. 119; April, 2001, Nina Lindsay, review of *Lizards, Frogs, and Polliwogs,* p. 129.

ON-LINE

Embracing the Child, http://www.eyeontomorrow.com/ (June 30, 2001), "Meet Douglas Florian."

Bulletin of the Center for Children's Books, http://alexia.lis.uiuc.edu/puboff/bccb/ (July 7, 2001), Deborah Stevenson, "True Blue: Douglas Florian."

Storybook Art, http://storybookart.com/ (July 7, 2001), "Douglas Florian."

OTHER

Florian, Douglas, "Artist/Author at a Glance" (publicity release), Harcourt, c. 1994.*

G

GAVIN, Jamila 1941-

Personal

Born August 9, 1941, in Mussoorie, Uttar Pradesh, India; daughter of Terence (a retired Indian civil servant) and Florence Jessica (a teacher; maiden name, Dean) Khushal-Singh; married Barrie Gavin (a television producer) in 1971 (divorced, 1990); children: Rohan Robert, Indra Helen. *Education:* Trinity College of Music, L.T.C.L. (piano performance and drama instruction); studied piano in Paris; attended Hochschul für Musik, Berlin, Germany. *Politics:* Labour Party. *Hobbies and other interests:* Theater.

Addresses

Home—"The Laurels," All Saints Rd., Uplands Stroud, Gloucestershire GL5 1TT, England. *Agent*—Jacqueline Korn, David Higham Associates, 5-8 Lower John St., Golden Square, London W1R 4HA, England.

Career

Freelance writer and lecturer. British Broadcasting Corporation (BBC), London, radio studio manager, then television production assistant, 1964-71. Member, Stroud Town Council; member of advisory committee, Cheltenham Literary Festival. Writer and co-director, Taynton House Children's Opera Group; affiliated with Children's Drama Group, Niccol Center, Cirencester. *Member:* PEN, Society of Authors, West of England Writers, Writers Guild.

Awards, Honors

Guardian award runner-up, 1993, for *The Wheel of Surya; Guardian* award special runner-up and Carnegie Medal nomination, both 1995, both for *The Eye of the Horse;* Whitbread Children's Book Award, and shortlisted for Carnegie Medal, both 2001, for *Coram Boy.*

Jamila Gavin

Writings

"SURYA" SERIES

The Wheel of Surya, Methuen (London, England), 1992.
The Eye of the Horse, Methuen (London, England), 1994.
The Track of the Wind, Methuen (London, England), 1997.

"GRANDPA CHATTERJI" SERIES

Grandpa Chatterji, illustrated by Mei-Yim Low, Methuen (London, England), 1993.

Grandpa's Indian Summer, illustrated by Mei-Yim Yow, Methuen (London, England), 1995.

OTHER

The Magic Orange Tree and Other Stories, illustrated by Ossie Murray, Methuen (New York, NY), 1979.

Double Dare and Other Stories, illustrated by Simon Willby, Methuen (New York, NY), 1982.

Kamla and Kate (short stories), illustrated by Thelma Lambert, Methuen (New York, NY), 1983.

Digital Dan, illustrated by Patrice Aitken, Methuen (New York, NY), 1984.

Ali and the Robots, illustrated by Sally Williams, Methuen (New York, NY), 1986.

Stories from the Hindu World, illustrated by Joanna Troughton, Macdonald, 1986, Silver Burdett (Morristown, NJ), 1987.

The Hideaway, illustrated by Jane Bottomley, Methuen (New York, NY), 1987.

(Reteller) *Three Indian Princesses: The Stories of Savitri, Damayanti, and Sita,* illustrated by Govinder Ram, Methuen (New York, NY), 1987.

The Singing Bowls, Methuen (New York, NY), 1989.

I Want to Be an Angel, Methuen (New York, NY), 1990.

Kamla and Kate Again (short stories), illustrated by Rhian Nest-James, Methuen (New York, NY), 1991.

Deadly Friend, Heinemann, 1994.

A Fine Feathered Friend, illustrated by Carol Walters, Heinemann, 1996.

The Mango Tree, illustrated by Rhian Nest-James, Heinemann, 1996.

Presents, illustrated by Rhian Nest-James, Heinemann, 1996.

Who Did It?, illustrated by Rhian Nest-James, Heinemann, 1996.

The Wormholers, Methuen (New York, NY), 1996.

Grandma's Surprise, illustrated by Rhian Nest-James, Heinemann, 1996.

Children Just Like Me: Our Favorite Stories from Around the World, Dorling Kindersley (London, England), 1997.

Out of India: An Anglo-Indian Childhood (memoir), Pavilion (London, England), 1997.

Forbidden Memories, illustrated by Mark Robertson, Mammoth (London, England), 1998.

Someone's Watching, Someone's Waiting, illustrated by Anthony Lewis, Mammoth (London, England), 1998.

Monkey in the Stars, illustrated by Anthony Lewis, Mammoth (London, England), 1998.

Star Child on Clark Street, Cambridge University Press, 1998.

Coram Boy, Mammoth (London, England), 2000, Farrar, Straus (New York, NY), 2001.

Monkey in the Stars (play; based on Gavin's book), produced in London, England, 2000.

Also author of the books *The Temple by the Sea,* Ginn; *The Demon Drummer,* Pavillion; *Pitchou; The Girl Who Rode on a Lion,* Ginn; *Forbidden Dreams,* Mammoth; *All Aboard,* Heinemann; *A Singer from the Desert,* Pavillion; *Forbidden Clothes,* Methuen; and *Just Friends,* Mammoth. Contributor of *The Lake of Stars* (a retelling) to *The Wolf and the Kids; The Straw House;* *Lake of the Stars; The Ugly Duckling,* four volumes, Heinemann Educational (Exeter, NH), 1996.

Also author of the musical *The Green Factor,* music by Nigel Stephenson.

Adaptations

The Demon Drummer was adapted as a play, Cheltenham Literary Festival, 1994; *Grandpa Chatterji* was adapted for television, 1996; a six-part adaptation of *The Wheel of Surya* was broadcast on BBC-TV, 1996.

Sidelights

Jamila Gavin brings her understanding of the special concerns of children with a multicultural heritage to her stories and novels for young readers. Born in India of an Indian father and a British mother, Gavin has focused on her Indian heritage in such books as *Three Indian Princesses: The Stories of Savitri, Damayanti, and Sita* as well as in her highly praised epic trilogy that begins with the 1992 novel *The Wheel of Surya.* In addition to her novels and short fiction for middle-school readers, Gavin, who has worked in television and in theater for many years, has also authored plays for younger viewers. Several of her works have been adapted for broadcast on British television. "I began writing to be published, rather than for fun in 1979, when I realized how few books for children reflected the multicultural society in which they lived," Gavin once explained. "As someone of mixed Indian and British origins, I wanted to see my mirror image, and felt that every child, no matter what their race or color, was entitled to see their mirror image."

Among Gavin's first books is *Kamla and Kate,* a collection of short stories featuring a young girl named Kate who gains a best friend when six-year-old Kamla and her family move from India to Kate's boy-dominated street. While engaging together in tasks and activities common to young British children, Kate joins her new friend in celebrating the Indian Festival of Light, or Diwali. The book reflects the author's belief that "people with different customs and beliefs [need] to find common ground," while also celebrating their differences, according to Margery Fisher of *Growing Point.* The two best friends return in *Kamla and Kate Again,* a second collection of stories that *School Librarian* contributor Julie Blaisdale cited as showing "with sensitivity and understanding" the many ways in which young people can "share in and celebrate a diversity of cultural influences."

Several other books by Gavin are steeped in Indian culture and tradition. In *The Singing Bowls,* a mixed Anglo-Indian teen named Ronnie delves into the mystery surrounding three wooden bowls that have mystical properties rooted in Tibetan history. The sixteen-year-old hopes that the bowls can help him find his Indian father, who disappeared ten years ago. While noting that the writing is "slightly uneven," a *Junior Bookshelf* reviewer praised *The Singing Bowls* for evoking "the dust, heat and beauty of India" and presenting a "revealing and thought-provoking" portrait of the multi-layered generations of Indian society. Indian culture also plays a significant role in *Grandpa Chatterji,* a collection of stories about Sanjay and Neeta, sisters who get to know their Indian grandfather when he makes a long-awaited visit from his home in Calcutta. A man of traditional, old-fashioned values, "Grandpa Chatterji is a wonderful character ... with his warmth and enthusiasm for life," according to *School Librarian* contributor Teresa Scragg. A *Junior Bookshelf* reviewer similarly noted that Gavin's "charming" book paints the portrait of a family with strong ties to two diverse cultures "and offers the hope that its members will draw the best from both." In *Children Just Like Me: Our Favorite Stories from Around the World,* Gavin brings together folktales from all over the world, including corresponding geographical and cultural information for each story in the book. A reviewer for *Publishers Weekly* lauded Gavin for an "unusually successful" project that presents information in an "engagingly personal way." And Chris Brown noted in *School Librarian* that Gavin's "straight-forward storytelling" provides both observations and commentary without intruding on the pace of each story.

First published in England in 1992, Gavin's *Wheel of Surya* is the first book of her "Surya" trilogy. Taking place in a small Indian village in the Punjab on the eve of India's war for independence, the novel follows the adventures of Marvinder and Jaspal Singh, siblings whose mother decides to bring the family to England to join her husband, who has been absent for many years in an effort to further his education. During the trip, the children's mother and grandmother both die, but the brother and sister remain determined to find the father whom they hardly remember. With little money, the pair find their way to Bombay and stow away aboard an ocean liner bound for England. When at last they find their father, Govind, he is not at all the person they expected to find—he has married an Irishwoman and has a son—and the two children must adjust to both a new family and a new culture. In a review of *The Wheel of Surya* for *School Librarian,* Linda Saunders praised Gavin for "the power of her descriptions and her portrayal of two different societies." A *Junior Bookshelf* critic called the novel "a tribute to the stubbornness of children the world over whose instinct is for survival first and prosperity second."

In the sequels to *The Wheel of Surya—The Eye of the Horse* and *The Track of the Wind*—readers continue to follow the adventures of Marvinder and her brother, Jaspal. *The Eye of the Horse* finds the children's father released from jail after a conviction for dealing in stolen goods; on the heels of his release, now abandoned by his Irish wife, Govind gathers his children together and returns to his native India, which is now free of British domination. The story threads in and out of many historic events during the 1940s, including the death of Mahatma Gandhi and the religious and political turmoil that troubled India during that decade. In a review for *Books for Your Children,* Val Bierman dubbed the novel a "powerful book of betrayal, sadness and anger" that also reveals the "power of healing and forgiveness." In a

School Librarian review, Peter Hollindale praised it as "an immensely readable, exciting story." In the last book of the series, *The Track of the Wind,* Gavin returns to the travails of Marvinder and Jaspal as they both struggle to understand the country they had fled in search of their father. Through Jaspal's efforts to understand India's history, and Marvinder's personal struggles as she is married off to a kindly but serious man named Bahadur, Gavin once again "encompasses all manner of clashes between East and West," said Susan Hamlyn in *School Librarian.* The trilogy covers over a quarter century of events in India and England, beginning from the period leading up to World War II and ending with the partition of India and Pakistan in the late 1940s. Characterizing the trilogy as a "rich weave of history, geography, myth and religion," Adrian Jackson wrote in *Books for Keeps* that this final book, full of "striking scenes," reflects the darker tones of its characters as they finally face the reality of their almost-adult lives.

Of her more recent works, Gavin once commented, "Perhaps, of all my books, *The Wormholers* represents my exploration of the inner world, but inspired by the glorious theories and astro-physical world of the physicist Stephen Hawking. That is the joy of writing; that there are so many doors waiting to be opened and be a source of inspiration."

Biographical and Critical Sources

PERIODICALS

Books for Keeps, May, 1986, p. 20; March, 1989; May, 1991; January, 1996; November, 1997, Jill Bennett, review of *Children Just Like Me: Our Favorite Stories from Around the World,* p. 21; November, 1997, Adrian Jackson, review of "The Surya Trilogy," p. 27.

Books for Your Children, summer, 1986, p. 8; summer, 1989, p. 12; summer, 1993, p. 10; spring, 1995, Val Bierman, review of *The Eye of the Horse,* p. 12.

Bulletin of the Center for Children's Books, September, 1997, Pat Mathews, review of *Children Just Like Me: Our Favorite Stories from Around the World,* p. 10.

Growing Point, September, 1979, p. 3578; September, 1982, p. 3943; May, 1983, Margery Fisher, review of *Kamla and Kate,* p. 4089.

Junior Bookshelf, October, 1979, p. 271; April, 1988, p. 93; October, 1989, review of *The Singing Bowls,* p. 237; April, 1992, p. 62; August, 1992, review of *The Wheel of Surya,* p. 153; June, 1993, review of *Grandpa Chatterji,* pp. 96-97; August, 1994, p. 134; February, 1995, pp. 35-36.

Publishers Weekly, April 28, 1997, review of *Children Just Like Me: Our Favorite Stories from Around the World,* p. 77.

School Librarian, February, 1988, p. 20; November, 1989, p. 160; November, 1991, Julie Blaisdale, review of *Kamla and Kate Again,* p. 144; November, 1992, Linda Saunders, review of *The Wheel of Surya,* pp. 157-158; August, 1993, Teresa Scragg, review of *Grandpa Chatterji,* p. 108; November, 1994, Peter Hollindale, review of *The Eye of the Horse,* p. 165; February, 1997, Celia Gibbs, review of *Fine Feathered*

Friend, p. 24; August, 1997, Chris Brown, review of *Children Just Like Me: Our Favorite Stories from Around the World,* p. 145; spring, 1998, Susan Hamlyn, review of *The Track of the Wind,* p. 48.
Times Educational Supplement, August 26, 1983, p. 20.

ON-LINE

ACHUKA, http://www.achuka.com/ (October, 2000), interview with Jamila Gavin.*

*   *   *

GLICK, Ruth (Burtnick) 1942- (Samantha Chase, Alexis Hill, Alyssa Howard, Alexis Hill Jordan, Amanda Lee, Tess Marlowe, Rebecca York, joint pseudonyms)

Personal

Born April 27, 1942, in Lexington, KY; daughter of Lester Leon (a physician) and Beverly (a teacher; maiden name, Miller) Burtnick; married Norman Glick (a computer scientist), June 30, 1963; children: Elissa, Ethan. *Education:* George Washington University, A.B., 1964; University of Maryland, M.A., 1967. *Politics:* Democrat.

Addresses

Home and Office—P.O. Box 1233, Columbia, MD 21044-0233. *E-mail*—rglick@capaccess.org.

Career

Writer, 1972—. *Member:* International Association of Culinary Professionals, Romance Writers of America, Authors Guild, Authors League of America, Sisters in Crime, Novelists Inc., Maryland Romance Writers, Washington Romance Writers.

Awards, Honors

Romantic Times, Lifetime Achievement Award, romantic suspense series, 1987, for books in "The Peregrine Connection" series, Career Achievement Award, series romantic mystery category, 1993, for work under pseudonym Rebecca York, WISH Award and Best Intrigue Award, both 1998, for *Nowhere Man,* and various award nominations; citation for one of twelve best cookbooks of the year, *USA Today,* 1994, for *100 Percent Pleasure;* Outstanding Achievement Award, Washington Romance Writers, 1996; Critics' Choice Award, best contemporary novel, *Affaire de Coeur,* 1998, for *Nowhere Man;* National Health Information Bronze Award, 1999, for *The Diabetes Snack Munch Nibble Nosh Book;* award nominations from Romance Writers of America.

Writings

NONFICTION

(With Nancy Baggett) *Dollhouse Furniture You Can Make,* A. S. Barnes (San Diego, CA), 1978.
(With Nancy Baggett) *Dollhouse Lamps and Chandeliers,* Hobby House (Cumberland, MD), 1979.
Dollhouse Kitchen and Dining Room Accessories, Hobby House (Cumberland, MD), 1979.
(With Nancy Baggett and Gloria Kaufer Greene) *Don't Tell 'Em It's Good for 'Em* (cookbook; excerpt published in *Family Circle*), Times Books (New York, NY), 1984.
(With Nancy Baggett and Gloria Kaufer Greene) *Eat Your Vegetables!,* Times Books (New York, NY), 1985.
(With Nancy Baggett) *Soup's On,* Macmillan (New York, NY), 1985.
(With Nancy Baggett) *The Oat Bran Baking Book,* Contemporary Books (Chicago, IL), 1989.
(Contributor) Jean McMillen and Ron McMillen, editors, *Cooking with Malice Domestic,* Mystery Bookshop (Bethesda, MD), 1991.
(With Nancy Baggett) *Skinny Soups,* Surrey Books (Chicago, IL), 1992, 2nd edition, 1997.
Skinny One-Pot Meals, Surrey Books (Chicago, IL), 1994, 2nd edition, 1997.
(With Nancy Baggett) *100 Percent Pleasure,* Rodale (Emmaus, PA), 1994.
(Recipe developer) Jean Rogers, editor, *Your Family Will Love It! Quick and Healthy Weekday Meals for the Hard-to-Please,* Rodale (Emmaus, PA), 1995.
(Recipe developer) Sue Spitler and Linda R. Yoakam, *1001 Low-Fat Recipes,* Surrey Books (Chicago, IL), 1995.
(Recipe developer) Jean Rogers, editor, *Prevention's Healthy One-Dish Meals in Minutes: 200 No-Fuss Low-Fat Recipes for Busy People,* Rodale (Emmaus, PA), 1996.
(With Nancy Baggett) *Skinny Italian Cooking,* Surrey Books (Chicago, IL), 1996.
The Diabetes Snack Munch Nibble Nosh Book, American Diabetes Association (Alexandria, VA), 1998.
Simply Italian, Surrey Books (Chicago, IL), 1999.
Fabulous Lo-Carb Cuisine, illustrated by Sanny Wroblewski, Light Street Press (Columbia, MD), 2000.

FICTION; UNDER NAME RUTH GLICK

Invasion of the Blue Lights (juvenile science fiction), Scholastic (New York, NY), 1982.
(With Eileen Buckholtz) *Space Attack* (juvenile novel with computer activities), Scholastic (New York, NY), 1984.
(With Eileen Buckholtz) *Mindbenders* (juvenile novel with computer activities), Scholastic (New York, NY), 1984.
(With Eileen Buckholtz) *Mission of the Secret Spy Squad* (juvenile fiction), Scholastic (New York, NY), 1984.
(With Eileen Buckholtz) *Doomstalker* (juvenile novel with computer activities), Scholastic (New York, NY), 1985.
(With Eileen Buckholtz) *Captain Kid and the Pirates* (juvenile novel with computer activities), Scholastic (New York, NY), 1985.

(With Eileen Buckholtz) *The Cats of Castle Mountain* (juvenile novel with computer activities), Scholastic (New York, NY), 1985.

(With Eileen Buckholtz) *Saber Dance* (young adult fiction), Pageant Books, 1988.

(With Eileen Buckholtz) *Roller Coaster* (young adult fiction), Pageant Books, 1989.

(With Kathryn Jensen) *The Big Score* (young adult fiction), Pageant Books, 1989.

(With Kathryn Jensen) *Night Stalker* (young adult fiction), Pageant Books, 1989.

The Closer We Get (romance novel), Harlequin (New York, NY), 1989.

Make Me a Miracle (romance novel), Harlequin (New York, NY), 1992.

"43 LIGHT STREET" SERIES; ROMANTIC SUSPENSE NOVELS; UNDER PSEUDONYM REBECCA YORK

(With Eileen Buckholtz) *Life Line,* Harlequin (New York, NY), 1990.

(With Eileen Buckholtz) *Shattered Vows,* Harlequin (New York, NY), 1991.

(With Eileen Buckholtz) *Whispers in the Night,* Harlequin (New York, NY), 1991.

(With Eileen Buckholtz) *Only Skin Deep,* Harlequin (New York, NY), 1992.

(With Eileen Buckholtz) *Trial by Fire,* Harlequin (New York, NY), 1992.

(With Eileen Buckholtz) *Hopscotch,* Harlequin (New York, NY), 1993.

(With Eileen Buckholtz) *Cradle and All,* Harlequin (New York, NY), 1993.

(With Eileen Buckholtz) *What Child Is This?,* Harlequin (New York, NY), 1993.

(With Eileen Buckholtz) *Midnight Kiss,* Harlequin (New York, NY), 1994.

(With Eileen Buckholtz) *Tangled Vows,* Harlequin (New York, NY), 1994.

(With Eileen Buckholtz) *Till Death Us Do Part,* Harlequin (New York, NY), 1995.

(With Eileen Buckholtz) *Prince of Time,* Harlequin (New York, NY), 1995.

(With Eileen Buckholtz) *Face to Face,* Harlequin (New York, NY), 1996.

(With Eileen Buckholtz) *For Your Eyes Only,* Harlequin (New York, NY), 1997.

(With Eileen Buckholtz) *Father and Child,* Harlequin (New York, NY), 1997.

Nowhere Man, Harlequin (New York, NY), 1998.

Shattered Lullaby, Harlequin (New York, NY), 1999.

Midnight Caller, Harlequin (New York, NY), 1999.

Never Too Late, Harlequin (New York, NY), 2000.

Amanda's Child, Harlequin (New York, NY), 2000.

The Man from Texas, Harlequin (New York, NY), 2001.

Never Alone, Harlequin (New York, NY), 2001.

Lassiter's Law, Harlequin (New York, NY), 2001.

FICTION; UNDER PSEUDONYM REBECCA YORK

(With Eileen Buckholtz) *Talons of the Falcon* ("The Peregrine Connection" series), Dell (New York, NY), 1986.

(With Eileen Buckholtz) *Flight of the Raven* ("The Peregrine Connection" series), Dell (New York, NY), 1986.

(With Eileen Buckholtz) *In Search of the Dove* ("The Peregrine Connection" series), Dell (New York, NY), 1986.

Bayou Moon (romantic suspense novel), Harlequin (New York, NY), 1992.

(With Kelsey Roberts) *Secret Vows,* Harlequin (New York, NY), 2000.

(With Metsy Hingle and Joanna Wayne) *Bayou Blood Brothers: Tyler/Nick/Jules* (contributor of *Tyler*), Harlequin (New York, NY), 2001.

The Man from Texas, Harlequin (New York, NY), 2001.

Work represented in anthologies, including *In Our Dreams,* Kensington Books, 1998; *Key to My Heart,* Harlequin (New York, NY), 1998; *After Dark,* Harlequin (New York, NY), 1999; and *Bayou Blood Brothers,* Harlequin (New York, NY), 2001.

ROMANCE NOVELS; UNDER PSEUDONYM ALEXIS HILL JORDAN; WITH LOUISE TITCHENER

Brian's Captive, Dell (New York, NY), 1983.

Reluctant Merger, Dell (New York, NY), 1983.

Summer Wine, Dell (New York, NY), 1984.

Beginner's Luck, Dell (New York, NY), 1984.

Mistaken Image, Dell (New York, NY), 1985.

Hopelessly Devoted, Dell (New York, NY), 1985.

Summer Stars, Dell (New York, NY), 1985.

Stolen Passion, Dell (New York, NY), 1986.

ROMANCE NOVELS; UNDER PSEUDONYM AMANDA LEE

(With Eileen Buckholtz) *End of Illusion,* Silhouette Special Edition (New York, NY), 1984.

More than Promises, Silhouette Desire (New York, NY), 1985.

(With Eileen Buckholtz) *Logical Choice,* Silhouette Desire (New York, NY), 1986.

(With Eileen Buckholtz) *Great Expectations,* Silhouette Desire (New York, NY), 1987.

(With Eileen Buckholtz) *A Place in Your Heart,* Silhouette Desire (New York, NY), 1988.

(With Eileen Buckholtz) *Silver Creek Challenge,* Silhouette Romance (New York, NY), 1989.

OTHER

(Under pseudonym Alyssa Howard; with Eileen Buckholtz, Carolyn Males, and Louise Titchener) *Love Is Elected* (romance novel), Silhouette Romance (New York, NY), 1982.

(Under pseudonym Alyssa Howard; with Eileen Buckholtz, Carolyn Males, and Louise Titchener) *Southern Persuasion* (romance novel), Silhouette Desire (New York, NY), 1983.

(Under pseudonym Alexis Hill; with Louise Titchener) *In the Arms of Love* (romance novel), Dell (New York, NY), 1983.

(Under pseudonym Tess Marlowe; with Louise Titchener) *Indiscreet,* Silhouette Desire (New York, NY), 1988.

(Under pseudonym Samantha Chase; with Eileen Buckholtz) *Postmark,* Tudor, 1988.

(Under pseudonym Samantha Chase; with Eileen Buckholtz) *Needlepoint,* Tudor, 1989.

Coeditor of "Micro Adventure" and "Magic Micro"
series of juvenile adventure books with computer
activities, Scholastic. Contributor to magazines, including *Good Health* and *Essence,* and to newspapers. Food
editor of *Columbia Flier,* 1977-80.

Work in Progress

Diabetes One-Pot Meal Book, for American Diabetes
Association; romantic suspense under pseudonym Re-
becca York, including the novels *From the Shadows,
Phantom Lover,* and *Intimate Strangers,* all for "43
Light Street" series, Harlequin (New York, NY), com-
pletion expected in 2002; "Wyatt," to be included in
Gypsy Magic, Harlequin (New York, NY), 2002; and
Lone Wolf, Berkley (New York, NY), 2003.

Sidelights

Ruth Glick commented: "I'm delighted to have the
chance to speak directly to my readers and answer some
questions that I'm frequently asked. At this point in my
career, I'm primarily writing fiction as Rebecca York. I
have also continued writing health-oriented cookbooks
under my own name.

"One frequently-asked question is: how did you get
started in your writing career, and why did it take such
an unconventional path? I began my writing career when
I was a stay-at-home mom with two small children. My
first sales were feature articles for my local newspaper,
articles which were sold for ten dollars each. At the
time, the idea of sitting down to write a novel would
have been too intimidating. I had written hundreds of
articles before I ever thought about a longer work.

"While I was getting a solid background in nonfiction, I
started taking a local community college class that was
run as a writing seminar. Participants brought what they
were working on and read it—articles, chapters of
books, poems, essays. I learned a lot about novel writing
by listening to the chapters and participating in the
critiques. Since I had always wanted to write fiction, the
class made me long to start my own novel. Because my
main reading as a teenager was science fiction, mystery,
and suspense, I started with what I knew. Since I was
still worried about length, I decided to try a juvenile
science fiction novel of about 40,000 words.

"I read my chapters in class, got feedback, and learned
how many more skills it takes to write fiction than
nonfiction. About a year later, I decided I'd absorbed
everything I could from the teacher and formed my own
critique group, where writers could bring their works in
progress and get feedback. (Twenty years later, we're
still meeting, with a number of the same people and
some newcomers.)

"I polished up my first novel and sent it off to publishers
of juvenile fiction and got four rejections. An editor at

Scholastic held the book for nine months and finally
wrote me a two-page letter telling me everything that
was wrong with my book. I knew it was a 'good'
rejection, because she'd taken the time to read my work
and make suggestions. I made the revisions she request-
ed and sold the book. When I saw the contract, I decided
there was no way I could deal with it intelligently, so I
got an agent.

"Many people think that, if they can just get published,
all their problems will be over. But after that first book,
if you want to continue your career, you have to keep
selling. I had started a second juvenile novel, when one
of the people in my writing group asked if I wanted to
collaborate on a romance, since the market for them was
really expanding. When I told her I'd never read one,
she brought me a shopping bag full of old Harlequin
novels, and I had two reactions. First, I loved them,
because I'd always loved the subplots in the books I read
that focused on the developing relationship between a
man and a woman. My other reaction was—I can do
this!

"So, to continue my atypical career pattern, I asked a
couple of other people if they wanted to learn how to
write a romance novel. They did, and four of us wrote a
book together—working in two teams of two people
each, and then critiquing the other team's work. Through
that experience I learned more about what it takes to
write a good novel—and a good romance. The surprising
part of this episode is that we sold the book. It was *Love
Is Elected* by Alyssa Howard. The editor said she liked
the author's writing style.

"For several years, I worked with one of the team
members, writing together. We began to specialize in
romantic suspense, which is a very difficult genre to do
well, because you must combine a carefully plotted
suspense or mystery story with a romance that engages
the emotions of the reader. In romantic suspense, the
romance and the suspense must be woven together so
tightly that neither element could be pulled from the
story. In other words, a romantic suspense novel focuses
on a man and a woman falling in love and trying to work
out an intimate relationship at the same time they are
trying to extricate themselves from a life-threatening
situation.

"Ultimately, team writing stopped being satisfying for
me, because I wanted to develop my own ideas in my
own way. Throughout my career I'd always written
some books by myself, and these were the stories I liked
best. Now I've been working strictly on my own for the
past few years, writing the popular '43 Light Street'
series for Harlequin Intrigue. At the same time, I've kept
up my nonfiction career, chiefly writing cookbooks
which specialize in great-tasting but healthy food.

"Another question that people frequently ask me is: what
is a romance novel, and why do you love writing them?
A romance novel is the story of the development of the
relationship between one man and one woman. It's part
of the reader's expectation that there will be a happy

ending, just as the mystery reader expects that the crime will be solved and the killer brought to justice. Romance readers want to identify with the characters and feel uplifted and fulfilled by the outcome of the relationship.

"Romance readers are drawn to these books because they're about women's lives and women's concerns (home, family, bonding, love, marriage, making relationships work). They're also books that touch the emotions of the reader. The reader laughs and cries with the hero and heroine. She becomes involved in their lives for a short time. She gets to experience the creation of a deep, abiding love that leads to a lifetime commitment.

"Long ago, when I was writing primarily nonfiction, I did some ghostwriting for a sexual therapist. She told me that the most basic fear of men was impotence, and the most basic fear of women was abandonment. A romance novel is the antithesis of abandonment. The female protagonist always gets what she wants at the end of the book. She forges a lasting relationship with the man she loves. The male protagonist gets what he wants, too—the same thing. The difference is that, at the beginning of the book, he doesn't know that's what he wants! Part of the satisfaction for the reader is in seeing the heroine set her sights on an 'Alpha male' and win him. So a romance novel is an affirmation of women's most basic values.

"In effect, every successful genre novel is a suspense novel. In a romance, the suspense comes from the uncertainty of whether the hero or heroine can overcome the conflicts that keep them apart and make their relationship work. The successful romance writer keeps the reader in doubt until the very end of the book. In the most successful romances, the conflicts are internal—conflicts arising from within the character which seemingly make it impossible for these people to forge a lasting relationship.

"Writing romances is deeply satisfying to me. My work involves reaching down into my own emotions and imagination and creating characters and stories that my readers tell me they love . . . .

"I think you could answer Freud's famous question, 'What do women want?' by reading romances. In fact, I'd go so far as to advise men to read a few if they want some insights into what women consider important."

Biographical and Critical Sources

PERIODICALS

Baltimore Sun, June 18, 1978; April 26, 1995; January 27, 1999; March 30, 1999; Maryland and Howard County Edition, November 11, 1999.
GW, spring, 1999.
Houston Post, March 19, 1984.
News (Frederick, MD), October 13, 1997.
Washington Post Book World, February 3-7, 1999.

ON-LINE

Ruth Glick Web site, http://www.rebeccayork.com/ (September 2, 2001).

* * *

GREENBERG, Jan 1942-

Personal

Born December 29, 1942, in St. Louis, MO; daughter of Alexander (a manufacturer) and Lilian (an advertising executive; maiden name, Rubenstein) Schonwald; married Ronald Greenberg (an art dealer), August 31, 1963; children: Lynne, Jeanne, Jacqueline. *Education:* Washington University, B.A. (English), 1964; Webster University, M.A.T. (communications), 1971. *Hobbies and other interests:* Skiing, jogging, drawing.

Addresses

Home and office—3 Brentmoor Park, St. Louis, MO 63105.

Career

Teacher and author. St. Louis Public Schools, St. Louis, MO, teacher, 1969-72; Forest Park Community College, St. Louis, instructor in English composition, 1973-75; Webster University, St. Louis, director and instructor in aesthetic education, 1974-79; *St. Louis Post-Dispatch,* St. Louis, book reviewer, 1975-80; CEMREL (National Education Laboratory), St. Louis, researcher, 1976-78; freelance writer, 1978—. Presenter of workshops and lectures on aesthetic education and writing for young readers. *Member:* PEN, Society of Children's Book Writers and Illustrators, Missouri Arts Council (member, literature committee, 1984—).

Awards, Honors

American Library Association Best Books for Young Adults citation, 1984, for *No Dragons to Slay;* Webster University Distinguished Alumni Award, 1986.

Writings

A Season in-Between, Farrar, Straus (New York, NY), 1979.
The Iceberg and Its Shadow, Farrar, Straus (New York, NY), 1980.
The Pig-out Blues, Farrar, Straus (New York, NY), 1982.
No Dragons to Slay, Farrar, Straus (New York, NY), 1983.
Bye, Bye, Miss American Pie, Farrar, Straus (New York, NY), 1985.
Exercises of the Heart, Farrar, Straus (New York, NY), 1986.
Just the Two of Us, Farrar, Straus (New York, NY), 1988.
(With Sandra Jordan) *The Painter's Eye: Learning to Look at Contemporary American Art,* Delacorte (New York, NY), 1991.

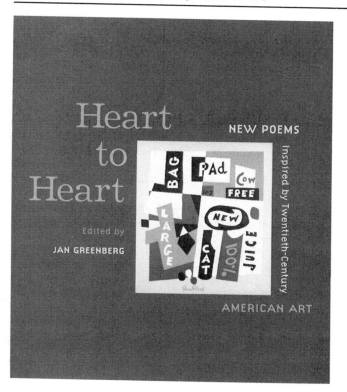

Greenberg's anthology includes more than forty poems that celebrate artistic expression ranging in form and style from cubism to pop art.

(With Sandra Jordan) *The Sculptor's Eye: Looking at Contemporary American Art,* DK Ink (New York, NY), 1993.

(With Sandra Jordan) *The American Eye: Eleven Artists of the Twentieth Century,* Delacorte (New York, NY), 1995.

(With Sandra Jordan) *Chuck Close up Close* (biography), DK Ink (New York, NY), 1998.

(With Sandra Jordan) *Frank O. Gehry: Outside In,* DK Ink (New York, NY), 2000.

(With Sandra Jordan) *Vincent Van Gogh: Portrait of an Artist,* Delacorte (New York, NY), 2001.

(Editor) *Heart to Heart: New Poems Inspired by Twentieth-Century American Art,* Abrams (New York, NY), 2001.

Sidelights

As the author of teen fiction, Jan Greenberg finds writing to be a process of discovery, as her young protagonists develop life skills by facing life's problems. "My books deal with domestic issues: illness or death in a family, sibling rivalry, or problems with friends or parents," Greenberg noted of such books as *The Pig-out Blues* and *Just the Two of Us.* Her writing focuses on "ordinary boys and girls who are experiencing ordinary, day-to-day problems growing up in a complex society. I am writing to cheer them on," Greenberg added, "to say, 'Yes, sometimes it's hard. But keep trying. Keep up the good work!'" In recent years Greenberg has expanded her writing for young people to include books that reflect her passion for contemporary American art, and has paired up with coauthor Sandra Jordan to provide several well-received overviews of modern art as well as biographies of individual artists.

Born in St. Louis, Missouri, in 1942, Greenberg quickly developed a love of books and reading. "My parents' library was filled with an assortment of books ranging from Plato's *Dialogues* to *Gone with the Wind,*" she once recalled to *SATA.* "It was there in that cozy room with a fireplace that I developed my eclectic tastes in literature." When Greenberg was ten, she began keeping a journal, a practice she has continued to maintain throughout her adult life.

Graduating with a degree in English in 1964, Greenberg worked for several years as a teacher, and went on to receive a master's degree in 1971. In the 1970s, Greenberg and her husband, Ronald Greenberg, began collecting contemporary American art, and soon their house was filled to overflowing, the walls "with bright canvases, the yard with large steel sculpture." The couple eventually opened an art gallery in their Midwest community that quickly became a center for young artists and musicians. "The energy and excitement engendered by my contact with other artists inspired me to write and develop my own creative skills," explained Greenberg.

Greenberg's first novel, *A Season in-Between,* is the story of a thirteen-year-old girl who must face the illness and death of her father while engaged in a host of adolescent worries, fears, and concerns. Published in 1979, it was followed a year later by *The Iceberg and Its Shadow.* In 1982 she released one of her most popular novels, *The Pig-out Blues,* which introduces Jodie as she struggles with weight fluctuations as well as a tense relationship with her ultra-thin mother. As a coveted part to play Juliet opposite a dishy Romeo in her school's annual play becomes available, a crash diet is the order of the day, with unforseen consequences.

Just the Two of Us, released in 1988, also finds a young teen coping none too well with the minefield of everyday life. It is not bad enough that Holly Hornby must struggle to finish the seventh grade; now her mother has totally disrupted her future by deciding to leave Manhattan and move to a small town in Iowa. Holly convinces her mom to let her remain in the city for the summer, and takes up residence at the Applebaum house, home of her best buddy, Max. By summer's end, Holly learns that life with the Applebaums is not as wonderful as she expected and looks forward to joining her mother in Iowa. Reviewing *Just the Two of Us* for *Booklist,* Barbara Elleman praised Greenberg for her "firm but easy touch with characters," adding that the book's "lively plot is believable and well paced."

When writing fiction, Greenberg thinks of herself as "a storyteller. I write books with a beginning, a middle, and an end. Most of my stories take place in the Midwest. But ... my books could take place in suburbia almost anywhere in America." According to Greenberg, when she meets with groups of young people, they often ask her "what kind of a miserable childhood did I have to invent such weird and cranky characters. The truth is that my childhood wasn't unusually miserable at all. Yes, I had eye allergies and boy troubles. I was too tall, I thought my parents too strict, my teachers unfair. But then," she added, "these complaints and a host of new ones cropped up in regular cycles with my own daughters as well." In fact, Greenberg credits her experiences parenting teens through a series of adolescent traumas as the impetus for her fiction-writing career. "The fact is," she once explained to *SATA,* "that trauma is the business of adolescence, and along with these traumas, large or small, come negative feelings.... After my first novel, some people told me how courageous I was to admit weakness and negative feelings in print. But writing is an act of sharing. A book is never a total figment of the imagination. It begins as a stomach ache, a slight quiver of discomfort. It's like falling in or out of love. If the feeling is strong enough, a book may evolve. Or maybe not. But when something happens and a year later I'm holding a new novel in my hand, I want to jump up and down, throw confetti, and stop everyone on the street and say, 'Look what I've done.'"

Beginning in the 1990s Greenberg paired up with Sandra Jordan, and the two began to publish books in the field of art. The first, 1991's *The Painter's Eye: Learning to Look at Contemporary American Art,* describes the basic elements of artistic composition amid a wealth of visual examples and interviews with artists, resulting in a work that a *Publishers Weekly* contributor dubbed "an ingeniously choreographed duet of text and image" that aids young people in understanding the role of contemporary art and the significance of their response to it. A companion volume, *The Sculptor's Eye,* was released two years later, its wealth of material "woven together with a clear and perceptive text," according to *Horn Book* contributor Lolly Robinson. In *American Eye: Eleven Artists of the Twentieth Century,* Greenberg and Jordan present biographies of such major artists as Thomas Hart Benton, Stuart Davis, Jackson Pollock, and Georgia O'Keeffe, and describe the significance of several modern masterworks. Calling their examination one of "clarity and insight," *Horn Book* reviewer Lolly Robinson added that the book's focus "is placed on understanding the artist as a person in order to begin to understand each artist's frame of reference for his or her work."

Individual artists Vincent Van Gogh, Chuck Close, and Frank O. Gehry also benefit as the subject of highly praised biographies by Greenberg and Jordan. In 1999's *Chuck Close up Close,* the life and work of the artist known in the 1960s for his oversized, highly detailed, and often outrageous neck-up portraits is examined. Published to coincide with a retrospective of Close's work in New York City, *Chuck Close up Close* "is a simply written yet fascinating account of how nearly insurmountable obstacles can often spur artistic growth," according to *New York Times Book Review* contributor Elizabeth Spires, who describes the disabilities endured by the artist throughout his life. A contributor to *Publishers Weekly* deemed the book equally praiseworthy, calling it "an ideal example of an artist biography." *Frank O. Gehry: Outside In* drew the same positive response from critics, as Greenberg and Jordan explain Gehry's approach to space and materials as it developed against the backdrop of his life and culminated in such whimsical, original works as the Guggenheim Museum in Bilbao, Spain. "This book is a journey through the creative process," noted Paul Goldberger in a laudatory appraisal for the *New York Times Book Review.* While noting that *Frank O. Gehry: Outside In* would not be suitable for readers under age ten, Goldberger went on to comment that the Goldberg-Jordan collaboration "may be one of the few books for young readers to address honestly not just the payoffs of artistic success but also the risks."

Commenting on the Greenberg-Jordan contributions to children's literature and art, *Bulletin of the Center for Children's Books* contributor Deborah Stevenson claimed that "no literary gallery can be complete without titles" from the pair. "The provocation of thought, encouragement of curiosity, and exploration of what all kinds of art can mean and do are the real contributions of this team's *oeuvre.* These books are truly state of the art."

Biographical and Critical Sources

PERIODICALS

Booklist, January 15, 1989, Barbara Elleman, review of *Just the Two of Us,* pp. 870-871; March 15, 1994, Stephanie Zvirin, review of *The Sculptor's Eye,* p. 1377; March 15, 1996, review of *The American Eye,* p. 1274; April 1, 1999, Stephanie Zvirin, review of *Chuck Close up Close,* p. 1382; December 15, 2000, Gillian Engberg, review of *Frank O. Gehry,* p. 810; March 15, 2001, Gillian Engberg, interview with Jan Greenberg, p. 1395.

Horn Book, March, 1994, Lolly Robinson, review of *The Sculptor's Eye,* p. 223; January-February, 1996, Lolly Robinson, review of *The American Eye,* p. 91; September, 2000, Lolly Robinson, review of *Frank O. Gehry,* p. 594.

New York Times Book Review, May 17, 1998, Elizabeth Spires, review of *Chuck Close up Close,* p. 32; November 19, 2000, Paul Goldberger, "The Master Builder," p. 30.

Publishers Weekly, April 25, 1994, review of *The Painter's Eye,* p. 81; July 3, 2000, review of *Chuck Close up Close,* p. 73; March 12, 2001, review of *Heart to Heart,* p. 87.

Voice of Youth Advocates, February, 1989, Beth E. Andersen, review of *Just the Two of Us,* p. 284; October, 1990, Susan Levine, review of *The Pig-out Blues,* p. 257.

ON-LINE

Bulletin of the Center for Children's Books Web Site, http://alexia.lis.uiui.edu/puboff/bccb/ (September 1, 2000), Deborah Stevenson, "True Blue: Jan Greenberg and Sandra Jordan."*

GUEST, Elissa Haden 1953-

Personal

Born January 10, 1953, in New York, NY; daughter of Peter Haden (a former ballet dancer, then editor) and Jean (a casting director; maiden name, Hindes) Guest; married Nicholas Smith (a film editor), May 30, 1981; children: Gena, Nathanael. *Education:* Attended Hampshire College and Bank Street College; Antioch College, West, B.A., 1975. *Hobbies and other interests:* "Spending time with my family and friends. Reading, walking in Golden Gate Park. Traveling, especially by train. Visiting schools and reading aloud to children."

Addresses

Agent—Phyllis Wender, 3 East 48th St., New York, NY 10017. *E-mail*—ehguest@yahoo.com.

Career

Children's book author and television writer; teaches creative writing. Has previously worked as a nursery school teacher, editorial assistant, and researcher for

From the ups and downs of friendship to worries about puberty, Elissa Haden Guest's collaboration with Margaret Blackstone lets girls of all ages know that "it's great that we're all in this together."

soap opera *One Life to Live.* Member: Society of Children's Book Writers and Illustrators, Authors Guild, Writers Guild of America (East), Northern California Children's Book Association.

Awards, Honors

Christopher Award, 1989, for NBC family drama *A Place at the Table;* Notable Book selection, American Library Association, Junior Literary Guild selection, Best Children's Book selection, *Publishers Weekly,* 2000, Blue Ribbon Book selection, *Bulletin of the Center for Children's Books,* 2000, and PEN Center USA West Literary Award, 2001, all for *Iris and Walter.*

Writings

The Handsome Man (young adult novel), Four Winds Press (New York, NY), 1980.
Over the Moon (young adult novel), Morrow (New York, NY), 1986.
(With Margaret Blackstone) *Girl Stuff: A Survival Guide to Growing Up,* illustrated by Barbara Pollack, Gulliver Books/Harcourt (San Diego, CA), 2000.
Iris and Walter, illustrated by Christine Davenier, Gulliver Books/Harcourt (San Diego, CA), 2000.
Iris and Walter: True Friends, illustrated by Christine Davenier, Gulliver Books/Harcourt (San Diego, CA), 2001.
Iris and Walter and Baby Rose, illustrated by Christine Davenier, Gulliver Books/Harcourt (San Diego, CA), 2002.
Iris and Walter: The Sleepover, illustrated by Christine Davenier, Gulliver Books/Harcourt (San Diego, CA), 2002.

TELEVISION SCREENPLAYS

A Place at the Table, first broadcast on NBC-TV (New York, NY), 1989.
(With Jenny Bogart and Mia Certic) *Frankie and Hazel,* first broadcast on Showtime, 2000.

Sidelights

Elissa Haden Guest told *SATA,* "I have always associated storytelling with closeness and comfort. My parents read and sang to me very often when I was little. My father, who was British, had a beautiful speaking voice and my brothers and I loved when he made up stories filled with hilarious and eccentric characters.

"I had a lot of freedom when I was a child. My best friend, Jenny, and I ran around Riverside Park in New York City climbing trees and sliding down rocks. We spent days on end making up stories and acting them out. Looking back, I see that in a very real sense I was writing from the time I was little."

Guest's first published work was *The Handsome Man,* a young adult love story in which teenager Alexandra Barnes falls in love with a "handsome man" whom she and her friend Angela notice around their town. While

In Iris and Walter, *Guest's first picture book, the author tells the story of a young girl whose move to the country is filled with wonderful experiences once she makes a new friend. (Illustration by Christine Davenier.)*

Alexandra's love is unrequited, she does get to know the man, who is a photographer. In addition to the love story, the book focuses on Alexandra and Angela's friendship, as well as Alexandra's family life and her relationship with her parents. Denise M. Wilms, writing for *Booklist,* noted the "trueness of character" in this work, praising Guest for treating Alexandra's emotional state with a great deal of sensitivity.

In 1986, Guest issued another young adult novel, *Over the Moon.* The story is narrated by Kate as she recalls events in the year her then-sixteen-year-old sister, Mattie, ran away with Dean Hartwell, a handsome twenty-eight-year-old man. Now Kate is sixteen and is still haunted by memories of a sister who simply vanished from her life. With no contact from Mattie in over four years, Kate is surprised when she suddenly receives a birthday gift from her. Despite the cold reactions of her brother, Jay, and Aunt Georgia, who has taken care of the children since their parents died in an accident, Kate decides to go in search of her sister. Although the journey seems destined for failure from the beginning (Kate loses her wallet; she misses her bus), she meets a young man along the way who helps her realize the reality of Mattie's situation. Kate eventually finds Mattie and her infant, bringing them both home to reunite the family. Writing for *Horn Book,* Mary M. Burns noted that "this remarkable novel is unforgettable" in its poignant presentation of the human condition.

Guest followed her young adult novels with *Girl Stuff: A Survival Guide to Growing Up,* a resource book for girls approaching puberty. Coauthored with Margaret Blackstone, this work offers information on physical, emotional, and social development for young girls. According to Katie O'Dell, writing in the *School Library Journal,* although the length of the work does not allow for detailed discussion of the topics covered, the "frank, realistic" questions and "accurate, straightforward" answers are "packed with facts." O'Dell recommended *Girl Stuff* as a "worthy addition" to any young girl's library.

For her next publication, Guest turned to a younger set of readers with *Iris and Walter,* the first of Guest's books about Iris, a little girl who has moved from the city to the country with her parents. Once there, although she misses her life in the city terribly, Iris's grandfather helps her make friends with a boy named Walter. Soon they are good friends, and although Iris continues to miss her old life, she also learns to enjoy living in the country. Reviewing this work for *Publishers Weekly,* a critic lauded Guest for her "economic eloquence," which pairs "in perfect sync" with the "elegant" illustrations in the book. *School Library Journal* reviewer Holly Belli also praised the story, noting that the work helps

The lively duo return in Iris and Walter: True Friends *to help each other deal with challenges, setbacks, and the first day of school.*

illustrate the "positive qualities of different lifestyles" while also teaching young readers that it is possible to make friends anywhere. Writing in the *Bulletin of the Center for Children's Books,* Janice M. Del Negro noted that Guest shows a "sense of what is important not only to her characters but to [her] readers" as well, having created a story that is both realistic and humorous.

Biographical and Critical Sources

PERIODICALS

Booklist, December 15, 1980, Denise M. Wilms, review of *The Handsome Man,* p. 574.

Bulletin of the Center for Children's Books, March, 1986, review of *Over the Moon,* p. 128; December, 2000, Janice M. Del Negro, review of *Iris and Walter.*

Growing Point, March, 1987, review of *Over the Moon,* pp. 4757-4762.

Horn Book, July, 1986, Mary M. Burns, review of *Over the Moon,* p. 455.

Publishers Weekly, September 18, 2000, review of *Iris and Walter,* p. 112.

School Library Journal, June, 2000, Katie O'Dell, review of *Girl Stuff: A Survival Guide to Growing Up,* p. 160; November, 2000, Holly Belli, review of *Iris and Walter,* p. 122.

Voice of Youth Advocates, February, 1981, Carol Morrison, review of *The Handsome Man,* p. 30.

H–I

HADDIX, Margaret Peterson 1964-

Personal

Born April 9, 1964, in Washington Court House, OH; daughter of John Albert (a farmer) and Marilee Grace (a nurse; maiden name, Greshel) Peterson; married Doug Haddix (a newspaper editor), October 3, 1987; children: Meredith, Connor. *Education:* Miami University, B.A. (English; summa cum laude), 1986. *Religion:* Presbyterian. *Hobbies and other interests:* Travel.

Addresses

Agent—Tracey Adams, McIntoch & Otis, 353 Lexington Ave., New York, NY 10016.

Career

Fort Wayne Journal-Gazette, Fort Wayne, IN, copy editor, 1986-87; *Indianapolis News,* Indianapolis, IN, reporter, 1987-91; Danville Area Community College, Danville, IL, adjunct faculty, 1991-93; freelance writer, 1991-94. *Member:* Society of Children's Book Writers and Illustrators, Phi Beta Kappa.

Awards, Honors

Honorable mention, *Seventeen* magazine fiction contest, 1983; fiction contest award, National Society of Arts and Letters, 1988; *American Bestseller* Pick of the Lists selection, Mystery Writers of America's Edgar Allan Poe award nomination, Young Adult Library Services Association (YALSA) Quick Pick for Reluctant Young Adult Readers and Best Book for Young Adults designations, listed as a Notable Children's Trade Books in the Field of Social Studies, National Council for Social Studies/Children's Book Council, Sequoyah Young Adult Book Award, Black-Eyed Susan Award, all 1996-97, and Arizona Young Readers' Award, 1998, all for *Running out of Time;* Children's Book Award (older reader category), International Reading Association, and YALSA Quick Pick for Reluctant Young Adult

Margaret Peterson Haddix

Readers and Best Book for Young Adults designations, all 1997, Black-Eyed Susan Award, 1998-99, Nebraska Golden Sower Award, 2000, all for *Don't You Dare Read This, Mrs. Dunphrey;* YALSA Best Books for Young Adults and *American Bookseller* Pick of the Lists, both for *Leaving Fishers;* YALSA Top Ten Best Books for Young Adults and Quick Picks Top Ten designations, both 2000, California Young Readers' Medal, Minnesota Maud Hart Lovelace Award, and Nevada Young Readers' Award, all 2001, all for *Among the Hidden; American Bookseller* Pick of the Lists, American Library Association Best Book for Young

Adults, American Library Association Quick Pick for Reluctant Young Adult Readers, and International Reading Association Young Adults' Choices List, 2001, all for *Just Ella; American Bookseller* Pick of the Lists, for *Turnabout, The Girl with 500 Middle Names,* and *Among the Imposters;* Junior Library Guild selection, for *Takeoffs and Landings.*

Writings

Running out of Time, Simon & Schuster (New York, NY), 1995.
Don't You Dare Read This, Mrs. Dunphrey, Simon & Schuster (New York, NY), 1996.
Leaving Fishers, Simon & Schuster (New York, NY), 1997.
Among the Hidden, Simon & Schuster (New York, NY), 1998.
Just Ella, Simon & Schuster (New York, NY), 1999.
Turnabout, Simon & Schuster (New York, NY), 2000.
The Girl with 500 Middle Names, Simon & Schuster (New York, NY), 2001.
Takeoffs and Landings, Simon & Schuster (New York, NY), 2001.
Among the Imposters, Simon & Schuster (New York, NY), 2001.

OTHER

Contributor of short stories to anthologies, including *Indiannual* and *The Luxury of Tears,* National Society of Arts and Letters, 1989; *On the Edge,* Simon & Schuster (New York, NY), 2000; and *I Believe in Water,* HarperCollins (New York, NY), 2000.

Adaptations

Just Ella, Leaving Fishers, Don't You Dare Read This, Mrs. Dunphrey, and *Among the Hidden* have all been adapted for audiocassette.

Work in Progress

Anya's Wig, a middle-grades novel; and *Among the Betrayed* and *Among the Barons,* further books in the *Among the Hidden* series.

Sidelights

Award-winning author Margaret Peterson Haddix has written a number of highly praised novels for young adults and juvenile readers that deal with topics from religious cults and futuristic dystopias to modern-day science fiction and reality-based fiction. Haddix's 1995 debut novel, *Running out of Time,* a time-slip story with a twist, has become something of a classic of the form, and was adopted for use in middle school classrooms around the United States. Other novels, both fanciful and realistic, from the pen of Haddix include *Don't You Dare Read This, Mrs. Dunphrey, Leaving Fishers, Among the Hidden, Just Ella, Turnabout, The Girl with 500 Middle Names, Takeoffs and Landings,* and *Among the Imposters.* A former journalist-turned-author, Haddix stumbled into writing for young readers. "In fact," noted

An isolated teen, the youngest of three children, assumes a fake identity to avoid discovery in a world where no family is permitted to have more than two children. (Cover illustration by Cliff Nielson.)

a contributor to the *Akron Beacon Journal* in an interview with Haddix, the author "was trying to 'get discovered' as a short-story writer when she fell into the world of children's literature, much as Alice tumbled down the rabbit hole." With the popularity of *Running out of Time,* and with several awards to her credit, Haddix decided that this particular rabbit hole was one worth exploring.

Haddix was born in Washington Court House, Ohio, in 1964, the daughter of a farming father and a mother who worked as a nurse. "I grew up on lots of stories," Haddix once commented, "both from books and in my family. My father in particular was always telling tales to my brothers and sister and me—about one of our ancestors who was kidnaped, about some friends who survived lying on a railroad bridge while a train went over the top of them, about the kid who brought possum meat to the school cafeteria when my father was a boy. So I always thought that becoming a storyteller would be the grandest thing in the world. But I didn't want to just tell stories. I wanted to write them down."

Through adolescence and on into high school, Haddix maintained her love of both reading and writing. "For a long time, I tried to write two different kinds of stories: real and imaginary," she once said. When the time came for college, Haddix chose Miami University, where she earned a B.A. summa cum laude with both university honors and honors in English. "In college I majored in both journalism and creative writing (and history, just because I liked it). After college, I got jobs at newspapers, first as a copy editor in Fort Wayne, then as a reporter in Indianapolis. It was a lot of fun, especially getting to meet and talk to people from all walks of life, from homeless women to congressmen."

All the time, on weekends and in the evenings, she continued to stretch her writing repertoire, working on short stories. "But this was frustrating," Haddix once observed, "because there was never enough time. So, in 1991, when my husband got a new job in Danville, Illinois, I took a radical step: I quit newspapers. I took a series of temporary and part-time jobs, such as teaching at a community college, and used the extra time to write."

The first large-story idea to percolate in Haddix's imagination was the seed of her first published book, *Running out of Time.* "I'd gotten the idea when I was doing a newspaper story about a restored historical village," Haddix recalled. "I kept wondering what it would be like if there was a historical village where all the tourists were hidden and the kids, at least, didn't know what year it really was." In the event, her first manuscript was quickly accepted by an editor at Simon and Schuster, and Haddix was on her way as a juvenile author.

In *Running out of Time,* thirteen-year-old Jessie Keyser lives with her family in a frontier village in 1840, but when the town's children are stricken with diphtheria, Jessie's mother reveals that it is actually the 1990s, and the village is a tourist exhibit and scientific experiment gone awry. Jessie is, in fact, sent to the outside world to get help; her mother is fearful that the one-time idealistic planners of this "ideal" village may have become evil. In fact, Jessie's mother is right: the idealism of Mr. Clifton, who started the community a dozen years before, has been subverted by researchers who have now introduced an outbreak of diphtheria in order to see what will happen to patients without modern medical care. Out in the real world of the 1990s, Jessie comes into contact with modernity with a vengeance: she has to deal with phones, traffic, flush toilets, and the seductions of fast food.

Reviewers were generally positive in their reception of this first novel. Writing in *School Library Journal,* Lisa Dennis dubbed the book "absorbing" and "gripping," further noting that the "action moves swiftly, with plenty of suspense" as Jessie attempts to make her way through the modern world, looking for help for her family and friends. "The suspense and the cataloguing of differences as they appear to Jessie are the best parts," wrote Mary Harris Veeder in a *Booklist* review of the novel.

Voice of Youth Advocates critic Ann Welton, however, complained that Jessie's adjustment to the drastic shift in time "is far too smooth, resulting in a lack of narrative tension." Welton did, however, go on to point out that the book had "potential as a model for writing assignments and provides an interesting perspective on American history." In his review of *Running out of Time, Bulletin of the Center for Children's Books* critic Roger Sutton also felt that Jessie's "disorientation upon discovering the modern world would surely have been more pronounced than it seems," but concluded that "many kids ... will be gripped by the concept, and the book, readable throughout, [is] exciting in spots." Dennis concluded in *School Library Journal* that young readers "will look forward to more stories from this intriguing new author." They did not have long to wait.

"I wrote my second book, *Don't You Dare Read This, Mrs. Dunphrey,* when I was eight months pregnant with my first child, and feeling a little bored," Haddix once explained. "The story should have been very difficult to write, because I had a happy childhood and wonderful parents, and should have had nothing in common with

When two one-hundred-year-old women participate in a scientific experiment that turns the biological clock backward, they face terrifying consequences. (Cover illustration by Cliff Nielson.)

the main character—tough-talking, big-haired Tish, whose parents abandoned her. But I'd once worked on a newspaper series where I talked to more than a dozen abused and neglected kids, and their stories haunted me for years. So writing *Don't You Dare* was almost like an exorcism—I did feel possessed by Tish's spirit. Actually, in a way, everything I've written has felt like that, like being possessed. When I'm writing, I feel like I *must* write."

Critics noted that Haddix relies on a much more familiar set-up for her second novel, placing Tish Bonner, the main character in *Don't You Dare Read This, Mrs. Dunphrey,* in an English class where she is required to keep a journal, giving the reader an insiders' view of her troubles. Since Tish has no one but her journal to confide in as she deals with an absent father, a depressed mother unable to care for her or her younger brother, and a part-time job where the manager subjects her to sexual harassment, "the tone here shifts only in terms of varying shades of anger," a reviewer observed in *Publishers Weekly.* The same writer further described this second book as a "tough-edged if familiar story of a beleaguered high school girl" who confides all her difficulties in her diary. The title of the book refers to the teacher who has promised to only read finished work inspired by her students' journal entries, and not the individual entries themselves. Tish's predicament goes from bad to worse when she has to shoplift from a local store to feed herself and her brother Matthew, and then she faces eviction from her home, as well. Finally Tish turns over the entire journal to her sensitive teacher who helps the young girl find help.

"Tish's journal entries have an authentic ring in phrasing and tone and will keep readers involved," Carol Schene claimed in *School Library Journal.* The result, according to Schene is a "brief, serious look at a young person who is isolated and faced with some seemingly overwhelming problems." Jean Franklin, writing in *Booklist,* called the book "a brief, gritty documentary novel ... a natural for reluctant readers." Jamie S. Hansen, writing in *Voice of Youth Advocates,* echoed this sentiment: "The breezy style, short diary-entry format, and melodramatic subject matter will ensure popularity for this title, particularly with reluctant readers."

After becoming the mother of two children, Meredith and Connor, Haddix admitted "amuse[ment] that I felt like I didn't have enough time to write before they were born. It's much harder now .... And a lot of times when I'm doing the ordinary things that go along with having two kids, a husband, and a house ... I'm listening to a voice in my head insisting, 'Write about me!' or suggesting things like, 'What if Dorry's dad confronts her before she goes to the mall?' Now, I'll be the first to admit that it sounds a little weird to have voices talking in my head, but I wouldn't have it any other way."

While Haddix's novels for young adults share little in terms of plot, setting, or theme, critics have commended the author's ability to involve even reluctant readers in the lives of her characters. Thus with her third novel,

Haddix moved to yet new themes and settings—this time dealing with religious cults and one youngster's attempts at extricating herself from such a group. In *Leaving Fishers,* Haddix tells the story of young Dorry, whose life has been uprooted both geographically and economically. Suffering from diminished circumstances, Dorry is also upset that she has not been able to make friends at her new school. When Angela, one of several attractive and friendly kids who congregate together, asks her to join her friends at lunch, Dorry is eager to blend in. Her enthusiasm is not much diminished when she learns that these students are all part of a religious group called the Fishers of Men. She is introduced to their parties and retreats, and soon these pizza parties turn into prayer groups. Dorry becomes caught up in the zeal at such retreats and becomes a member of the Fishers. Increasingly, Dorry finds all her time taken up with the cult's activities, and begins to fear that she will go to hell if she does not do everything she is told to do by Angela and her assortment of fellow adherents. Neglecting family and school, Dorry is soon caught in the grips of the Fishers. Only when she discovers herself terrifying young baby-sitting charges with threats of hell if they do not convert does Dorry finally see what has been happening to her. She shakes off the bonds of the cult, unlike other young practitioners.

"Haddix gives a fine portrayal of a teenager's descent into a cult," wrote *Booklist's* Ilene Cooper, who further noted that the book was a "good read and an informative one for young people who are constantly bombarded with challenges to their beliefs." Reviewing the same title in *Voice of Youth Advocates,* Beverly Youree felt *Leaving Fishers* "is a definite page-turner, full of excitement and pathos." Youree concluded that "Dorry and readers learn that the world is neither black nor white, good nor bad, but shades of gray." A critic for *Kirkus Reviews* called the novel "a chilling portrait of an insecure teenager gradually relinquishing her autonomy to a religious cult," and a "wholly convincing picture of the slow, insidious stages by which Dorry is 'caught.'" The same reviewer went on to note that Haddix's novel, "[t]ightly written, with well-drawn characters," is "in no way anti-religious." In the end, indeed, Dorry does not turn against religion, but against the sort of mind-numbing cult that seeks total domination over its believers. She continues her spiritual quest, but on her own terms. "Haddix's even-handed portrayal of the rewards of Christian fellowship and the dangers of a legalistic or black-and-white approach to religion" are, according to a reviewer for *Publishers Weekly,* the "book's greatest strength[s]."

Haddix next turned her hand to a future dystopia à la *1984* or *Brave New World.* With *Among the Hidden,* the novelist tells the story of a future totalitarian regime that strictly observes a two-children-only policy. Luke, twelve, is the third child of a farming family and is thus illegal. When the government starts to cut the woods around the family home to make way for new housing, Luke must hide from view, looking at the world outside through a small air vent in the attic. From this vantage point, he one day sees a shadowy figure in a nearby house and begins to suspect that this might be another hidden person like himself. One day he breaks into the seemingly empty house only to find Jen, a hidden child with a tough exterior who has been secreted in this neighboring house. Through Jen, Luke learns of an entire subculture of hidden children via chat rooms on the Internet. He learns through such discussions, and through literature given to him by Jen, of the repressive policies of the government. When Jen organizes a rally of other hidden children that ends in bloodshed and her death, Luke must finally make a decision as to how far he will go to defy the government in order to have a life that is worth living.

Critics responded positively to the theme of this futuristic novel, applauding, as did a *Publishers Weekly* contributor, for example, "the unsettling, thought-provoking premise [which] should suffice to keep readers hooked." Susan L. Rogers, writing in *School Library Journal,* observed that, as with Haddix's debut novel, *Running Out of Time,* this fourth novel took as its theme the loss of free will. Describing *Among the Hidden* as "exciting and compelling," Rogers remarked that readers "will be captivated by Luke's predicament and his reactions to it." Debbie Earl noted in *Voice of Youth Advocates* that Haddix presents a "chilling vision of a possibly not-too-distant future" in this "bleak allegorical tale."

Among the Imposters is a sequel to *Among the Hidden* which picks up the story of Luke Garner as he is sent to a boarding school under the name of Lee Grant. Hendricks School for Boys is a place of violence and fear, where the terrified students quietly follow orders and Luke suffers nightly hazing at the hands of older boys. He soon discovers that some of the boys, along with girls from a neighboring girls' school, are meeting secretly in the woods to plot their escape. Luke must decide whether to join the plotters in their dangerous plan. Brenda Moses-Allen in the *Voice of Youth Advocates* found the story to be filled with "tension and excitement."

With *Just Ella,* her fifth novel, Haddix presented herself yet another creative challenge: rethinking a traditional fairy tale, and putting, as a *Publishers Weekly* reviewer commented, "a feminist spin on the Cinderella story." Haddix starts her revisionist tale at the point in action where the fairy tale ends. Planning to live happily ever after with her Prince Charming who has saved her from her evil step-family, Ella Brown is sorely disappointed upon arrival at the prince's castle. An energetic and resourceful person, Ella has found her own way to the ball where she met the prince, without the aid of a magical fairy godmother. Now she is sorely in need of such divine intervention, for she discovers her husband-to-be is yawningly boring; neither is a continual diet of needlepoint enough to keep her intellectually challenged. Ella's independent nature is assaulted by the etiquette lessons which Madame Bisset dishes out, but her young tutor, Jed, does talk to her about things that matter, and soon she sees that there is no way she can go through with her planned marriage. But then Ella discovers it is

not all that easy to walk away from the prince, for she finds herself locked away in a dungeon when her fiancé gets wind of her resolve. However, with the help of a servant girl she has befriended, Ella manages to tunnel her way to freedom and to a life that has meaning for her.

Once again, readers and critics responded warmly to Haddix's writing and invention. "In lively prose, with well-developed characters, creative plot twists, wit, and drama, Haddix transforms the Cinderella tale into an insightful coming-of-age story," wrote Shelle Rosenfeld in a *Booklist* review. Rosenfeld also commented that *Just Ella* was a "provocative and entertaining novel." The contributor for *Publishers Weekly* concluded that Ella's "straightforward, often gleefully glib narrative breathes fresh life into the tale," while Connie Tyrrell Burns, writing in *School Library Journal,* called the book an "imaginative retelling," and recommended it for older readers who could "enjoy this new take on a strong heroine." "Make room in the canon of retold tales for a spirited, first-person retelling of 'Cinderella'," proclaimed Cynthia Grady in *Voice of Youth Advocates.* "Ella," concluded Grady, "is a thoughtful heroine who overcomes her youthful 'foolishness'." Similarly, Natalie Soto, reviewing the novel in the *Rocky Mountain News,* felt that "Ella is a strong and sensitive character sure to make girls cheer."

Haddix returned to the future with *Turnabout,* a novel set in 2085, when the pavement is made of foam rubber and society favors singles. As with her first novel, this one involves a scientific experiment gone wrong. At the heart of this novel is the question, "What if people could turn back the aging clock?" Haddix explores this question through two characters, Melly and Anny Beth, aged respectively 100 and 103 in the year 2001 and residing in a nursing home. Part of an experiment to "un-age," the two are given PT-1, a drug in the Project Turnabout program that will reverse the aging process, allowing the participant to grow younger every year until they reach a self-determined perfect age. At that point, they will receive another injection which will stop the process. The only problem is that this second shot proves fatal, and now the members of Project Turnabout are doomed to continue "unaging" until they reach zero. The novel switches between the present and 2085 when Melly and Anny Beth are teenagers and must find someone to parent them as they grow increasingly younger. Upping the stakes is a reporter who has gotten wind of the project and is trying to track Melly; this would destroy any chance of privacy these refugees from age have, and they have to flee from unwanted exposure. In the telling, Haddix also offers her own view of what the future will be like, with toothpaste so perfect that dentists are no longer necessary, cars that drive themselves, and a society so smitten with news that individual privacy is a thing of the past.

"The story is irresistible," noted an interviewer for the *Akron Beacon Journal,* and "good reading for adults too." Haddix told this writer that she thought she would have trouble picturing the future. "But then I decided to

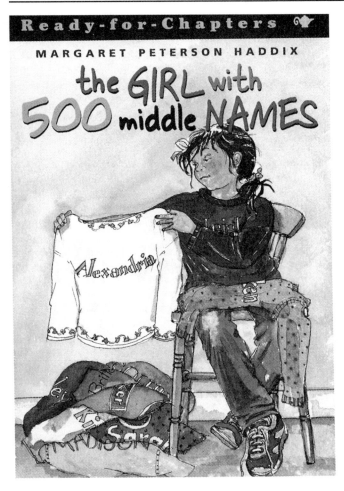

Janie Sams finds herself in a new school where everyone else lives in a bigger house and wears trendier clothes than she does. (Cover illustration by Jacqui Thomas.)

have some fun with it and not be so concerned. I extrapolated from trends I see in society today and pushed them farther." A contributor for *Publishers Weekly* called *Turnabout* a "thought-provoking science fiction adventure," and further noted that Haddix "keeps the pacing smooth and builds up to a surprising face-off." Debbie Carton, reviewing the novel in *Booklist,* felt that the need for love and protection "is poignantly conveyed, as is the isolation of the elderly in society." Carton also thought that the book "will provoke lively discussion in middle-school book clubs." *School Library Journal* contributor Beth Wright commented that the futuristic setting "is scarily believable," and that the theme of the book would spark "thoughtful discussion about human life and human potential."

Haddix continues to have many works in progress, from sequels to her own works to shorter novels for young readers. Her background in journalism and novels is apparent in her meticulous and informed writing, and her appreciation for and belief in the written word. Yet she is not draconian about forcing children to read, remaining doubtful about the effects of programs that push

reading. "Like the library programs where you read so many minutes and win a prize at the end of the summer," Haddix commented in her interview for the *Akron Beacon Journal.* "I like seeing the emphasis on reading, but I'm almost afraid the more we push it, the more [young readers] will think of it like broccoli or spinach, that it doesn't taste good or isn't fun. I'd like to see them pick up a book and read it and not think 'I've read for 15 minutes.' The more they read and begin to enjoy it, the more likely they are to continue."

Biographical and Critical Sources

PERIODICALS

Akron Beacon Journal, October 12, 2000, p. C3; November 2, 2000, "'Turnabout' Author at Hudson Store" (interview), p. E10.

Booklist, October 1, 1995, Mary Harris Veeder, review of *Running out of Time,* p. 314; October 15, 1996, Jean Franklin, review of *Don't You Dare Read This, Mrs. Dunphrey,* p. 413; December 15, 1997, Ilene Cooper, review of *Leaving Fishers,* p. 691; September 1, 1999, Shelle Rosenfeld, review of *Just Ella,* p. 123; October 15, 2000, Debbie Carton, review of *Turnabout,* p. 431.

Bulletin of the Center for Children's Books, November, 1995, Roger Sutton, review of *Running out of Time,* p. 91; January, 1997, p. 172; November, 1999, pp. 93-94.

Detroit Free Press, October 20, 2000, p. D8.

Horn Book Guide, spring, 1996, p. 62; spring, 1997, p. 79.

Kirkus Reviews, October 1, 1997, review of *Leaving Fishers,* p. 1532; July 15, 1998, p. 1035.

Publishers Weekly, August 12, 1996, review of *Don't You Dare Read This, Mrs. Dunphrey,* p. 85; November 24, 1997, review of *Leaving Fishers,* p. 75; August 31, 1998, review of *Among the Hidden,* p. 76; January 11, 1999, p. 26; May 24, 1999, p. 81; October 11, 1999, review of *Just Ella,* p. 77; February 7, 2000, p. 87; October 16, 2000, review of *Turnabout,* p. 77.

Rocky Mountain News, September 5, 1999, Natalie Soto, review of *Just Ella,* p. E4.

School Library Journal, October, 1995, Lisa Dennis, review of *Running out of Time,* p. 133; October, 1996, Carol Schene, review of *Don't You Dare Read This, Mrs. Dunphrey,* p. 147; October, 1997, p. 132; September, 1998, Susan L. Rogers, review of *Among the Hidden,* p. 203; September, 1999, Connie Tyrrell Burns, review of *Just Ella,* p. 225; September, 2000, Beth Wright, review of *Turnabout,* p. 230; August, 2001, B. Allison Gray, review of *Takeoffs and Landings,* pp. 182-183.

Times Educational Supplement, May 19, 2000, p. FR123.

Voice of Youth Advocates, December, 1995, Ann Welton, review of *Running out of Time,* p. 302; Jamie S. Hansen, review of *Don't You Dare Read This, Mrs. Dunphrey,* p. 270; February, 1998, Beverly Youree, review of *Leaving Fishers,* p. 386; October, 1998, Debbie Earl, review of *Among the Hidden,* p. 283; December, 1999, Cynthia Grady, review of *Just Ella,* p. 346; August, 2001, Brenda Moses-Allen, review of *Among the Imposters,* p. 213.

—Sketch by J. Sydney Jones

HALPERIN, Wendy Anderson 1952-

Personal

Born April 10, 1952, in Joliet, IL; daughter of John B. (a lawyer) and Marion S. (an artist) Anderson; children: Kale, Joel, Lane. *Education:* Attended Syracuse University, 1971-72, Pratt Institute, 1973-74, California College of Arts and Crafts, 1979-80, and the American Academy (Chicago, IL), 1982-83; received private instruction from David Hardy, 1979-81.

Addresses

Home and office—76990 14th Ave., South Haven, MI 49090.

Career

Leo Burnett (ad agency), Chicago, IL, art director, 1973-74; Benton & Bowles (ad agency), New York, NY, art director, 1975-77; freelance art director, New York, NY, 1977-79; freelance fine art painter, 1980-90. Art workshop teacher for various elementary school programs and at a local art center. *Exhibitions:* Work exhibited at various galleries, including the Art Institute of Chicago Sales and Rental Gallery, 1982 and 1985; Kalamazoo Institute of the Arts, Kalamazoo, MI, 1988; Works Gallery, New York, NY, 1993; and Elizabeth Stone Gallery, Birmingham, MI, 1997-2001.

Awards, Honors

Honorable mention, Palette & Chisel Award, 1985; Best of Show Award, South Haven Center for the Arts, 1990; *New York Times* Notable Book, American Booksellers Association/Bank Street College Children's Book of the Year, *Boston Globe* Book of the Year, and *Parents Magazine* Pick of the List selection, all for *The Lampfish of Twill;* American Library Association Notable Children's Book selection, New York Public Library's Best Children's Books selection, 1993, Marion Vannett Ridgway Memorial Award honor book, 1993, and National Council of Teachers of English Notable Children's Books in the Language Arts selection, 1994, all for *Hunting the White Cow;* Notable Social Studies Trade Books for Young People, National Council for the Social Studies/Children's Book Council, 1999, for *Once upon a Company.*

Writings

ILLUSTRATOR

Janet Taylor Lisle, *The Lampfish of Twill,* Orchard Books (New York, NY), 1991.

Tres Seymour, *Hunting the White Cow,* Orchard Books (New York, NY), 1993.

Anne Shelby, *Homeplace,* Orchard Books (New York, NY), 1995.

Sarah Orne Jewett, *A White Heron,* Candlewick Press (Cambridge, MA), 1997.

Jim Aylesworth, *The Full Belly Bowl,* Atheneum (New York, NY), 1998.

Kathryn Lasky, *Sophie and Rose,* Candlewick Press (Cambridge, MA), 1998.

Polly Horvath, *The Trolls,* Farrar, Straus (New York, NY), 1999.

Marsha Wilson Chall, *Bonaparte,* Dorling Kindersley (New York, NY), 2000.

Cynthia Rylant, *Let's Go Home: Some Wonderful Things about a House,* Simon & Schuster (New York, NY), 2000.

Elizabeth Spurr (adaptor) *The Peterkin's Christmas* (adapted from one episode of Lucretia P. Hale's *Peterkin Papers*), Atheneum (New York, NY), 2002.

SELF-ILLUSTRATED

(Reteller) *When Chickens Grow Teeth: A Story from the French of Guy de Maupassant,* Orchard Books (New York, NY), 1996.

Once upon a Company, Orchard Books (New York, NY), 1998.

Love Is, Simon & Schuster (New York, NY), 2000.

Wendy Anderson Halperin adds depth to Janet Taylor Lisle's **The Lampfish of Twill** *with her intricately wrought illustrations.*

*ILLUSTRATOR; "COBBLE STREET COUSINS" SERIES;
WRITTEN BY CYNTHIA RYLANT*

In Aunt Lucy's Kitchen, Simon & Schuster (New York, NY), 1998.
A Little Shopping, Simon & Schuster (New York, NY), 1998.
Special Gifts, Simon & Schuster (New York, NY), 1999.
Some Good News, Simon & Schuster (New York, NY), 1999.
Summer Party, Simon & Schuster (New York, NY), 2001.
Wedding Flowers, Simon & Schuster (New York, NY), 2002.

Sidelights

Children's author and illustrator Wendy Anderson Halperin has earned a reputation among critics for her detailed and expressive pencil and watercolor paintings. Throughout her career, she has not only illustrated for award-winning writers, including Cynthia Rylant, Janet Taylor Lisle, and Kathryn Lasky, but has also created and adapted stories of her own, including a 1996 version of a Guy de Maupassant story in *When Chickens Grow Teeth.* Set in a small French village, a jovial café owner finds himself confined to his bed for several weeks after falling from a ladder. Unfortunately, Antoine's prescribed convalescence is anything but restful, for his ill-tempered wife, Madame Colette, sees his elbows as potential incubators for her beloved chickens' eggs. Despite initial protests, Antoine keeps the eggs under his arms for twenty-one days, eventually feeling like a proud father when his new brood emerge from their shells. Writing in the *New York Times Book Review,* Scott Veale observed that "the paintings' rich detail rewards repeated readings, as does the lively, nuanced text, which feels more reimagined than translated." "Halperin," according to a *Kirkus Reviews* critic, "draws readers in with highly detailed, multiple paneled drawings of the French countryside."

For her 1998 work *Once upon a Company,* Halperin follows the story of her own three children's efforts at raising money to pay for their future college education. Told from the viewpoint of her son, Joel, the book details how the trio set about organizing a company, first selling Christmas wreaths before moving on to a summer snack stand. Along the way, readers learn about many of the aspects of running a business, including investing, selling, and marketing. In a starred *Booklist* review, GraceAnne A. DeCandido called the book "an absolutely winning, and not easily classifiable, picture book." Describing *Once upon a Company* as a "warm and lively introduction to the world of business," a *Publishers Weekly* contributor predicted that "this down-to-earth success story could inspire a whole generation of young entrepreneurs."

Using the popular Bible verse I Corinthians 13:4-8, Halperin illustrates the many different ways love can be expressed in *Love Is.* For example, on one side of the double spread illustration, Halperin depicts an individual behaving selfishly, while on the opposite page the same person acts out the scene in a more loving manner,

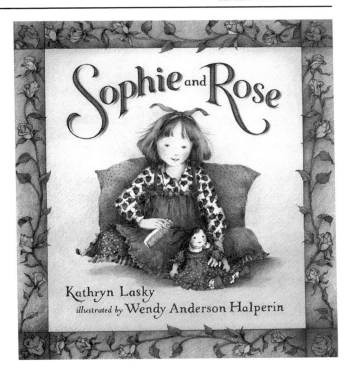

Halperin illustrated this work about a young girl's affection for a hand-me-down doll named Rose.

reflecting the text running along the bottom. Noting that the book is "by no means limited to religious education," *School Library Journal* critic Patricia Pearl Dole observed that Halperin's "precepts are universally valid." Writing in *Booklist,* Shelley Townsend-Hudson called *Love Is* "a fresh, splendid picture book," praising Halperin's "delightful, elaborately detailed, contrasting illustrations."

Halperin is also noted for her work with other children's authors. In 1998, she set to pictures Kathryn Lasky's words for *Sophie and Rose,* "a book that any doll lover will want to look at over and over," predicted Ilene Cooper in a *Booklist* review. When Sophie finds an old doll once belonging to her mother and grandmother, she immediately falls in love with her new playmate she names Rose. Despite the wear and tear Rose suffers, Sophie finds herself more and more attached to the tattered doll. While commenting on the absence of a strong storyline, *School Library Journal* critic Judith Gloyer maintained that "the book is more a reflection of a loving relationship heightened by artwork that visually reinforces the pair's closeness."

Two other books illustrated by Halperin also received high praise from critics, *The Full Belly Bowl* and *Bonaparte.* In Jim Aylesworth's *The Full Belly Bowl,* a poor and often hungry old man saves a "wee small man" from the jaws of a fox. In return, the small man presents the old man with a bowl that will multiply its contents. Quickly, the old man must learn to treat the full belly bowl wisely, carefully following the small man's warnings to always store it upside down. "From the dainty pictures on the endpapers ... to the equally charming artwork inside, this book is a feast for the eyes," claimed Stephanie Zvirin in a *Booklist* review.

Written by Marsha Wilson Chall, *Bonaparte* reveals the story of a faithful dog of the same name who will attempt anything to stay with his owner, Jean Claude, a young boy who attends a school off-limits to canines. Dressing-up as the boy's mother, a new student, a member of the school band, a cafeteria worker, and a custodian, the dog tirelessly tries to break school rules to be with his master. "The real winner is Bonaparte himself; however garbed, whatever *chapeau,* Bonaparte *est charmant,*" claimed a *Horn Book* critic. *Booklist* reviewer Lauren Peterson found "Halperin's highly detailed, realistic watercolor-and-pencil illustrations ... wonderfully expressive and humorous."

In 1998 Halperin teamed up with Cynthia Rylant to illustrate that author's "Cobble Street Cousins" series. Featuring nine-year-old cousins Lily, Rosie, and Tess, the series recounts the exploits of the threesome as they live with their Aunt Lucy while their respective parents, all ballet dancers, spend a year on tour. Designed for new readers ready to make the transition to chapter books, the titles feature pencil-and-watercolor illustrations throughout the text. Reviewing *Some Good News* and *Special Gifts,* Sarah O'Neal wrote in *School Library Journal* that Halperin's "artwork ... reveals the unique personalities of the girls and creates a wonderfully serene setting." "Halperin's generous sprinkling of pencil-and-watercolor illustrations throughout capture a warm family dynamic and provide energetic expressions for a family cast," remarked a *Publishers Weekly* critic in a review of *In Aunt Lucy's Kitchen* and *A Little Shopping.*

Halperin once told *SATA,* "I love Lake Michigan and its ever-changing environment. I enjoy children and get very excited by their drawings and paintings. My parents live next door and we (my family) all enjoy each other. We have lots of animals around. I especially like raising chickens. I enjoy solitude. I enjoy listening to the radio and books on tape."

Biographical and Critical Sources

BOOKS

Jim Aylesworth, *The Full Belly Bowl,* Atheneum (New York, NY), 1998.

PERIODICALS

Booklist, September 1, 1993; September 1, 1998, Grace-Anne A. DeCandido, review of *Once upon a Company,* p. 112; September 15, 1998, Ilene Cooper, review of *Sophie and Rose,* p. 238; November 1, 1999, Stephanie Zvirin, review of *The Full Belly Bowl,* p. 524; October 15, 2000, Lauren Peterson, review of *Bonaparte,* p. 444; January 1 & 15, 2001, Shelley Townsend-Hudson, review of *Love Is,* p. 950.

Bulletin of the Center for Children's Books, October, 1993.

She was chasing around in a frenzy, doing her best, but not knowing which mouse to go after first.
Thinking fast, the very old man picked her up, gently folded her legs, and set her down in the Full Belly Bowl.

As soon as he took his hands away, Angelina jumped out again. And just that fast, she was replaced by another cat that looked exactly like her. That cat jumped out to be replaced by a third, and so on until the house was wild with black-and-white cats chasing hundreds of mice.

Jim Aylesworth's **The Full Belly Bowl,** *about a kindly old man who receives a magical gift, features Halperin's detailed illustrations.*

In Aunt Lucy's Kitchen, *a work by Cynthia Rylant, three lively nine-year-olds attempt to make money by having a cookie sale. (Illustration by Halperin.)*

Horn Book, November-December, 1993; September, 2000, review of *Bonaparte,* p. 548.
Kirkus Reviews, August 15, 1993; July 15, 1996, review of *When Chickens Grow Teeth,* p. 1048.
New York Times Book Review, November 14, 1993; March 2, 1997, Scott Veale, review of *When Chickens Grow Teeth,* p. 25.
Publishers Weekly, August 10, 1998, review of *Once upon a Company,* p. 388; August 24, 1998, review of *Sophie and Rose,* p. 56; October 19, 1998, review of *In Aunt Lucy's Kitchen* and *A Little Shopping,* p. 81.
School Library Journal, January, 1994; January, 1999, Judith Gloyer, review of *Sophie and Rose,* p. 97; February, 1999, Pam Hopper Webb, review of *A Little Shopping* and *In Aunt Lucy's Kitchen,* p. 88; April, 1999, Christy Norris Blanchette, review of *The Trolls,* pp. 97-98; June, 1999, Sarah O'Neal, review of *Some Good News* and *Special Gifts,* pp. 106-107; October, 1999, Rosalyn Pierini, review of *The Full Belly Bowl,* p. 102; February, 2001, Patricia Pearl Dole, review of *Love Is,* p. 111.

ON-LINE

Wendy Anderson Halperin Web site, http://www.wendyhalperin.com/ (June 30, 2001).

*   *   *

HARPER, Ellen
See NOBLE, Marty

*   *   *

HEISEL, Sharon E(laine) 1941-

Personal

Born September 20, 1941, in Tower, MN; daughter of Douglas Eugene (a mechanic) and Florence Celina (a homemaker; maiden name, Hall) Johnson; married Manville Marion Heisel (an attorney), May 31, 1974. *Education:* Attended Southern Oregon State College and Reed College; George Washington University, B.S.; Portland State University, M.S., 1975. *Hobbies and other interests:* Transformation of wood, fiber, and clay into objects of functional and aesthetic value.

Addresses

Home—3775 Roads End Blvd., Central Point, OR 97502. *E-mail*—shesel@cdsnet.net. *Agent*—Jean V. Naggar Literary Agency, 216 East 75th St., New York, NY 10021.

Career

Sacred Heart Junior High School, Medford, OR, science teacher, 1978-87; Providence Hospital, Medford, OR, health educator, 1988-93; middle school science teacher, 1998—. Also active in children's advocacy and literacy (Laubach teacher). *Member:* PEN, Society of Children's Book Writers and Illustrators, Mensa.

Awards, Honors

Western Heritage Wrangler Award, 2000, and Notable Book for a Global Society selection, International Reading Association, 2001, both for *Precious Gold, Precious Jade.*

Writings

A Little Magic, Houghton (Boston, MA), 1991.
Wrapped in a Riddle, Houghton (Boston, MA), 1993.
Eyes of a Stranger, Delacorte (New York, NY), 1996.
Precious Gold, Precious Jade, Holiday House (New York, NY), 2000.

Sidelights

When Sharon E. Heisel went back to college at the age of twenty-six, she explained to SATA, "I decided to study something about which I was truly ignorant. I majored in biology. A new and wonder-filled world opened to me." After earning a master's degree in invertebrate zoology, Heisel "formed a personal mission. I would reveal the unexpectedly beautiful world of science to young people in order to enrich their lives. Writing was the vehicle for that mission. Being childless, I quickly encountered my own ignorance about the language and customs of American youth. That led me to become a junior high science teacher." Heisel continued writing as she taught, and in the early 1990s she began accomplishing her mission with the publication of two mysteries for young adults that feature "many concepts from history and science," *A Little Magic* and *Wrapped in a Riddle.*

Heisel explained to *SATA* that a "second constant in my books is the essential goodness of ordinary people. This comes directly from my experience as a teacher. My books may have evil or misguided characters since those people are common in the world and they add the element of tension which is essential in a story, but most of the characters are simple, decent human beings, doing the best they can every day."

"The theme of *A Little Magic* is a concept from the philosophy of science: our first step in explaining the universe is the creation of myth and magic," Heisel related to *SATA*. "Eventually, the rational processes develop, but both views are part of a single continuum." *A Little Magic* begins when Jessica and her cousin Corky begin to worry about the strange figures and noises they notice in the forest. While Corky, whose father has just died, is sure that the activity is supernatural, Jessica is skeptical, but she is too busy with a science project and preoccupied with her social life to worry about it. When one of Jessica's guests disappears from her carefully planned thirteenth birthday party, however, she and Corky are forced to confront their fears in order to find the girl. According to Patricia Gosda in *Voice of Youth Advocates, A Little Magic* is "an engaging and well-paced mystery." Tatiana Castleton stated in *School Library Journal* that Heisel "strikes a good balance between Jessica's concerns with school, friends, and a first romance" and solving the mystery.

Like *A Little Magic, Wrapped in a Riddle* also includes facts about science and history. In this book, Jessica and other characters from *A Little Magic* join eleven-year-old Miranda as she investigates some strange happenings at her grandmother's Jumping Frog Inn. Although her grandmother, GrandAnn, is not very concerned when the housekeeper is hit on the head or when things disappear from the fruit shed, she is upset when she finds that someone has stolen a packet of letters that Mark Twain wrote to her great-grandmother. Miranda begins to watch the inn's boarders for clues and is ultimately trapped by a criminal in an underground gold mine adjoining the fruit shed. Miranda not only solves the mystery and escapes but, as Kathryn Jennings noted in the *Bulletin of the Center for Children's Books,* she "turns out to be a real hero in the tradition of Nancy Drew." Heisel told *SATA* that she included "a lot of information about the writings of Mark Twain" in

Sharon E. Heisel

Wrapped in a Riddle, and that "riddles and puns permeate the book."

Eyes of a Stranger is another mystery-thriller by Heisel, a story about a lonely teenage girl who works at the ticket booth of her uncle's carousel. Merissa, the protagonist, is a shy girl who has a limp; she blossoms when she is behind the ticket counter at the booth, though, because no one can see her legs. She watches with envy as a handsome young stranger comes to ride the carousel accompanied by a pretty blond girl. The young man returns over the course of several days, each time with a different young, teenage girl, and each time Merissa watches him, she is increasingly attracted to him. However, she learns via the newspaper about several young teenage girls who have been found murdered. As the book reaches its climax, Merissa realizes that the handsome young stranger she had developed a crush on is the culprit. Accompanied by "sinister cover art and full characterizations," this book makes fascinating reading, according to Debbie Earl in *Voice of Youth Advocates.* Writing for *Booklist,* Hazel Rochman lauded Heisel's ability to build up tension in the story, calling the book a "memorable" read.

In her next book, *Precious Gold, Precious Jade,* Heisel tackles issues of economic hardship and race relations in the United States during the gold rush. Set in southern Oregon, the narrative tells the story of Angelina and Evangeline, two sisters who befriend the first Chinese student to attend their school. Other students in the class, however, are hostile towards the Chinese student, reflecting the attitudes of several townspeople. Barbara Chatton noted in the *School Library Journal* that via the story of the young girls, Heisel is able to impart detailed and realistic descriptions of the era, including social and technological information.

While Heisel continues to further her goal of educating and entertaining young adult readers, she told *SATA* that "writing is the hardest work I have ever done. I write five days a week, usually from six o'clock in the morning until two in the afternoon. Each book develops differently, but always the fun comes when the story starts to flow. The writing reaches a point where it is like a whirlpool. It sucks you in and drags you along and, although you may struggle so that the perturbations show in the water, the overall effect is a kind of inevitable drowning. Apparent inevitability is my goal in writing fiction. Like anything that seems effortless, it requires hard work."

In Heisel's 1993 mystery, Miranda finds that living with her grandmother at a quiet inn is not as dull as she expected, especially when the search for a bundle of her grandmother's valuable letters draws a host of suspicious characters. (Cover illustration by Pat Grant Porter.)

Biographical and Critical Sources

PERIODICALS

Booklist, May 15, 1991, p. 1798; October 1, 1993, p. 344; June 1, 1996, Hazel Rochman, review of *Eyes of a Stranger,* p. 1698.
Bulletin of the Center for Children's Books, November, 1993, Kathryn Jennings, review of *Wrapped in a Riddle,* p. 84; June, 1996, Lisa Mahoney, review of *Eyes of a Stranger,* pp. 337-338.
Horn Book Guide, spring, 1994, p. 77.
Kirkus Reviews, September 15, 1993, review of *Wrapped in a Riddle,* p. 1202.
School Library Journal, April, 1991, Tatiana Castleton, review of *A Little Magic,* p. 119; February, 1994, p. 102; April, 2000, Barbara Chatton, review of *Precious Gold, Precious Jade,* p. 136.
Voice of Youth Advocates, June, 1991, Patricia Gosda, review of *A Little Magic,* pp. 96-97; August, 1996, Debbie Earl, review of *Eyes of a Stranger,* p. 156.

*   *   *

HIGGINS, Joanna 1945-

Personal

Born February 20, 1945, in Alpena, MI; daughter of Frank (a railroad worker) and Clara Jill (a homemaker and clerk) Wojewski; married Gerald Higgins (a stockbroker), December 20, 1969; children: Kaili. *Education:* Aquinas College, B.A., 1967; University of Michigan, M.A., 1968; State University of New York at Binghamton, Ph.D., 1977. *Politics:* Democrat. *Religion:* "Catholic, with Zen Buddhist overtones." *Hobbies and other interests:* Piano, gardening.

Addresses

Office—R.R.1, Box 1544, Bowbridge Rd., Little Meadows, PA 18830; 21 Gardner Rd., Vestal, NY 13850.

Career

Grand Rapids Junior College, Grand Rapids, MI, instructor in English, 1968-69; University of Maryland Overseas Program, England, instructor in English, 1970-71; Keystone Junior College, La Plume, PA, instructor in English, 1974-77; Hilo College (now University of Hawaii-Hilo), Hilo, HI, assistant professor of English, 1977-78; University of Hawaii, West Oahu College, Pearl City, HI, assistant professor of English, 1978-79; State University of New York-Binghamton, Binghamton, NY, adjunct member of creative writing faculty, 1982; writer, 1982—.

Awards, Honors

Fellow of Pennsylvania Council on the Arts, 1983, and National Endowment for the Arts, 1989; Syndicated Fiction Award, International PEN, 1983.

Writings

The Magic Crystal (for children), Bell Offset, 1987.
Quest for the Golden Flower (for children), Bell Offset, 1988.
In the Treasure House of the Ten Masters (for children), Bell Offset, 1990.
The Importance of High Places (stories and a novella), Milkweed Editions (Minneapolis, MN), 1993.
A Soldier's Book (novel), Permanent Press (Sag Harbor, NY).

Author of the plays *Grant*, 1983, and *Dreamers*, 1985. Work represented in anthologies, including *The Best American Short Stories 1982*, edited by John Gardner and Shannon Ravenel, Houghton (Boston, MA), 1982; *The Best American Short Stories 1983*, edited by Anne Tyler and Shannon Ravenel, Houghton, 1983; and *Passages North Anthology*, edited by Elinor Benedict, Milkweed Editions, 1990. Contributor of stories and articles to periodicals, including *American Fiction, Prairie Schooner, Passages North, MSS, Indiana Review,* and *Writer.*

Sidelights

Joanna Higgins is the author of several children's books as well as short stories and novels for adults. Higgins once commented: "The worthy Irish name Higgins, taken in marriage, masks my background as a fourth-generation Polish-American. When I was growing up in the small town of Alpena, Michigan, Polish was the primary language in our house until my maternal grandmother died in 1947, when I was two years old. Then it became the language of choice when family and friends came to visit my grandfather, with whom we lived. At church on Sundays, our priest read the Gospel in Polish and English, and gave the sermon in both languages as well. This was well before the self-conscious efforts, two or so decades later, to return to one's roots.

"So in my early life there was Polish—and Latin, too, a mysterious language that, like Polish, seemed to extend life in invisible, though tangibly real, dimensions that flowed backward to ancient times and simultaneously upward to the 'holy.' English was for the everyday world of school and play, but somewhere in there, I got hooked on English words, the words in books. When I found out about library books, I'd walk the two miles or so to the elegant, wood-paneled library at the public high school. It was like being in church, almost—the high ceilings and art deco lamps and dark wood everywhere, the church vestibule-smell of wood and wax. There I discovered Jack London and John Steinbeck, Anton Chekhov and Maxim Gorky, and I was a goner.

"In those days creative writing wasn't given much academic attention at my liberal arts college, though the chairman of the English department did offer a creative writing course, which I took. That's when I wrote my first story, about a young boy and a wild duck that gets shot. Heavily naturalistic and broody, and also heavily edited by my teacher, the story won an honorable mention in an *Atlantic Monthly* contest for college students. Critiques from five judges came back with it, and at least one of the readers had some sharp things to say about stereotyping. It was a new word for me, yet this was a victory nonetheless, and it whetted my appetite. I didn't take a single writing course in graduate school, however. I was on a fellowship and worried about the demanding course work. Writing seemed too extra-curricular, too off-the-track.

"Much later, years later, I was teaching a literature course in the short story at Hilo College in Hawaii when the urge to write came back. The moment was exhilarating and scary. You get idiotic for quite a while when that happens, and maybe it's a good thing. I was able to write all the awful stuff that has to get written before a sentence appears that's finally worth something.

"A few months later, I learned that John Gardner, the writer, critic, and medieval scholar, was teaching writing at the State University of New York at Binghamton, where I'd done my doctoral work. My husband and I had been renting out our hillside farmhouse near there and were lonesome for those windy hills, the woods, the 'seasons.' I gave up a tenure-track teaching position, and we came back to start over again. When I overcame my fears enough to send a story to John Gardner and to ask to sit in on one of his fiction workshops, he—unfailingly, unstintingly generous with all young writers—consented. I studied informally with him for the next three years, eventually helping with the literary magazine, *MSS,* he'd started up again. John Gardner died in a motorcycle accident on September 14, 1982, on a warm, brilliant fall afternoon. The horror of that day nearly broke us—his students and friends. The only thing that helped at all, then, was knowing that we had to keep writing, to prove that his faith in us had not been misplaced.

"Now I'm on my own, writing and hiking these hills known locally as "The Endless Mountains," part of the great Appalachian chain, and sometimes teaching little kids in the schools about writing; or rather, they teach me. When I'm not teaching, I try to write every day. And as for my Irish name, it's okay. It stays. The Irish are great storytellers too, after all, and why not tap into whatever magic the world chooses to offer us? For the journey."

Higgins published three children's tales in the late 1980s: *The Magic Crystal, Quest for the Golden Flower,* and *In the Treasure House of the Ten Masters.* Then, in 1993, she brought out her first adult collection, four short stories and a novella, *The Importance of High Places,* published by Milkweed Editions. In one of the stories a man buys a dilapidated dinosaur theme park and attempts, unsuccessfully, to breathe new life into it. Another story tells of an elderly gentleman who courts a Polish widow by bringing his curtains to her for laundering. Yet another tale recounts the misadventures of a quarry worker who also sings opera. Deserted by his wife, he cares for his elderly aunt. In the novella,

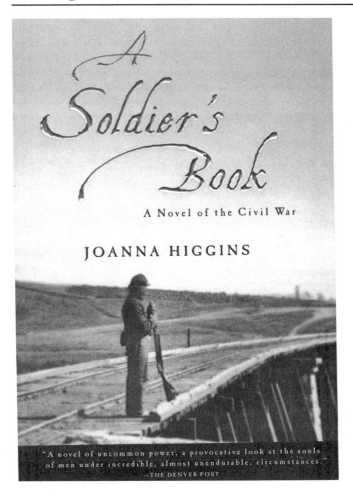

The terrifying realities of war are brought to life in Higgins's novel about a captured Union soldier held at the notorious Andersonville prison during the U.S. Civil War. (Photo courtesy of the Library of Congress.)

Higgins tells of a priest who lives in Hawaii. A contributor for *Publishers Weekly* found the short stories in the collection to be a "delight," while the novella "disappoints." The reviewer went on to explain: "While a certain deftly handed opaqueness adds layers to the stories, the same quality obfuscates the meaning of the novel." However, the same reviewer concluded that Higgins displayed "delicate prose" in the tales.

"The writing process is difficult if not impossible to describe," Higgins commented, "and maybe one shouldn't even attempt to do so, but here I am, giving it a try. The impulse to write a particular piece seems to come out of nowhere. It's as if something needs to be born and is latching onto whatever available matter happens to be nearby. A thought can generate the impulse, or a feeling, or something read, or an image, sometimes a person, a comment, a memory, a newspaper story, a dream, and of course raw experience itself. There's a necessary gestation period, then the writing—more like groping, for me, pure trial and error—then the rewriting, or—better word, 'unwriting,' where I work at getting rid of all the junk I've written in my haste,

sometimes, to create a form that might do justice to the impulse, the flash, the whatever-thing that happens at the onset.

"Obsession helps, which was the case for me with *A Soldier's Book,* an historical novel set during the Civil War and revised over an eight- or ten-year period. It's a matter of having faith—blind, mad faith—that something greater than the sum of your parts as a writer will eventually take over and fly you there."

Higgins's "obsession" paid off, according to critics, in *A Soldier's Book.* Her first published novel won critical praise, reprint publication by a major house, and a readership which spanned from young adults to adults. *A Soldier's Book* tells of the incarceration of a Union soldier, young Ira Cahill Stevens, an apothecary's apprentice, captured along with hundreds of others at the 1864 Battle of the Wilderness. Transferred to the infamous Confederate prison at Andersonville, Georgia, and from there to another prison at Florence, South Carolina, Stevens keeps a journal of the vicissitudes of incarceration, including continual hunger, disease, and pillaging by other prisoners. The friendship of a group of fellow prisoners keeps Stevens going, despite the death and deprivation all around. A reviewer for *Publishers Weekly* called this novel a "wrenching fictional diary" rendered in "tightly packed prose with expertly rendered bits of dialogue" which "brings to vivid life one of the most atrocious episodes in the history of warfare." "One of the many strengths of the novel is that Ira's experiences are typical of any prisoner of war," wrote Nancy Pearl in a *Booklist* review. Compared favorably with the 1955 Pulitzer Prize winning *Andersonville* by MacKinlay Kantor, and with Charles Frazier's *Cold Mountain,* Higgins's *A Soldier's Book* is a "remarkable debut novel, laced with historical detail," according to Jill Smolowe writing in *People Weekly.* Smolowe concluded, "Though Higgins's taut prose is unsparing in its cruel detail, she ultimately delivers a message of hope."

Biographical and Critical Sources

PERIODICALS

Booklist, March 15, 1993, p. 1297; June 1, 1998, Nancy Pearl, review of *A Soldier's Book,* p. 1725.
Library Journal, March 1, 1984, p. 468; February 1, 1993, p. 115; March 15, 1999, p. 52.
People Weekly, August 31, 1998, Jill Smolowe, review of *A Soldier's Book,* p. 40.
Publishers Weekly, January 25, 1993, review of *The Importance of High Places,* p. 82; May 18, 1998, review of *A Soldier's Book,* p. 66.*

*   *   *

HILL, Alexis
See GLICK, Ruth (Burtnick)

HOPKINS, Lee Bennett 1938-

Personal

Born April 13, 1938, in Scranton, PA; son of Leon Hall Hopkins (a police officer) and Gertrude Thomas. *Education:* Newark State Teachers College (now Kean College; Union, NJ), B.A., 1960; Bank Street College of Education, M.Sc., 1964; Hunter College of the City University of New York, Professional Diploma in Educational Supervision and Administration, 1967.

Addresses

Home—307 Kemeys Cove, Briarcliff Manor, NY 10510.

Career

Public school teacher in Fair Lawn, NJ, 1960-66; Bank Street College of Education, New York, NY, senior consultant, 1966-68; Scholastic Magazines, Inc., New York, NY, curriculum and editorial specialist, 1968-74; full-time writer, 1976—. Lecturer on children's literature; host and consultant to children's television series "Zebra Wings," Agency for Instructional Television, beginning 1976. Consultant to school systems on elementary curriculum; literature consultant with various publishers. National trustee, National Center for Children's Illustrated Literature, 1991—. *Member:* International Reading Association, American Library Association, National Council of Teachers of English (member

Lee Bennett Hopkins

of board of directors, 1975-78; chair of 1978 and 1991 Poetry Award Committees; member of Commission on Literature, 1983-85; member of Children's Literature Assembly, 1985-88; honorary board member of Children's Literature Council of Pennsylvania, 1990—).

Awards, Honors

Don't You Turn Back: Poems by Langston Hughes, Rainbows Are Made, Surprises, and *A Song in Stone* were chosen as American Library Association notable books; Outstanding Alumnus in the Arts award, Kean College, 1972; Notable Book selection, National Council for the Social Studies, for *Mama; To Look at Any Thing* was chosen as choice book of the 1978 International Youth Library exhibition, Munich, Germany; Children's Choice Award, International Reading Association/Children's Book Council, 1980, for *Wonder Wheels;* honorary doctor of laws, Kean College, 1980; Phi Delta Kappa Educational Leadership Award, 1980; International Reading Association Broadcast Media Award for Radio, 1982; Ambassador Extraordinary in the Order of the Long Leaf Pine, presented by Governor James B. Hunt of North Carolina, 1982; International Reading Association Manhattan Council Literacy Award, 1983; National Children's Book Week Poet, 1985; Pick-of-the-List selection, American Booksellers Association (ABA), 1988, for *Side by Side: Poems to Read Together,* and 1988, *Voyages: Poems by Walt Whitman;* University of Southern Mississippi Medallion; Pennsylvania Author of the Year award, 1989; ABA Choice Award, 1991, for *Good Books, Good Times!;* recipient of Child Study Committee Children's Books of the Year award, for *Ring Out, Wild Bells: Poems of Holidays and Seasons* and for *Questions: An I Can Read Book,* both 1992; Pick of the List selection, ABA, and winner of Southern California Council of Literature and Young People Excellence in Illustration award, both 1994, both for *Extra Innings: Baseball Poems;* Outstanding Children's Book, Westchester Library System, 1994, for *The Writing Bug: An Autobiography;* New York Public Library Best Children's Books of 1994, "Few Good Books of 1994" selection, *Book Links,* Notable Children's Trade Books in the Field of Social Studies, Children's Book Council/National Council for the Social Studies, and winner of ABC 1995 Choice Award, all for *Hand in Hand: An American History through Poetry;* Best Books of the Year selection, *School Library Journal,* 1995, for *Been to Yesterdays: Poems of a Life;* Pick of the List, ABA, 1995, for *Blast Off: Poems about Space: An I Can Read Book; The Best of Book Bonanza* was an *Instructor* Book-of-the-Month Club selection; *Me!: A Book of Poems* was a Junior Literary Guild selection; *Side by Side: Poems to Read Together* was a Book-of-the-Month Club selection.

Writings

(With Annette F. Shapiro) *Creative Activities for Gifted Children,* Fearon, 1968.
Books Are by People, Citation Press (New York, NY), 1969.

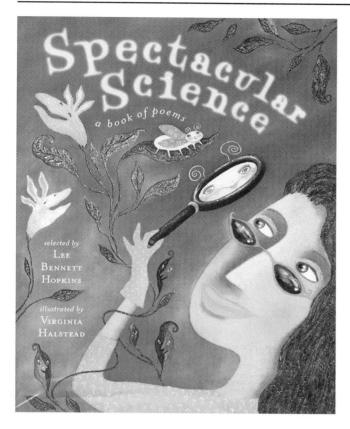

Hopkins's poetry anthology explores the mysteries of biology, chemistry, and physics through the words of such poets as Carl Sandburg, Valerie Worth, and David McCord.

Let Them Be Themselves: Language Arts Enrichment for Disadvantaged Children in Elementary Schools, Citation Press, 1969, second edition published as *Let Them Be Themselves: Language Arts for Children in Elementary Schools,* 1974, third edition, Harper, 1992.

(With Misha Arenstein) *Partners in Learning: A Child-Centered Approach to Teaching the Social Studies,* Citation Press, 1971.

Pass the Poetry, Please!: Bringing Poetry into the Minds and Hearts of Children, Citation Press, 1972, third revised edition, HarperCollins, 1998.

More Books by More People, Citation Press, 1974.

(With Misha Arenstein) *Do You Know What Day Tomorrow Is?: A Teacher's Almanac,* Citation Press, 1975.

The Best of Book Bonanza, Holt (New York, NY), 1980.

The Writing Bug: An Autobiography, Richard C. Owen (Katonah, NY), 1993.

Been to Yesterdays: Poems of a Life, Boyds Mill Press (Honesdale, PA), 1995.

Pauses: Autobiographical Reflections on 101 Creators of Children's Books, HarperCollins (New York, NY), 1995.

YOUNG ADULT NOVELS

Mama, Dell, 1977, reprinted, Boyds Mill Press (Honesdale, PA), 2000.

Wonder Wheels, Dell (New York, NY), 1980.

Mama and Her Boys, Harper, 1981, reprinted, Boyds Mill Press (Honesdale, PA), 2000.

FOR CHILDREN

Important Dates in Afro-American History, F. Watts (New York, NY), 1969.

This Street's for Me (poetry), illustrated by Ann Grifalconi, Crown (New York, NY), 1970.

(With Misha Arenstein) *Faces and Places: Poems for You,* illustrated by Lisl Weil, Scholastic Book Services (New York, NY), 1970.

Happy Birthday to Me!, Scholastic Book Services, 1972.

When I Am All Alone: A Book of Poems, Scholastic Book Services, 1972.

Charlie's World: A Book of Poems, Bobbs-Merrill (New York, NY), 1972.

Kim's Place and Other Poems, Holt, 1974.

I Loved Rose Ann, illustrated by Ingrid Fetz, Knopf (New York, NY), 1976.

A Haunting We Will Go: Ghostly Stories and Poems, illustrated by Vera Rosenberry, Albert Whitman (Chicago, IL), 1976.

Witching Time: Mischievous Stories and Poems, illustrated by Vera Rosenberry, Albert Whitman, 1976.

Kits, Cats, Lions, and Tigers: Stories, Poems, and Verse, illustrated by Vera Rosenberry, Albert Whitman, 1979.

Pups, Dogs, Foxes, and Wolves: Stories, Poems, and Verse, illustrated by Vera Rosenberry, Albert Whitman, 1979.

How Do You Make an Elephant Float and Other Delicious Food Riddles, illustrated by Rosekranz Hoffman, Albert Whitman, 1983.

Animals from Mother Goose, Harcourt, 1989.

People from Mother Goose, illustrated by Kathryn Hewitt, Harcourt, 1989.

Good Rhymes, Good Times!, illustrated by Frane Lessac, HarperCollins, 1995.

Mother Goose and Her Children, illustrated by JoAnn Adinolfi, Emilie Chollat, and Gerardo Suzan, Sadlier-Oxford, 1999.

COMPILER

I Think I Saw a Snail: Young Poems for City Seasons, illustrated by Harold James, Crown, 1969.

Don't You Turn Back: Poems by Langston Hughes, illustrated by Ann Grifalconi, forward by Arna Bontemps, Knopf, 1969.

City Talk, illustrated by Roy Arnella, Knopf, 1970.

The City Spreads Its Wings, illustrated by Moneta Barnett, F. Watts, 1970.

Me!: A Book of Poems, illustrated by Talavaldis Stubis, Seabury (New York, NY), 1970.

Zoo!: A Book of Poems, illustrated by Robert Frankenberg, Crown, 1971.

Girls Can Too!: A Book of Poems, illustrated by Emily McCully, F. Watts, 1972.

(With Misha Arenstein) *Time to Shout: Poems for You,* illustrated by Lisl Weil, Scholastic, 1973.

(With Sunna Rasch) *I Really Want to Feel Good about Myself: Poems by Former Addicts,* Thomas Nelson (Nashville, TN), 1974.

On Our Way: Poems of Pride and Love, illustrated by David Parks, Knopf, 1974.

Hey-How for Halloween, illustrated by Janet McCaffery, Harcourt, 1974.

Take Hold!: An Anthology of Pulitzer Prize Winning Poems, Thomas Nelson, 1974.

Poetry on Wheels, illustrated by Frank Aloise, Garrard, 1974.

Sing Hey for Christmas Day, illustrated by Laura Jean Allen, Harcourt, 1975.

Good Morning to You, Valentine, illustrated by Tomie de Paola, Harcourt, 1976.

Merrily Comes Our Harvest In, illustrated by Ben Shecter, Harcourt, 1976.

(With Misha Arenstein) *Thread One to a Star,* Four Winds (New York, NY), 1976.

(With Misha Arenstein) *Potato Chips and a Slice of Moon: Poems You'll Like,* illustrated by Wayne Blickenstaff, Scholastic, 1976.

Beat the Drum! Independence Day Has Come, illustrated by Tomie de Paola, Harcourt, 1977.

Monsters, Ghoulies, and Creepy Creatures: Fantastic Stories and Poems, illustrated by Vera Rosenberry, Albert Whitman, 1977.

To Look at Any Thing, illustrated by John Earl, Harcourt, 1978.

Easter Buds Are Springing: Poems for Easter, illustrated by Tomie de Paola, Harcourt, 1979.

Merely Players: An Anthology of Life Poems, Thomas Nelson, 1979.

My Mane Catches the Wind: Poems about Horses, illustrated by Sam Savitt, Harcourt, 1979.

By Myself, illustrated by Glo Coalson, Crowell (New York, NY), 1980.

Elves, Fairies and Gnomes, illustrated by Rosekranz Hoffman, Knopf, 1980.

Moments: Poems about the Seasons, illustrated by Michael Hague, Harcourt, 1980.

Morning, Noon, and Nighttime, Too!, illustrated by Nancy Hannans, Harper, 1980.

I Am the Cat, illustrated by Linda Rochester Richards, Harcourt, 1981.

And God Bless Me: Prayers, Lullabies and Dream-Poems, illustrated by Patricia Henderson Lincoln, Knopf, 1982.

Circus! Circus!, illustrated by John O'Brien, Knopf, 1982.

Rainbows Are Made: Poems by Carl Sandburg, illustrated by Fritz Eichenberg, Harcourt, 1982.

A Dog's Life, illustrated by Linda Rochester Richards, Harcourt, 1983.

The Sky Is Full of Song, illustrated by Dirk Zimmer, Harper, 1983.

A Song in Stone: City Poems, illustrated by Anna Held Audette, Crowell, 1983.

Crickets and Bullfrogs and Whispers of Thunder: Poems and Pictures by Harry Behn, Harcourt, 1984.

Love and Kisses (poems), illustrated by Kris Boyd, Houghton (Burlington, MA), 1984.

Surprises: An I Can Read Book of Poems, illustrated by Meagan Lloyd, Harper, 1984.

Creatures, illustrated by Stella Ormai, Harcourt, 1985.

Munching: Poems about Eating, illustrated by Nelle Davis, Little, Brown (Boston, MA), 1985.

Best Friends, illustrated by James Watts, Harper, 1986.

The Sea Is Calling Me, illustrated by Walter Gaffney-Kessel, Harcourt, 1986.

Click, Rumble, Roar: Poems about Machines, illustrated by Anna Held Audette, Crowell, 1987.

Dinosaurs, illustrated by Murray Tinkelman, Harcourt, 1987.

More Surprises: An I Can Read Book, illustrated by Meagan Lloyd, Harper, 1987.

Voyages: Poems by Walt Whitman, illustrated by Charles Mikolaycak, Harcourt, 1988.

Side by Side: Poems to Read Together, illustrated by Hilary Knight, Simon & Schuster, 1988.

Still as a Star: Nighttime Poems, illustrated by Karen Malone, Little, Brown, 1988.

Good Books, Good Times!, Harper, 1990.

On the Farm, illustrated by Laurel Molk, Little, Brown, 1991.

Happy Birthday: Poems, illustrated by Hilary Knight, Simon & Schuster, 1991.

Questions: An I Can Read Book, illustrated by Carolyn Croll, HarperCollins, 1992.

Through Our Eyes: Poems and Pictures about Growing Up, illustrated by Jeffrey Dunn, Little, Brown, 1992.

To the Zoo: Animal Poems, illustrated by John Wallner, Little, Brown, 1992.

Ring Out, Wild Bells: Poems of Holidays and Seasons, illustrated by Karen Baumann, Harcourt, 1992.

Pterodactyls and Pizza: A Trumpet Club Book of Poetry, illustrated by Nadine Bernard Westcott, Trumpet Club, 1992.

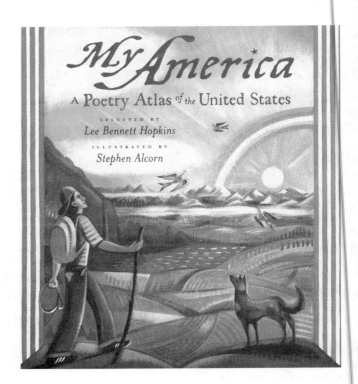

The vastness of the American landscape and the dreams of the American people are among the subjects in Hopkins's anthology that includes selections from Nikki Giovanni, Lilian Moore, and Carl Sandburg.

Flit, Flutter, Fly!: Poems about Bugs and Other Crawly Creatures, illustrated by Peter Palagonia, Doubleday, 1992.

Ragged Shadows: Poems of Halloween Night, illustrated by Giles Laroche, Little, Brown, 1993.

Extra Innings: Baseball Poems, illustrated by Scott Medlock, Harcourt, 1993.

It's about Time: Poems, illustrated by Matt Novak, Simon & Schuster, 1993.

Hand in Hand: An American History through Poetry, illustrated by Peter Fiore, Simon & Schuster, 1994.

April, Bubbles, Chocolate: An ABC of Poetry, illustrated by Barry Root, Simon & Schuster, 1994.

Weather: An I Can Read Book, illustrated by Melanie Hill, HarperCollins, 1994.

Blast Off!: Poems about Space: An I Can Read Book, illustrated by Melissa Sweet, HarperCollins, 1995.

Small Talk: A Book of Short Poems, illustrated by Susan Gaber, Harcourt, 1995.

School Supplies: A Book of Poems, illustrated by Renee Flower, Simon & Schuster, 1996.

Opening Days: Sports Poems, illustrated by Scott Medlock, Harcourt, 1996.

Marvelous Math: A Book of Poems, illustrated by Karen Barbour, Simon & Schuster, 1997.

Song and Dance, illustrated by Cheryl Munro Taylor, Simon & Schuster, 1997.

All God's Children: A Book of Prayers, illustrated by Amanda Schaffer, Harcourt Brace, 1998.

(With Mary Perrotta Rich) *Book Poems: Poems from National Children's Book Week, 1959-1989,* Children's Book Council, 1998.

Climb into My Lap: First Poems to Read Together, illustrated by Kathryn Brown, Simon & Schuster, 1998.

Dino-Roars, illustrated by Cynthia Fisher, Golden Books, 1999.

Lives: Poems about Famous Americans, illustrated by Leslie Staub, HarperCollins, 1999.

Spectacular Science: A Book of Poems, illustrated by Virginia Halstead, Simon & Schuster, 1999.

Sports! Sports! Sports!: An I Can Read Book, illustrated by Brian Floca, HarperCollins, 1999.

My America, illustrated by Stephen Alcorn, Simon & Schuster, 2000.

Yummy!: Eating through a Day, illustrated by Renee Flower, Simon & Schuster, 2000.

Hoofbeats, Claws, and Rippled Fins: Creature Poems, illustrated by Stephen Alcorn, HarperCollins, 2001.

OTHER

Also author of "Poetry Plus" column in *Creative Classroom* magazine.

Sidelights

Lee Bennett Hopkins is "one of America's most prolific anthologists of poetry for young people," according to Anthony L. Manna in *Children's Literature Association Quarterly.* The compiler of well over eighty children's verse collections, "Hopkins has spent his career trying to make the crystal image accessible to children," noted Manna. His collections encompass a variety of topics, including animals, holidays, the seasons, and the works of noted poets like Walt Whitman and Carl Sandburg. Poetry, Hopkins stated in *Instructor* magazine, "should come to [children] as naturally as breathing, for nothing—*no thing*—can ring and rage through hearts and minds as does this genre of literature."

Born in Scranton, Pennsylvania, in 1938, Hopkins grew up in a poor but close family. At age ten, his family moved in with other relatives to make ends meet, and he spent most of his youth in Newark, New Jersey. The oldest child in the family, Hopkins had to help out with the family finances, often missing school so he could work. Though the family was able to get on its feet again and rent a basement apartment, relations soon deteriorated between Hopkins's parents, leading to divorce (the circumstances of his youth would later play a prominent part in his fiction writing for young adults). Early reading encompassed everything from comic books and movie magazines to the occasional adult novel, and in spite of his frequent absences, Hopkins maintained passing grades in school, excelling in English classes. Then a schoolteacher reached out to young Hopkins and helped to change his life. "Mrs. McLaughlin saved me," Hopkins wrote in the *Something about the Author Autobiography Series* (*SAAS*). "She introduced me to two things that had given me direction and hope—the love of reading and theatre."

After graduating from high school, Hopkins determined that he would like to teach. To pay his way through a teacher's training college, he worked several jobs. Taking a job in a suburban, middle-class school district after graduation, he soon became the resource teacher, gathering and organizing materials for the other teachers. It was during this time he came up with using poetry as an aid in reading. However, it quickly became apparent to him that poetry could be expanded to introduce all subject areas. In the 1960s, Hopkins was a consultant at Bank Street College of Education, where he again used poetry as a learning tool. In 1968 he became an editor at Scholastic, a post he held until 1976 when he became a full-time writer and anthologist.

During his years at Scholastic, Hopkins hit on his charmed formula for poetry anthologies, a pattern apparent in one of his earliest volumes, the award-winning *Don't You Turn Back: Poems by Langston Hughes.* Writing in *SAAS,* Hopkins describes key elements in his compilations. "Balance is important in an anthology. I want many voices within a book, so I rarely use more than one or two works by the same poet. I also envision each volume as a stage play or film, having a definite beginning, middle, and end. The right flow is a necessity for me. Sometimes a word at the end of a work will lead into the title of the next selection. I want my collections to read like a short story or novel—not a hodgepodge of works thrown together aimlessly." Since 1969, Hopkins has compiled scores of poetry anthologies employing this same successful formula. Further anthologies of individual poets include *Rainbows Are Made: Poems by Carl Sandburg* and the award-winning *Voyages: Poems by Walt Whitman.* Reviewing the latter title, *Booklist*'s Hazel Rochman called it a "spacious, handsome edition that helps make accessible a poet of vigor and sensitivity." *Horn Book*'s Nancy Vasilakis felt *Voyages* was a "well-conceived and elegantly produced anthology."

Hopkins often works with single themes for his anthologies. One of his seasonal collections, *The Sky Is Full of Song,* was described by a *Language Arts* reviewer as a "rare gem [that] poetically radiates the unique sense of each season." The reviewer added that each poem is "short, crisp, and in tune with the quartet of seasons." Steven Ratiner commented in the *Christian Science Monitor* that *The Sky Is Full of Song* "is an attractive packet of poetry for a young reader, pleasing to both the ear and eye." Holidays are presented in *Ring Out, Wild Bells,* and Halloween in particular is celebrated in *Ragged Shadows,* a "collection of well-chosen and cleverly illustrated poetry [that] will claim a place of its own," according to Meg Stackpole in *School Library Journal.*

Other individual themes are presented in *Weather, It's about Time* and *Blast Off!: Poems about Space.* Reviewing *Blast Off!* in *Horn Book,* Maeve Visser Knoth thought the volume is a "perfect match of subject, format, and interest level," making the collection for beginning readers "a sure winner." Food is served up in *Yummy!,* a "book to be savored in many delicious bites," according to Kathleen Whalin in *School Library Journal.* Whalin further observed that "Hopkins's mastery of the art of creating a delectable anthology is quite clear." Bugs and insects take center stage in *Flit, Flutter, Fly!,* a "charming assortment of 20 easy-to-read creature features," according to *Booklist* critic Quraysh Ali, who further commented that young readers "will find the book a dance for the senses." Musical and dance themes come to play in *Song and Dance,* "an inspired and free-spirited arrangement of poems with musical themes," as a reviewer for *Publishers Weekly* described the collection. Hopkins turns his editorial gaze to school days with *School Supplies,* "one of his best collections," according to a contributor for *Publishers Weekly.* School subjects also crop up in *Marvelous Math* and *Spectacular Science,* which collect poems dealing with those seemingly non-poetic subjects. Reviewing *Marvelous Math* in *Bulletin of the Center for Children's Books,* Elizabeth Bush concluded that the anthology is a "delight for independent readers" and a "boon to teachers attempting to integrate math across the curriculum." Lee Bock Brown, writing in *School Library Journal,* called the same book a "delightful collection." In *Spectacular Science,* Hopkins gathers verse dealing with topics from what happens to insects in winter to magnets. "Hopkins, familiar poet and anthologizer, has rounded up a satisfying variety of works," noted Stephanie Zvirin in a *Booklist* review. Carolyn Angus, reviewing *Spectacular Science* in *School Library Journal,* wrote that it is a "delightful, thought-provoking anthology that is—in short—spectacular."

From science, Hopkins turns his compiler's attention to sports in several volumes, including *Extra Innings,*

Sports! Sports! Sports!, and *Opening Days.* In *Sports!, Spots! Sports!,* Hopkins gathers verse about scuba diving, baseball, and ice skating, among other sports in an easy reader that is "a good way to attract new readers to poetry," according to *Booklist*'s Zvirin. American history, geography, and biography are presented in other anthologies by Hopkins. *Hand in Hand* delivers seventy-eight verse selections that offer "a singular outlook on American history as viewed by some of America's foremost poets, past and present," according to Nancy Vasilakis in *Horn Book.* Vasilakis concluded, "This well-conceived anthology should be a welcome supplement to any study of American history." Noted Americans are celebrated in *Lives: Poems about Famous Americans,* an anthology with many poems specially commissioned for inclusion. Thomas Edison, Sacagawea, and Rosa Parks are among the fourteen featured Americans. "Teachers looking for poetry to enhance social-studies units will find several good choices here," noted Carolyn Phelan in a *Booklist* review. *My America* is a geographical description of the country in verse form, focusing on eight regions. Barbara Chatton, writing in *School Library Journal,* concluded that "this volume will enrich literature and social-studies units."

The multi-talented Hopkins has also penned his own works, including autobiographies, classroom materials, poetry, picture books, and novels for young adults. Two of his novels, *Mama* and *Mama and her Boys,* tell about a resourceful single mother and her two sons. In *Mama,* the reader is confronted with a nonstop talker, shoplifter, and slightly obnoxious single mom who is a pain to live with, but who is a loving and caring person nevertheless. Narrated by her older son, the story presents Mama going from job to job while the family barely keeps its head above water. Reviewing *Mama,* a contributor for *Publishers Weekly* called the work a "not-to-be-missed first novel." "You'll remember Mama," wrote Zena Sutherland in a *Bulletin of the Center for Children's Books* review, noting how the mother is "tough, cheerfully vulgar in her tastes ... passionately dedicated to see that her two sons whose father has decamped have everything they need." Mama makes a curtain call in *Mama and Her Boys,* in which the boys are now worried that their mother might marry her boss, Mr. Jacobs; a better match, as far as they are concerned, is the school custodian, Mr. Carlisle. Reviewing the sequel to the first novel, another contributor for *Publishers Weekly* concluded, "The author packs the ensuing incidents with merriment and an understated lesson about different kinds of love and companionship."

Hopkins's novel, *Wonder Wheels,* tells the story of Mick Thompson and his love of roller skating; his second passion is for Kitty Rhoades, whom he meets at his local roller rink. When Kitty is murdered by a psychotic ex-boyfriend, Mick is left to learn one of the toughest lessons in life: the fragility and brevity of existence.

Hopkins's poetry has also won high praise. His 1995 volume of verse, *Good Rhymes, Good Times!,* is a "joyous collection of 21 original poems," according to a reviewer for *Publishers Weekly,* who further noted that

In his anthology **School Supplies: A Book of Poems**, *illustrated by Renee Flower, Hopkins captures a child's excitement upon entering the world of learning.*

"Hopkins brings freshness and immediacy to his subjects" and "deftly depicts a sense of delight and wonder in everyday experience." *Been to Yesterdays: Poems of a Life* is a gathering of poems that look at the psychology of Hopkins at age thirteen when his parents divorced. "This autobiographical cycle of poems is a rare gift, a careful exploration of one life that illumines the lives of all who read it," wrote Kathleen Whalin in a *School Library Journal.*

Hopkins is also behind the work of *Pauses: Autobiographical Reflections of 101 Creators of Children's Books, Pass the Poetry, Please!,* and *The Writing Bug,* a short autobiographical sketch. In the last-named book, Hopkins tells the secret of his amazing productivity: "There isn't a day that goes by that I'm not reading poetry or working on a poem of my own." This simple work ethic has made him one of the most popular and best known anthologists of poetry at work today. He has helped make poetry accessible to young readers in over a hundred volumes of his own writings and in his compilations. As a reviewer for *Juvenile Miscellany* concluded, "Hopkins' immersion in poetry, past and

present, text and illustration, places him at the heart of children's literature."

Biographical and Critical Sources

BOOKS

Children's Books and Their Creators, edited by Anita Silvey, Houghton, 1995.
Children's Literature Review, Volume 44, Gale (Detroit, MI), 1997.
Hopkins, Lee Bennett, *The Writing Bug,* Richard C. Owen, 1993.
Something about the Author Autobiography Series, Volume 4, Gale (Detroit, MI), 1987.

PERIODICALS

Best Sellers, August, 1979.
Booklist, November 15, 1988, Hazel Rochman, review of *Voyages: Poems by Walt Whitman,* p. 565; December 15, 1992, Quraysh Ali, review of *Flit, Flutter, Fly!* p. 739; July, 1995, p. 1881; February 15, 1996, pp. 1015, 1018; March 15, 1996, p. 1274; April 1, 1998, p. 1323; November 15, 1998, p. 592; March 1,

1999, p. 1224; March 15, 1999, Carolyn Phelan, review of *Lives: Poems about Famous Americans,* pp. 1340, 1343; April 1, 1999, Stephanie Zvirin, review of *Sport! Sport! Sport!,* pp. 1418-1419; July, 1999, Stephanie Zvirin, review of *Spectacular Science,* pp. 1948-1949; June 1, 2000, p. 1904; October 1, 2000, p. 361; November 15, 2000, p. 637.

Bulletin of the Center for Children's Books, July-August, 1977, Zena Sutherland, review of *Mama,* p. 175; February, 1993, p. 179; April, 1995, p. 277; December, 1995, p. 147; September, 1997, Elizabeth Bush, review of *Marvelous Math,* pp. 13-14; May, 1999, p. 336.

Children's Literature Association Quarterly, summer, 1985, Anthony L. Manna, "In Pursuit of the Crystal Image: Lee Bennett Hopkins's Poetry Anthologies," pp. 80-82.

Christian Science Monitor, June 29, 1983, Steven Ratiner, review of *The Sky Is Full of Song.*

Early Years, January, 1982.

Horn Book, January-February, 1989, Nancy Vasilakis, review of *Voyages: Poems by Walt Whitman,* pp. 86-87; September-October, 1993, p. 616; July-August, 1994, p. 467; March-April, 1995, Nancy Vasilakis, review of *Hand in Hand,* p. 209; May-June, 1995, p. 338; July-August, 1995, Maeve Visser Knoth, review of *Blast Off!: Poems about Space,* pp. 472-473; May-June, 1996, p. 344; January-February, 1999, p. 77.

Instructor, March, 1982, Lee Bennett Hopkins interview.

Juvenile Miscellany, summer, 1989, p. 4.

Language Arts, November-December, 1978; September, 1983; December, 1984; September, 1986.

New York Times Book Review, April 8, 1979; October 5, 1986; October 31, 1993, p. 26; November 13, 1994, p. 32.

Publishers Weekly, February 21, 1977, review of *Mama,* p. 79; December 11, 1981, review of *Mama and Her Boys,* p. 62; August 31, 1992, p. 80; July 3, 1995, review of *Good Rhymes, Good Times!,* pp. 60-61; August 12, 1996, review of *School Supplies,* p. 84; March 31, 1997, review of *Song and Dance,* p. 77; July 29, 1997, p. 76; June 21, 1999, p. 70; January 10, 2000, p. 70; July 31, 2000, p. 95.

School Library Journal, September, 1994, p. 208; May, 1995, p. 99; September, 1995, Kathleen Whalin, review of *Been to Yesterdays: Poems of a Life,* p. 209; December, 1995, p. 38; March, 1997, p. 113; September, 1997, Meg Stackpole, review of *Ragged Shadows,* p. 224; October, 1997, Lee Bock Brown, review of *Marvelous Math,* p. 118; March, 1998, p. 196; December, 1998, p. 106; September, 1999, Carolyn Angus, review of *Spectacular Science,* p. 213; August, 2000, Kathleen Whalin, review of *Yummy!,* p. 170; September, 2000, Barbara Chatton, review of *My America,* p. 248.

—Sketch by J. Sydney Jones

*   *   *

HOSSELL, Karen Price
See PRICE, Karen

HOWARD, Alyssa
See GLICK, Ruth (Burtnick)

*   *   *

ISBELL, Rebecca T(emple) 1942-

Personal

Born 1942. *Education:* University of Tennessee, B.S., 1964, Ed.D., 1979; East Tennessee State University, M.S., 1974.

Addresses

Home—Johnson City, TN. *Office*—Center of Excellence in Early Childhood Learning and Development, East Tennessee State University, Box 70434, Johnson City, TN 37614-0434. *E-mail*—isbell@etsu.edu.

Career

Teacher at elementary schools in Knoxville, TN, 1964, and Greeneville, TN, 1965-70 and 1972-75; East Tennessee State University, Johnson City, instructor, 1975-80, assistant professor, 1980-85, associate professor, 1985-91, professor of early childhood education, 1991—, director of Child Study Center, 1980-82, director of pilot project for Tennessee Early Childhood Training Alliance, 1992—, director of Center of Excellence in Early Childhood Learning, 1998—. University of Virginia, adjunct faculty member, 1981-84; Walters State Community College, member of advisory board, 1984—. Holston Methodist Children's Home, member of advisory board, 1985—; Families First, member of Tennessee state steering committee, 1995-96. Participant in National Storytelling Festival. *Member:* Association for Childhood Education International (member of board of directors, Division of Early Childhood Education, 1989—), National Association of Early Childhood Teacher Educators, National Association of Educators of Young Children, Southern Early Childhood Association, Tennessee Association on Young Children (member of governing board, 1987—), Delta Kappa Gamma, Phi Delta Kappa, Phi Kappa Phi.

Awards, Honors

Grants from Bureau of Education for the Handicapped, Association of Childhood Educators, and Tennessee Higher Education Commission; Award of Merit for Outstanding Educational Research, Eastern Educational Research Conference, 1989, for the research study "An Analysis of the Oral Language Production of Young Children Participating in Three Types of Play Centers"; Certificate of Merit for outstanding research paper, Eastern Educational Research Conference, 1991, for "A Study of Four-Year-Olds with Low Book Interest Behaviors in Three Classroom Contexts"; Distinguished Faculty Award, East Tennessee State University, 1994, for outstanding teaching.

Writings

(With Shirley C. Raines) *Stories: Children's Literature in Early Education,* and sole author of teacher's guide, Delmar Publishers (Albany, NY), 1994.

The Complete Learning Center Book: An Illustrated Guide for 32 Different Early Childhood Learning Centers, Gryphon House (Mount Rainer, MD), 1995.

(With Shirley C. Raines) *Tell It Again! Easy-to-Tell Stories with Activities for Young Children,* illustrated by Joan C. Waites, Gryphon House (Mount Rainer, MD), 1999.

(With Shirley C. Raines) *Tell It Again! 2: Easy-to-Tell Stories with Activities for Young Children,* illustrated by Joan C. Waites, Gryphon House (Beltsville, MD), 2000.

(With Betty Exelby) *Early Learning Environments That Work!,* illustrated by Garry Exelby, photographs by Mike Talley, Susan Lachmann, and Su Lorencen, Gryphon House (Beltsville, MD), 2001.

Creative Arts for Young Children, Thomson Learning, 2001.

Contributor of articles and reviews to periodicals, including *Young Children, Childhood Education, Dimensions, Tennessee Education, Family Health and Human Relations, Oklahoma Children,* and *Education Digest.*

Biographical and Critical Sources

PERIODICALS

School Library Journal, January, 2000, Grace Oliff, review of *Tell It Again! Easy-to-Tell Stories with Activities for Young Children,* p. 164; March, 2001, Jennifer M. Parker, review of *Tell It Again! 2: Easy-to-Tell Stories with Activities for Young Children,* p. 289.*

J–K

JORDAN, Alexis Hill
See GLICK, Ruth (Burtnick)

*   *   *

KEACH, James P. 1950-

Personal

Born December 7, 1950, in New York, NY; son of Walter Stacy and Mary Caine (Peckham) Keach; married Jane Seymour; children: John Stacy, Kristopher Steven, Kalen James, Sean, Katie, Jenny. *Education:* Northwestern University, B.S., 1970; Yale University, M.F.A., 1971. *Hobbies and other interests:* Martial arts, golf, skiing, horseback riding.

Addresses

Home—23852 Pacific Coast Hwy., Malibu, CA 90265-4879. *Office*—c/o James Palmer Associates, 1901 Avenue of the Stars, Fl. 7, Los Angeles, CA, 90067-6001. *E-mail*—jkeach@aol.com

Career

Actor, author. Has appeared as an actor in over fifty films, including *The Wings of Kitty Hawk* (1978), *Comes a Horseman* (1978), *Love Letters* (1983), *National Lampoon's Vacation* (1983), *The Razor's Edge* (1984), *Moving Violations* (1985), and *Wildcats* (1986); performed at Body Politic Theatre in Chicago, IL, and at the New York Shakespeare Festival. Producer and writer, *Armed and Dangerous;* director and producer, *The Young Riders* (television series); writer, director, and producer, *The Forgotten;* producer, *A Winner Never Quits;* producer and director, *The Long Riders* (television series); director, *The Stars Fell on Henrietta* and *Camouflage;* director of television movies, including *Sunstroke, False Identity, A Passion for Justice, The Absolute Truth, The New Swiss Family Robinson,* and *A Marriage of Convenience;* executive producer and director, *Dr. Quinn Medicine Woman* (television series), 1999; director, *Camouflage,* 1999; executive producer and director, *Enslavement* and *Murder in the Mirror,* both 1999.

Awards, Honors

Christopher Award; Ace Award; Western Heritage Award.

James P. Keach

Writings

WITH WIFE, JANE SEYMOUR; "THIS ONE 'N THAT ONE" SERIES; ILLUSTRATED BY GEOFFREY PLANER

Splat! The Tale of a Colorful Cat, Putnam (New York, NY), 1998.

Yum! A Tale of Two Cookies, Putnam (New York, NY), 1998.

Boing! No Bouncing on the Bed, Putnam (New York, NY), 1999.

WITH WIFE, JANE SEYMOUR; "THIS ONE 'N THAT ONE" SERIES; ILLUSTRATED BY GEOFFREY PLANER; BOARD BOOKS

Play, Putnam (New York, NY), 1999.
Eat, Putnam (New York, NY), 1999.
Talk, Putnam (New York, NY), 1999.
Me and Me, Putnam (New York, NY), 1999.

Sidelights

Film and television actor, director, producer, writer James P. Keach has paired up with his wife, actress Jane Seymour, to produce a series of picture books featuring a pair of mischievous twin kittens named This One and That One. The authors make their own appearances in the stories as Lady Jane and Big Jim, the erstwhile parents of This One and That One. In *Splat!: The Tale of a Colorful Cat,* Lady Jane leaves This One and That One with Big Jim to go out shopping, and Big Jim allows the kittens to get into Lady Jane's paints. He lazily suggests himself as a subject for their art and then falls asleep, giving the kittens the opportunity to truly *paint* their father. In *Yum! A Tale of Two Cookies,* Lady Jane's plan to surprise her husband with a late night picnic of freshly baked cookies on the beach is foiled by her mischievous offspring, who sneak out of bed and into the picnic hamper. There they eat all the cookies and jump out of the hamper during their parents' intended time alone. These "slaphappy stories," as a reviewer in *Publishers Weekly* characterized them, are "hardly essential purchases," but they remain "cheerful little capers" nonetheless, this critic concluded.

Biographical and Critical Sources

PERIODICALS

Publishers Weekly, September 28, 1998, review of *Splat! The Tale of a Colorful Cat* and *Yum! A Tale of Two Cookies,* p. 100.

School Library Journal, February, 1999, Blair Christolon, review of *Splat! The Tale of a Colorful Cat* and *Yum! A Tale of Two Cookies,* pp. 88-89.*

* * *

Autobiography Feature

David Kherdian

1931-

I had heard that J. I. Case Company came to the docks of New York to hire the Armenians and other émigrés for their factory in Racine, Wisconsin. The story was never corroborated. It had the fictive sound of truth and appealed to my sense of drama.

This is where I began, if there can be said to be beginnings, and if one can extricate one's own history and lore from that of one's father, and then of one's mother, and then at last from all one's ancestry.

But then my father did not begin his American citizenry as a laborer for J. I. Case; he began as a chef—but even that is not quite right, for it was after serving in the U.S. Army (where he learned to cook) that he became a chef. Upon his discharge he was made an American citizen, and soon after he became a short order cook at Nelson's Hotel. It was only then that he began searching for a mail-order bride. Being the sole support of his family—who had fled Turkey for Armenia (where the Massacres stopped but the starvation continued)—and having two wastrel brothers, who were also his dependents, he decided on an orphan bride—one who would not bring further family problems and obligations.

My mother had been the sole survivor of her immediate family, all of them having died from cholera or heartbreak on their forced march from Turkey to the desert wastes of Mesopotamia. My father's family found her in Greece (they were in Piraeus on their way to Armenia) and after a series of refusals which consumed a year, she finally agreed to an engagement by proxy, and thereby said *Yes* to America (for this is how it must have seemed to her) and *No* to England, to where she might have gone, having been offered an opportunity for free schooling (college, she said—a dream she would take to her grave, along with some far-fetched aristocratic needs that she thought were her birthright but really belonged to a need in her to balance the loss caused by the horrors of her early life).

Seven years later I was born.

I do not have my own first memory of being—or rather, *thinking* of myself as an Armenian. Instead, I have a series of memories connected to the dawning realization that I *was* an American—the realization, that is, that I was American-born, and that the soil I was standing on was therefore America's, not Armenia's, as I mistakenly thought it was. When I was four my mother enrolled me in nursery school at Central Association, to correct the most conspicuous aspect of the problem: I needed to learn English.

By five I was bilingual, but of course I hadn't noticed, as I also had not noticed that a huge psychological problem was beginning to be formed in me.

I do remember an evening when a group of us boys, aged six to eight—the Superior Street gang in embryo: Mikey Kaiserlian, Dickie Steberl, Junior Rognerud, and probably one or more of the Mieneckes—were gathered under the street light at the end of our block. All at once God was mentioned, and then at once his nationality was named. Someone insisted that God did not have a nationality, while another claimed that God was American. All at once I knew—or thought I knew—God was Armenian. If I was the son of God, and surely I was, then God was Armenian. Everyone insisted that I was mistaken; the consensus being that either God did not have a nationality, of if he did, he was American.

I felt cheated, deprived, insulted. And that is all I remember, except that the ramifications of that experience would haunt my life—and perhaps I became a writer that night, in order to redress the error that turned into a "fault" in me—for something had been set in my being that night, and it would take years of self-study, for which writing was the means, before I could see and begin to correct this problem, begun so innocently, but that had gone on by momentum and had caused me to spoil everything in my life.

It was said that I was a loner. Can this be traced, can anything that belongs to our nature be traced? Or can it only be identified and named and then worked with, if we are to be delivered to a place from which real action and choice can take place.

I remember now my solitary wanderings. I discovered Lake Michigan first, perhaps, where I fished for perch with all the others, but more important I discovered Root River, both from the city bridges, where it seemed choked and bloated and largely lifeless, until I traveled outward toward its source, where it was alive with fish and the life that is nurtured by the freedom of moving water. My greatest memories of childhood are memories of fishing. I named two of my books *I Remember Root River* and *Root River Run.* Re-return and then deliverance: the process of inner freedom that cannot be understood unless experienced.

In our homes, in our community, in my immediate and extended surroundings there was no art, no writing, and no culture but the wisdom of an ancient race living an alien and distorted life. What beauty there was I had to find for myself. Its need was in me and I had therefore to transform

David Kherdian

the ordinary into something that, although it did not seem to be there, was there, if one could expand one's awareness and see beneath the surface. The invisible world clothed in visible life.

I found it in nature and in the common and preposterous acts of man: my father marching in a parade, the rock-garden across the bridge from Island Park that contained a replica of the bridge I viewed it from, the Saturday matinees at the Mainstreet Theatre, and especially the serials: *Lone Ranger, Batman, Green Hornet, Mask of Zorro,* and many others. But the most special event of all from that time—for it indicated a possibility—was the colored-pencil drawing of an Indian that was done by one of my mother's students during her Armenian language class in the basement of our church. The drawing must have been a gift for my mother, who brought it home to me, never guessing the effect it would have on my life. By now I was drawing myself and it was assumed I would be an artist. I was awarded a blue ribbon for my rendering of a red-headed woodpecker, that resulted in an invitation to study at the Wustum Art Museum at the edge of town. My only memory of the one or two sessions I attended was that of discomfort, for I had been discriminated against at Garfield Elementary School and by now I hated classrooms of any kind. Had I stayed I would have no doubt studied with Nancy Ekholm Burkert, who, I found out many years later, had also taken classes there with Sylvester Jerry.

School. Or to be specific, Garfield Elementary School. I hated it with an unrelenting passion, and for good reason—I was made to feel dumb. Having flunked the second grade I flunked the fifth grade twice, once in the regular year and then again in summer school. To this day I cannot pass a test, do not know how to listen, and resort to imitation in most things, on the theory that I-will-not-be-able-to-get-it-on-my-own. But there were sports, and here I excelled. Largely because, like my teammates, I was older (by the time we reached sixth grade all of my Armenian teammates had flunked at least two grades). Ours was the first softball team to win the championship three years running, which meant that we could keep the traveling trophy. And it was our sixth-grade basketball team that scored 100 points in a single game. It had never been done before and probably hasn't been done since. We made the papers and won the championship: Horse Kamakian, Lotch Oglanian, Ed Chobanian, Ralph Molbeck, and myself. All Armenians but one. Our softball coach was Gustave (Shypoke) Sheibach, the janitor, and our basketball coach was Herbert Von Haden, the principal. They respected us and looked out for us and I cherish their memory to this day, as I cherish the memory of my companions.

And then in the sixth grade, finally, there was a teacher who cared for us as well—Mrs. McKinney. She read us Mark Twain and she loved her work—and her work was us. She alone prepared me for Washington Junior High School, where I found myself, quite unexpectedly, at the top of the class. I set a record for the greatest number of book reports given by a seventh grader. The writer I remember best, having discovered him on my own, was J. W. Schultz, who wrote countless books about his life as a squaw man.

But then I got bored. The teachers were still horrible, and the routine of being a good student was as deadly as the routine of being an incorrigible one. The fact is I was neither of these things, but *what* I was I did not know. It was in the ninth grade that we wrote reports on the professions we intended to follow. This was the first and last writing I can remember doing in school. I wrote that I wanted to be a conservationist. I was by now an expert

David Kherdian at Garfield Elementary School, Racine, Wisconsin, 1945

fisherman, and I wanted to be a hunter as well. I flunked typing (my only failure) and went on to Horlick High School. You might say that my preparation for life was proceeding on a decline.

It was on one side or another of my nineteenth birthday, and before my first semester of my junior year of high school was completed, that I walked out of what was for me Incarcerated Hell. I didn't even clean out my locker, and I refused to return to complete my act of departure-despite an admonishing phone call from the principal. It does me no credit to say that I didn't even realize that he was angry. I paid the price of my insensitivity when he refused (a few years later) to honor my Army certificate of high school equivalency, causing me to drive to the South Side of town, where it was honored by our rival, Park High School.

I am now nineteen years old, certified stupid, totally unprepared for life, full of great undefined hopes and daydreams, with an unabiding hatred of authority, and hopelessly armed with an upper lip that curls at one corner into a snarl to announce and declare my defiance of the world.

Thus armed I am about to embark—rather clumsily and very luckily—on one of the best years of my life. But not before I am fired from my first job. I do not realize, perhaps fortunately, that this will establish a pattern for my life that will endure until I am able to find my own work. But now, after several found and lost jobs, I answer an ad promising travel and adventure, and find myself several stories up in the old Baker Block on Main Street entering a door marked Crowell-Collier Publishing Company.

I was about to become a door-to-door magazine salesman, traveling throughout Wisconsin and northern Illinois. This was a job I would not have to worry about being fired from: if you produced you ate, and if you didn't, you starved. It was self-producing, self-regulating work. I could not have known then that it was preparing me for an even harder ordeal to come—for the first thing a writer must discipline is himself.

I found myself among a mixed company of misfits of every cloth and description. Wayne Kruse—who would be my sidekick—had signed on the same week, and together we grafted ourselves to such seasoned veterans as Bob Hill, the cocky ace of the crew; Pliney Olson, the maroon-shirted hobo with aristocratic manners; Charley Metcalf, the pint-sized alcoholic for whom the manager—Milton (Smitty) Smith—had a soft spot; and also Max Dembroski, who was our field manager. This was the nucleus, around which others came and went: newcomers who lasted only a week or a month, as well as veteran travelers, who followed the sun and their own lazy natures.

My first week on the job I sold twenty orders and joined the magic circle (from which I would soon plummet), making the mimeo newsletter that traveled the circuit. An order was worth $5 to the salesman, and $100 in 1951 was Big Money. It wouldn't happen often but it didn't need to, for the great excitement was not money but adventure. And romance. I fell in love with the life, beginning with my first drink in a tavern—the famous Mully's American Bar, which was downstairs and next door to the Baker Building. And then I fell in love with all the cities, concluding with Janesville, Smitty's home (he lived with his family in the old Park Hotel that was run by his wife), which became my favorite city of all, for it was there that I fell in love with Smitty's daughter, Barbara.

About this time Max Dembroski left, not being cut out for the game, and I was named field manager, "the youngest in the history of Crowell-Collier Publishing Company," the mimeo said. I bought my first car, a gray 1941 Plymouth with a sailboat hood ornament. How I scraped together $200 for the purchase I cannot imagine, unless the company chipped in half. My job consisted of driving the crew from city to city, registering at the local police station, where we were fingerprinted, checking the crew into a hotel (the weekly rates at the best hotels in town was twenty dollars average—and we always went first class, doubling up when we'd had a bad week, but taking our own room when we didn't), placing the men in their territories, verifying orders, drying out the drunks, making reports, and paying the men on Saturday mornings when the vouchers from the home office reached the territory.

It lasted an entire year, until I got drafted into the U.S. Army. I would never again experience such camaraderie and adventure and high-spirited innocent fun. I felt worldly, cocky, and ready for anything.

Anything but the Army, that is. Here my innocence was shattered. There was something deadlier and dirtier than school, after all. But then wasn't the Army a part of society's education also? Hadn't we merely traded in the spinster teacher, full of prejudice and hatred, for the bully-boy sergeant, but with the stakes and the risks suddenly and dangerously escalated?

Once again I was forced to rebel.

And once again something saved me—for, as the Armenian proverb goes, *God never closes every door.* In my final week as a magazine salesman I discovered Theodore Dreiser. The book was *The Stoic.* I was beside myself with an excitement that bordered on shock. It was as if what I had been groping for and secretly believing/hoping existed, not only *did* exist, was not only true and possible, but had been made manifest by a man in a book. It had to do with being—that I knew. And that was all I knew. The written word, the book, became for me a god. Something did exist that had the power to deliver me to another reality, a truth that was somehow already within me, but buried, unrealized, and without a means for expression and ultimate usage.

Had it not been for that book at that particular moment it is hard to say what would have become of me. I was far less prepared for the Army than I had been for school—although I was as innocent as a babe on entering kindergarten.

We gathered at Memorial Hall in Racine and were driven by bus to Fort Sheridan. The first days were tolerable, partially because I shared a barracks with old friends: Jerry Hansen, Sam Balian, Johnny Musurlian, and Jack Levonian, among others. Then we were shipped to Fort Knox, where, from the start, I began to show my stripes—no pun intended. I skipped reveille whenever I could, and in the middle of maneuvers I would wander off by myself. I refused to listen, I refused to learn. I was on the golf course when news reached me that I was being shipped to Korea.

I remember my mother and father standing on the porch, waving goodbye as a neighbor drove me to the airport to catch my plane for Seattle. They were sure I'd never return and they were powerless to do anything about it (this was Korea, remember, not Vietnam). Father had told Mother, "He'll fall asleep on guard duty, they'll shoot him." He was right about the first part, but he didn't know his son. Once, while guarding officers' quarters, I sneaked into the colonel's room and fell asleep on the chair beside his bed. If he awoke I figured I would awake, too. I'd say I heard something under his bed.

The ship bound for Korea took thirteen days to make its first port—Japan. I was AWOL the entire time. I cannot remember now what precipitated my decision. Was there duty I wanted to get out of; did I want to eat wherever and whenever I could; was the puking in the cramped quarters getting to me; or was it simply that I wanted to sit on deck and watch the ocean, which I was seeing for the first time.

It wasn't long before I was missed and a search was put into effect. Passes were issued for meals, bulletins went out and calls were made over the loudspeaker. Everyone was being questioned. A few of the soldiers knew who I was but they, more than all the others, were enjoying the game, and they were not about to turn me in. I found a different place to sleep every night, and different places to eat as well.

It got to be amusing. On the last night I thought I would enjoy the pleasure of my own arrest so I got in a line that was being checked by the lieutenant in charge of my case. I couldn't suppress a smile when I stood in front of him and told him my name.

He sputtered, "Put this man under arrest." There weren't any MPs in sight, and so the job fell to some innocent private, who fumbled my arm and tried to look stern and in possession of himself. I was marched to the kitchen where the mess sergeant was ordered to make me work throughout the night at KP.

The mess sergeant was huge, black, and inscrutable. I stood before him and waited. He turned and walked away and didn't speak until the others had left his kitchen. Then he said, "Whats you wants to eat, boy?"

I sat down before a dish of fresh-baked apple pie, enjoying the taste of fame. The climax was yet a week away, but the following day, while walking to the PX, I passed the lieutenant who had arrested me. He was so flustered when he saw me he saluted. I didn't return his salute, instead I smiled faintly and walked on, without breaking my stride. I thought, "What can they do, send me to Korea!" One week later all of the five thousand pathetic souls that had journeyed over the waters—that I alone had enjoyed—were give their orders: Korea—except for five hundred men, of which I (of all people) was numbered. We would remain in Japan. My life had been saved, for looking back on it now I know that I would never have returned from Korea alive.

The Korean Conflict, as it was called, had ended; my two years were up, and I was discharged. I returned home, thoroughly disillusioned with life, my nerves shot, and with no prospects or plans for the future. Reading had kept me alive in the Army, and now, aged twenty-three, I began a novel of my own. My subject was the Kaiserlians—the troubled, eccentric, colorful family that had had such a strong influence on my youth. I had this idea that I could solve their problems by writing a novel about their life. It was a preposterous idea and it fizzled to a halt by page twenty-five. I now knew for myself the great gulf that lay between writing home and writing fiction. I had discovered in the Army that I enjoyed writing letters, and also that I was good at it. I don't remember now all the people I wrote to, but it remains vivid in my memory that Joyce Southwell (who must have taken it on as a morale-building assignment) was the one I most enjoyed writing to. There was nothing at stake, nothing to be gained or lost, and so I simply wrote, letter after letter, indulging my newly discovered bent for writing.

But a novel! It would be several years before I would try to write anything creative again.

There was something to be learned—but just what it was and how it was to be acquired remained a mystery.

I went back to being nervous. My mother's cooking was too rich for me, our house too cramped, and once again I found myself being fired from one job after another.

What to do?

I knew that I could get $110 a month if I attended college. I had already gotten my high school equivalency exam certified and I learned that the University of Wisconsin had a two-year extension course downtown.

The GI Bill, as I believe it was called, combined with what I was making selling shoes Friday evenings and Saturdays at Mary Jane's Shoe Store, would be enough for my purposes.

Everyone said you had to have a college degree if you wanted to get ahead. If "ahead" was the place to get, then I wanted to get there, too. I wanted to show "them," whoever "they" were, that I could "do it." I had forgotten, temporarily, about being a writer. But in the second semester I took a composition class and it became clear to everyone that I could write.

Time moves slowly when you are not sure what you want, or even how to get what you think you do want. It was a sad and boring year, drinking every night, going to class hung-over, contemplating suicide, hating Racine and my life—and the prospect of doing the same thing all over again the following year seemed senseless. Where I got the idea I do not know, but I decided to go to Europe.

I drove to Bridgeport, Connecticut, to visit an old Army buddy, got a night time job at Sikorsky Aircraft (building helicopter propellers) and worked as a busboy in their cafeteria afternoons. Before leaving home I had cashed out an insurance policy my mother had on me (worth $500) and after six months of hard work I had $1,500 to my name—a lot of money! I booked passage on the *Queen Elizabeth* and went to Europe for four months, traveling first to England and then to nearly every country on the continent. It was the-wildest-of-dreams-come-true! Europe at that time (1954) was everything America was not: cultured, sophisticated, with great restaurants to eat in, wine to drink and learn about, sights to see, and best of all friendships and adventures. And of course romance. I bought a notebook and wrote in it every night.

I need to back up for a moment and remember my six months in Connecticut, because it was during this time that I discovered New York, and the experiences (one in particular) that prepared me for Europe. I visited New York often on weekends in order to go to jazz clubs, theatres, and art galleries and museums—and it was at the Metropolitan Museum that I saw my first work of original art. I had mounted the stairs, and walking down the corridor I saw ahead of me in one of the rooms a painting by Van Gogh. I knew about art through reproductions, but I had no idea! I literally stopped in my tracks, so overcome with emotion that I could not move. It was an experience on the level of my first reading of Theodore Dreiser. Again a flower unknown to me peeled back another petal and revealed a portion of its heart that was my own heart. Although I had not forgotten that I wanted to write, I suddenly found myself plunged into the world of art, and once I reached Europe I began visiting museum after museum, feeding a hunger so deeply buried that it had as yet no name or identity.

I had hoped to find work in Europe but it was not to be, so I returned again to boring and hopeless America. I re-enrolled in college, my reason for doing so unchanged—there was simply nothing better to do. But there were two subjects now that interested me: writing *and* art history. I went from selling shoes to tending bar. And I continued to read on my own. College itself meant nothing to me but a paycheck, although I did have an idea in the back of my head that a degree was important, perhaps even necessary, to have. Had I been able to trust my own experience and intelligence I would have seen the utter absurdity and futility of college life and college learning.

I don't think any writer worth his salt ever learned to write in college, and whether or not I believed, or even thought about this at the time, I will say this: it never occurred to me even to try.

I scribbled on in secret, and for my third year of schooling I went to Madison, where I enjoyed for the second time in my life a camaraderie with friends of like spirit (Ardie Kaiserlian, Ted Burdosh, Jerry Zwiefel, and Jack Danelski). It would last for only one year. During the following summer my father was stricken with cancer and so I transferred to the University of Wisconsin in Milwaukee in order to be near the Veteran's Hospital.

My father was to live another year, and then, before the start of my final term, my mother and sister moved to Fresno. By now my Uncle Jack, who had been a second father to me, had also died. There was talk of my inheriting his 1924 Model-A Ford (that he had bought new), as his son Chuckie had years before inherited my Red Racer. But upon his death it somehow got interred in the garage beyond the garden he had loved so much. Had I noticed—had I been able to notice—I would have seen that the old world was coming to an end. But I hadn't yet made the beginning of a new world for myself.

On the day following my final exam I got in my car and drove to California. I knew what I needed to do next: meet William Saroyan. I had discovered his books, and through his books I had rediscovered my heritage. Now I needed to meet him, although I did not as yet know the reasons why.

A writer's apprenticeship is a never-ending thing. It cannot be chosen—as apprenticeship—because it is impossible to know what it is, or how to acquire it, or how it ends and when it will end—or even if it ever *will* end: that is, when/if it will turn into writing, and then evolve into writing that will sell (it is assumed it will fulfill its other purpose, if there *is* another purpose—and there *must be* another purpose for the great fight to have been worth the waging), or even what the final form of that writing will be.

I had read and read and read. I had traveled and would continue to travel, I had listened everywhere to the speech patterns of people, and I had practiced dialogue. But above all I had tried to understand how the artist could transform life into literature; that is, chaos into order, the stuff of ordinary existence into the imperishable materiality of extraordinary art.

Saroyan was about to leave for Europe when I arrived in San Francisco, but I was not deterred. I had begun his bibliography and wrote to tell him so. By now I was collecting his books. I had to own them all and read them all. And then I moved to Fresno to manage the Book House on Tulare Street so I could meet and know the people and places that were the subjects and objects of Saroyan's art. I wanted to see, if I could, how his writing was done, for up until now all I had managed on my own that I considered "creative" were two finished stories and what I suppose would have to be called a poem.

More than twenty years later, upon Saroyan's death and at the bidding of my hometown newspaper, I would write:

> . . . I had arrived on the scene just in time, because the old Armenian town was still standing, with the churches and bakeries and dairies and assorted buildings that he had written about, still somehow intact. And not only were the streets still there, carrying their immortal names, but the courthouse was still standing with the postal telegraph office facing it, just as I had found it in *The Human Comedy*.
>
> It was all there and I went out to all of it, to unravel, if I could, the mystery of writing.

Saroyan came and went. We met and talked and I kept pecking away at his bibliography. It was finished at last and published in 1965. I had returned once again to San

Kherdian (right) and friend Gerry Hausman, fellow author and poet

Francisco, and now, with my book circulating in the great world, I received a letter one day from an editor in New York proposing a bibliography of some of the Beat poets living in San Francisco.

But I seem to have gotten ahead of myself, for the memory of that offer by an editor I had never met reminds me of one of the handful of important decisions I have made in my life. It had occurred a few years earlier at an employment agency in Chicago. Having failed to find meaningful work in San Francisco, not yet having begun to write, and suddenly feeling homesick and lost, I packed my car and began the long drive home. Everyone said I should be able to get a good job on the strength of my college degree, especially in a big city like Chicago. But the questions I was being asked by the man in the agency were disturbing me. At one point he asked me to turn around and look at something in the corner of the room. Then he asked to see my hand. He was examining my fingernails, apparently, and when I turned he had looked to see if my neck was cleanly shaved.

I felt degraded by the interview, and by the time I reached the street I had made an irrevocable decision: I would never again in my life fill out an application form. Instead, I would work at my life until my name itself became what I was and what I would be employed for. It was a bold, desperate decision. It meant, as I knew, that I could never seek regular employment again, that I would have to drift from job to job.

I couldn't have known at the time that this decision would give my apprenticeship the boost it needed. It was now do-or-die, which is the perfect framework and condition for a near-impossible goal. No one in my line had been a writer, no one I knew had been a writer, Racine had never produced a writer, I myself had not yet even *met* a writer—and writing, I was convinced, was the highest activity of man.

Who did I think I was to imagine I could become a writer? The few people I mentioned it to looked at me with either scorn or pity. I decided that in the future I would keep it to myself.

I remained in Racine for one year, opened a used-book store called *The Sign of the Tiger,* sold shoes at Zahn's, and tended bar at the Hotel Racine—where I met my first writer: Glenway Wescott. But the most important thing about that year was that I began to look at my city with a writer's eye.

Everywhere I looked there was a story, and everywhere I looked I saw the remnants of my own confused past. How could meaning and order and beauty be brought to bear on this life—and this city—that I both loved and hated? And what was its truth? and who was I? and how could I use writing to help me in my search?

I struggled. I drifted. I dreamed. I waited. And I watched.

Ted Burdosh, my college chum, whose home was in northern Wisconsin, had talked to me about trout fishing. Ted was an expert fly caster and when he invited me to his parents' home in Little Suamico for a weekend of trout fishing, I readily accepted. I did not think then that at the age of thirty a completely new, totally unknown experience would still be possible for me.

I stood on a high bank and looked down at my first trout stream: swift, crystal clear, pure, and undefiled. It was the single most beautiful sight I had witnessed in nature, in great part because it was the home of fish, and not just any fish, but the swift and speckled leaping trout.

One other memory of that year, very different from the above, stands out as an influence that would also affect my life. Ardie Kaiserlian and I were watching a boxing match on the television. It might have been Jake La Motta's last fight, and he was taking a merciless beating. He had somehow stayed on his feet (he had managed an entire career without once being knocked down) for the entire fight. When it was finally over he was asked at ringside why he hadn't gone down for a nine-count in order to take a rest. As I recall he replied, "I didn't want to start any bad habits."

I had just been given my first piece of literary advice. My worst beatings were yet ahead of me, but I knew to stand my ground, no matter what. What Jake La Motta had said to me was, Don't set a bad precedent, establish good working habits and don't let yourself off.

Back to San Francisco, 1965. Who were the Beat poets? And what was poetry, for that matter? I had taken more English courses than philosophy (my major) and so, inevitably, I had read some poets. I did like Yeats, along with Housman, and—I am ashamed to say—Khalil Gibran and Walter Benton. But none of this had prepared me for contemporary American poetry.

In my last year of college I had heard of Allen Ginsberg and Jack Kerouac, but neither of them were in San Francisco when I got there, although Allen Ginsberg soon showed up. Gregory Corso had also left town, but there were plenty of others to choose from.

The poets I finally settled on for my book were David Meltzer (who was the only one I knew personally—he was working at Discovery Book Store and I would soon be working there as well), Michael McClure, Gary Snyder, Philip Whalen, Brother Antoninus (William Everson), and Lawrence Ferlinghetti, whose City Lights Bookstore was two doors down from Discovery.

It had occurred to me to write portraits of the poets, as well as checklists of their works.

About this time I met Robert Hawley, who was just then starting Oyez. He read my portrait of David Meltzer, whose poetry he was just about to publish, and offered me $100 outright. Not counting my $200 advance for the Saroyan bibliography (bibliographies are *compiled,* not *written*) this was my first money and my most thrilling moment as a writer.

I moved into a fleabag hotel on Columbus Street—inhabited for the most part by bums, drunks, and derelicts—and set to work. I was simultaneously as poor and as happy as I had ever been in my life. I would have a donut and a cup of coffee in the morning and start my day. I would write all morning and spend the afternoons reading and preparing the next day's work. In the evenings I would wander over to Chinatown—there was a restaurant that served a regular meal, including dessert for seventy-five cents—and also in Chinatown there was a movie house that showed old American movies for fifty cents. If I could afford a beer I'd go to Vezuvio's (the Bohemian bar facing the alley that separated Discovery and City Lights).

The David Meltzer monograph was published with a frontispiece drawing of the poet by my friend Peter LeBlanc. I had stolen a line ("otter brown eyes") from a short story in a typescript by another friend, Jacob Needleman, who was also trying to write. His wife, Carla, said I had been hiding my light under a bushel. Jerry and I decided to begin a literary magazine. He had the perfect title: *Tired Horse Review,* as I remember. He thought the title so outstanding he swore me to secrecy, and together we sat down to write our credo. I put a piece of paper in the typewriter and ten minutes later, presto! a perfect manifesto. From that day on Jerry was convinced I was a born writer.

I visited Gary Snyder's class at Berkeley; Brother Antoninus at his monastery in Marin County; Phil Whalen at his apartment on Beaver Street; Michael McClure at Holmes's Bookstore in Oakland, where Bob Hawley worked; and finally Lawrence Ferlinghetti at his studio on Potrero Hill. Even if I didn't think much of the writing or bearing of these poets, it was still a very high time in my life. Jack Spicer was holding court nightly at Gino & Carlo's tavern, where I began to drink and play pool with other unknown writers like myself. Richard Brautigan was writing *Trout Fishing in America.* I had considered including him in my book but disqualified him on the basis of his poems, that seemed to me minimal at best—but we had long, involved talks about Saroyan, whose work he admired as much as I did.

As I went on with the writing of the book I began to see that the thing that interested me most about these poets was not so much their writing but their manhood. It seemed to me that it wasn't enough to be a good writer—or a good anything else—what mattered most was a man's character and being. I felt that if a man did important work then he himself should be the equal of that work. The outside should match the inside. For good or ill, the writing of the portraits for that book was founded on this premise.

The book was finally completed, and at the same time I sold my Saroyan collection to the Fresno Public Library. I had $5,000 in my pocket and, at the same time, a publishing offer from Kent State University for *Six Poets of the San Francisco Renaissance.* Once again I packed my car and headed for Racine, where I showed the letter from Kent State to my childhood friend, Chuck Pehlivanian, who was now a lawyer. Kent State University Press wanted to put the word "Beat" in the title, and they offered me a $500 advance—with a tiny royalty, as I remember. I didn't want to make a title change, and I didn't think $500 was enough money for a year's work. I asked Chuck to do something about it. Whatever it was he did, the offer was rescinded and I went off to Europe for the summer, wondering if I had done the right thing.

But first I lingered in Racine, visiting old haunts and gathering material from a past that seemed to be increasing its hold on me. I wrote "Highway America," that would eventually become the booklet, *An Evening with Saroyan.*

By the time I boarded a Belgian freighter in Pensacola, Florida, I had visited six southern states.

I had sold my Volkswagen in New Orleans, but in Germany I bought another and drove slowly, leisurely to Greece, where I spent a very happy month in the city of Pylos on the sea, and met Erik Haugaard and his family. Erik was working mornings on a novel, but from afternoon till evening he, along with his wife Myrna, and their two sprightly children, made excellent companions. The stretch of country we drove through nearly every day on our way to a secluded beach will ever be etched in my memory—in particular the time we heard the sheeps' bells and waited for them to appear over a hillock and roam across the road past our halted car.

I had this idea that I would not marry until I had established my life work. I wanted my work to be a part of my identity, as well as my reality. I wanted the woman I married to know what she was getting, and I wanted her to understand that she was getting something special. I was by now nearing my middle thirties but I still knew very little about life. I had always been naive, which my mother was wont to excuse by declaring that I had a "good heart." Alas, it didn't make me less a fool.

As I journeyed home from Europe I sensed that the time of my marriage was approaching. But the marriage I made was doomed from the start. When it finally ended I couldn't help but believe that it never should have happened. While it was on and after it was over, its result for me seemed to be nothing but pain, suffering, and remorse. But there is no school for marriage but marriage itself, and it was because of the suffering and because of the remorse that I was able to marry Nonny Hogrogian, a woman my age, who was also an artist, and whose ancestry was the same as mine. It was proof of graduation. My "failed" marriage had resulted in my making a true and real marriage.

But it was my first marriage that helped me to become a poet. There is a reason why poetry, love, and youth are connected in our minds. Perhaps one has to be mad to write poetry, and being in love makes this madness seem desirable.

I had not yet become the writer of my writing, but now—at once—something that *appeared* to be writing was occurring to *me.* I found myself wandering out of the house and into the back yard, and then wandering back inside, where I would scribble something on paper that seemed to have something to do with what I had just seen. It was all very confusing. I didn't know what poetry was, but whatever it was I couldn't imagine that *I* was writing it. And yet there was nothing else to call the stuff I was getting down on paper—and in fact, in its form at least, it did *look* like poetry.

Saroyan and I had made a friendship, which began about the time I started writing *Six Poets of the San Francisco Renaissance,* for which he had contributed an introduction. He had admired the writing—in part, I am sure, because it was so unlike the kind of writing he did. He had been away while I was writing my poems, but upon his return he phoned and asked that I come over to his place— he was the owner of two adjoined tract homes in Fresno, one for his papers and junk, the other for his living. Fortunately, before leaving, I thought to take a sheaf of poems with me. Surely the Master would know what I had done and whether or not my poems were any good. He had let me know on an earlier occasion that my short stories, although showing talent, were not publishable.

Saroyan, as it turned out, had called to offer me a job as his secretary, but immediately after reading my poems he changed his mind. I had my own writing to do now, he said (he had called the poems "A-1"), and my writing, combined with my plans for my press, would be full-time work. I had founded the Giligia Press (named after my father's birthplace, which was the site of the last Armenian kingdom) in order to make money from my book (it did), and now Saroyan was able to see something I myself had not yet seen: I would soon be publishing poetry—my own—and, inevitably, the work of other poets with whom I would feel a kinship. This kind of literary practice (for poets, especially) seemed to be in the American tradition, as I was soon to find out.

Poem followed poem, while the proceeds from my book kept us afloat. One day Andy Brown, whom I had met at Discovery Book Store, and who had helped me get the job as literary consultant at Northwestern University (the twenty-five dollars-a-week unemployment checks resulting from this job had given me the money with which to write my book about the poets) called to say he had purchased Gotham Book Mart. Would I come and help him out?

My wife and I set out at once by car, stopping on the way to visit her relatives in New Mexico. To make a long story short, I fell in love with New Mexico, and after our brief stay in New York we moved to Santa Fe, for what would prove to be a very important year in my life. I had done very little writing in New York (the place didn't agree with me) but now I was writing again—poems about the haunting landscape, so different and strange from anything I had previously seen or experienced.

Santa Fe was a city with a culture, a past, and a tradition. I began meeting other writers with whom I exchanged views and shared my work. Then I met Gerald Hausman, an unpublished poet like myself and a student in Las Vegas, New Mexico. It wasn't long before we gave our first poetry reading—at a coffee shop off campus, that we followed with a reading at St. John's College in Santa Fe, celebrating the event with a chapbook of poems.

There is an inestimable value in the friendships beginning writers make. Together they share their hopes and dreams, and, knowing each other's work intimately, they are able to keep each other honest, while boosting morale and providing an audience for one another's work. This kind of sharing and healthy criticism can happen but once in a writer's life—for once you are published you are alone and compelled to know for yourself what you are doing, as well as when you go off and how you must get back on.

But the real fun is in the beginning, because, so much of it being dream, anything seems possible and perhaps everything *is* possible. Gerry Hausman's enthusiasm for poetry in general, and my own in particular, was the greatest benefit I could have received at what was certainly a crucial time in my life. I had a friend in the literary wars, a comrade-in-arms.

I had been living in Santa Fe for one year when I learned there was an Armenian *oud* player living in Albuquerque, who had in turn learned there was an Armenian poet living in Santa Fe. The *oud* player turned out to be Avak Akgulian, the great oral historian of the

folkways of the people of Racine, in particular the Armenians. We soon got together and, as he talked, his stories began evoking in me a longing for something—I knew not what. In my mind I was puzzled, but my feelings knew: I was not where I needed to be. There was something calling me. It had to do with my people, it had to do with my childhood, and it had to do with an understanding of my past—without which I could not inhabit the future.

I had by now written the poem "On the Death of My Father," and soon after my meeting with Avak I had a dream about my father that I tried to get into a poem. In the dream he is standing in front of me, " . . . his back to me bare." What did it mean? After a great deal of pondering I realized that I needed to see the Armenians again.

We packed up and moved once again to Fresno.

During my years as an antiquarian book dealer I had gotten to know Henry Madden, the head librarian at Fresno State College. I went to him now and asked for a part-time job as a library consultant. It was at a time when libraries had been allocated more money than they knew how to reasonably spend.

The pay was poor but the hours were right and I set to work writing the poems I felt I had been called to write. Every evening, immediately after dinner, I would go to my work room and write for a minimum of three hours.

After four months' time *Homage to Adana* was completed. In writing this book I had found my material and my voice. I also learned how to take a theme and sustain it for the length of an entire book. From here on this would characterize all of my books of poetry—they would not be collections of poems—a book being the excuse to gather them together—but a book in the way that a novel or a biography is a book.

Still another thing happened while writing that book: my mind finally came forward and took its proper place alongside my feeling. It felt as if my mind had finally caught up, and as it did, I realized why it had taken me so long to become a writer—I had been mentally unprepared. Or should I say, undeveloped.

We are a body, we are a mind, and we are also our feelings. When all three participate in an activity it has a quality and force that no one part—no matter how highly developed it may be—can bring. But now, with my mind and my feelings suddenly aligned, I wondered, what was the function of the mysterious third ingredient, the body. It took a long time before I found the answer, but at last I saw what it was—the breath. It made me wonder if our only mark of individuality is not our breath. We are breathed into life, and we are all breathed differently. In poetry, all talk of cadence, music, measure, line break, etc., is really talk of breath. We write as we breathe, for as we breathe we write. This is how the body accompanies the mind and feelings, as they participate together in the act of making a poem.

There was another reason why it had taken me so long to come to my writing, which *Homage to Adana* also made evident. It revealed once and for all what the subject of my writing would be: myself. This of course had been the reason for my attraction to Saroyan's work. I had a deep, abiding need to understand my life—and writing, I instinctively knew, was the instrument through which I would conduct my search. But this by itself was not enough: writing had to be interesting to others as well, and this being the case how, I wondered, would my writing ever qualify in the marketplace, since here I was a son of immigrant parents, and a person who not only did not have any special qualities of his own, but one who had in fact gotten himself raised in what amounted to a ghetto, in a city that had to be one of the most forlorn places in all America.

These attitudes—call them beliefs—were in my bones. My mother remembered my accosting her when I was ten with the accusation that there were no great men in Racine. She said *our* great men had been assassinated by the Turks. What about the Americans then, I had asked, what was their excuse? I needed models, figureheads, examples—and there were none in sight.

All of these notions, I knew, had kept me from writing. But little by little, principally through a gradual understanding of Saroyan's work, I began to see that for the purpose of art one life is as good as another, and that no life is unworthy of the attention of art.

I had had my models all along, as the writing of *Homage to Adana* would reveal. I had had them because I had to have them, and so I had, unwittingly, transformed the material that surrounded me as a child into something meaningful, instructive, and intelligent for myself. The river, the lake, the rock garden, the pavilions and gazebos—all of nature itself—as well as the people I knew: United States Tony, Umbashi, Joe Perch, State Street Harry—there was a meaning to their lives. *There was a meaning to their lives for me.* It was so because I required it, and because I did they would become what they needed to become for me.

I had learned to make a poem, and because I had, I was beginning to find out about my life. It seemed obvious to me now that a man could live a lifetime and never get the first twelve years of his life understood. And yet, those years would determine everything that followed. Nearly all my writing from now on would be concerned with an attempt to do just that.

Soon after I completed *Homage to Adana,* James Baloian, a young poet who had studied with Philip Levine and Robert Mezey at Fresno State College, approached me with the suggestion that we do a poetry magazine together. I was against doing a magazine, but I had another idea. Because of the times, and because of all the teacher-poets—who were also a product of the times—Fresno was crawling with poets. It seemed to me that if they were gathered together, an interesting city anthology would result.

It was a new concept in publishing. By now the Giligia Press was going strong. I had published several books of poetry, so why not, I reasoned, do an anthology to add to the list. Together, Baloian and I selected work from the twenty best local poets we could find. Then we got Tom Peck to bring his camera down to the old Santa Fe train station to photograph the poets in the book, to which we added the presences of William Saroyan and William Everson, as elder statesmen-poets.

It was a happy moment and no one, least of all myself, suspected that we were making history. A hundred and more city anthologies followed from all around the country, as poets everywhere saw that they didn't have to be dependent on traditional publishing procedures to get their work out into the world. We titled our book *Down at the Santa Fe Depot: Twenty Fresno Poets.* It was an instant success locally, selling out the first thousand copies in one month. By good timing or fortune it was issued almost simultaneously with my first book of poems, to which Saroyan added an introduction, after changing the title from *A Family of Four* to *On the Death of My Father and Other Poems.* I had arrived: I was a poet, a publisher, and I had made a name in the world—just as I had avowed I would.

The year was 1970. My life was changing and changing fast. The dissolution of my marriage had finally occurred. I read Castaneda's *Don Juan: A Yaqui Way of Knowledge,* which would influence my next book of poems, but more important, would show me, both through the teachings of that book and the indications revealed by my own poems, that there was another level of life that was beckoning me.

I had moved to Lenox, Massachusetts, and I took up residence with the Hausmans at Windsor Mountain School, where Gerry was teaching—its campus being the summer home of the resident musicians at Tanglewood, just down the road. There I wrote *Looking over Hills* in a month's time and realized that the "higher states" in which poets often find themselves when creating do not belong to them, cannot be beckoned at will, and in fact, the poet at such times is nothing more than a radio transmitting messages between levels of reality. I knew—that is to say, I was convinced—from having read Castaneda, that these states could only be achieved by being earned. A poet was a channel, yes, but nothing was his for the keeping. A need was growing in me—a need I could not name but that was nonetheless mysteriously knowable.

By the end of that summer I was offered the editorship of *Ararat,* the Armenian-American literary magazine. For some years I had been reviewing books and contributing poems to their pages, and I had some very definite ideas about changes that needed to be made in the magazine—both to serve its audience and community, and to fulfill the needs of writers like myself who were grappling with their past. I was beginning to see that my Armenian heritage had been, from the beginning of my life, both a blessing and a curse.

What did it mean to be an Armenian? I had rejected the implications as a child, seeing that I did not want to align myself with a dying culture and a forlorn race of people—but I *was* an Armenian after all. I could not deny my blood simply because it disturbed me—nor even because it attracted me. Was this then the material of my life—to understand, transform, and thereby transcend? Perhaps—but at the time I was only confused, anxious, troubled, angry at the Armenians—and angry at the world. What was the meaning of this life we had been given—and more specifically: what was the meaning and purpose of my *own* life? No one could tell me. I had to find out for myself. And I had to find out in the only way I knew—by following my instincts and by insisting—and persisting—in my search.

I had made a beginning with my poems of childhood, the title a clear and conscientious declaration of homage to my race. Now I had to take another harder step, for I had to actually work with the Armenians, and as I well knew, one

Armenian cannot get along with another Armenian. This too had to be understood.

I had had a clue when, several summers previous, driving through the Yugoslavian village of Tito Valdez, I stopped in a coffee house, and there, for the first time in my life, saw a party of Turkish men seated round a table. What I had heard about the Turks did not prepare me for this moment, for this demonstration of comradeship that was being enacted before my eyes. It was so un-Armenian, and yet so familiar, as if I understood through my emotions alone what I was witnessing. Their camaraderie, their well-wishing toward one another, the way they embraced the last member of their party to arrive, their obvious generosity and openness with each other—all of this startled me, both because they were so rarely evinced in relationships among Armenian men, but also because it did not conform with all the horrible stories I had heard about the Turks. In fact, I thought at the time: there is something of their gentility in Armenian women, but certainly not in our men. Why?

I could see better now why Armenian and Turk had lived in enmity. The Armenian, perhaps because he had lost his country, was ambitious, clever, driven, and suspicious—and therefore suspect. But more important, the Armenian belonged to the West—both because he was Christian, but also for other reasons that I could not understand as yet.

Nonny was now my art director and it occurred to me that we should do a special issue from Armenia—on its people and its arts. We were invited to Yerevan as guest of the Armenian government, to attend a writer's congress and to do our work.

My difficulties with the Armenians of Armenia was even greater than my difficulties with the Armenians of America—who were after all free men, at least politically, and who were also, like my parents, from western Armenia—that is, Turkey—whereas these Armenians had been Russianized. Part of the difficulty of course was the

Kherdian with his wife, Nonny Hogrogian, and his cat, Sossi, Aurora, Oregon, 1984

Communist government: by way of reminder, tanks in formation would come roaring into Lenin Square once a week. But it was also the realization that I was not a part of this world: whether as it existed in the present (Armenia itself) or in the past: America (with its Armenians clinging to a vanished world).

Well, didn't I know this as a child? Yes! But something had to be actualized, and it was *being* actualized by the work I was doing: in my poetry, as editor of *Ararat* magazine, and by working with Armenians and traveling to their country. I was earning my deliverance by facing it, for the alternative would be to deny or run away from it.

Little by little I began to free myself, both of my ancestral past as well as my actual past. That is, Racine, Wisconsin: the limiting land I was born onto, out of the limiting race I inherited with my birth.

From New Hampshire, where we took up residence after our marriage in 1971, we moved to upstate New York. My poems now were concerned exclusively with the present, and they began to unfold as naturally as breathing. Had I really done the impossible, and I resolved my early life and made it possible for me to inhabit the present: with art *and* with living? The poems, for the moment, seemed to say so. And yet there was this search for something more that had begun with the reading of that strange book by Castaneda that was composed of fact and fiction, but that gave the lie to both, thereby creating a new reality. And it was this reality, I felt, that I had come in touch with when I wrote my Berkshire poems, that were so unlike my previous work.

Then one day I began writing poems of childhood again—but so different from the poems in the previous volume, that had been content only to look back. The first poem I wrote would serve as the book's epigraph:

At the bottom of Liberty Street,
the Island Park Bridge—
(the hollow heart of the city);
and I return there now for
the soundings:
pavilion dead, river dead,
city all but dead,
with only the breathless
remains of the imitation
rock-garden city in the yard
almost touching the bridge
it imitates (on which I stand)
and there
on that spot—
just beyond the heart
but palpitating with it, the
new city, the city that
sings these poems,
is going up

I had returned again, but this time to reclaim my life. I had paid homage to the past, and now, with the poems of *I Remember Root River,* I had slain the demon that would hold me to that past. I was ready to declare my life.

Just a month before I had completed *Taking the Soundings on Third Avenue,* concluding (though I hadn't known it then) the trilogy of poems that began with *The*

Nonny Poems and that was followed by *Any Day of Your Life.*

Three was a good number, two was not. But now, without any thought that there would one day be a fitting and concluding third volume to my childhood poems, my writing life suddenly changed. Ever since I was a little boy my mother had said to me, "Someday you grow up and tell my story." No doubt this lament echoed through all of the surrounding homes in our community. How the other children responded I did not know. I only knew that for me her story was too painful to listen to; it was a hell she had passed through and that I had no intention of entering.

And so here I was, well past the age of forty, never having heard her story of persecution and starvation, but with the promise made at last, that since I was a writer, even though only a poet, I would take it upon myself to bear witness to her life.

I flew my mother to New York so I could hear about her life for the first time. She arrived, clutching her story in hand: Fourteen handwritten pages in Armenian. We began by taping the reading of her script. When she came to the part of her story where her mother dies of a broken heart she began weeping—the first time she had ever wept in my presence—and said, "I cannot any more today."

I could see that this was going to be a book of suffering but I did not see then that, because the suffering was ours, the reader would be the beneficiary.

It is the writer that must suffer, not the reader.

One year later the book was completed and upon its acceptance I phoned my mother to give her the news. But apparently she and her family already knew, as her dream of the night before had made known. She said, "Last night in my dream my entire family was gathered into a circle and Virginia (my sister) was moving inside our circle and pouring tea into each of our cups. This is the first dream I have ever had with all of my family present. As Virginia poured tea into each of our cups I could see a look of peace come over all their faces. David, it is because of your book. Now there is rest and joy and peace for our family at last."

The Road from Home would go on to make my name, but long before it won any awards—in fact while it was still in typescript—my mother declared, "Now you can go on and write anything." And suddenly I saw that it was true. I would not only be able to write both fiction and nonfiction, but I had found a way at last to make a living exclusively from writing. I had known all along that as far as money was concerned I could expect nothing from my poetry. This had never troubled me because I had had no choice: I had not chosen poetry, it had chosen me, and also I was using poetry to explore my life—and this was more important to me than making money.

From the time I began writing *The Road from Home,* Nonny had insisted that the real book I needed to write was my own childhood story of growing up in Racine, Wisconsin. But first I wrote *Finding Home,* the inevitable sequel to *The Road from Home.*

By then I was going back and forth between poetry and prose, and one bright day, without any preparation or indication, I awoke and began writing the poems for *Place of Birth,* taking just one week to complete the book, thereby concluding my trilogy of childhood poems.

As I write two books are in the process of being published both of which are, again, concluding volumes in trilogies: *Root River Run,* my autobiography, and the third volume of "Farm" poems, which are, appropriately, the least known of my books of poems, perhaps even more so than *Looking over Hills,* which was, I suppose, their predecessor. These poems embody the spiritual home, not only of my work but of my life. What I am now, what I have learned, what I hope to be!

POSTSCRIPT, 2000

The concluding paragraph of my autobiographical entry for *SATA* alluded to a book of poems emanating from my "spiritual home," whose identity I did not wish at that time to reveal. I did not know then that my time of departure from "The Farm" (the title of that book of poems) was imminent, and that the book I would soon write—about my experiences in what was a Gurdjieff school and quasi community—would make my time (highly private in its occurrence) a public declaration.

I called it a quasi community because only my wife and I, our teacher, the schoolmaster and his family, a caretaker and family, and our resident "farmer" were live-ins, with the latter two positions in rotation among the hundred or so, ever in flux, "members" of the school. Soon after we moved to Oregon to join the Gurdjieff group, we persuaded our teacher to allow us to move onto the property and convert an unused hop barn into a residence for ourselves and as a site for Two Rivers Press, where we would learn, for the first time, typesetting and letterpress printing, marbling and hand bookbinding. During the nine years we spent on The Farm, that came to be called Two Rivers Farm after our press name, we produced a number of books in limited editions, and an odd assortment of labels, menus, posters, broadsides and, most importantly, keepsakes for the annual Gurdjieff birthday dinners.

My wife and I were both over fifty years old when the time came for us to leave The Farm. Having intentionally burned our bridges—when we sold our house in upstate New York in order to fund the press—and having no savings or safe haven to return to, we put our worldly goods in storage and headed East.

For the next two years we lived in upstate New York, where we started our own Gurdjieff group and began printing again, but we soon saw that we were merely imitating the form of the school we had left, and also that the teaching, at least in its traditional form, was not right for us.

To improve our earnings, Nonny had her first one-woman show of illustrated art. Soon after her successful showing, she was invited to exhibit permanently in a gallery devoted exclusively to children's book art in Vermont. Meanwhile, we were completing the last of the books we had contracted for with Knopf. It was during this period, when we were just beginning to get on our feet, that my closest friend from childhood, Michael (Mikey) Kaiserlian came down with cancer. Throughout his illness we remained in close contact by phone and through the mails. But our plans for a visit with him and his family in Racine was never realized because he quickly went from remission into his final illness. Although we had drifted apart after I left Racine, following my graduation from the University of Wisconsin, we had just a few years prior to his illness resumed our friendship by an odd set of circumstances. A

friend of his, while visiting Portland, had seen our faces on the cover of the *Oregonian*'s Sunday magazine. He took the copy home with him to give to his friend. At about the same time Mikey's pastor had given him the assignment of writing a letter to someone once close to him that he was no longer in contact with, with the result that a long correspondence ensued, followed by my visits whenever I returned to Racine to research new projects.

I took his death very hard. He was the first of my friends to die, and it faced me not only with my own mortality but with the realization that a part of me disappeared with his going; that his memories of our friendship were now no longer available to me. What was the lesson in this? What was the experience? I learned that I had to deal with the personal loss and the grief I was enduring by turning to my writing, to discover all that I didn't know I knew about my life, his life, and the life we knew together.

Years before, when writing *Homage to Adana,* which I dedicated to my Father, I learned that death does not—nor need not—end a relationship between two people, and that by working consciously for resolution and understanding the effort can result in our repairing the past; and since the past is our present, it is only in this way that we can prepare the future. The book I was writing, to be dedicated to Michael Kaiserlian, would be titled *The Dividing River/The Meeting Shore.* In the writing I realized that I had not completely put the ghosts of the past to rest, and that this was not to be the last book I would write about my childhood years. It was but the first book in a new phase, in what would bring to finality what I saw were the linked volumes in what I was now calling my Root River Cycle—poetry, novellas, and memoirs, of which there are presently thirteen volumes, all of them concerned with the town's history and my childhood years in that place: Racine, Wisconsin.

Circumstances led us to Charlottesville, to be close to my sister, Virginia, her son, Michael, and husband, Edwin Hedge. My sister had met Edwin in England, his home, and as a result we had not met until after their marriage, and now, for the first time, we were becoming acquainted. We soon established a close and enduring friendship. Because of our troubled parting from our teacher, who resisted our leaving the Farm in every way she could, Edwin suggested I write a book about those years to purge myself of the hurt I was still feeling, and also to record the teaching as I had received and understood it. The ideas of Gurdjieff had become the central governing principle in Nonny's life and mine. Although no one had ever suggested a book idea to me before, it became obvious that this was something I needed to do. It was a hard book to write, and I found it necessary to scrap the first draft and start again from scratch. In the end it was a deeply satisfying experience and proved to be beneficial to other Gurdjieffians as well, especially since it was the first published work by someone of our generation about the actual practice of the Work. Unfortunately, it was its very success that defeated it *and* the publisher, for when it was reviewed on the front page of the *New York Times Book Review,* it was between printings, and so the people who most wanted to read the book were unable to purchase a copy. The second printing, therefore, soon remaindered and the publisher gave up the ghost. Since then the book—*On a Spaceship with Beelzebub: By a*

Grandson of Gurdjieff—has been republished with an additional Afterword by Inner Traditions.

We remained in Charlottesville for two years, and for the entire time I conducted what I called my "Writing Class," where I continued teaching the Gurdjieff Work by a method I had devised while at the Farm, using what I had learned about myself from writing about my own past, together with Gurdjieff's psychological ideas about man.

Nonny had been thinking of doing a children's book of the famous Asian classic *Monkey*. She asked if I would do a translation of the text for a thirty-two-page picture book. I agreed and found two complete literal translations in the University of Virginia library, but I soon saw that I needed to give the book its due by doing a fuller version, and not for children. *Monkey* would be published by Shambhala, becoming an instant success, and was quickly adopted by the Book-of-the-Month club, and also sold to television.

Philomel, who had published others of our more recent books, including *Asking the River,* now proposed our first coffee table book, a collection of folktales from around the world, that I would retell and that Nonny would illustrate. I found, not surprisingly, that the book was excruciatingly difficult for me to write because it was my least favorite of all the literary forms. Nonny reminded me that I had been creating over many years my own mythology, both of myself, as well as the time, and the people, and the place I had come from. Perhaps it was for this reason that I had to fix all of it in a myth-like reality, making it believable by my own insistent need to create my life from the inside out, rather than accept the life that had been largely imposed on me. The book was titled *Feathers and Tails* and became Nonny's favorite of all the books we did together.

Two earlier books that I had written while in Oregon would soon be published: the first, *A Song for Uncle Harry,* which I had aborted during the first draft, but that I found among my papers and completed after we moved East. The other, my first memoir, *I Called It Home,* that I had written years before, finally found a brave publisher. It had been rejected numerous times because it was episodic, impressionistic, and, not surprisingly, very poetic. The critics were right in terms of a mass audience, and the book sank without a trace, but it and *A Song for Uncle Harry* remain my own favorites of my works in prose.

When I was a young boy growing up in Racine, I hunted Scouts Woods with my buddy Chuck (Horse) Kamakian, and others. We walked to Scouts Woods from our homes, skirting the Horlick Malted Milk plant on the outskirts of town while peering through the fence at their private pond, rumored to hold fourteen bluegills. Why bluegills, and why fourteen in particular since no one was allowed to fish there, was something I never questioned. I believed it absolutely and, with the others, dreamed and made preliminary plans to scale the fence at night and catch these large, beguiling bluegills. But we never did, and so it remained all my youth one of the unfulfilled fantasies that—lo and behold—one day magically reappeared in the form of a short story of a fishing contest for boys and girls at our own zoo pond in Racine (which I had witnessed from a distance as an adult). The pond, that was really a shallow cement-bottom pool for youngsters to swim in, was filled with small panfish for the contest. However, this pond was connected by a foot bridge to a larger, deeper pond that was fenced off to protect the animals that were sequestered on

Kherdian with his sister, Virginia K. Hedge, on the porch swing

its grounds. In the story, two buddies get the idea of fishing beside the bridge in the hope that a large bluegill, possibly fourteen in length, might wander from the off-limits pond into ours, and that if one did and we caught it, we would surely win the top prize in the contest.

Philomel contracted for *The Great Fishing Contest,* and Nonny did the illustrations. We had a friend in Racine take photos of the zoo pond and surrounding buildings, and our nephew, Michael Hedge became Nonny's model for the story's hero.

Soon after this my sister and her family moved to Africa where Edwin assumed a teaching post, and we ventured to Maine, first on an invitation from Janwillem van de Wetering, who had blurbed my book *On a Spaceship with Beelzebub*. After a week's stay, we decided we liked what we saw and bought a large home in Blue Hill upon selling our home in Charlottesville. We turned an unfinished portion of the house into an art gallery for children's book artists and others, and our first show included Janwillem's unusual sculptures made almost entirely from found objects that he had collected around his seaside home. It was his first show, and also included his wife's Columbian influenced pottery and sculptures. Of the artists we met through our exhibitions, two became our good friends, Jeannette and Roger Winters.

Once again I found that there was still material from my childhood that needed transforming. One day, again unexpectedly, I found myself writing a portrait of one of my childhood friends. The next day I wrote of another friend about yet another incident from my childhood. By the following day I began to wonder aloud if I was onto another book. All of my books of poems—which are always thematic—occur in just this way: a poem appears direct from the subconscious, and then possibly one or two more that are clearly related, before I realize that something has formed itself inside me that now wants release and completion.

In a period of weeks I had fifty-one poems and an epigraph, which had been written sometime earlier, without my knowing that it was the herald for a new book. Each poem bore the name of an individual friend or friends. I learned from this book that my peers were also my teachers, and in some cases my models for attributes of character that I felt were missing in myself. It was a heartwarming book and a number of writers told me it had inspired them to make a similar journey with their work. I also realized that the moments in which we are truly awake stay with us forever, and it is this that we are composed of. Why we were awake to some moments and not to others tells us who we are. For the shock of recognition occurs differently in each of us, and our task is to find ourselves and know ourselves, and finally to *become* ourselves. And it is from this that a larger understanding of our connection to all humanity is possible. It is for this reason that the thrust of my work, which is also the central concern of my life, is built around relationships. There is nothing more important than this. Art by itself can do nothing, is nothing, if it does not lend itself to this.

The harsh winters of Maine along with the sense of isolation that we felt living there, impelled us—when our home wouldn't sell—to rent a home in the Berkshires (near Chatham, again) for the winter.

My friend, Gerry Hausman, suggested that I do an anthology of Beat poetry, which I knew at once was a project that would interest my editor at Henry Holt. So that winter was spent on this project (*Beat Voices* was the title I finally settled on) and also another surprise book of poems, this one called *My Racine.* I had lived long enough to see the city of my birth become another place, almost unrecognizable to me, and so I wanted to distinguish with the title what I remembered from what I was now seeing on my rare return visits to the city.

Our house in Maine finally sold and once again we moved back to the Chatham area, this time the village of Spencertown. It was here that my twenty-year-old dream to publish a multiethnic literary magazine came to fruition. We called it *Forkroads,* and despite a highly favorable press, we were not able to go beyond six issues. Although I had always been a proponent for one world, I felt that before this could be achieved we had not only to accept our differences but learn to cherish them, and also to exchange with others and thereby benefit from our differences. Until *Forkroads* came along, ethnic meant minorities only, but it became quickly evident that those of the majority were often just as ethnic conscious and ethnic proud. However, as always with things human, there was a greater interest in being known than in knowing the other. Perhaps our journal was not ahead of its time, but behind it, because the changes we were promulgating were occurring, if not in art, then certainly in the public square, which is not always where artists look for their material. Still, it was an interesting experiment and what we learned about magazines and journals would come back into play in the very near future.

It was around this time that an independent filmmaker, Jim Belleau, approached me with the idea of doing an hour-long film on my life and work. As we were bound for Chicago to attend a library conference, where we would be launching our new journal, it was arranged that we meet in Racine and begin shooting film. Later episodes took place in Spencertown, and at a filmed reading I gave in Oneonta, New York. The end result was a film I was proud of, thanks

to the fine work of Jim Belleau. Although it never sold to television, as intended, it became a video and enjoyed a modest success. It is called *The Dividing River/The Meeting Shore,* after the title of one of my books of poems.

We had been living in Spencertown for two years when we were invited to attend a week-long seminar in Sebastopol, California, that a small existing Gurdjieff group was sponsoring. At their prompting we decided to move to Sebastopol and participate in the experiment of peers working with peers. By now, all of the people that Gurdjieff had trained were dead, and all of us who had followed his ideas were thrown back on ourselves. Most had gone off on their own, continuing the inner work as best they could, while others remained in groups, and still others began the new experiment of working with peers across the various lineages.

Although our particular experiment failed in six months, resulting in the dispersion of its members, we remained close with nearly all of them, while each of us continued our search.

In our case it meant moving to Oregon to be near our closest friends from the Farm days. The former schoolmaster was suffering from cancer. The last thing I did before moving to Oregon was to write a life of the Buddha on contract from Shambhala. Shortly after we settled in, we launched a Gurdjieff Work journal. This seemed to be an important way to work with peers, but more importantly we needed to begin to identify and recognize who our peers were, for we realized that there were many who had gone off on their own, conducting their own experiments and ventures, and needed to share what they had come to or were coming to in their understanding and practice of the Work. It seemed that a new phase of the Work was beginning and perhaps our journal, *Stopinder: A Gurdjieff Journal for Our Time,* would be a handmaiden that could play a crucial role in this new octave of the Work.

A longtime champion of my poetry, David Shevin, who was associated with Bottom Dog Press, a Midwestern publisher, asked if I had any unpublished works in my Root River Cycle. I had in fact been revising a book of poems on and off for two years or more that belonged to that cycle. The new work was titled *The Neighborhood Years.* Bottom Dog Press became its publisher, with an introduction by David Shevin. I selected for the cover a photo of myself with Bob Hill and Wayne Kruse. I had been out of touch with both of them since our days as door-to-door magazine salesmen. But now, out of the blue, Bob Hill sent me the photo that seemed just right for the cover of my book. As a result, our friendship was renewed and when the book was published Bob sent me an engraved plaque with an Irish blessing, beneath which my name was engraved, followed by his message: My friend and the youngest boss I ever had. Buddies awhile, friends forever. Bob Hill.

It was the most touching present I had ever received, and the only one of my many plaques and awards that I put on my wall. As I said to Bob, it is one thing to be praised by strangers, but there is nothing comparable to being thanked by one's friends.

It is now fifty years, give or take a month or three, since that photo was taken. As I type this I am sixty-nine years old to the day. Where does a life go, and where do we go when it is gone? Just yesterday, while driving to the home of my acupuncturist friend to have him look at my suddenly troublesome left leg, I realized that the process of aging is a gift, as all of life is, with each time or aspect in our life of slow aging having a self-contained, built-in-apparatus-fulfilling opportunity for us to see and know what we need to understand to advance our slow evolution to truth and conscious completion. The special gift of aging, as we approach our own end, is the opportunity to drop our illusions, which more than anything else inhibits reality. The preparing of our departure that ageing induces brings us before ourselves in ways that were seemingly never possible before. In seeing this yesterday, I knew in a moment the freedom I had been struggling all my life to attain. It was brief, it was real, and it was whole. But as with everything that is not perfectly achieved, it will pass— but it *will* return. Our journey is not linear, it is circular. We will arrive again at the place we have been, but we will see it from above, as something seen before, with the recognition of what we could be, and will inevitably become.

Writings

POETRY

(With Gerald Hausman) *Eight Poems,* Giligia Press (Aurora, OR), 1968.

On the Death of My Father and Other Poems, with introduction by William Saroyan, Giligia Press (Aurora, OR), 1970.

Homage to Adana, Perishable Press, 1970, Giligia Press (Aurora, OR), 1971.

Looking over Hills, illustrations by wife, Nonny Hogrogian, Giligia Press (Lyme Center, NH), 1972.

A David Kherdian Sampler, edited and with an introduction by Moses Yanes, Community of Friends Press (Boulder Creek, CA), 1974.

The Nonny Poems, Macmillan (New York, NY), 1974.

Any Day of Your Life, Overlook Press/Bookstore Press (Woodstock, NY), 1975.

Country Cat, City Cat (poems for children), illustrated by Hogrogian, Four Winds Press (New York, NY), 1978.

I Remember Root River, Overlook Press (Woodstock, NY), 1978.

The Farm, with introduction by Brother Jeremy Driscoll, Two Rivers Press (Aurora, OR), 1979.

Taking the Soundings on Third Avenue, Overlook Press (New York, NY), 1981.

The Farm: Book Two, Two Rivers Press (Aurora, OR), 1982.

Place of Birth, with introduction by Martha Heyneman, Breitenbush (Portland, OR), 1983.

Threads of Light: The Farm Poems, Books Three and Four, with introduction by A. L. Staveley, Two Rivers Press (Aurora, OR), 1985.

Poems to an Essence Friend, The Press at Butternut Creek, 1987.

The Dividing River/The Meeting Shore, Lotus Press (Santa Fe, NM), 1990.

Friends: A Memoir, Globe Press Books (New York, NY), 1993.

My Racine, Forkroads Press (Spencertown, NY), 1994.

Seven Poems for Mikey, Forkroads Press (Spencertown, NY), 1997.

Chippecotton: Root River Tales of Racine, Gatehouse (Sebastopol, CA), 1998.

The Neighborhood Years, with introduction by David Shevin, Bottom Dog Press (Huron, OH), 2000.

FICTION

It Started with Old Man Bean, Greenwillow (New York, NY), 1980.

Beyond Two Rivers, Greenwillow (New York, NY), 1981.

The Song in the Walnut Grove, Knopf (New York, NY), 1983.

Asking the River: A Novel, Orchard Books (New York, NY), 1993.

FICTION; FOR CHILDREN; ILLUSTRATED BY NONNY HOGROGIAN EXCEPT AS NOTED

Right Now, Knopf (New York, NY), 1983.

The Mystery of the Diamond in the Wood, Knopf (New York, NY), 1983.

The Animal, Knopf (New York, NY), 1984.

A Song for Uncle Harry, Philomel Books (New York, NY), 1989.

The Cat's Midsummer Jamboree, Philomel Books (New York, NY), 1990.

The Great Fishing Contest, Philomel Books (New York, NY), 1991.

By Myself, Holt (New York, NY), 1993.

Juna's Journey, Philomel Books (New York, NY), 1993.

Lullaby for Emily, Holt (New York, NY), 1995.

The Rose's Smile: Farizad of the Arabian Nights, illustrated by Stephano Vitale, Holt (New York, NY), 1997.

The Golden Bracelet, Holiday House (New York, NY), 1998.

NONFICTION

The Road from Home: The Story of an Armenian Girl, Greenwillow (New York, NY), 1979.

Finding Home, Greenwillow (New York, NY), 1981.

Root River Run (memoir), Carolrhoda (Minneapolis, MN), 1984.

Bridger: The Story of a Mountain Man, Greenwillow (New York, NY), 1987.

On a Spaceship with Beelzebub: By a Grandson of Gurdjieff (autobiography), Globe Press (New York, NY), 1991.

I Called It Home, Blue Crane Books (Watertown, MA), 1997.

The Revelations of Alvin Tolliver, Hampton Roads Publishing (Charlottesville, VA), 2001.

EDITOR

(With James Baloian) *Down at the Santa Fe Depot: Twenty Fresno Poets,* Giligia Press (Fresno, CA), 1970.

Visions of America, by the Poets of Our Time, Macmillan (New York, NY), 1973.

Settling America: The Ethnic Expression of Fourteen Contemporary Poets, Macmillan (New York, NY), 1974.

Traveling America with Today's Poets, Macmillan (New York, NY), 1976.

Poems Here and Now, illustrated by Nonny Hogrogian, Greenwillow (New York, NY), 1976.

The Dog Writes on the Window with His Nose and Other Poems (poetry for children), illustrated by Nonny Hogrogian, Four Winds Press (New York, NY), 1977.

If Dragon Flies Made Honey (poetry for children), illustrations by Jose Aruego and Ariane Dewey, Greenwillow (New York, NY), 1977.

I Sing the Song of Myself: An Anthology of Autobiographical Poems, Greenwillow (New York, NY), 1978.

Beat Voices: An Anthology of Beat Poetry, Holt (New York, NY), 1995.

BROADSIDES

Letter to Virginia in Florence from Larkspur, California, Giligia Press (Aurora, OR), 1966.

Mother's Day, Gary Chafe and Sanford M. Dorbin, 1967.

Kato's Poem, Giligia Press (Aurora, OR), 1967.

Christmas, 1968, privately printed, 1968.

My Mother Takes My Wife's Side, illustrations by Judi Russell, Giligia Press (Aurora, OR), 1969.

O Kentucky, Giligia Press (Aurora, OR), 1969.

Outside the Library, privately printed, 1969.

Root River, illustrations by Bob Totten, Perishable Press, 1970.

Anniversary Song, Bellevue Press (Binghamton, NY), 1975.

Remembering Mihran, Massachusetts Council for the Arts, 1975.

The Toy Soldier, Bookstore Press (Freeport, ME), 1975.

Melkon, Isat Pragbhara Press, 1976.

October 31, 1980, privately printed, 1980.

Letter to Charles J. Hardy from David Kherdian, privately printed, 1981.

Solstice, Two Rivers Press (Aurora, OR), 1983.

The Press at Butternut Creek, The Press at Butternut Creek, 1987.

Also author of broadside *Island Park,* Isat Pragbhara Press.

BROADSIDES; ILLUSTRATED BY NONNY HOGROGIAN

Bird in Suet, Giligia Press (Lyme Center, NH), 1971.

Of Husbands and Wives, privately printed, 1971.

Hey Nonny, privately printed, 1972.

Poem for Nonny, Phineas Press, 1973.

Onions from New Hampshire, privately printed, 1973.

In the Tradition, University of Connecticut (Storrs, CT), 1974.

16:IV:73, Arts Action Press, 1975.

Dafje Vartan, Prescott Street Press (Portland, OR), 1978.

OTHER

David Meltzer: A Sketch from Memory and Descriptive Checklist, Oyez (Berkeley, CA), 1965.

A Biographical Sketch and Descriptive Checklist of Gary Snyder, Oyez (Berkeley, CA), 1965.

A Bibliography of William Saroyan, 1934-1964, Roger Beacham (San Francisco, CA), 1965.

(Compiler) *William Saroyan Collection* (catalog), Fresno County Free Library (Fresno, CA), 1966.

Six Poets of the San Francisco Renaissance: Portraits and Checklists, with introduction by William Saroyan, Giligia Press (Fresno, CA), 1967, new edition with introduction by Kherdian published as *Six San Francisco Poets,* Giligia Press (Fresno, CA), 1969.

(Author of introduction) Gerald Hausman, compiler, *The Shivurrus Plant of Mopant,* Giligia Press (Aurora, OR), 1968.

An Evening with Saroyan, The Ghost of Shah-Mouradian: A Review of "Short Drive, Sweet Chariot," Monday, May 9, 1966, Giligia Press (Aurora, OR), 1970.

(Author of introduction) Art Cuelho and Dean Phelps, editors, *Father Me Home, Winds,* Seven Buffaloes Press, 1975.

(Reteller; published anonymously) *The Pearl: Hymn of the Robe of Glory,* illustrated by Hogrogian, Two Rivers Press (Aurora, OR), 1979.

(Translator) *Pigs Never See the Stars: Proverbs from the Armenian,* woodcuts by Hogrogian, Two Rivers Press (Aurora, OR), 1982.

(Author of introduction) William Saroyan, *Births,* Creative Arts Book Co. (Berkeley, CA), 1983.

(Author of introduction) A. L. Staveley, *Themes III,* Two Rivers Press (Aurora, OR), 1984.

(Translator) Wu Ch'eng-en, *Monkey: A Journey to the West,* Shambhala Publications (Boston, MA), 1992.

(Reteller) *Feathers and Tails: Animal Fables from around the World,* illustrated by Nonny Hogrogian, Philomel Books (New York, NY), 1992.

Contributor to books, including *New to North America: Writing by U.S. Immigrants, Their Children, and Grandchildren,* edited by Abby Bogomolny, Burning Bush (Santa Cruz, CA), 1997; *The Mythology of Cats: Feline Legend and Lore through the Ages,* edited by Gerald and Loretta Hausman, St. Martin's (New York, NY), 1998; and *How Much Earth: The Fresno Poets,* edited by Christopher Buckley, David Oliveira, and M. L. Williams, Roundhouse Press (Berkeley, CA), 2001. Contributor to periodicals, including *Spirit Horse, Prairie Schooner, Shambhala Sun, Impressions,* and *Door Voice.* Featured in *The Dividing River/The Meeting Shore. The Poetry of David Kherdian,* a video production by Jim Belleau, produced by Acorn Productions, 1997.

KIMMEL, Eric A. 1946-

Personal

Born October 30, 1946, in Brooklyn, NY; son of Morris N. (a certified public accountant) and Anne (an elementary school teacher; maiden name, Kerker) Kimmel; married Elizabeth Marcia Sheridan (a professor of education), April 7, 1968 (divorced, 1975); married Doris Ann Blake, June 16, 1978; children: Bridgett (stepdaughter). *Education:* Lafayette College, A.B., 1967; New York University, M.A., 1969; University of Illinois, Ph.D., 1973. *Politics:* Democrat. *Religion:* Jewish.

Addresses

Home and office—2525 Northeast 35th Ave., Portland, OR 97212-5232. *E-mail*—kimmels@earthlink.net.

Career

Indiana University at South Bend, assistant professor of education, 1973-78; Portland State University, Portland, OR, professor of education, 1978-94. Full-time writer, 1994—. *Member:* International Reading Association, Authors Guild, Authors League of America, PEN Northwest, Society of Children's Book Writers and Illustrators, Phi Beta Kappa, Phi Delta Kappa, Kappa Delta Pi.

Awards, Honors

Juvenile Book Merit Award, Friends of American Writers, 1975, for *The Tartar's Sword;* Ten Best Books of 1989, Association of Booksellers for Children, for *Anansi and the Moss-Covered Rock;* Present Tense—Joel A. Cavior Award for Notable Children's Book, National Council of Teachers of English, 1990, for *Hershel and the Hanukkah Goblins;* Sydney Taylor Picture Book Award, Association of Jewish Libraries (AJL), 1990, and National Jewish Book Award nomination, both for *The Chanukkah Guest;* Notable Children's Trade Book in the Field of Social Studies, Children's Book Council/National Council for the Social Studies (CBC/NCSS), 1992, for *The Greatest of All;* Notable Children's Trade Book in the Field of Social Studies, CBC/NCSS, 1992, and Aesop Prize, Children's Folklore Section of the American Folklore Society, 1993, both for *Days of Awe: Stories for Rosh Hashanah and Yom Kippur;* Parents' Choice Award, 1994, for *The Three Princes;* Paul A. Witty Short Story Award, International Reading Association, for *Four Dollars and Fifty Cents;* Anne Izard Storytellers' Choice Award, for *The Spotted Pony;* Irma and James H. Black Award, Bank Street College of Education, for *Three Sacks of Truth;* Sydney Taylor Award, AJL, National Jewish Picture Book Award finalist, Zena Sutherland Award, University of Chicago Lab School, Notable Children's Book selection, American Library Association, Best Children's Books of 2000, *Publishers Weekly,* and One Hundred Titles for Reading and Sharing, New York Public Library, 2000, all for *Gershon's Monster: A Story for the Jewish New*

Eric A. Kimmel

Year; Best Children's Books of 2001, Bank Street College of Education, for *The Runaway Tortilla;* Notable Book selection, AJL, for *The Jar of Fools: Eight Hanukkah Stories from Chelm;* White House Easter Egg Roll featured book, 2001, for *The Birds' Gift: A Ukrainian Easter Story.*

Several of Kimmel's books have been nominated or won state awards from organizations in Colorado, Georgia, Nebraska, Nevada, Oregon, Utah, Kentucky, Pennsylvania, and Washington, and have been named to numerous "best books," "children's choice," and "teachers' choice" lists from various organizations, including the New York Public Library, the American Booksellers Association, and the Children's Book Council/International Reading Association.

Writings

FOR CHILDREN

The Tartar's Sword (novel), Coward, 1974.

Mishka, Pishka and Fishka, and Other Galician Tales, illustrated by Christopher J. Spollen, Coward, 1976.

Why Worry?, illustrated by Elizabeth Cannon, Pantheon, 1979.

Nicanor's Gate, illustrated by Jerry Joyner, Jewish Publication Society, 1979.

Hershel of Ostropol, illustrated by Arthur Friedman, Jewish Publication Society, 1981.

(With Rose Zar) *In the Mouth of the Wolf,* Jewish Publication Society, 1983.

(Reteller) *Anansi and the Moss-Covered Rock,* illustrated by Janet Stevens, Holiday, 1988.

The Chanukkah Tree, illustrated by Giora Carmi, Holiday House (New York, NY), 1988.

Charlie Drives the Stage, illustrated by Glen Rounds, Holiday House (New York, NY), 1989.

Hershel and the Hanukkah Goblins, illustrated by Trina Schart Hyman, Holiday House (New York, NY), 1989.

The Chanukkah Guest, illustrated by Giora Carmi, Holiday House (New York, NY), 1990.

Four Dollars and Fifty Cents, illustrated by Glen Rounds, Holiday House (New York, NY), 1990.

(Reteller) *Nanny Goat and the Seven Little Kids,* illustrated by Janet Stevens, Holiday House (New York, NY), 1990.

I Took My Frog to the Library, illustrated by Blanche Sims, Viking (New York, NY), 1990.

(Reteller) *Baba Yaga: A Russian Folktale,* illustrated by Megan Lloyd, Holiday House (New York, NY), 1991.

(Adapter) *Bearhead: A Russian Folktale,* illustrated by Charles Mikolaycak, Holiday House (New York, NY), 1991.

(Reteller) *The Greatest of All: A Japanese Folktale,* illustrated by Giora Carmi, Holiday House (New York, NY), 1991.

(Adapter) *Days of Awe: Stories for Rosh Hashanah and Yom Kippur,* illustrated by Erika Weihs, Viking (New York, NY), 1991.

(Reteller) *Anansi Goes Fishing,* illustrated by Janet Stevens, Holiday House (New York, NY), 1992.

(Reteller) *Boots and His Brothers: A Norwegian Tale,* illustrated by Kimberly Bulcken Root, Holiday House (New York, NY), 1992.

(Adapter) *The Four Gallant Sisters,* illustrated by Tatiana Yuditskaya, Holt (New York, NY), 1992.

Kimmel retells **Count Silvernose: A Story from Italy** *as a tale of good conquering evil. (Illustration by Omar Rayyan.)*

(Adapter) *The Old Woman and Her Pig,* illustrated by Giora Carmi, Holiday, 1992.

(Reteller) *The Spotted Pony: A Collection of Hanukkah Stories,* illustrated by Leonard Everett Fisher, Holiday House (New York, NY), 1992.

(Reteller) *The Tale of Aladdin and the Wonderful Lamp,* illustrated by Ju-Hong Chen, Holiday House (New York, NY), 1992.

(Adapter) *Three Sacks of Truth: A Story from France,* illustrated by Robert Rayevsky, Holiday House (New York, NY), 1993.

(Adapter) *The Witch's Face: A Mexican Tale,* illustrated by Fabricio Vanden Broeck, Holiday House (New York, NY), 1993.

Asher and the Capmakers: A Hanukkah Story, illustrated by Will Hillenbrand, Holiday House (New York, NY), 1993.

(Reteller) *The Gingerbread Man,* illustrated by Megan Lloyd, Holiday House (New York, NY), 1993.

(Reteller) *Anansi and the Talking Melon,* illustrated by Janet Stevens, Holiday House (New York, NY), 1994.

One Good Tern Deserves Another (novel), Holiday, 1994.

(Adapter) *I-Know-Not-What, I-Know-Not-Where: A Russian Tale,* illustrated by Robert Sauber, Holiday House (New York, NY), 1994.

(Adapter) *Iron John: A Tale from the Brothers Grimm,* illustrated by Trina Schart Hyman, Holiday House (New York, NY), 1994.

Bernal and Florinda: A Spanish Tale, illustrated by Robert Rayevsky, Holiday House (New York, NY), 1994.

(Reteller) *The Three Princes: A Tale from the Middle East,* illustrated by Leonard Everett Fisher, Holiday House (New York, NY), 1994.

(Reteller) *The Valiant Red Rooster: A Story from Hungary,* illustrated by Katya Arnold, Holt (New York, NY), 1994.

(Reteller) *The Goose Girl: A Story from the Brothers Grimm,* illustrated by Robert Sauber, Holiday House (New York, NY), 1995.

(Adapter) *Rimonah of the Flashing Sword: A North African Tale,* illustrated by Omar Rayyan, Holiday House (New York, NY), 1995.

Bar Mitzvah: A Jewish Boy's Coming of Age, Viking (New York, NY), 1995.

(Reteller) *The Adventures of Hershel of Ostropol,* illustrated by Trina Schart Hyman, Holiday House (New York, NY), 1995.

Billy Lazroe and the King of the Sea: A Tale of the Northwest, illustrated by Michael Steirnagle, Harcourt (San Diego, CA), 1996.

(Reteller) *Count Silvernose: A Story from Italy,* illustrated by Omar Rayyan, Holiday House (New York, NY), 1996.

The Magic Dreidels: A Hanukkah Story, illustrated by Katya Krenina, Holiday House (New York, NY), 1996.

One Eye, Two Eyes, Three Eyes, illustrated by Dirk Zimmer, Holiday House (New York, NY), 1996.

The Tale of Ali Baba and the Forty Thieves: A Story from the Arabian Nights, illustrated by Will Hillenbrand, Holiday House (New York, NY), 1996.

Onions and Garlic: An Old Tale, illustrated by Katya Arnold, Holiday House (New York, NY), 1996.

(Adapter) *Sirko and the Wolf: A Ukrainian Tale,* illustrated by Robert Sauber, Holiday House (New York, NY), 1997.

(Adapter) *Squash It!: A True and Ridiculous Tale,* illustrated by Robert Rayevsky, Holiday House (New York, NY), 1997.

(Reteller) *Ten Suns: A Chinese Legend,* illustrated by YongSheng Xuan, Holiday House (New York, NY), 1998.

(Reteller) *Seven at One Blow: A Tale from the Brothers Grimm,* illustrated by Megan Lloyd, Holiday House (New York, NY), 1998.

When Mindy Saved Hanukkah, pictures by Barbara McClintock, Scholastic (New York, NY), 1998.

Be Not Far from Me: The Oldest Love Story: Legends from the Bible, illustrated by David Diaz, Simon & Schuster (New York, NY), 1998.

(Editor) *A Hanukkah Treasury,* illustrated by Emily Lisker, Holt (New York, NY), 1998.

(Reteller) *Easy Work!: An Old Tale,* illustrated by Andrew Glass, Holiday House (New York, NY), 1998.

(Reteller) *The Birds' Gift: A Ukrainian Easter Story,* illustrated by Katya Krenina, Holiday House (New York, NY), 1999.

(Reteller) *The Rooster's Antlers: A Story of the Chinese Zodiac,* illustrated by YongSheng Xuan, Holiday House (New York, NY), 1999.

Sword of the Samurai: Adventure Stories from Japan, Harcourt (New York, NY), 1999.

The Runaway Tortilla, illustrated by Randy Cecil, Winslow (Delray Beach, FL), 2000.

(Reteller) *Gershon's Monster: A Story for the Jewish New Year,* illustrated by Jon J. Muth, Scholastic (New York, NY), 2000.

The Jar of Fools: Eight Hanukkah Stories from Chelm, illustrated by Mordecai Gerstein, Holiday House (New York, NY), 2000.

Grizz!, illustrated by Andrew Glass, Holiday House (New York, NY), 2000.

Montezuma and the Fall of the Aztecs, illustrated by Daniel San Souci, Holiday House (New York, NY), 2000.

(Reteller) *The Two Mountains: An Aztec Legend,* illustrated by Leonard Everett Fisher, Holiday House (New York, NY), 2000.

Zigazak: A Hanukkah Story, illustrated by Jon Goodell, Random House (New York, NY), 2001.

A Cloak for the Moon, illustrated by Katya Krenina, Holiday House (New York, NY), 2001.

Website of the Warped Wizard (chapter book), illustrated by Jeff Shelly, Dutton (New York, NY), 2001.

(Reteller) *Anansi and the Magic Stick,* illustrated by Janet Stevens, Holiday House (New York, NY), 2001.

Robin Hook, Pirate Hunter!, illustrated by Michael Dooling, Scholastic (New York, NY), 2001.

Pumpkinhead, illustrated by Steve Haskamp, Winslow Press (Delray Beach, FL), 2001.

Website of the Cracked Cookies (chapter book), illustrated by Jeff Shelly, Dutton (New York, NY), 2001.

Why the Snake Crawls on Its Belly, illustrated by Allen Davis, Pitspopany Press (New York, NY), 2001.

OTHER

Contributor to periodicals, including *Ladybug* and *Cricket.*

Sidelights

The author of dozens of picture books and novels, Eric A. Kimmel is well known for his adaptations or retellings of folktales from around the world, especially Yiddish tales. This award-winning author is further noted for his blend of sardonic wit with traditional storyteller motifs: mistaken identities, tests of courage and intelligence, wise fools, and tricksters. The result is a body of tales that both entertain and teach and that are filled with broad, slapstick humor as well as moral lessons. Popular retellings by Kimmel include *Hershel and the Hanukkah Goblins, The Chanukkah Guest, The Greatest of All, Baba Yaga, Bearhead, The Four Gallant Sisters, The Valiant Red Rooster,* and *Gershon's Monster,* among many others. Kimmel has also written contemporary novels for young readers, including *One Good Tern Deserves Another,* and chapter books, such as *Website of the Warped Wizard.*

Folktales and their resonance form the centerpiece of Kimmel's work. It is no coincidence that he deals so heavily in folktales, for as Kimmel once told *SATA,* "I've been a storyteller for [more than] twenty years. When you stand in front of an audience of a hundred people or more, you learn very quickly what works and what doesn't. Folktales are oral stories, so it's important for the writer to be firmly rooted in oral traditions."

Kimmel himself is rooted not only in the oral tradition but also in a multicultural one, which his work celebrates. "I grew up in Brooklyn, New York," he told *SATA,* "in a very mixed neighborhood. Our neighbors were Armenian, Italian, Chinese, Puerto Rican, Irish, and German. You could hear five different languages in a walk around the block. I spoke Yiddish as a child and spent lots of time with my grandmother. She had come over [to America] as an adult, so she remained European in her thinking throughout her life." Kimmel's grandmother was to prove an important influence on his writing. Coming from western Ukraine and speaking five languages, she was full of stories.

More of a reader than an athlete as a child, Kimmel loved the books of Dr. Seuss as well as the tales of the brothers Grimm, which were introduced to him by an illustrated volume given to him by his uncle. Kimmel remembered reading that book "until it fell to pieces." He told *SATA,* "That's how I came to be a storyteller, telling other kids stories that I remembered from Grimm and from my grandmother." From storyteller to writer is not a large jump, but first Kimmel needed to earn a living. He majored in education and taught at the college level for many years, writing and telling stories in his spare time. His first book appeared in 1974; by 1994 he had left teaching to write full time. Beginning as a storyteller in schools, parks, and libraries, Kimmel adapted those skills when it came to writing his tales down rather than telling them. "When I write a story,"

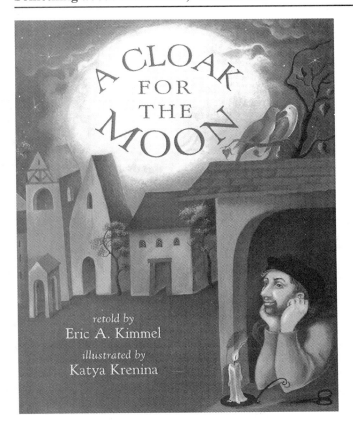

The story of a tailor determined to find a magic thread so he can weave a cloak flexible enough to encompass the moon as she waxes and wanes is retold by Kimmel.

Kimmel explained in an online interview for Scholastic's *Author's Online Library,* "I'm very aware of [spoken] rhythms, and I try to capture in my writing the experience of telling. And that's also important because a picture book, which most of my books are, is usually read aloud to an audience, which is very close to storytelling. So, when I write a story, I read it aloud over and over again many times, trying to capture the music and rhythm of the words. So you might say that what I'm trying to do is capture in written words the experience of listening to the spoken word."

Kimmel's first book was a historical novel set in Russia, *The Tartar's Sword.* Then came a number of picture books, including *Why Worry?,* a humorous tale about a neurotic cricket and a carefree grasshopper, and *Nicanor's Gate,* a legend about the building of the Second Temple. However, as Kimmel once noted, most of his early titles seemed to "sink without a trace." Then came his big break: a request to stand in for Nobel Prize-winner Isaac Bashevis Singer to write a Hanukkah story. Kimmel dusted off a story that he had filed in his dead box after several rejections. The tale was based on a folkloric character, the storyteller and wanderer Hershel Ostropoler. His subsequent picture book, *Hershel and the Hanukkah Goblins,* tells the original story of how Hershel gets rid of goblins who are haunting a synagogue and keeping the locals from celebrating Hanukkah. "This book is welcome both as a Hanukkah story

and as a trickster tale," noted *Horn Book* critic Hanna B. Zeiger. It was welcome to Kimmel, as well, for the book set Kimmel's writing career on a firm course. Although he had only published a handful of books in the eight years prior to *Hershel,* the years since its publication have seen scores of books published by Kimmel that explore folktales from Eastern and Western Europe, the Middle East, Mexico, Asia, Africa, and both South and North America. Kimmel reprised Hershel in *The Adventures of Hershel of Ostropol,* this time featuring a medley of ten adventures of the wandering Hershel, the "Jewish first cousin of tricksters like Brer Rabbit and Till Eulenspiegel," according to Rodger Kamenetz, writing in the *New York Times Book Review.* "Mr. Kimmel has a good ear, makes clever use of repetition and knows how to structure a story that has a good joke, with a hearty punch line," Kamenetz concluded.

Kimmel's *The Chanukkah Guest* continues his series of holiday books in a story of mistaken identity in which a bear is taken for a rabbi by a nearsighted woman. "Festivity, generosity and cooperation are all celebrated in this wintry holiday tale that children of all religions will enjoy," wrote a critic in *Publishers Weekly.* In the 1998 title *A Hanukkah Treasury,* Kimmel brings together a potpourri of holiday information and tales and poems in an "outstanding choice for holiday sharing," according to Anne Connor in the *Los Angeles Times Book Review.* A contributor for *Publishers Weekly* felt *A Hanukkah Treasury* was "one of the best Hanukkah titles in recent years" with "more than enough material to keep a family going for eight days and nights." In *Jar of Fools* Kimmel tells eight Hanukkah stories from Chelm, the legendary Yiddish town of fools. A "true gem," declared a reviewer for *School Library Journal.* A kindhearted fool is also presented in *Onions and Garlic,* adapted from a Jewish folktale about the poor merchant Getzel, who ultimately makes good while his acquisitive older brothers are left short. A contributor for *Kirkus Reviews* observed that Kimmel "retells the Jewish folktale (carefully sourced in an author's note) with lively dialogue and a comic twist at the end." Less comic is *Gershon's Monster,* a story for the Jewish New Year, Rosh Hashanah, from a Hasidic legend. In this tale, Gershon the baker finally repents his wicked ways when his sins threaten the lives of his beloved twin children. "The story will achieve its full impact when children, with adult help, begin to understand why it is so important to recognize the wrongs they've committed and try to right them," wrote *Booklist*'s Ilene Cooper in a featured review.

Many of Kimmel's retellings take place in Russia and Eastern Europe, the result of his grandmother's storytelling influence. In *Baba Yaga* Kimmel retells a Russian folktale replete with an evil stepmother and the sweet stepdaughter who outwits her and the local witch, Baba Yaga. "This engrossing story is both fanciful and suspenseful," wrote a *Publishers Weekly* reviewer. Kimmel retold another Russian folktale in *Bearhead,* about a half man/half bear who is raised by a human and grows into the wise fool of popular folk legend. "Kimmel's lively text plays up the broad, almost slapstick humor of the story," remarked Denise Anton Wright about this tale in *School Library Journal*. In the 1996 title *Billy Lazroe and the King of the Sea*, Kimmel transplants a Russian folktale to his own part of the world, setting the retelling in Oregon at the turn of the century. "Kimmel's lyrical text ... has a strong sense of frontier adventure," noted *Booklist*'s Hazel Rochman, while a contributor for *Publishers Weekly* wrote that Kimmel "lets the creative juices flow in his Oregonian version of an old Russian seafaring tale."

One Eye, Two Eyes, Three Eyes was originally told to Kimmel by his grandmother; it is the story of a young girl, cast into slavery, who, with the help of a magic goat, is finally freed to marry a prince. Further Ukrainian influences are found in *The Birds' Gift*, an Easter story that deals with the origin of the intricate process of decorating eggs for the spring holiday. "Filled with warmth, the story is illustrated with charming folk-art paintings," commented Patricia Pearl Dole in *School Library Journal*. "Kimmel reserves the full force of his storytelling for folkloric rather than religious elements," noted a reviewer for *Publishers Weekly*.

Kimmel's beloved Grimm Brothers provide a host of stories for successful retellings. In *The Four Gallant Sisters*, Kimmel adapted "The Four Artful Brothers" into a story that is "real reading pleasure," according to Linda Boyles in *School Library Journal*. Boyles further commented that Kimmel "couches his adaptation in the strong direct language of a master storyteller." His retelling of another Grimm story in *The Goose Girl* is "polished," according to *Booklist* reviewer Janice Del Negro. Similarly, Kimmel's *Iron John* is a "seamless" retelling, as a reviewer for *Publishers Weekly* described the picture book. A *Booklist* Editors' Choice for 1994, *Iron John* was described by a reviewer from that magazine as a dramatic retelling that "flows from scene to scene with a clear sense of adventure and romance and an underlying sense of mystery." And Grace Oliff, writing in *School Library Journal*, called Kimmel's *Seven at One Blow* a "thoroughly enjoyable retelling of a traditional tale" with "only minor deviations from the original Grimm story."

The 1993 book *Three Sacks of Truth* ventures to France for inspiration, employing the familiar motif of a suitor who must pass tests to win the hand of the fair princess. "In this crisp and sprightly interpretation, storyteller Kimmel takes full advantage of the plot's sly humor," wrote Penny Kaganoff in *Publishers Weekly*. Other European tales include the Hungarian folktale *The Valiant Red Rooster, Count Silvernose*, a tale from Italy, *Squash It!*, from Spain, and *Easy Work*, a Norwegian folktale transplanted to America. In *Count Silvernose*, ugly Assunta comes to the rescue of her beautiful sisters, using her skill of cleverness. In a starred *Booklist* review of *Count Silvernose*, Susan Dove Lempke noted that Kimmel's storytelling "combines humor and suspense, pitting good against evil and delivering a magnificently satisfying conclusion." Reviewing the Spanish tale of a flea and a royal louse, a contributor for *Kirkus Reviews* felt that Kimmel's retelling in *Squash It!* is peppered

with "judiciously chosen details" and "is good for reading aloud to kids who relish a bit of grossness in their story-hour diet."

Other published books by Kimmel have gone farther afield for material, including locations such as the Middle East, Africa, Asia, Mexico, and South America. Teaming up with illustrator Will Hillenbrand, Kimmel produced a retelling of *The Tale of Ali Baba and the Forty Thieves*. "Kimmel captures the flavor of *The Thousand and One Nights*," wrote *Booklist*'s Carolyn Phelan, who concluded that *Ali Baba* is an "entertaining picture-book version of the classic story." Turning to Asia, Kimmel features a mouse living in Japan's imperial palace in *The Greatest of All* and presents adventure stories from Japan in *Sword of the Samurai*. "Reluctant readers looking for a short book of high adventures will be especially pleased," noted Karen Morgan in a *Booklist* review of *Sword of the Samurai*. Barbara Scotto, writing in *School Library Journal*, thought that readers "who delight in stories of knights will be happy to discover" *Sword of the Samurai*. China also provides inspiration for several Kimmel titles. An old legend is presented in *Ten Suns* in which "narrative and the dramatic illustrations ... work wonderfully together to create a beautiful tale of Chinese gods, misuse of power, and heroism that restores the faith of a people," according to *Booklist* contributor Helen Rosenberg. And a story from the Chinese zodiac is featured in *The Rooster's Antlers*, which relates how the Jade Emperor chose twelve animals to represent the years in his calendar.

Closer to home, Kimmel adapts an Aztec legend in *Two Mountains* to explain the formation of two mountains overlooking the Valley of Mexico. "Youngsters are likely to find the connection between the story and the geological formations intriguing," wrote a contributor for *Publishers Weekly*, "and its parallels with Adam and Eve may make for some lively discussion." More Aztec lore, this time historical, is served up in *Montezuma and the Fall of the Aztecs*. Cooper, reviewing the title in *Booklist*, felt Kimmel presents this complicated story "with ease" in a book that makes a "good introduction to a pivotal event in the Americas."

In *Website of the Warped Wizard*, a chapter book, young Jess and Matthew are drawn into a computer game and must defeat an evil wizard to save, among others, an elf, a centaur, and King Arthur. A reviewer for *Publishers Weekly* noted that Kimmel "ventures far off his well-beaten path as a folktale reteller for this madcap chapter book." And in the 2001 title, *Robin Hook, Pirate Hunter!*, Kimmel "gleefully plunders Sherwood Forest, Peter Pan, Dr. Dolittle and pirate lore for ... [a] hybrid tale of a stout-hearted lad bent on ending piracy," according to a writer for *Publishers Weekly*.

"I'm always looking for good stories," Kimmel told *SATA*. "But I have no hesitation about making changes if I feel for some reason the original doesn't work, or if I can think of a way to make it better. There is no 'authentic' version. Stories evolve over centuries as tellers add and subtract. I think of myself as one link in a long, long chain."

Biographical and Critical Sources

BOOKS

Children's Books and Their Creators, edited by Anita Silvey, Houghton, 1995.

PERIODICALS

Booklist, November 15, 1992, pp. 596, 598; January 15, 1995, review of *Iron John,* p. 863; March 1, 1995, p. 1245; October 15, 1995, Janice Del Negro, review of *The Goose Girl,* pp. 398, 400; December 15, 1995, p. 715; March 15, 1996, Susan Dove Lempke, review of *Count Silvernose,* p. 1263; November 1, 1996, p. 503; December 1, 1996, Carolyn Phelan, review of *The Tale of Ali Baba and the Forty Thieves,* p. 667; December 15, 1996, Hazel Rochman, review of *Billy Lazroe and the King of the Sea,* p. 730; May 1, 1997, Helen Rosenberg, review of *Ten Suns,* p. 1520; September 15, 1997, p. 238; April 15, 1998, pp. 1448-1449; September 1, 1998, p. 133; March 15, 1999, Karen Morgan, review of *Sword of the Samurai,* p. 329; April 15, 1999, p. 1533; December 15, 1999, p. 787; January 1, 2000, Ilene Cooper, review of *Montezuma and the Fall of the Aztecs,* pp. 910, 914; May 1, 2000, p. 1678; September 1, 2000; p. 133; October 1, 2000, Ilene Cooper, review of *Gershon's Monster,* p. 362.

Inspired by the pirate stories of Howard Pyle, Kimmel's novel mixes the adopted son of the notorious Captain Hook, a band of lost boys, and a deserted island into a rousing adventure for young readers.

Bulletin of the Center for Children's Books, January, 1995, Roger Sutton, review of *One Good Tern Deserves Another,* p. 169.

Horn Book, January-February, 1990, Hanna B. Zeiger, review of *Hershel and the Hanukkah Goblins,* pp. 52-53; January-February, 1991, p. 57; November-December, 1991, p. 721; September-October, 1995, p. 620; January-February, 1996, p. 83; January-February, 1997, p. 72; July-August, 1997, p. 467; September-October, 2000, p. 587.

Kirkus Reviews, March 15, 1996, review of *Onions and Garlic,* p. 449; May 15, 1997, review of *Squash It!,* p. 801; November 1, 1998, p. 1600.

Los Angeles Times Book Review, October 25, 1998, p. 7; December 6, 1998, Anne Connor, review of *A Hanukkah Treasury,* p. 4.

New York Times Book Review, April 12, 1992, p. 28; October 22, 1995, p. 41; December 17, 1995, Rodger Kamenetz, review of *The Adventures of Hershel of Ostropol,* p. 28; June 16, 1996, p. 33; October 13, 1996, p. 26; December 8, 1996, p. 78; May 17, 1998, p. 26; December 3, 2000, p. 85.

Publishers Weekly, November 9, 1990, review of *The Chanukkah Guest,* p. 57; May 3, 1991, review of *Baba Yaga,* p. 71; August 2, 1991, p. 73; April 19, 1993, Peggy Kaganoff, review of *Three Sacks of Truth,* p. 60; March 4, 1996, review of *Iron John,* p. 67; September 16, 1996, review of *The Tale of Ali Baba and the Forty Thieves,* p. 82; November 4, 1996, review of *Billy Lazroe and the King of the Sea,* p. 75; March 10, 1997, p. 69; October 6, 1997, p. 53; March 23, 1998, p. 95; September 28, 1998, review of *A Hanukkah Treasury,* p. 52; February 22, 1999, review of *The Birds' Gift,* p. 94; October 4, 1999, p. 75; February 7, 2000, review of *Two Mountains,* p. 84; February 7, 2000, review of *Montezuma and the Fall of the Aztecs,* p. 86; August 28, 2000, p. 35; January 22, 2001, review of *Website of the Warped Wizard,* p. 324; February 19, 2001, review of *Robin Hook, Pirate Hunter!,* p. 90; February 26, 2001, p. 85.

School Library Journal, November, 1990, p. 94; October, 1991, Denise Anton Wright, review of *Bearhead,* p. 110; May, 1992, Linda Boyles, review of *The Four Gallant Sisters,* p. 105; March, 1995, p. 198; May, 1995, p. 100; May, 1998, p. 134; June, 1998, p. 130; December, 1998, Grace Oliff, review of *Seven at One Blow,* p. 106; June, 1999, Barbara Scotto, review of *Sword of the Samurai,* p. 132; July, 1999, Patricia Pearl Dole, review of *The Birds' Gift,* p. 86; October, 1999, p. 138; March, 2000, pp. 209, 228; April, 2000, p. 121; October, 2000, review of *Jar of Fools,* pp. 64-65; October, 2000, p. 148.

Voice of Youth Advocates, April, 1995, Marian Rafal, review of *One Good Tern Deserves Another,* p. 24.

ON-LINE

Author's Online Library, http://teacher.scholastic.com/ (June 12, 2001).

Meet Major Authors and Illustrators, http://www. childrenslit.com/ (June 12, 2001).

—*Sketch by J. Sydney Jones*

KROHN, Katherine E(lizabeth) 1961-

Personal

Born February 5, 1961, in Bitburg, Germany; daughter of Don Ray (a physician) and Betty Jo (a homemaker; maiden name, Stevens) Krohn. *Education:* University of Michigan, B.A., 1983. *Hobbies and other interests:* Traveling, hiking, camping, photography, painting, cooking gourmet vegetarian dinners, baking cookies.

Addresses

Home and office—Eugene, OR. *Agent*—c/o Lerner Publications, 241 First Ave. N., Minneapolis, MN 55401.

Career

Freelance writer, 1991—.

Awards, Honors

Young Adult Choice Award, International Reading Association (IRA), 1994, for *Lucille Ball: Pioneer of Comedy;* Children's Choice Award, IRA, 1994, for *Roseanne Arnold: Comedy's Queen Bee.*

Writings

Lucille Ball: Pioneer of Comedy, Lerner (Minneapolis, MN), 1992.
Roseanne Arnold: Comedy's Queen Bee, Lerner (Minneapolis, MN), 1993.
Elvis Presley: The King, Lerner (Minneapolis, MN), 1994.
Marilyn Monroe: Norma Jeane's Dream, Lerner (Minneapolis, MN), 1997.
Marcia Clark: Voice for the Victims, Lerner (Minneapolis, MN), 1997.
Princess Diana, Lerner (Minneapolis, MN), 1999.
Rosie O'Donnell, Lerner (Minneapolis, MN), 1999.
Women of the Wild West, Lerner (Minneapolis, MN), 2000.
You and Your Parents' Divorce, Rosen (New York, NY), 2000.
Everything You Need to Know about Birth Order, Rosen (New York, NY), 2000.
Everything You Need to Know about Living on Your Own, Rosen (New York, NY), 2000.
Ella Fitzgerald: First Lady of Song, Lerner (Minneapolis, MN), 2001.
Is This Funny, or What? (part of "Full House Michelle and Friends" series), Pocket Books, 2001.
Oprah Winfrey, Lerner (Minneapolis, MN), 2002.

Work in Progress

A biography, for children, of Opal Whiteley, "the child-diarist and naturalist who lived in the Eugene area of Oregon in the early part of the century."

Katherine E. Krohn fills Women of the Wild West *with inspiring stories of women who broke new ground in areas formerly open only to men. (Photograph courtesy of the Ohio Historical Society.)*

Sidelights

Katherine E. Krohn is the author of several informative biographies for grade-school and teen readers. Her first published title is *Lucille Ball: Pioneer of Comedy.* Both this and her next work, *Roseanne Arnold: Comedy's Queen Bee,* earned honors from the International Reading Association. Her biography of a 1950s film star, *Marilyn Monroe: Norma Jeane's Dream,* was hailed as "an appealing overview" of Monroe's life and career by *School Library Journal* reviewer Janet Woodward. As Krohn's text relates, the actress overcame a tough, impoverished childhood to become one of the biggest celebrities of her era before she died in 1962 in what some say was an accidental overdose. Woodward predicted that "young people will be quickly drawn into the compelling story."

Krohn has also written about the Los Angeles-area prosecutor who gained fame in the criminal trial of former football star O.J. Simpson in 1997's *Marcia Clark: Voice for the Victims.* In 1999, Krohn penned biographies of the late Diana, Princess of Wales, and television personality Rosie O'Donnell. In the latter, Krohn recounts O'Donnell's early life and career start as a stand-up comedian in what *School Library Journal* contributor Tim Wadham called "a breezy, interesting look at a pop-culture icon." Krohn moved away from the specific biography format with her 2000 title *Women of the Wild West,* in which she reveals the little-known stories of American women who became part of the historic, nation-making westward migration in the nineteenth century. Her subjects range from author Laura Ingalls Wilder, who wrote about her prairie childhood in the popular "Little House" series, to gunslingers Calamity Jane and Belle Starr.

Krohn has also written insightful books about family matters. *You and Your Parents' Divorce* and *Everything You Need to Know about Birth Order* were both published in 2000. For the latter title, she distills contemporary psychological and sociological findings about birth order and personality traits into a readable work for teens. An interactive book as well, *Birth Order* aims to help readers discover just how well they match with the characteristics attributed to the oldest, middle, and youngest offspring in a family. Marilyn Fairbanks, writing in *School Library Journal,* commended the work and Krohn's explanation of the theories behind birth

In her biography **Princess Diana,** *Krohn covers both the joyous and the sad occasions of the late princess' life. (Photograph courtesy of AP/Wide World.)*

order for "helping youngsters to affirm their perceptions of self, family, and friends."

"When I was in grade school in the 1960s, I liked to read biographies of famous people," Krohn once said. "I enjoyed peering inside someone else's world—nosing around a bit. More than anything, my reading a biography gave me a sense of possibility. So much could be accomplished if a person set their mind to it. I saw how someone could overcome difficulties to achieve their goals in life. I saw how life, for everyone, has its ups and downs, and that nothing great is accomplished without faith and perseverance.

"I grew up to be a biographer for young readers. I have written books on artists of all kinds—movie stars, singers, writers, a television personality, and a comedian. I enjoy my work very much. I research each subject thoroughly, and by the time the biography is written I feel like I know my subject personally. Sometimes I am so engrossed in a book project that I even dream about a subject. During the writing of *Roseanne Arnold: Comedy's Queen Bee,* I dreamed I was a guest on TV's 'Roseanne,' and she even invited me over to her house for a big homemade dinner after the show! I guess you could say I really get into my work!

"I believe that much can be learned from the story of an exceptional individual. Fortunately, children today have the opportunity to choose from a vast and diverse selection of biography titles."

Biographical and Critical Sources

PERIODICALS

Horn Book Guide, fall, 1997, Peter D. Sieruta, review of *Marcia Clark,* p. 325; fall, 1997, Gail Hedges, review of *Marilyn Monroe,* p. 381.

School Library Journal, July, 1997, Janet Woodward, review of *Marilyn Monroe,* p. 107; February, 1999, Tim Wadham, review of *Rosie O'Donnell,* p. 120; September, 2000, Patricia Ann Owens, review of *Women of the Wild West,* p. 243; December, 2000, Marilyn Fairbanks, review of *Everything You Need to Know about Birth Order,* p. 163.*

*　　　*　　　*

KROLL, Steven 1941-

Personal

Born August 11, 1941, in New York, NY; son of Julius (a diamond merchant) and Anita (a business executive; maiden name, Berger) Kroll; married Edite Niedringhaus (a children's book editor), April 18, 1964 (divorced, 1978); married Abigail Aldridge (a milliner), June 3, 1989 (divorced, 1994); married Kathleen Beckett (a journalist), October 4, 1997. *Education:* Harvard University, B.A., 1962. *Politics:* "Committed to change." *Religion:* Jewish. *Hobbies and other interests:* Walking, traveling, and playing tennis.

Addresses

Home—25 Fifth Avenue, Apt. 4F, New York, NY 10003. *Office*—64 West Eleventh St., New York, NY 10011.

Career

Transatlantic Review, London, England, associate editor, 1962-65; Chatto & Windus, London, reader and editor, 1962-65; Holt, Rinehart & Winston, New York, NY, acquiring editor, adult trade department, 1965-69; freelance writer, 1969—. Instructor in English, University of Maine at Augusta, 1970-71. *Member:* PEN American Center (former chairman of children's authors' book committee and former member of executive board), Authors Guild, Authors League of America, Harvard Club (New York, NY).

Writings

FOR CHILDREN

Is Milton Missing?, illustrated by Dick Gackenbach, Holiday House (New York, NY), 1975.

That Makes Me Mad!, illustrated by Hilary Knight, Pantheon (New York, NY), 1976.

The Tyrannosaurus Game, illustrated by Tomie de Paola, Holiday House (New York, NY), 1976.

Gobbledygook, illustrated by Kelly Oechsli, Holiday House (New York, NY), 1977.

If I Could Be My Grandmother, illustrated by Lady McCrady, Pantheon (New York, NY), 1977.

Sleepy Ida and Other Nonsense Poems, illustrated by Seymour Chwast, Pantheon (New York, NY), 1977.

Santa's Crash-Bang Christmas, illustrated by Tomie de Paola, Holiday House (New York, NY), 1977.

T. J. Folger, Thief, illustrated by Bill Morrison, Holiday House (New York, NY), 1978.

Fat Magic, illustrated by Tomie de Paola, Holiday House (New York, NY), 1979.

The Candy Witch, illustrated by Marylin Hafner, Holiday House (New York, NY), 1979.

Space Cats, illustrated by Friso Henstra, Holiday House (New York, NY), 1979.

Amanda and the Giggling Ghost, illustrated by Dick Gackenbach, Holiday House (New York, NY), 1980.

Dirty Feet, illustrated by Toni Hormann, Parents Magazine Press (New York, NY), 1980.

Monster Birthday, illustrated by Dennis Kendrick, Holiday House (New York, NY), 1980.

Friday the Thirteenth, illustrated by Dick Gackenbach, Holiday House (New York, NY), 1981.

Giant Journey, illustrated by Kay Chorao, Holiday House (New York, NY), 1981.

Are You Pirates?, illustrated by Marylin Hafner, Pantheon (New York, NY), 1982.

Banana Bits, illustrated by Maxie Chambliss, Avon (New York, NY), 1982.

Bathrooms, illustrated by Maxie Chambliss, Avon (New York, NY), 1982.

The Big Bunny and the Easter Eggs, illustrated by Janet Stevens, Holiday House (New York, NY), 1982.

The Goat Parade, illustrated by Tim Kirk, Parents Magazine Press (New York, NY), 1982.

One Tough Turkey, illustrated by John Wallner, Holiday House (New York, NY), 1982.

The Hand-Me-Down Doll, illustrated by Evaline Ness, Holiday House (New York, NY), 1983.

Otto, illustrated by Ned Delaney, Parents Magazine Press (New York, NY), 1983.

Pigs in the House, illustrated by Tim Kirk, Parents Magazine Press (New York, NY), 1983.

Toot! Toot!, illustrated by Anne Rockwell, Holiday House (New York, NY), 1983.

Woof, Woof!, illustrated by Nicole Rubel, Dial (New York, NY), 1983.

The Biggest Pumpkin Ever, illustrated by Jeni Bassett, Holiday House (New York, NY), 1984.

Loose Tooth, illustrated by Tricia Tusa, Holiday House (New York, NY), 1984.

Happy Mother's Day, illustrated by Marylin Hafner, Holiday House (New York, NY), 1985.

Mrs. Claus's Crazy Christmas, illustrated by John Wallner, Holiday House (New York, NY), 1985.

Annie's Four Grannies, illustrated by Eileen Christelow, Holiday House (New York, NY), 1986.

The Big Bunny and the Magic Show, illustrated by Janet Stevens, Holiday House (New York, NY), 1986.

I'd Like to Be, illustrated by Ellen Appleby, Parents Magazine Press (New York, NY), 1987.

I Love Spring, illustrated by Kathryn E. Shoemaker, Holiday House (New York, NY), 1987.

It's Groundhog Day!, illustrated by Jeni Bassett, Holiday House (New York, NY), 1987.

Don't Get Me in Trouble!, illustrated by Marvin Glass, Crown (New York, NY), 1988.

Happy Father's Day, illustrated by Marylin Hafner, Holiday House (New York, NY), 1988.

Looking for Daniela: A Romantic Adventure, illustrated by Anita Lobel, Holiday House (New York, NY), 1988.

Newsman Ned Meets the New Family, illustrated by Denise Brunkus, Scholastic (New York, NY), 1988.

Oh, What a Thanksgiving!, illustrated by S. D. Schindler, Scholastic (New York, NY), 1988.

Big Jeremy, illustrated by Donald Carrick, Holiday House (New York, NY), 1989.

The Hokey-Pokey Man, illustrated by Deborah Kogan Ray, Holiday House (New York, NY), 1989.

Newsman Ned and the Broken Rules, illustrated by Denise Brunkus, Scholastic (New York, NY), 1989.

Branigan's Cat and the Halloween Ghost, Holiday House (New York, NY), 1990.

Gone Fishing, illustrated by Harvey Stevenson, Crown, 1990.

It's April Fools' Day!, illustrated by Jeni Bassett, Holiday House (New York, NY), 1990.

Annabelle's Un-Birthday, illustrated by Gail Owens, Macmillan (New York, NY), 1991.

Howard and Gracie's Luncheonette, illustrated by Michael Sours, Holt (New York, NY), 1991.

Mary McLean and the St. Patrick's Day Parade, illustrated by Michael Dooling, Scholastic (New York, NY), 1991.

Princess Abigail and the Wonderful Hat, illustrated by Patience Brewster, Holiday House (New York, NY), 1991.

The Squirrels' Thanksgiving, illustrated by Jeni Bassett, Holiday House (New York, NY), 1991.

The Magic Rocket, illustrated by Will Hillenbrand, Holiday House (New York, NY), 1992.

Andrew Wants a Dog, illustrated by Molly Delaney, Hyperion Books (New York, NY), 1992.

The Hit and Run Gang, volumes 1-4, illustrated by Meredith Johnson, Avon (New York, NY), 1992.

The Pigrates Clean Up, illustrated by Jeni Bassett, Henry Holt (New York, NY), 1993.

Queen of the May, illustrated by Patience Brewster, Holiday House (New York, NY), 1993.

Will You Be My Valentine?, illustrated by Lillian Hoban, Holiday House (New York, NY), 1993.

I'm George Washington and You're Not!, illustrated by Betsy Lewin, Hyperion Books (New York, NY), 1994.

By the Dawn's Early Light: The Story of the Star-Spangled Banner, illustrated by Dan Andreasen, Scholastic (New York, NY), 1994.

Patrick's Tree House, illustrated by Roberta Wilson, Macmillan (New York, NY), 1994.

The Hit and Run Gang, volumes 5-8, illustrated by Meredith Johnson, Avon (New York, NY), 1994.

Steven Kroll vividly brings to life the Massachusetts rebellion against British taxation that sparked the American Revolutionary War. (Cover illustration by Peter Fiore.)

Lewis and Clark: Explorers of the American West, illustrated by Richard Williams, Holiday House (New York, NY), 1994.

Doctor on an Elephant, illustrated by Michael Chesworth, Henry Holt (New York, NY), 1994.

Eat!, illustrated by Diane Palmisciano, Hyperion Books (New York, NY), 1995.

Ellis Island: Doorway to Freedom, illustrated by Karen Ritz, Holiday House (New York, NY), 1995.

Pony Express!, illustrated by Dan Andreasen, Scholastic (New York, NY), 1996.

The Boston Tea Party, illustrated by Peter Fiore, Holiday House (New York, NY), 1998.

Oh, Tucker!, illustrated by Scott Nash, Candlewick Press, 1998.

Robert Fulton: From Submarine to Steamboat, Holiday House (New York, NY), 1999.

William Penn: Founder of Pennsylvania, Holiday House (New York, NY), 2000.

Patches Lost and Found, Winslow Press, 2001.

YOUNG ADULT BOOKS

Take It Easy, Four Winds (Bristol, FL), 1983.

Breaking Camp, Macmillan (New York, NY), 1985.

Multiple Choice, Macmillan (New York, NY), 1987.

Sweet America, Jamestown Publishers (Chicago, IL), 2000.

When I Dream of Heaven, Jamestown Publishers (Chicago, IL), 2000.

Dear Mr. President: John Quincey Adams' Letters from a Southern Planter's Son, Winslow Press, 2001.

OTHER

Also contributor of book reviews to *Book World, Commonweal, Village Voice, Listener, New York Times Book Review, Spectator, Times Literary Supplement,* and *London Magazine.* Contributor to poetry anthologies. Some of Kroll's works have been translated into French, Spanish, Danish, Italian, and Japanese.

Adaptations

The Biggest Pumpkin Ever and Other Stories (includes *The Biggest Pumpkin Ever; Sleepy Ida and Other Nonsense Poems; T. J. Folger, Thief;* and *Woof, Woof!*) have been recorded on audiocassette for Caedmon, 1986; *The Biggest Pumpkin Ever, The Big Bunny and the Easter Egg, Will You Be My Valentine?* and *Oh, Tucker!* have been recorded on audiocassette for Scholastic.

Sidelights

According to reviewers, children's author Steven Kroll possesses a unique ability to view his stories as a child would, so he understands what interests and entertains his young audience. Even though it took him years to commit himself to writing and he fell into children's writing by chance, the author has never regretted his career choice. Writing for children affords Kroll a special connection with his own youth—something he values greatly. "What is most important is the feeling that I am somehow in touch with my own childhood,"

Kroll has said. "To be in touch with your own childhood is to be, in some way, touched with wonder, and when I write for children, that is what I feel."

After working as an editor in London, England, and New York City, Kroll went off to Maine to write full time and began writing for children in the early 1970s upon the suggestion of his first wife, then a children's book editor, and other friends in children's book publishing. Although he resisted the idea at first, once he began writing for children he discovered he loved it. His first book, *Is Milton Missing?*, was published in 1975, and since then Kroll has steadily produced at least two books per year, once as many as nine, for Holiday House and other publishers.

For his story ideas and settings Kroll sometimes recalls places and instances from his own childhood. "When I write about a child's room, that room is often my own— the one in the Manhattan apartment house where I grew up," Kroll commented. "When I write about an urban street or an urban school, it is often my street or my school, taken out of time into a situation I have invented. And sometimes," the author continued, "if I'm writing about a suburb or a small town, that place will resemble the home of a summer camp friend I visited once, and longed to see again."

Kroll's stories appeal greatly to young readers, evidenced by the number of letters the author constantly receives. His favorites are those from children who are not afraid to share their enthusiasm. "The best letter I ever got was from a first grader in Connecticut where I was going to speak the following week," Kroll recollected in *Behind the Covers*. "This one read, 'Dear Mr. Kroll, My heart is beating because it's so anxious to see what you look like.' The little girl was wonderful! She signed everything she wrote with her name and 'Made in U.S.A.'"

Kroll's collection of works includes several that help bring to life stories from American history. From *The Boston Tea Party* to *Pony Express!*, these colorful volumes are designed for readers of various elementary school levels. *The Boston Tea Party*, for example, is geared toward the third-to sixth-grade set and uses vivid impressionistic illustrations to recount the events leading up to the famous uprising of December 16, 1773. Setting the protest in context, *The Boston Tea Party* opens with an explanation of how the Seven Years War placed England in debt, and how the country planned to raise money by taxing the colonies. Carolyn Phelan noted in a *Booklist* review that the lack of a central character makes the narrative more difficult for young readers, but observed that Kroll still does a "credible job of summarizing history."

Another colonial-era story is recounted in Kroll's picture book, *William Penn: Founder of Pennsylvania*. Aimed at a slightly older audience (ages 9-12), *Penn* focuses on the rebellious personality of a man who, though born to privilege, chose a more challenging path of spreading

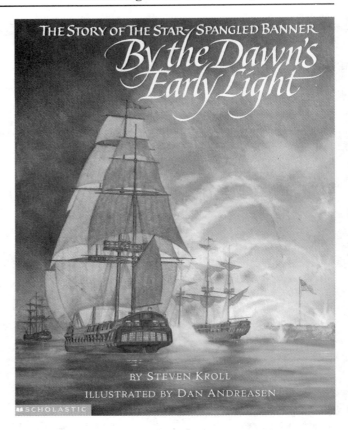

In Kroll's highly praised biography of Francis Scott Key, readers learn the background behind the writing of The Star-Spangled Banner, *the national anthem of the United States.*

religious and political freedom. In another *Booklist* review, Phelan expressed concern that the subject matter may be too advanced for the young readership, citing Penn's background of civil disobedience and debt problems. Still, she recommends the book to school libraries as "a useful and certainly handsome addition" to history collections. Likewise, an article in *Kirkus Reviews* singled out Kroll's "highly event-oriented and [information-]packed" text as notable. In *Robert Fulton: From Submarine to Steamboat*, Kroll produces what a *Kirkus Reviews* critic called "a handsomely illustrated biography" that "will make readers yearn for more information" on the visionary marine designer.

Kroll invited youngsters in grades three and older to saddle up with the *Pony Express!* Oil paintings underline the text as the hunt for "young skinny wiry fellows not over eighteen, orphans preferred" brought scores of riders to the fledgling mail delivery system of 1860-61. The book earned high marks from *Horn Book, Booklist* and *Publishers Weekly*, all of whom found the depth of information (detailed route maps are provided), sharp graphic detail, and compelling narrative valuable for its intended audience. "An absorbing and enlightening dose of history and adventure," *Publishers Weekly* elaborated.

History for older readers is served up in Kroll's novel-length titles for young adults, including *Sweet America* and *When I Dream of Heaven.* In the former title, Kroll presents an immigrant's story in the guise of fourteen-year-old Tonio who gradually is transformed into Tony in late nineteenth-century New York. In *When I Dream of Heaven,* "the appalling conditions of the New York City sweatshops at the turn of the 20th century and the plight of young immigrant girls come to life," according to Linda Bindner, writing in *School Library Journal.* In this piece of historical fiction, Gina Petrosino tries to balance her familial duties with her own wishes to continue her education.

On a lighter note, Kroll has also created contemporary picture books for young readers. His 2001 title, *Patches Lost and Found,* "is a masterful blend of text and illustration," according to Barbara Buckley in *School Library Journal.* Jenny would much rather draw than write stories, so when her beloved guinea pig, Patches, goes missing, she designs "missing" posters for the pet and distributes them all over town. The posters do the trick—her pet is found and returned. This incident happily coincides with a difficulty at school: Jenny has been unable to come up with a writing assignment for her teacher. Now her mother points out that Jenny's pictures tell a story; all she needs to do is add some words to complete her assignment. Buckley found *Patches Lost and Found* "a suspenseful, kid-friendly picture book that works on several levels," while *Booklist*'s Phelan noted that the book was written "with a sure sense of narrative and an understanding of the concerns and the learning styles of children." Phelan concluded, "A fresh, fine offering." For still younger readers, Kroll has published such whimsical stories as *The Biggest Pumpkin Ever, The Squirrel's Thanksgiving* and, in 1998, *Oh, Tucker!* In the 1998 work, young children are introduced to a playful, oversized pup whose ability to generate household havoc is matched only by his loving personality. "Wherever he goes— 'WHAM!'—he creates a trail of disaster," proclaimed a *Publishers Weekly* critic, who went on to predict that early readers were likely to "get swept up in the momentum" of Tucker's well-meaning rampages. *Book-*

A bad day at school is made worse when Jenny comes home to find her beloved guinea pig missing in Kroll's Patches Lost and Found.

list's Ellen Mandel noted that Tucker's "slapstick race through the house" led straight "into readers' hearts."

Kroll never regrets leaving his full-time job to become a children's author. "I really love writing for children," he remarked. "I love starting the fireworks, love that explosion of emotion, of excitement, terror, and enthusiasm that comes with putting those words on paper and sometimes, if the mood is right, doing a draft of a whole picture-book story in one sitting. I've been doing a lot more picture books, but I've also become much more involved in writing chapter books, American history for middle grade readers, and historical fiction for young adults." Writing for children is what Kroll feels most content doing. "It's part of me now," the author concluded, "and I'd like other adults to let down the barriers and feel the wonder in their own lives that I feel in these books."

Biographical and Critical Sources

BOOKS

Behind the Covers: Interviews with Authors and Illustrators of Books for Children and Young Adults, Libraries Unlimited (Littleton, CO), 1985.

Something about the Author Autobiography Series, Volume 7, Gale (Detroit, MI), 1989.

PERIODICALS

Booklist, March 1, 1996, review of *Pony Express!,* p. 177; May 1, 1998, Ellen Mandel, review of *Oh, Tucker!,* p. 521; September 15, 1998, Carolyn Phelan, review of *The Boston Tea Party,* p. 222; February 15, 2000, Carolyn Phelan, review of *William Penn: Founder of Pennsylvania,* p. 1108; March 1, 2001, Carolyn Phelan, review of *Patches Lost and Found,* p. 1277.

Horn Book, September-October, 1996, review of *Pony Express!,* p. 616.

Junior Literary Guild, September, 1975.

Kirkus Reviews, February 1, 1999, review of *Robert Fulton: From Submarine to Steamboat;* January 1, 2000, review of *William Penn: Founder of Pennsylvania,* p. 60.

Publishers Weekly, February 5, 1996, review of *Pony Express!,* p. 90; May 4, 1998, review of *Oh, Tucker!,* p. 212.

School Library Journal, March, 2000, p. 234; September, 2000, Linda Bindner, review of *When I Dream of Heaven,* p. 233; May, 2001, Barbara Buckley, review of *Patches Lost and Found,* p. 126.

L

LaROSE, Linda

Personal

Born in Regina, Saskatchewan, Canada; daughter of Malcolm (a farmer) and Glenn (a homemaker) LaRose; married Barry Polowick, 1975; children: Christopher. *Education:* University of Regina, B.Ed. (with distinction), 1976; University of Calgary, M.Ed., 1987. *Hobbies and other interests:* Reading, swimming, tennis, weightlifting, walking.

Linda LaRose

Addresses

Home—Calgary, Alberta, Canada. *Office*—c/o Author Mail, Annick Press, 15 Patricia Ave., Toronto, Ontario, Canada, M2M 1H9. *E-mail*—Lalarose@home.com.

Career

Calgary Board of Education, Calgary, Alberta, researcher and writer in educational communications. Also worked as an elementary school teacher in Calgary and Regina, Saskatchewan, and as an educational consultant.

Writings

Jessica Takes Charge, illustrated by Leanne Franson, Annick Press (Willowdale, Ontario), 1999.

Contributor to periodicals, including *Educational Leadership, Canadian Education Association Newsletter,* and *Research Forum.*

Work in Progress

A story for a picture book; a novel and a mystery novel, both for young readers.

Sidelights

Linda LaRose told *SATA:* "I have always loved to write, beginning with meager, untutored efforts as a child through serious efforts that began when my son was born.

"I love humor in the books I read and try to incorporate humor into the picture books that I write for children and the novels that I write for young readers. As a dedicated reader of mysteries, I have recently become interested in writing mysteries for young readers. My efforts in this area were spurred on when I taught grades two to five and found an insufficient supply of mysteries available at a variety of levels for the children to read.

"My stories, whether for picture books or novels, usually start with a situation, sometimes real, but more often imaginary, that appeals to me. On some occasions, however, I think of an ending that I like for a story, then work backwards to figure out how to get to the end. At other times, an opening sentence or a title occurs to me, sparking ideas for characters and/or situations to carry it forward.

"Regardless of how I start, once I have placed a character into a situation, the character takes over. In the beginning, I spend a good deal of time puzzling over a 'just right' name for the main character; for me, a name will sometimes influence the way that a character develops. From there I begin writing dialogue, which is my favorite part of story writing and is the way that I get to know and develop the characters. Often I write the dialogue for most of a book first, then go back and write the narrative and description later.

"Most often, I know how the major problem of the story will be resolved when I begin, but occasionally I discover it along with and through the main character. For example, I am writing a novel for young readers about a boy named Max and his efforts to help an unexpected backyard guest—a dragon with tendencies toward practical joking. Max and I resolved the main problem together—in the second last chapter! As I worked on the first draft, I went to bed night after night thinking, 'How on earth is Max going to solve that dragon's problem?' Although it was worrisome not knowing, it was also exciting wondering what would happen—just like when you read a book to find out what's going to happen in the end. When the ending finally occurred to me, it seemed as if it was the solution that was meant to be all along. As much as I love reading, writing is even more engaging and more fun!

"My best and most creative thinking for stories is done in the dark, after I go to bed. (In the case of *Jessica Takes Charge,* the idea and the story definitely emerged during the night!) I keep a hardcover, black notebook and gold mechanical pencil beside me to jot down ideas and dialogue. As I don't turn on the light during my jotting, I have a great deal of difficulty deciphering it the next day."

LaRose commented that her work in progress includes, in addition to the story of Max and the dragon, "a story for a picture book about two small farm girls, one a dedicated climber, the other a brave rescuer, who give their mother a scare" and "a mystery novel for young readers about two eleven-year-olds, a boy and a girl, who are reluctantly thrust into the role of detectives."

Biographical and Critical Sources

PERIODICALS

Calgary Herald, February 17, 2000, Annie McCinnis, review of *Jessica Takes Charge.*

Feminist Bookstore News, fall, 1999, review of *Jessica Takes Charge.*

Library Lane, spring, 1999, review of *Jessica Takes Charge.*

London Free Press (London, Canada), August 14, 1999, Barbara Novak, review of *Jessica Takes Charge.*

Montreal Review of Books, spring-summer, 1999, Joanne Stanbridge, review of *Jessica Takes Charge,* p. 22.

Prairie Books Now, summer, 1999, review of *Jessica Takes Charge.*

Resource Links, April, 1999, Sally Bender, review of *Jessica Takes Charge.*

School Library Journal, September, 1999, review of *Jessica Takes Charge.*

ON-LINE

CM: Canadian Review of Materials Web Site, http://www.umanitoba.ca/outreach/cm/ (May 21, 1999), Harriet Zaidman, review of *Jessica Takes Charge.*

*   *   *

LEE, Amanda
See GLICK, Ruth (Burtnick)

*   *   *

LeMIEUX, A(nne) C(onnelly) 1954-
(Anne LeMieux, Anne C. LeMieux)

Personal

Born December 15, 1954, in Bridgeport, CT; daughter of John D., Sr. and Elizabeth (Magee) Connelly; married Charles P. LeMieux III, January 7, 1977 (divorced, April, 1996); married Timothy D. Pocock, May, 1997; children: Sarah Elizabeth, Brendan Wolfe. *Education:* Simmons College, B.A., 1976; attended University of Bridgeport School of Music, 1976-78. *Politics:* Democrat. *Religion:* Roman Catholic. *Hobbies and other interests:* Music, acoustic fingerstyle guitar, sailing, golf.

Addresses

Home—490 Pequot Ct., Southport, CT 06490. *Agent*—Fran Lebowitz, Writer's House, 21 West 26th St., New York, NY 10010. *E-mail*—Swan522@aol.com.

Career

Freelance journalist, 1982-87; writer, 1987—. Cofounder and comoderator of the Children's Writer's Chat on America Online. *Member:* Authors Guild, Authors League of America, Society of Children's Book Writers and Illustrators, Williams Syndrome Association.

Awards, Honors

Best Book for Young Adults, American Library Association, 1994, and nominated for Garden State Teen Book Award, 1996, both for *The TV Guidance Counselor;* Children's Choice selection, International Reading Association, 1994, for *Super Snoop Sam Snout: The Case*

A. C. LeMieux—writing as Anne LeMieux—tells the story of a budding horticulturalist, Sylvia Widden, who suddenly finds herself caretaker to a magical world when a packet of seeds sprouts a fairy garden. (Cover illustration by Richard Bober.)

of the Missing Marble; Notable Book, Society of School Librarians International, and Silver Honors Award, Parents' Choice, both 1995, both for *Do Angels Sing the Blues?; Fruit Flies, Fish and Fortune Cookies* was named to the Sequoia Young Adult Master List by the Oklahoma Library Association, 1996-97.

Writings

The TV Guidance Counselor, Tambourine, 1993.
Super Snoop Sam Snout: The Case of the Yogurt Poker, Avon, 1994.
Super Snoop Sam Snout: The Case of the Stolen Snowman, Avon, 1994.
Super Snoop Sam Snout: The Case of the Missing Marble, Avon, 1994.
Fruit Flies, Fish and Fortune Cookies, illustrated by Diane de Groat, Tambourine, 1994.
Do Angels Sing the Blues?, Tambourine, 1995.
Dare to Be, M.E.!, Avon, 1997.
(As Anne LeMieux) *The Fairy Lair: A Special Place,* Aladdin, 1997.
(As Anne C. LeMieux) *The Fairy Lair: A Hidden Place,* Aladdin, 1998.
(As Anne C. LeMieux) *The Fairy Lair: A Magic Place,* Aladdin, 1998.
All the Answers, Avon, 2000.

Contributor to anthologies, including a poem to *Food Fight,* Harcourt, 1996, a short story, "Just Say . . . ," to *New Year, New Love,* Avon, 1996, and *My America: A Poetry Atlas of the United States,* Simon & Schuster, 2000. Contributor to *Family Issues* volume of the "Using Literature to Help Troubled Teens" series, edited by Joan Katwell, Greenwood Press, 1999. Author of unpublished screenplays, including *Music of the Sphere, The TV Guidance Counselor,* and *Mulligans.*

Work in Progress

Jester's Quest, Lovespeed, and *Brewtopia,* young adult novels; *Sea-Sar Salad,* a poetry collection; and *Being and Becoming: Journeying Though Life with a Special Child,* adult nonfiction.

Sidelights

"For me, writing is a process of finding connections," writer A. C. LeMieux once commented. "It's not only connecting words, but connecting ideas, symbols, events—and connecting them all to people." LeMieux further elaborated on this fundamental fact of writing in *ALAN Review:* "If I had to characterize the core of my writing process, I'd describe it as making connections. Connecting small graphic symbols into groupings which carry meaning. Connecting words into ordered strings which hopefully compound the meaning. Connecting sentences until the constructs of language are as laden with meaning as I can make them—ideas, events, symbols, all connected to character—the whole hopefully forming a conduit for human meaning, leading to a reader, the final connection." In this "final connection," LeMieux has been eminently successful, attracting loyal teenage and preteen readers for problem novels like *The TV Guidance Counselor,* which deals with teen depression and suicide, and *Do Angels Sing the Blues?,* which looks at the impact of the death of a friend. LeMieux also employs humor to connect her readers to lighter novels such as *Fruit Flies, Fish and Fortune Cookies* and its sequel, *Dare to Be, M.E.!,* and to the comedy-laden *All the Answers.* Or perhaps LeMieux connects with a younger audience with her trio of easy to read mysteries featuring "Super Snoop Sam Snout," or with early middle grade readers favoring fantasy with her "Fairy Lair" trilogy. With all of her books, LeMieux follows the edict of the British writer, E. M. Forster: "only connect." "I interpret this," LeMieux wrote in *ALAN Review,* "as a call to unite our ideals with our daily efforts and second, as a call to reach out and cultivate relationship."

Born in Bridgeport, Connecticut, in 1954, LeMieux was the second oldest of seven children—six boys and one girl. Growing up with so many boys around inevitably led to a deeper understanding of the young male psyche and may, as LeMieux once commented, "have contributed to the fact that I often write from a boy's point of view." An avid reader as a child, she would often run out of her own titles and have to borrow one of her brothers' more guy-oriented tales. Something of a tomboy, she and the rest of the neighborhood congregated at the local golf course, sledding on the fairways in the winter and dodging golf balls in the summer, and generally using the space like a giant backyard.

As a seventh grader, LeMieux first ventured into novel writing, "a neighborhood saga called *From My Porch,*" as she once stated. "It was one of those tell-all exposes, written from the point of view of a crow who spied on all the neighborhood kids, and it got more than a few people mad at me when Sister Robert Ann read it out loud to the English class at school." In high school, LeMieux read Harper Lee's *To Kill a Mockingbird,* and studying it with her freshman English teacher is what LeMieux credits as being most influential in making her a writer herself. "Immersed in the story, I first encountered a living concept of justice in the unshakable ethics of the gentle Atticus Finch," LeMieux noted in the *ALAN Review.* "I first realized the complexity of morality, and the decisions we face, and the choices we must make, witnessing, through Scout's perception, the renegade against-the-rules heroism of Boo Radley." Already a patient observer as a teenager, LeMieux filed away one character she encountered for future use. While working after school as a cashier in a supermarket, she observed one young man who came into the store continually, went to the magazine rack, and then skimmed through the pages of *TV Guide* with a worried look on his face. For two years the young man did this, without ever buying the magazine. Much later LeMieux would use this character in her first young adult novel, *The TV Guidance Counselor.*

Attending Simmons College in Boston, LeMieux majored in writing and minored in illustration. Intimidated by the idea of writing fiction, she stuck with nonfiction and journalism, publishing an article on Arthurian legends while still in college. Graduating from Simmons in 1976, she went on to study music for two years at the Bridgeport School of Music. Married in 1977, she soon had a daughter. In the 1980s, LeMieux worked part time as a freelancer, writing about sailing and music. "Doing freelance journalism, I also learned another important writing rule: writing is rewriting," LeMieux once commented. With the birth of a son in 1987, LeMieux finally felt she had lived enough and experienced enough to actually have something to say in fiction. To that end, she signed up for a children's book writing course at Fairfield University; after a dozen manuscripts and five years of slogging away at the writing process, LeMieux finally published her first work, *The TV Guidance Counselor.*

The narrator of LeMieux's first novel, seventeen-year-old Michael Madden, relates the events that led to his suicide attempt and hospitalization. Employing both flashbacks and conversations with his psychiatrist, Michael tells the reader about his parent's divorce,

which turned his life upside down, and his ultimate withdrawal from society. Michael and his mother live much less affluently than they had when his photographer father was part of the family. Michael takes a job at a supermarket to help out, and here he comes across the "guidance counselor" of the title, dubbed so by his best friend, Ricky. Harking back to the real-life character she had observed as a teenage shop clerk, LeMieux made this character a central metaphor of her first novel, an early subject for Michael's lens. Soon Michael is taking more and more photos with a camera his father once gave him and discovers he has a real talent for photography. Despite his new hobby, encouraged by the photography teacher, Mr. Dorio, and the attentions of a girlfriend, Melissa, Michael becomes increasingly withdrawn and is finally a victim to sadness and despair which, in the end, brings him to a near-fatal jump off a bridge.

"That such an ordinary young man can find himself plunging off a bridge will shock readers," observed a contributor for *Kirkus Reviews.* However, this same writer felt that the first-person narration "offers enough

As the magic in the Fairy Lair becomes unbalanced, Sylvia and Dana find problems spilling over to the human world in the second book of LeMieux's fantasy trilogy. (Cover illustration by Doug Beekman.)

insights into Michael's world, and into the depth of his feelings, to make his actions comprehensible," and concluded that this was a "well-wrought first novel." A writer for *Publishers Weekly* applauded LeMieux for her excellent handling of "adolescent anguish," saying "this first novel admirably explores a young man's injured soul." While criticizing LeMieux for having Michael recite "adult pop psychology," Kathy Piehl, writing in *School Library Journal,* nevertheless commended the author for creating a character with "an authentic teen voice" and "masterfully depict[ing] various aspects of depression." Reviewing this debut novel in *Booklist,* Karen Hutt wrote that readers would "appreciate Michael's vulnerability and understand his despondency," while the first-person narration "will sweep them into the goings-on."

LeMieux's next novel, the 1994 *Fruit Flies, Fish and Fortune Cookies,* deals with teen and preteen issues of a less serious nature. One evening, Mary Ellen Bobowick has the misfortune of eating a fortune cookie which warns, "Reflect carefully, or your deeds will bring bad luck." Shrugging off the ominous prediction, Mary Ellen notices that suddenly nothing seems to go her way: she shatters her mother's antique mirror, gets sprayed by a skunk, and learns that her best friend is moving to France for a year. After she drops a jar of fruit flies at school on Career Day, Mary Ellen becomes convinced that the cookie was telling the truth. However, Mary Ellen's luck eventually improves, and she even finds a new boyfriend. Leslie Barban, in *School Library Journal,* called *Fruit Flies, Fish and Fortune Cookies* a "lighthearted, funny novel" and enjoyed LeMieux's "believable, likable ... characters." Carolyn Phelan, writing in *Booklist,* maintained that some of the minor characters in the story "are not well developed," but added that Mary Ellen is an "easily identifiable" heroine for middle-grade readers.

LeMieux has also written a trio of easy to read mysteries featuring "Super Snoop Sam Snout" which earned a place on the International Reading Association Children's Book Choice List. However, in 1995, she returned to a world where teenagers must overcome more serious problems in their lives with *Do Angels Sing the Blues?*. "I knew I wanted the book to be about the death of a best friend," LeMieux once stated. "My own best friend, who grew up across the street from me in my neighborhood, died when I was twenty-six. And I knew I wanted the book to be about music. I was listening to Stevie Ray Vaughan one day, singing 'Life Without You,' and that's when the connection clicked: I knew that the music in the book had to be the blues." The result is a book about friendship, a story of love and loss, and also a musical tale all told from the point of view of a sixteen-year-old narrator, James "Boog" Buglioni.

Boog recounts the events of one year in high school and his friendship with Theodore Haley Stone, his buddy since grade school. Together Boog and Theo formed a band called "Blues Thing," and the two are basically inseparable until the advent of Carey Harrigan. Seeing her one day in Mrs. Brockmeyer's class, Theo falls instantly in love with her, and then everything changes between Boog and Theo. A depressive girl from a troubled family, Carey forms an unlikely triangle with Theo and Boog at first. She begins writing lyrics for the band, and for a time Boog and Carey try to get along well together. Pressure plays on the triangle when Theo gets into trouble in a bid to protect Carey, caught drinking at school. Grounded, Theo cannot play in the local "Battle of the Bands." Carey subsequently runs away when she learns that old family friends have died in a fire. Boog and Theo go looking for her and find her alongside the road. Crossing the misty road to get Carey a hot chocolate at a shop, Theo is hit by a passing car and killed. Boog cannot forgive Carey for what he sees as her responsibility for his buddy's death; he confronts her at the funeral, where she is drunk. Thereafter, he leaves his music behind and spends the summer tucked away in his room. Finally, letters from Theo's mother and from Carey give him some perspective on the incidents and allow him to put the death of Theo behind him and forgive Carey.

Again, critics generally responded favorably to LeMieux's problem novel. Although criticizing the slightly heavy-handed foreshadowing of Theo's death, Renee Steinberg in *School Library Journal* believed that LeMieux created teenagers who "can deal with unexpected tragedy" in a way that is neither condescending or unbelievable. Maeve Visser Knoth in *Horn Book* complimented LeMieux for the emotional depth of her characters, describing Boog and Theo as "sympathetic, richly drawn characters with human complexities," and concluding that LeMieux presented "an emotional but never maudlin story of tragedy and growth." "LeMieux writes well," commented *Booklist*'s Merri Monks, "evoking some favorite teen fantasies in a believable first-person male voice." A reviewer for *Publishers Weekly* felt that *Do Angels Sing the Blues?* surpassed LeMieux's first novel "in its power and sensitivity," and was an "absorbing exploration of adolescent hopes, dreams and vulnerability" which "contains undertones as resonant and melancholy as a blues melody."

Such resonance is not a matter of chance in LeMieux's books. "Especially in the early stages of a book," LeMieux once commented, "I often feel my way into a story with a pen—I see what it's about as it emerges on the page. I write all my drafts longhand, then edit them into the word processor. Using the computer actually seems to activate a different part of my 'writing brain'— a part that's as tuned into the sounds of language as the sense itself, and that thinks hypertextually, associatively. In fact, I write all my poetry directly on the computer.

"I find the act of writing to be a process of exploration and discovery. Much of the 'think-work' I do as a writer involves asking questions and postulating answers. When I sit down to write the first draft of the story, I consider two things: what is going to happen, a general plot, but even more important, to whom it is going to happen. I spend a lot of time getting to know my characters, who they are, what they're like, how they think, so that they really do take on a life of their own inside my head. Parts of me wind up in all my characters, both male and female, adult and young people."

LeMieux lets laughter do the work in her sequel to *Fruit Flies, Fish and Fortune Cookies,* the 1997 *Dare to Be, M.E.!.* Reprising the gang from *Fruit Flies,* LeMieux brings Mary Ellen to stage center, initially saddened by the departure of friend Ben just before the start of the seventh grade. However, Mary Ellen soon has something to be happy about when she learns that another friend is coming back into her life. Recently returned from Paris where her parents split up, Justine is having difficulty re-adjusting to her old life. She insists on dieting, even though she does not need to lose weight, and obsesses about her looks. Only slowly does Mary Ellen come to understand that her friend's obsession with dieting is really a sickness—bulimia. Touching on issues from nose rings to peer pressure and body image, the book follows Mary Ellen and Justine through a difficult readjustment until Justine is finally willing to admit her problem and see a therapist.

In the conclusion to her popular trilogy, LeMieux follows Sylvia and Dana as they seek to prevent the destruction of their fairy kingdom at the hands of a ruthless real estate developer. (Cover illustration by Doug Beekman.)

"In a story filled with subplots and modeled behavior, LeMieux offers a primer for students entering junior high," wrote a contributor for *Kirkus Reviews,* who also felt that "the lessons slide down easily." *Booklist*'s Ilene Cooper thought that even though some of the writing in *Dare to Be, M.E.!* was "cliched," "the story does bring the issue of eating disorders to the forefront." A *Publishers Weekly* reviewer also commented on the "issues-oriented" nature of the story, touching on eating disorders, body image and other "sources and symptoms of preteen angst."

With *All the Answers,* LeMieux once again let laughter do the work for her in a preteen novel. Witty, eighth-grade Jason at first appears to have all the answers, except for those that he desperately needs to pass algebra class. His stressed-out dad is becoming alienated from wise-cracking Jason, and at school things are not going so rosy outside of algebra class, either. The arrival of twins, Philip and Phelicia, is putting another strain on Jason's life: Philip is something of a bully to Jason, both on the basketball court and off, and the beautiful though shallow Phelicia becomes the object of Jason's flirting attentions. Things come to a head when Jason pays a friend to copy her math homework and then must face the wrath of his teacher when she finds out about the cheating.

Reviewing the novel in *Publishers Weekly,* a contributor noted that male and female readers alike would find Jason "both likable and authentic; his incessant string of wisecracks would make any standup comic envious." A writer for *Kirkus Reviews* found the novel "[b]riskly engaging though strictly skin deep," with LeMieux's narrative "consistently amusing and peppered with witty dialogue." *Booklist*'s Shelle Rosenfeld also observed LeMieux's "snappy dialogue," but felt in addition that Jason's troubles "are insightfully portrayed," and that the "well-written novel champions the value of honesty and integrity."

The versatile LeMieux has also penned a trilogy of fantasy novels aimed at early middle grade readers. Her "Fairy Lair" novels take readers on a magical trip to a fairy glade, featuring Sylvia and Dana who learn with bitter results that man can upset the fragile balance of the fairy realm. Additionally, LeMieux has written poetry and short stories that have been anthologized in young adult story collections.

"As a writer, I think of myself as a miner of life," LeMieux once observed, "digging for meaning, for raw ore to refine into characters of genuine mettle, and forge into building blocks to create a world. My aim is to produce work that will be so genuinely evocative of and so true to life, that a reader will experience it as real." In *ALAN Review* she expounded on her use of humor in her books. "How to connect with today's adolescent readers by means of laughter and literature?" she wrote. "As a writer, my foremost aim is to write with honesty, and without condescension, with humor which encompasses the paradoxes, incongruities, and even absurdities of life. My hope is that my characters' voices will catch kids' attention, and connect with their hearts, and that my stories might help expand their emotional vocabularies. I believe a writer can be an agent of connection."

Biographical and Critical Sources

PERIODICALS

ALAN Review, spring, 1998, A. C. LeMieux, "The Problem Novel in a Conservative Age"; winter, 2000, Anne C. LeMieux, "Only Connect," pp. 11-16.

Booklist, December 15, 1993, Karen Hutt, review of *The TV Guidance Counselor,* p. 746; March 15, 1994, p. 1358; November 1, 1994, Carolyn Phelan, review of *Fruit Flies, Fish and Fortune Cookies,* p. 497; September 1, 1995, Merri Monks, review of *Do Angels Sing the Blues?,* p. 66; June 1 & 15, 1997, Ilene Cooper, review of *Dare to Be, M.E.!,* p. 1703; January 1 & 15, 2000, Shelle Rosenfeld, review of *All the Answers,* p. 906.

Bulletin of the Center for Children's Books, October, 1993, p. 50; February, 2000, p. 213.

Horn Book, November-December, 1995, Maeve Visser Knoth, review of *Do Angels Sing the Blues?,* p. 746.

Kirkus Reviews, August 15, 1993, review of *The TV Guidance Counselor,* p. 1075; November 15, 1994, p. 1534; July 1, 1995, p. 949; May 15, 1997, review of *Dare to Be, M.E.!,* p. 802; December 1, 1999, review of *All the Answers,* p. 1887.

Publishers Weekly, July 12, 1993, review of *The TV Guidance Counselor,* p. 81; July 10, 1995, review of *Do Angels Sing the Blues?,* p. 58; June 2, 1997, review of *Dare to Be, M.E.!,* p. 73; January 17, 2000, review of *All the Answers,* p. 57.

School Library Journal, October, 1993, Kathy Piehl, review of *The TV Guidance Counselor,* p. 151; October, 1994, Leslie Barban, review of *Fruit Flies, Fish and Fortune Cookies,* p. 124; September, 1995, Renee Steinberg, review of *Do Angels Sing the Blues?,* p. 219; June, 1997, p. 94; July, 1997, p. 94; February, 2000, p. 122.

Voice of Youth Advocates, February, 1994, p. 370; August, 1995, p. 160.*

—*Sketch by J. Sydney Jones*

LeMIEUX, Anne
See LeMIEUX, A. C.

* * *

LeMIEUX, Anne C.
See LeMIEUX, A. C.

* * *

LINDBERGH, Anne (Spencer) Morrow 1906-2001

OBITUARY NOTICE—See index for *SATA* sketch: Born 1906, in Englewood, NJ; died February 7, 2001, in Passumpsic, VT. Pilot and author. Lindbergh was a writer and the wife of pilot Charles A. Lindbergh, who flew the first transatlantic flight from New York to Paris in 1927. Co-pilot and radio operator on several missions with her husband, Lindbergh wrote of their travels and adventures in over a dozen published works. Her first book, *North to the Orient,* was published in 1935 and was followed by her *Listen! The Wind* in 1938. Some of her best-known works were her published diaries, including *Bring Me a Unicorn* and *Hour of Gold, Hour of Lead.* Lindbergh's final work, *War Within and Without,* was published in 1980. In 1934 the National Geographic Society honored Lindbergh with the Hubbard Gold Medal for her work as co-pilot and radio operator in numerous flight missions.

OBITUARIES AND OTHER SOURCES:

PERIODICALS

Chicago Tribune, February 8, 2001, section 2, p. 11.
Los Angeles Times, February 8, 2001, p. A1, A28.
New York Times, February 8, 2001, p. A26.
Times (London, England), February 9, 2001.

M

MACKAY, Constance D'Arcy 1880-1966

Personal

Born August 15, 1880, in St. Paul, MN; died August 21, 1966; daughter of Robert G. and Anne (D'Arcy) Mackay; married Roland Holt (a publishing executive), April 11, 1923 (died, 1931). *Education:* Attended Boston University, 1903-04.

Career

Writer. Director of theatrical events for War Camp Community Service, 1918-19; associated with various community theaters, including some presenting productions for children. *Member:* Festival Society of America, PEN, Society of American Dramatists and Composers, Pen and Brush Club (New York, NY), Town Hall Club.

Writings

Costumes and Scenery for Amateurs, Holt (New York, NY), 1915.

How to Produce Children's Plays, Holt (New York, NY), 1915.

The Little Theatre in the United States, Holt (New York, NY), 1917.

Patriotic Drama in Your Town: A Manual of Suggestions, Holt (New York, NY), 1918.

Play Production in Churches and Sunday Schools, Playground and Recreation Association of America (New York, NY), 1921.

(Editor) *Suggestions for the Dramatic Celebration of the Three-Hundredth Anniversary of the Purchase of Manhattan, 1626-1926*, Playground and Recreation Association of America (New York, NY), 1926.

The Shepherdess and the Chimneysweep: A Christmas Opera in One Act: Founded on the Story by Hans Christian Andersen, Mowbray Music Publishers (New York, NY), 1978.

Also author of *Rural Drama Bibliography*, Playground and Recreation Association of America.

PLAYS

The Queen of Hearts (three-act), first produced in Boston, MA, 1904.

The House of the Heart, and Other Plays for Children, Holt (New York, NY), 1909.

The Silver Thread, and Other Folk Plays for Young Children, Holt (New York, NY), 1910.

The Pageant of Patriotism, first produced in Brooklyn, NY, at Prospect Park, May, 1911.

The Pageant of Schenectady (first produced in Schenectady, NY, at Union College, May 30, 1912), Gazette Press, 1912.

Patriotic Plays and Pageants for Young People, Holt (New York, NY), 1912.

The Historical Pageant of Portland, Maine (first produced in Portland, ME, 1913), Southworth, 1913.

The Beau of Bath, and Other One-Act Plays of Eighteenth Century Life, Holt (New York, NY), 1915.

Plays of the Pioneers: A Book of Historical Pageant-Plays, Harper & Brothers (New York, NY), 1915, reprinted, Core Collection Books (Great Neck, NY), 1976.

The Forest Princess, and Other Masques, Holt (New York, NY), 1916.

Memorial Day Pageant, Harper & Brothers (New York, NY), 1916.

William of Stratford: Shakespeare's Tercentenary Pageant, first produced in Baltimore, MD, 1916.

Pageant of Sunshine and Shadow (also see below), first produced in New York, NY, 1916.

Patriotic Christmas Pageant, first produced in San Francisco, CA, 1918.

Victory Pageant, first produced in New York, NY, 1918.

Franklin, Holt, 1922.

America Triumphant, D. Appleton (New York, NY), 1926.

Midsummer Eve: An Outdoor Fantasy, Samuel French (New York, NY), 1929.

Youth's Highway, and Other Plays for Young People (includes *Pageant of Sunshine and Shadow*), Holt (New York, NY), 1929.

Ladies of the White House, Baker's Plays, 1948.

A Day at Nottingham: A Festival at Which All the Playgrounds of a City Can Take Part, National Recreational Association of America (New York, NY), 1952.

OTHER

Contributor of plays and articles to periodicals, including *Woman's Home Companion* and *St. Nicholas.* Mackay's papers are stored at the New York Public Library and at the University of North Carolina at Chapel Hill.

Sidelights

Constance D'Arcy Mackay was well known during her lifetime for her promotion of community and children's drama. The author of many books on the subject—and even more plays that could be used in community or outdoor settings—Mackay was a twentieth-century pioneer in her field. According to Christian H. Moe in *Twentieth-Century Children's Writers,* "Her productive writing career, extending from 1904 to 1952, encompassed a variety of dramatic forms from folk and history plays to pageant dramas and morality plays. Believing that youth yearns for the heroic and the wonderful, she peopled her dramas with leading characters who realize heroic and humane virtues by overcoming danger and difficulty."

By the time she married publishing executive Roland Holt in 1923, Mackay had been publishing with his company for fourteen years. She was also renowned, especially in New York City, for staging the dramas and pageants that she had written. If she was unable to direct the production herself, she included copious notes on how it should be done, and these evolved into a series of "how-to" books aimed at rural communities, Sunday Schools, and little theaters.

Mackay's plays are rarely performed today, but in their era they were quite popular. Her talents ranged across a wide area of drama and were many times aimed at a youthful audience, as the author was particularly dedicated to introducing children to the theater arts. As might be expected, given the decades in which she was most productive, Mackay concentrated on patriotic themes, fairy tales, and dramas intended to promote civic pride. Moe concluded, "Mackay's dramas display worthy content and literary quality, imaginative theatricality, and a respect for the intelligence of the young. That her dramas are not produced today does not diminish their worth and their historical influence. She stands tall as an early leader in her field."

Biographical and Critical Sources

BOOKS

Twentieth-Century Children's Writers, 4th edition, St. James Press (Detroit, MI), 1995, pp. 615-616.*

MacMILLAN, Dianne M(arie) 1943-

Personal

Born August 26, 1943, in St. Louis, MO; daughter of Luckie Stradtman (in used car sales) and Dee (a homemaker and in real estate sales; maiden name, Maniscalco) Webb; married James Robert MacMillan (a general contractor), August 14, 1965; children: Jennifer Dorand-Fisher, Kathy, Shannon. *Education:* Miami University (Oxford, OH), B.S. (education). *Politics:* Independent. *Religion:* Catholic. *Hobbies and other interests:* Reading, hiking, golf, bowling, traveling.

Addresses

Home—6901 E. Avenida de Santiago, Anaheim, CA 92807. *E-mail*—mac826@earthlink.net.

Career

Elementary school teacher in St. Louis, MO, 1965-71; tutor for children with reading and learning problems, 1972-78; freelance writer, 1977—; writing instructor, 1996—. Homeless Ministry Coordinator, 1987-91. *Member:* Society of Children's Book Writers and Illustrators (regional advisor of Orange, Riverside, and San Bernardino counties), Authors Guild, PEN Center USA West, Southern California Council on Literature for Children and Young People.

Dianne M. MacMillan describes the rituals and festivities associated with a Vietnamese new year's celebration. (Cover illustration by Charlott Nathan.)

Awards, Honors

Patriotic Feature of the Year, *Highlights for Children*, 1992; Outstanding Science Trade Books for Children, National Science Teachers Association/Children's Book Council, 1998, and Best Book for Children selection, *Science Books and Films*, 1999, both for *Cheetahs.*

Writings

(With Dorothy Freeman) *My Best Friend Martha Rodriguez: Meeting a Mexican-American Family,* illustrated by Warren Fricke, Julian Messner (Englewood Cliffs, NJ), 1986.

(With Dorothy Freeman) *My Best Friend Duc Tran: Meeting a Vietnamese-American Family,* illustrated by Mary Jane Begin, Julian Messner (Englewood Cliffs, NJ), 1987.

(With Dorothy Freeman) *My Best Friend Mee-Yung Kim: Meeting a Korean-American Family,* illustrated by Bob Marstall, Julian Messner (Englewood Cliffs, NJ), 1989.

Martin Luther King, Jr. Day, Enslow (Hillside, NJ), 1992.

(With Dorothy Freeman) *Kwanzaa,* Enslow (Hillside, NJ), 1992.

Easter, Enslow (Hillside, NJ), 1993.

Jewish Holidays in the Fall, Enslow (Hillside, NJ), 1993.

Elephants: Our Last Land Giants, Carolrhoda (Minneapolis, MN), 1993.

Chinese New Year, Enslow (Hillside, NJ), 1994.

Jewish Holidays in the Spring, Enslow (Hillside, NJ), 1994.

Ramadan and Id al-Fitr, Enslow (Hillside, NJ), 1994.

Tet: Vietnamese New Year, Enslow (Hillside, NJ), 1994.

Missions of the Los Angeles Area, Lerner (Minneapolis, MN), 1996.

Diwali: Hindu Festival of Lights, Enslow (Springfield, NJ), 1997.

Japanese Children's Day and the Obon Festival, Enslow (Springfield, NJ), 1997.

Mardi Gras, Enslow (Springfield, NJ), 1997.

Presidents Day, Enslow (Springfield, NJ), 1997.

Thanksgiving Day, Enslow (Springfield, NJ), 1997.

Mexican Independence Day and Cinco de Mayo, Enslow (Springfield, NJ), 1997.

Cheetahs, photographs by Gerry Ellis, Carolrhoda (Minneapolis, MN), 1997.

Destination Los Angeles, Lerner (Minneapolis, MN), 1997.

Contributor of articles and stories to periodicals, including *Jack & Jill, Christian Science Monitor, Christian Adventure, Cobblestone, The Vine, The Beehive, Highlights for Children, Alive for Young Teens, Children's Playmate, Parish Family Digest, The Friend,* and *On the Line.*

Sidelights

Dianne M. MacMillan writes informative nonfiction works for elementary-age readers. Many of them delve into other cultures and explain how immigrants to the United States celebrate their heritage through various feast days and festivals. As the author once commented, "I live in a wonderful world of books. I began writing

Focusing on the development of Catholic missions during the eighteenth century, MacMillan's book explains how the arrival of European priests affected the lives of Native Americans living in the Los Angeles area. (Cover photograph by Don Eastman.)

for children officially in 1977, but deep inside I've always been a writer. I've always been able to express my feelings and emotions better on paper. (Everyone in my family knows to watch out for one of my 'letters.') In grade school, I looked forward to the monthly visits of the bookmobile. I was happiest when I was lost in a Nancy Drew mystery or a historical pioneer adventure."

Born in St. Louis, Missouri, in 1943, MacMillan earned a degree in education from Miami University in Ohio and began her career as an elementary school teacher in her hometown. She married and became a mother, and by the mid-1970s was working as a tutor for children with reading and learning problems. As the author recounted, "The world of children's books was still a big part of my life. When I stopped teaching, I missed the daily interaction with children and children's books. So I began to write. I choose to write for children because children are open to life, honest, and filled with enthusiasm. Their curiosity and sense of wonder give new meaning and hope to each generation. When writing, I try to tap into that honesty and curiosity. I love research and I'm fascinated by discoveries of little-known facts and trivia. I think kids share that fascination. Libraries and bookstores are pieces of 'heaven' for me and there never is enough time to spend as long as I'd like."

MacMillan's earliest works explored multicultural friendships from a young person's viewpoint. The titles, written with Dorothy Freeman, include *My Best Friend Duc Tran: Meeting a Vietnamese-American Family* and *My Best Friend Mee-Yung Kim: Meeting a Korean-American Family.* She also wrote titles about holidays—*Martin Luther King, Jr. Day, Kwanzaa,* and *Easter*—before penning *Elephants: Our Last Land Giants* for Carolrhoda Books in 1993. Here, she details the physiognomy of the massive beasts and discusses their particular social characteristics. She returned to the holiday theme with the books *Jewish Holidays in the Spring, Ramadan and Id al-Fitr, Tet: Vietnamese New Year,* and *Chinese New Year* in the mid-1990s. All of them focus on the way in which residents of the United States celebrate their heritage in their own communities, and how these observances link them to their homeland or culture. Dot Minzer, reviewing *Tet* and *Chinese New Year* in *School Library Journal,* stated that "the texts are well researched and have a great deal of information."

MacMillan has also penned a nonfiction work for young readers interested in Southern California history. *Missions of the Los Angeles Area,* published in 1996, provides historical details about the centers of education and Roman Catholic faith that missionaries of Spain's Franciscan order established on behalf of the Spanish throne in the 1700s. She also writes about the Native American civilization and culture against which these goals clashed; the friars' desire to educate California's Indians, and the ultimate mixed results of such colonization, are also explored. MacMillan tracks the ultimate decline of the missions, then describes the movement to restore the grand structures, including the historical sites of San Gabriel Archangel and San Fernando Rey de Espana. Specific missions are discussed in detail, a pattern also found in two other companion volumes by

other authors: *Missions of the Southern Coast* and *Missions of the San Francisco Bay Area.* Reviewing all three for *School Library Journal,* Rosalyn Pierini termed each "attractive, balanced, and age appropriate." MacMillan also wrote another work on the City of Angels, *Destination Los Angeles,* which focused on a little-known aspect of the megalopolis best known as the center of the entertainment industry: its port. MacMillan's book chronicles the history of the harbor, discusses the West Coast shipping industry, and alerts readers to the sheer volume of goods from around the globe that arrive daily in this little-known part of the city. *School Library Journal* reviewer Lucy Rafael called it "a well-rounded presentation" and "useful for reports on harbors."

In 1997 alone, MacMillan published an impressive eight titles, nearly all of them discussing various holidays around the world. In *Diwali: Hindu Festival of Lights,* MacMillan writes about one of India's most important celebrations and how Hindu believers observe it through costumes, rituals, and food—"giving readers a full picture of the meaning and value of this festival," noted Sabrina L. Fraunfelter in *School Library Journal. Japanese Children's Day and the Obon Festival, Mardi Gras, Thanksgiving Day,* and *Mexican Independence Day and Cinco de Mayo,* all present the history of the festivities and provide details about how Americans observe them in their respective ethnic communities. In 1997, MacMillan also wrote *Cheetahs,* published with photographs by Gerry Ellis. Like her earlier work about elephants, here the author sketches out the unique physical characteristics of the felines and how these fierce and fast cats live, eat, work, and play. It also discusses how conservationists have worked to help cheetahs survive. Carolyn Phelan, reviewing the title for *Booklist,* termed the book an "informative and attractively illustrated book" that "will satisfy many readers."

As MacMillan noted, creating such informative works for young readers presents agreeable challenges for her: "The initial writing of a story or nonfiction book is difficult because I'm trying to sort in my mind the details, words, and scenes to put down. Which will be most interesting? Most clear? Entertaining? There are as many choices as words. Once my first draft is complete, I attack rewriting with zeal and gusto. This is the fun part. If I can give my readers new information, or a sense of belonging, perhaps a chuckle, or a bit of entertainment, then I have succeeded. The best part of living constantly in a world of books is that I keep learning, exploring, growing, and asking 'Why?'"

Biographical and Critical Sources

PERIODICALS

Booklist, February 15, 1998, Carolyn Phelan, review of *Cheetahs,* p. 1005.
Bulletin of the Center for Children's Books, January, 1990, p. 115.
Horn Book, July, 1989, p. 75.
Horn Book Guide, fall, 1997, Peter D. Sieruta, review of *Thanksgiving Day* and *Presidents Day,* p. 330; spring,

In this work, Macmillan writes about the traditional day of celebration when Japanese honor the talents of their young people through festivities, gifts, and religious customs. (Cover photograph by James R. MacMillan.)

A Carolrhoda Nature Watch Book
by Dianne M. MacMillan / photographs by Gerry Ellis

Compiled with the help of wildlife experts throughout the United States, MacMillan's book describes the physical characteristics, way of life, and threats to one of the planet's most beautiful—and endangered—creatures.

1998, review of *Mexican Independence Day* and *Mardi Gras,* p. 107; fall, 1998, Kelly Ault, review of *Cheetahs,* p. 386, and *Destination Los Angeles,* p. 428.

Kirkus Reviews, July 1, 1987, p. 995.

Los Angeles Times Book Review, August 18, 1996, Kathleen Krull, review of *Missions of the Los Angeles Area,* p. 15.

School Library Journal, April, 1987, p. 99; September, 1987, p. 180; January, 1993, p. 92; February, 1994, review of *Elephants,* p. 113; March, 1995, Dot Minzer, review of *Tet* and *Chinese New Year,* p. 215; August, 1996, Rosalyn Pierini, review of *Missions of the Los Angeles Area, Missions of the Southern Coast* and *Missions of the San Francisco Bay Area,* p. 157; August, 1997, Pamela R. Bomboy, review of *Mexican Independence Day and Cinco de Mayo, Mardi Gras,* and *Japanese Children's Day,* p. 149; August, 1997, Sabrina L. Fraunfelter, review of *Thanksgiving Day* and *Diwali,* p. 171; March, 1998, Lucy Rafael, review of *Destination Los Angeles,* p. 236.

*   *   *

MARLOWE, Tess
See GLICK, Ruth (Burtnick)

MAROL, Jean-Claude 1946-

Personal

Born July 27, 1946, in Paris, France; son of Roger (an artist) and Lucienne (Roudier) Marol; married Elvire Ferle (an artist), 1969. *Education:* Received diploma in architecture from Fine Arts School of Paris.

Addresses

Home and Office—10 rue d'Orchampt, 75018 Paris, France.

Career

Writer and artist.

Writings

SELF-ILLUSTRATED CHILDREN'S BOOKS; IN ENGLISH TRANSLATION

Vagabul and His Shadow, Creative Education (Mankato, MN), 1982.
Vagabul Escapes, Creative Education (Mankato, MN), 1982.
Vagabul Goes Skiing, Creative Education (Mankato, MN), 1982.
Vagabul in the Clouds, Creative Education (Mankato, MN), 1982.

FOR CHILDREN; IN FRENCH

Nuarbre, Ecole des Loisirs, 1979.
Les Petits Chemins de Veille-en-Bulle, Grasset (Paris, France), 1979.
Feudou Dragon Secret, Ipomee, 1983.
Les Sauts de l'Auge Cascade, Ipomee, 1985.
Le Banc Vert, Terre Vivante, 1988.
J'ai Pas Faim, Limailles, 1992.
J'ai Pas Envie, Limailles, 1992.
J'ai Pas d'Idees, Limailles, 1992.
J'ai Pas Sommeil, Limailles, 1992.
Quel Micmac, Syros, 1992.
Contes d'Amour et de Sagesse, Le Fennec, 1994.
Tu m'Fais Pas Peur, Le Seuil (Paris, France), 1994.
Le Ralobolo, Pastel-Ecole des Loisirs, 1996.
Paroles de Troubadours, Albin-Michel (Paris, France), 1998.

Coauthor (with Robert Morel) of the books *J'Embrasse Ma Cousine, (Mon Cousin), J'Apprends Rien, Je Crois au Pere Noel,* and *J'Aime Pas les Vacances,* published in 1980. Children's albums include *Ding Dong Fair la Sieste* and *Dingdong Dans la Tempete,* both Lis-Moi une Histoire, 1991.

FOR ADULTS; IN FRENCH

La Tete Ailleurs, Editions du Felin, 1984.
Pli Urgent, L'Originel, 1985.
Secret, Le Fourneau, 1986.
Loup, Tiens ta Langue, Lis-Moi une Histoire, 1989.
Tout Reprendre a Zero, Dervy, 1991.

(With G. Sorval) *La Mise en Demeure* (essays), L'Originel-Accarias, 1994.

(With D. Roumanof) *Sois Sage!*, La Table Ronde, 1994.

En Tout et Pour Tout (essays), Le Fennec, 1995.

Vie en Jeu (essays), L'Originel-Accarias, 1995.

Blason Langue Vivante (essays), Dangles, 1995.

Une Fois Ma Anandamoyi (essays), Courrier du Livre, 1996.

Jeu t'Aime, Jouvence, 1997.

(With A. Gauer) *Au Coeur du Vent, Les Bauls* (essays), L'Originel-Accarias, 1997.

L'Amour Libere(e) ou l'Erotique Initiale des Troubadours (essays), Dervy, 1998.

La Fin 'Amor (essays), Le Seuil, (Paris, France), 1998.

Le Rire du Sacre (essays), Albin-Michel (Paris, France), 1999.

Le Fier Basier: Aux Sources de L'amour Chevaleresque, Relié (Gordes, France), 2001.

Work in Progress

La Cle des Mots, a book about the image of words, for Nathan.

Sidelights

Jean-Claude Marol commented: "I draw for magazines, make postcards and posters, tales for children, exhibitions, and books of poetry, and I tell my stories in public. Through humor or painting or poetry or stories, I try first to live, and to look with others between the lines, if there is space."

Biographical and Critical Sources

PERIODICALS

School Library Journal, May, 1983, p. 64.*

*   *   *

MASSIE, Diane Redfield 1938-

Personal

Born in 1938, in Los Angeles, CA; daughter of James Gilbert (an insurance agent) and Marion (a teacher; maiden name, Haskell) Redfield; married David M. Massie (a mathematics professor); children: Caitlin, Tom. *Education:* Attended Los Angeles City College and Occidental College; studied oboe with Los Angeles Philharmonic musician Henri DeBuscher.

Addresses

Home—Hunterdon County, NJ. *Office*—c/o Author Mail, Atheneum/Simon & Schuster, 1230 Avenue of the Americas, New York, NY 10020.

Career

Author and illustrator of books for children; art teacher; designer. Professional oboist with Honolulu Symphony for five seasons.

Awards, Honors

Honor Book Award, *Book Week* Children's Spring Book Festival, 1965, for *A Turtle and a Loon;* design award, Chicago's Book Clinic, and Best Books selection, New York Public Library, both 1966, both for *A Birthday for Bird;* Best Children's Book selection, Library of Congress, Edgar Allan Poe Special Award, Mystery Writers of America (MWA), Children's Book of the Year selection, Child Study Association, Best Books selection, *School Library Journal,* all 1979, Children's Choices selection, International Reading Association/Children's Book Council, 1980, and Utah Children's Book Award, Children's Literature Association of Utah, 1981, all for *Chameleon Was a Spy;* Edgar Allan Poe Award nomination (Best Juvenile Novel category), MWA, 1984, for *Chameleon the Spy and the Case of the Vanishing Jewels;* Junior Literary Guild selection, for *Lobster Moths;* Best Children's Books of the Year selection, Bank Street College, 2001, and Buckeroo Award nomination (Wyoming), 2001-02, both for *The Baby Beebee Bird.*

Writings

FOR CHILDREN; AND ILLUSTRATOR

The Baby Beebee Bird, Harper (New York, NY), 1963, republished with pictures by Steven Kellogg, HarperCollins (New York, NY), 2000.

Tiny Pin, Harper, 1964.

A Turtle and a Loon, Atheneum (New York, NY), 1965.

MacGregor Was a Dog, Parents' Magazine Press (New York, NY), 1965.

A Birthday for Bird, Parents' Magazine Press (New York, NY), 1966.

Cockle Stew and Other Rhymes, Atheneum (New York, NY), 1967.

Magic Jim, Parents' Magazine Press (New York, NY), 1967.

King Henry the Mouse, Atheneum, (New York, NY) 1968.

Dazzle, Parents' Magazine Press (New York, NY), 1969.

Walter Was a Frog, Simon & Schuster (New York, NY), 1970.

The Monstrous Glisson Glop, Parents' Magazine Press (New York, NY), 1970.

Zigger Beans, Parents' Magazine Press (New York, NY), 1971.

Good Neighbors, McGraw (Middletown, CT), 1972.

Briar Rose and the Golden Eggs, Parents' Magazine Press (New York, NY), 1973.

Turtle's Flying Lesson, Grosset, 1973.

The Lion's Bed, Weekly Reader Children's Book Club (Middletown, CT), 1974.

The Komodo Dragon's Jewels, Macmillan (New York, NY), 1975.

The Thief in the Botanical Gardens, Weekly Reader Children's Book Club (Middletown, CT), 1975.

Sloth's Birthday Party, Weekly Reader Children's Book Club (Middletown, CT), 1976.

Brave Brush-Tail Possum, Weekly Reader Children's Book Club (Middletown, CT), 1978.

Chameleon Was a Spy, Crowell (New York, NY), 1979.

Chameleon the Spy and Terrible Toaster Trap, Crowell (New York, NY), 1982.

Cocoon, Crowell (New York, NY), 1983.

Chameleon the Spy and the Case of the Vanishing Jewels, Crowell (New York, NY), 1984.

Lobster Moths, Atheneum (New York, NY), 1985.

Also author of several one-act plays and musicals. Contributor of poems to *Humpty Dumpty.* The author's work has also been published in Japan.

Work in Progress

"A large book of rhymes for children with illustrations in pen and ink."

Sidelights

Diane Redfield Massie has written and illustrated a number of charming picture books for children during a twenty-year career. Her first published work, *The Baby Beebee Bird,* is now considered a classic bedtime story. In 2000 it was reissued in a larger format with new illustrations, thirty-seven years after its debut.

Born in Los Angeles in 1938, Massie studied at Los Angeles City College and Occidental College. Auditioning in Los Angeles, she was hired to play first oboe in the Honolulu Symphony. She spent five seasons with the orchestra in Hawaii, met her husband (who was in the U.S. Navy) there, and after he was discharged, came to the East Coast. "It was not easy to find work in New York," Massie said. "I joined Local 802 (a musician's union), but in the music business, one needs to know contractors and other musicians. I didn't in New York, hence, no work. After my daughter, Caitlin, was born and had reached the age for stories, I began to think in terms of children's books."

"As a child, I loved to make up stories. I used to put on plays and puppet shows for my family and neighbors. The theater fascinated me. Years later, while in Honolulu working as a musician, I wrote, directed, and acted in several comedies, using my musician friends as actors. So story telling to my daughter began this interest anew. Sometimes with an especially liked story, I would go downstairs later and write it down. The next day, I would simplify the language, etc.

"Often I would make a 'dummy' with pictures accompanying the text. These first dummies are the ones I showed to publishers when I decided to try to sell my stories. Harper and Row published my first book, *The Baby Beebee Bird,* and I have been involved with children's books ever since."

First published in 1963 with Massie's illustrations, *The Baby Beebee Bird* was reissued by HarperCollins in 2000 with new illustrations from Steven Kellogg. The title character is a gangly, red-headed new arrival at the zoo who keeps his animal neighbors awake when he sings "beebeebobbi, beebeebobbi" all night long. The other animals then conspire to keep the little bird awake

during the day—so that for once he might sleep through the night and not disturb them. Amy Brandt, writing for *Booklist,* called it "a worthy revival" and "a story big on child appeal." *School Library Journal* critic Julie Cummins termed it "delightful" and predicted that "this newly hatched effort is bound to invite enthusiastic participation."

Massie has enjoyed an active career in children's publishing. Several of her works, including *A Turtle and a Loon* and *A Birthday for Bird,* have won industry honors. Some of her later books revolve around an endearing Chameleon, a feisty and curious lizard whose ability to change color to match his surroundings helps him solve mysteries. In *Chameleon Was a Spy,* published in 1979, Chameleon is hired by the Pleasant Pickle Company as their industrial counterspy and is given a mission to retrieve their stolen pickle recipe. Chameleon winds up inside a jar of pickles from competitor Perfect Pickle Company, and is duly discovered by a horrified shopper on a supermarket shelf. The lizard/pickle scandal forces the rival company to go under, and when Chameleon meets with his bosses at Pleasant Pickle, he peels off the secret formula from his body, thus putting them back in business. *New York Times* contributor Jane O'Connor wrote that "Unlike her inconspicuous hero, Diane Redfield Massie clearly stands out from the crowd.... Her dithery, unlabored drawings and straight-faced delivery is distinctively, disarmingly her own." *Booklist* critic Barbara Elleman predicted that young readers will view the prankster lizard "as a friend and find his natural disguise abilities a clever ploy for this funny cloak-and-dagger story."

Massie also wrote *Chameleon the Spy and Terrible Toaster Trap* and *Chameleon the Spy and the Case of the Vanishing Jewels.* The plot of this latter work relies on pig-Latin to clue readers in on the overall joke. When a royal pair from the "Isle of Unksay" visit Chameleon's hometown, the city hosts a lavish gala in their honor—during which the jewels of the guests vanish. Chameleon turns himself into a bracelet to help solve the crime and nabs the Prince and Princess Ookcray.

In *Lobster Moths,* another humorous fantasy, a selfish scientist named Willis Matlock compulsively collects the rare lobster-moth species. His cat, Puffin, derisively remarks that Willis has no idea what they even taste like; Matlock must constantly replenish his collection because of Puffin's eating habit. A Lobster Fairy Moth descends to teach both a lesson by turning them into their prey. The resulting uproar even involves the federal government, and authorities suspect that Matlock and Puffin are not lobster moths but rather Soviet spies. To escape the chaos, the pair are forced to join the annual lobster moth migration, which helps the scientist learn much more about the moths than he ever expected. "The cartoonist illustrations are airy and amusing," said Xenda Casavant in *School Library Journal.*

"I think my favorite occupation is writing rhymes," Massie once said. "Several of my books are in rhyme and two are collections of rhymes. A rhyme offers fascinating possibilities with a strict form. I find it like working a puzzle."

During her self-described "vacation from the field of children's books," Massie penned six musical plays for children, taught art, and worked as a designer of canvas bags in the shape of fish for a company in the Virgin Islands. With the republication of *The Baby Beebee Bird,* Massie intends to continue writing and illustrating. "Its something I love to do," she said. Massie's other interests include painting in oils, pastels, and watercolor. She lives with her husband in an old stone house in the country surrounded by trees and woods. "These circumstances, I think," Massie said, "color the stories I write, which are about animals (however anthropomorphic) in their natural surroundings."

Biographical and Critical Sources

PERIODICALS

Booklist, April 15, 1979, Barbara Elleman, review of *Chameleon Was a Spy,* p. 1296; April 15, 1984, Ilene Cooper, review of *Chameleon the Spy and the Case of the Vanishing Jewels,* p. 1192; December 15, 2000, Amy Brandt, review of *The Baby Beebee Bird,* pp. 827-828.
Bulletin of the Center for Children's Books, April, 1984, review of *Chameleon the Spy and the Case of the Vanishing Jewels,* p. 152.
Children's Book Review Service, March, 1983, review of *Cocoon,* p. 76
Kirkus Reviews, March 1, 1979, review of *Chameleon Was a Spy,* p. 259.
New York Times Book Review, June 10, 1979, Jane O'Connor, review of *Chameleon Was a Spy,* p. 51; November 1, 1981, review of *Chameleon Was a Spy,* p. 47.
Publishers Weekly, July 19, 1985, review of *Lobster Moths,* p. 52.
School Library Journal, August, 1983, Carol Hurd, review of *Cocoon,* p. 55; December, 1985, Xenda Casavant, review of *Lobster Moths,* p. 79; September, 2000, Julie Cummins, review of *The Baby Beebee Bird,* p. 205.

*   *   *

MAVOR, Salley 1955-

Personal

Born April 14, 1955, in Boston, MA; daughter of James W., Jr. and Mary (Hartwell) Mavor; married Robert G. Goldsborough III; children: Peter, Ian. *Education:* Attended Syracuse University, 1973-75; Rhode Island School of Design, B.F.A., 1978.

Addresses

Home—P.O. Box 152, Woods Hole, MA 02543. *Agent*—Studio Goodwin-Sturges, 146 West Newton St., Boston, MA 02118. *E-mail*—weefolk@cape.com.

Career

Artist and illustrator. Owner and founder, Wee Folk Studio, Woods Hole, MA. *Exhibitions:* Mavor's work has been displayed in exhibitions across the United States and Japan, including at "Children's Book Art," Henry Feiwel Gallery (New York, NY), 1991; "Playful Narratives: Children's Book Illustrations," Central Piedmont Community College (Charlotte, NC), 1993; "DMC International Embroidery Exhibit," Japan, 1994; "Mary Had a Little Lamb" (solo exhibit), Worcester Craft Center (Worcester, MA), 1995; "Baa's Relief" (solo exhibit), Cahoon Museum of American Art (Cotuit, MA), 1995; "Tales Galore—The Fine Art of Children's Books," New Britain Museum of American Art, 1996; "Telling Stories with Pictures: The Art of Children's Book Illustration," DeCordova Museum and Sculpture Park (Lincoln, MA), 1997; "Beyond Once upon a Time: A Celebration of Contemporary Children's Book Illustration," Creative Arts Workshop (New Haven, CT), 1998; "Family and Friends: Picture Books from Studio Goodwin-Sturges," Kraft Education Center and Art Institute of Chicago (Chicago, IL), 1998; and "Fantastic Fibers" (solo exhibit), Muscatine Art Center (Muscatine, IA), 1999. *Member:* Society of Children's Book Writers and Illustrators.

Salley Mavor

Writings

SELF-ILLUSTRATED

(Compiler) *You and Me: Poems of Friendship,* Orchard Books (New York, NY), 1997.

ILLUSTRATOR

Judith Benet Richardson, *The Way Home,* Macmillan (New York, NY), 1991.

Judith Benet Richardson, *Come to My Party,* Macmillan (New York, NY), 1993.

Sarah Josepha Hale, *Mary Had a Little Lamb,* Orchard Books (New York, NY), 1995.

Martin Waddell, *The Hollyhock Wall,* Candlewick Press (Cambridge, MA), 1999.

Ann Turner, *In the Heart,* HarperCollins (New York, NY), 2001.

Work in Progress

Designs and projects for a how-to book.

Sidelights

Salley Mavor told *SATA:* "I call my artwork *fabric relief,* which incorporates a unique combination of materials and techniques that is forever changing and evolving. My pictures are embroidered, dyed, appliqued, wrapped, painted, carved, and molded. A variety of materials are used to create a scene, including cloth of all kinds, leather, yarn, wire, wood, cardboard, and clay. I also use artificial flowers and leaves, beads, buttons, and miscellaneous found objects. The materials and objects are held together and attached with thread or glue. All sewing is done by hand.

"The fantasy scenes in the pot in *Hollyhock Wall* are photographs taken of a live miniature garden. The four-foot landscape is planted with mosses, young herbs, and succulents. Beach stones line the stream bed which is filled with water and tinted with a drop of blue food coloring. Tree branches make a forest and young flowering plants brighten the spectacle."

Mavor's mixed-media illustrations bring unexpectedly tactile pleasures to her picture books, according to enthusiastic reviewers. Her early work, an edition of *Mary Had a Little Lamb,* was credited with bringing new life to the traditional children's poem through illustrations that combine intricate stitchery, fabric, buttons, bits of wood, pebbles, and other found objects to create a homey atmosphere of nineteenth-century farm life. Robert D. Hale, writing in *Horn Book,* proclaimed: "Mavor has taken the well-loved poem and turned it into an artistic achievement." According to information on *Wee Folk Studio,* each intricately detailed illustration takes about a month to execute by hand, after careful planning by Mavor and approval by an in-house editor.

In addition to providing illustrations to accompany the stories of several other authors, Mavor has selected a series of poems for children on the subject of friendship.

Along with her signature illustrations, these poems are collected in her book *You and Me: Poems of Friendship.* The simple pieces by Jack Prelutsky, Myra Conn Livingston, Lucille Clifton, and others are described as cheerful evocations of the many joys of friendship with peers, with family members, and even with pets. Through the combination of artwork and poetry, "the book becomes a treasure to the eye and ear," remarked Barbara McGinn in *School Library Journal.* For a *Publishers Weekly* reviewer, however, the photographs of Mavor's artwork are the "main attraction" of *You and Me.* There the illustrator uses an astounding array of materials, resulting in "an imaginative doll-inhabited landscape of delicate pattern and unexpected, palpable texture," according to the *Publishers Weekly* critic.

Biographical and Critical Sources

PERIODICALS

Horn Book, November-December, 1995, Robert D. Hale, review of *Mary Had a Little Lamb,* p. 768.

Kirkus Reviews, July 1, 1997, review of *You and Me,* p. 1033.

Publishers Weekly, August 18, 1997, review of *You and Me,* p. 95; June 4, 2001, review of *In the Heart,* p. 80.

School Library Journal, September, 1997, Barbara McGinn, review of *You and Me,* p. 206.

ON-LINE

Wee Folk Studio, http://www.weefolkstudio.com/ (October 9, 2000).*

*   *   *

MEDDAUGH, Susan 1944-

Personal

Surname is pronounced "*med*-aw"; born October 4, 1944, in Montclair, NJ; daughter of John Stuart (a naval captain and insurance executive) and Justine (Leach) Meddaugh; married Harry L. Foster (an editor), November, 1982; children: Niko (son). *Education:* Wheaton College (Norton, MA) B.A., 1966. *Politics:* "Unaffiliated and opinionated." *Hobbies and other interests:* Reading mysteries, parenting.

Addresses

Home and Office—56 Maple St., Sherborn, MA 01770.

Career

Author and illustrator. Houghton Mifflin, Co., Boston, MA, designer and art director in trade division of the children's book department, 1968-78; freelance writer and illustrator of children's books, 1978—.

Awards, Honors

Children's Choice Award, International Reading Association/Children's Book Council (IRA/CBC), for *Beast;* Parents' Choice Literature Award (with Verna Aarde-

Susan Meddaugh and friend

ma), 1985, for *Bimwili and the Zimwi: A Tale from Zanzibar;* Best Books selection, *Parenting* magazine, for *Hog-Eye;* Reading Magic Award, *Parenting* magazine, for *Cinderella's Rat;* Oppenheim Toy Portfolio Platinum Award, for *The Best Place;* Notable Book selection, American Library Association, Children's Choice Award, IRA/CBC, Notable Book selection, National Council of Teachers of English, California Young Readers Award, Georgia State Readers Award, *New York Times* Best Illustrated Books citation, 1992, Charlotte Award, New York State Reading Association, Keystone State Reading Association award, both 1994, Pennsylvania Young Reader's Award, Nebraska Golden Sower Award, both 1995, and Parents' Choice Award, all for *Martha Speaks;* Parents' Choice Illustration Award, 1994, Volunteer State Award, Tennessee Association of School Librarians, 1999, Reading Magic Award, *Parenting* magazine, and Oppenheim Toy Portfolio Platinum Award, all for *Martha Calling;* Parent's Choice Award, Pick of the List, American Bookseller Association, and Reading Magic Award, *Parenting* magazine, all for *Martha Blah Blah;* Children's Book Award, New England Booksellers Association, 1998, for body of work; Parents' Choice Award, for *Five Little Piggies;* Children's Choice Award, IRA/CBC, 2001, and Oppenheim Toy Portfolio Platinum Award, for *Martha and Skits.*

Writings

SELF-ILLUSTRATED

Too Short Fred, Houghton (Boston, MA), 1978.

Maude and Claude Go Abroad, Houghton (Boston, MA), 1980.
Beast, Houghton (Boston, MA), 1981.
Too Many Monsters, Houghton (Boston, MA), 1982.
Tree of Birds, Houghton (Boston, MA), 1990.
The Witches' Supermarket, Houghton (Boston, MA), 1991.
Surprise! (wordless picture book), Houghton (Boston, MA), 1991.
Martha Speaks, Houghton (Boston, MA), 1992.
Martha Calling, Houghton (Boston, MA), 1994.
Hog-Eye, Houghton (Boston, MA), 1995.
Martha Blah Blah, Houghton (Boston, MA), 1996.
Cinderella's Rat, Houghton (Boston, MA), 1997.
Martha Walks the Dog, Houghton (Boston, MA), 1998.
The Best Place, Houghton (Boston, MA), 1999.
Martha and Skits, Houghton (Boston, MA), 2000.
Lulu's Hat, Houghton (Boston, MA), 2002.

Meddaugh's books have been translated into Spanish, French, Japanese, Chinese, Swedish, and Danish.

ILLUSTRATOR

Anne Merrick Epstein, *Good Stones,* Houghton (Boston, MA), 1977.
Carol-Lynn Waugh, *My Friend Bear,* Atlantic Monthly (Boston, MA), 1982.
Jean and Claudio Marzollo, *Red Sun Girl,* Dial (New York, NY), 1983.
Jean and Claudio Marzollo, *Blue Sun Ben,* Dial (New York, NY), 1984.
Jean and Claudio Marzollo, *Ruthie's Rude Friends,* Dial (New York, NY), 1984.
Verna Aardema, *Bimwili and the Zimwi: A Tale from Zanzibar,* Dial (New York, NY), 1985.
Jean and Claudio Marzollo, *The Silver Bear,* Dial (New York, NY), 1987.
Ruby Dee, *Two Ways to Count to Ten: A Liberian Folktale,* Holt (New York, NY), 1988.
Beatrice Schenk de Regniers, *The Way I Feel—Sometimes,* Clarion (New York, NY), 1988.
John Ciardi, *The Hopeful Trout and Other Limericks,* Houghton (Boston, MA), 1989.
Eve Bunting, *No Nap,* Clarion (New York, NY), 1989.
Eve Bunting, *In the Haunted House,* Clarion (New York, NY), 1990.
Eve Bunting, *A Perfect Father's Day,* Clarion (New York, NY), 1991.
Susan Wojciechowski, *The Best Halloween of All,* Crown (New York, NY), 1992.
Linda Breiner Milstein, *Amanda's Perfect Hair,* Tambourine (New York, NY), 1993.
Jennifer Armstrong, *That Terrible Baby,* Tambourine (New York, NY), 1994.
Sarah Wilson, *Good Zap, Little Grog,* Candlewick Press (Cambridge, MA), 1995.
Jennifer A. Ericsson, *The Most Beautiful Kid in the World,* Tambourine (New York, NY), 1996.
David Martin, *Five Little Piggies* (stories), Candlewick Press (Cambridge, MA), 1998.

A loquacious pet turns a normal household upside down in Martha Speaks, *written and illustrated by Meddaugh.*

Sidelights

Susan Meddaugh writes and illustrates children's books with the eye of someone who knows the trade inside and out. This is no coincidence; Meddaugh worked as a designer and art director for children's books at the Boston-based publishing house Houghton Mifflin before setting out on her own as a writer and illustrator of such books as *Too Many Monsters, Martha Speaks,* and *The Witches' Supermarket.* "Meddaugh has a gift for building a picture book out of one funny scene after another," wrote Mary Lou Burket in *Five Owls.* Her quirky and humorous picture books have won awards as well as earned her a large audience for her canine character Martha, a hound with an attitude.

Meddaugh was born in Montclair, New Jersey, in 1944. "Growing up in my family was a little like being in an extended George Burns and Gracie Allen routine," she once explained to *SATA.* "My younger brother, John, and I were the audience for our parents' performance. There was also a fine supporting cast of characters (relatives) contributing to the plot. Housework was not high on my mother's list of priorities. She was dramatic and whimsical." Meddaugh's father, a retired Navy captain, had participated in African landings and in the South Pacific theater during World War II; his "wry comments and a sort of humorous view of the world" kept the Meddaugh family living on the lighter side.

A shy child, Meddaugh enjoyed fantasy games and loved to draw. Books were an important ingredient of her childhood, with stories by Dr. Seuss and *Curious George* by H. A. Rey particular favorites. Meddaugh's father was a fine storyteller, and her mother read to her

regularly. But it was drawing and painting that attracted Meddaugh the most, and the two came together during an innovative class she attended while in high school. "We had a combined art and English section," Meddaugh explained. "And it was a revelation for me. It was very new for its day, and the instructors were enthusiastic. They said, 'Just be original. Have one original thought and you'll get an A.'"

After graduation, Meddaugh enrolled at Wheaton College, where she majored in French while also taking an equal number of art classes where she learned painting techniques. Following college, Meddaugh realized that her French degree was not going to lead her into any career, so she went to New York, portfolio in hand, and landed a job as a "Girl Friday" at an advertising agency. From New York City, Meddaugh moved on to Boston, where she took a temporary job at Houghton Mifflin that eventually became a ten-year stint in children's books. "Publishing was different then," Meddaugh recalled. "I even applied for the job wearing white gloves. The pace was leisurely, and I basically learned on the job."

As a designer of children's books, she learned the basics of the thirty-two-page format and the technique of pre-separated art in which illustrators did the work computer scanners now do, drawing separate black and white sketches for the addition of yellow, red, and blue in each illustration. She was also responsible for hiring illustrators for book projects, and increasingly began to wonder if her own illustration skills could be put to use some day. "A good picture book is a very specific form," Meddaugh explained to *SATA.* "Both art and text move the story.... There can be no superfluous parts, not in such a short format."

Meddaugh's first book, *Too Short Fred,* was a transitional work. She once told *SATA,* "I needed to move away from fine art, which I had been doing, to a more expressive and exaggerated form for children's books, so I chose to portray animals at first." In *Too Short Fred,* the title character, an undersized cat, faces five trials in which he must overcome his height disadvantage. The school bully stealing Fred's lunch gets worm sandwiches for his troubles; at a school dance Fred is partnered with a girl much taller than himself but who turns out to be a great dancer; and a race down a snowy hill turns into victory for Fred when he falls and rolls to the bottom first. Working in colored pencils, Meddaugh drew her cats to easily bring to mind humans, and her trademark whimsy and humor was already detectable. A *Publishers Weekly* contributor suggested that *Too Short Fred* would be "fun and reassuring for boys and girls who are different, in any way" and also described the illustrations as "rich in texture."

Meddaugh's 1980 book, *Maude and Claude Go Abroad,* was inspired by a brother-sister relationship like her own, in which the older sister looks out for the younger sibling. The Foxes put their two children, Maude and Claude, aboard an ocean liner sailing for France. En route, Claude falls overboard, and Maude—who has been instructed by her parents to watch out for him—

does the only sensible thing: she jumps in after him. Told in punning and humorous rhyme, the story follows the adventures of the two as they hitch a ride with a whale who, before delivering them safely to France, must first outwit the harpooners following him. Maude solves this problem, sitting on the whale's spout so that it looks like they are riding a floating island. Dubbed a "gem of a story" by a *Publishers Weekly* critic, the book also suffered under several less-favorable reviews.

Despite the criticism of *Maude and Claude Go Abroad,* Meddaugh remained undaunted; her third book, *Beast,* introduces human characters in the form of a little girl and her family, as well as a big, furry beast that comes out of the forest to terrorize them. The young child does not think the beast is as bad as her family believes and, more curious than scared, she learns that the beast has need for more than food: it is lonely and needs a friend, too. Using "singularly imaginative color paintings" and a rhythmic text, Meddaugh created a story that children, according to a *Publishers Weekly* reviewer, would be "thrilled to discover."

In *Too Many Monsters,* Howard lives with ninety-nine other monsters—the difference between them being that kindly Howard wants no part of their dirty tricks. His wish is fulfilled when the tree they chase him up comes crashing down, letting light into the forest and scaring the meanies away. A *Publishers Weekly* critic called attention to the "meticulously colored" pencil illustrations: green monsters except for lavender Howard, and the change from blue-green forest depths to warm and bright colors at the end when the tree comes down.

After *Too Many Monsters,* Meddaugh took time out to be a wife and full-time mother, although she did continue to illustrate the works of other authors. In 1985, she teamed up with Verna Aardema on the award-winning *Bimwili and the Zimwi: A Tale from Zanzibar,* and she later illustrated several books for the prolific Eve Bunting, among others. Meddaugh once revealed to *SATA,* "It's clearly not as rewarding doing illustrations for somebody else's book as for your own. But it is still enjoyable. Still a challenge. It's the kind of work that gives me both freedom and structure. I need that mix."

She returned to the role of author/illustrator in 1990's *Tree of Birds,* the story of Harry, a boy who brings an injured bird home with him one day, only to be inundated by an enormous flock of birds—all Green Tufted Tropicals, according to Harry's bird book—in search of their lost member. The flock nests outside his house and refuses to leave, even when Harry tries dressing up in a cat costume or when the temperature drops and snow is on the way. Although Harry grows attached to his bird and does not want to lose her, when the birds outside turn blue from the cold, he sets his bird free. In a surprise ending, the entire flock ends up wintering at Harry's house. Mary M. Burns, writing in *Horn Book,* praised *Tree of Birds* for its "expressive watercolors" and "tongue-in-cheek text," calling it "funny without being forced." "Children will reach for it again and again," maintained a *Publishers Weekly*

reviewer, while Zena Sutherland, reviewing the book for *Bulletin of the Center for Children's Books,* dubbed the picture book "wildly anthropomorphic."

Meddaugh's son, Niko, was the inspiration behind *The Witches' Supermarket* and *Martha Speaks.* "It was at Halloween," Meddaugh explained to *SATA,* "and Niko asked me where the witches got all their stuff—the dried spiders and all that. And then he wondered if they didn't have a witches' supermarket. Well, I just couldn't let that one go." The result was the story of young Helen and her dog Martha (the first incarnation of the Meddaugh family pet in print) who end up in a very strange supermarket indeed, where all the customers are dressed in witches' garb. Helen realizes these are not just Halloween costumes at about the same time as the witches realize that Helen is only in costume for Halloween. Martha the dog, in a cat costume, saves the day when she wreaks a bit of havoc with the witches' real cats. A *Kirkus Reviews* critic called the book "Imaginative Halloween fun," while Liza Bliss, writing in *School Library Journal,* called *The Witches' Supermarket* "a book that's as much fun as Halloween itself."

In her self illustrated work Cinderella's Rat, *Meddaugh presents readers with a new slant on a classic fairy tale, as a rat scurrying within wand's reach of Cinderella's fairy godmother suddenly finds himself in human form, but with his rodent instincts still intact.*

If Martha the dog ate alphabet soup, Niko asked his artist mom, would she be able to talk? This question supplied Meddaugh with a mental image of their pet pit bull swallowing noodle alphabets; instead of going to her stomach, they go directly to her brain. The resulting book, *Martha Speaks,* not only has Martha talking, but talking too much. Martha redeems herself, however, by saving the family from burglars with her newfound speech. The popularity of *Martha Speaks* led Meddaugh to use the crafty canine again in *Martha Calling,* in which the talking dog enters a radio call-in contest and wins the family a vacation weekend. Martha soon learns, however, that there are no dogs allowed in the hotel where the family is booked. Not to worry: Martha disguises herself as an invalid grandmother in a wheelchair and enjoys one adventure after another. Again the art work is loose and cartoon-like, done in simple colored pencil. A reviewer in *Parents' Choice* applauded the sequel while cautioning that adult readers might suffer "hoarseness from constant requests to 'Read it again!'" A *Publishers Weekly* contributor praised the droll illustrations, noting that young readers would be sure to be "drawn in once again by Meddaugh's witty and unaffected cartooning." The critics were not the only ones to award the loquacious pit bull best in show: the first two Martha books won their author numerous industry honors.

"I am frankly amazed and puzzled at the success of the Martha books," Meddaugh admitted to *SATA.* "You just never know what is going to work with the readers. I know what works for me, what makes me laugh. But it's not always what makes others laugh. Ultimately what I am striving for is to have kids get involved with the images I create, to find some meaning and, yes, humor in them. And that's a pretty tall order in today's world with all the competing images we have around us all the time. Doing picture books is a sort of funny field. In one way it's hard to take it seriously, but on the other hand it *is* serious. It's important to get kids reading. If they laugh at Martha and it helps them to read, fine. I've done my job. But my work is also a great self-indulgence. Here I am drawing pictures of dogs and making up stories just like I did when I was a kid."

Although the real Martha would pass on to doggie heaven in 1996, Meddaugh has continued to keep her beloved pet alive through a continuous stream of Martha stories, among them *Martha Blah Blah, Martha Walks the Dog,* and *Martha and Skits.* In *Martha Blah Blah,* published in 1996, Martha's vocabulary suffers when the soup manufacturer introduces a cost-cutting measure that involves shortening the noodle alphabet. Fortunately, the curious pooch does some scouting around and sets the soup world to rights again in a book that *Booklist* contributor Ilene Cooper noted was "marked by sly humor." *Martha Blah Blah* "is a superb blend of humor, pathos, and Martha's brave panache," felt Roger Sutton in his *Horn Book* review of the third Martha book.

In *Martha and Skits,* Meddaugh introduces another family member: a rambunctious puppy named Skits.

Trying to follow in Martha's pawsteps proves impossible for the newcomer when a dose of alphabet soup yields no chatter. But Skits has other skills, among them an ability to chew everything in sight and a talent to catch things in flight. Calling Meddaugh's illustrations "loving and playful," *School Library Journal* contributor Laura Scott added that the book contained "several laugh-out-loud moments," while a *Publishers Weekly* contributor noted that the author's "fitting addition to Martha's family acknowledges time's passage, invigorating both her canine heroine and her series."

Meddaugh took a departure from dogs with several other picture books, including her 1995 work *Hog-Eye* in which an adventurous pig outsmarts a hungry wolf in Meddaugh's updated twist on the old folktale scenario that involves pig soup. *Cinderella's Rat* is another fairy tale outtake, as one of the rats turned by the fairy godmother into a coachman recounts his night at the ball. "Humor permeates the tale, while clever twists shape it," commented a reviewer from *Kirkus Reviews,* who compared Meddaugh's treatment to the works of author-illustrator William Steig. And in 1999's *The Best Place,* an elderly wolf is prompted to leave his cosy home when he suspects that it may not be "the best place" after all. Journeying far and wide, he encounters nothing to surpass his home, but alas, he returns home to find it has been sold to a family of rabbits. The rabbits

Trick-or-treating is a torment to young Ben when his parents concoct a series of ridiculous costumes in Susan Wojciechowski's **The Best Halloween of All,** *illustrated by Meddaugh.*

have no intention of vacating in favor of the former owner, no matter how long his teeth. Ultimately, the neighborhood pitches in to construct a new home for the wolf that is just as "best" as the old one. "Meddaugh combines understated humor with her expressive watercolor illustrations to produce a delightful book," claimed *School Library Journal* contributor Tom S. Hurlburt, while in *Publishers Weekly,* a critic maintained that Meddaugh's "airy, lighthearted watercolors evoke a pleasant animal idyll" in "a clever picture book about attitude."

"Ideas are everywhere," Meddaugh explained to *SATA.* "You relax and wait for them; they can't be forced." Picture book illustrating continues to be "something I love to do. And that's important. With all the commercialization of children's books that is happening now— the blockbuster bestseller mentality that is taking over children's publishing just as it has the adult market—it's important to remember that the best children's books are the ones that are timeless. They are the ones created by people who are in it not so much for the money, but because they just love doing picture books."

Biographical and Critical Sources

PERIODICALS

Booklist, January 15, 1995, review of *Martha Calling,* p. 863; September 1, 1995, Stephanie Zvirin, review of *Hog-Eye,* p. 88; September 15, 1996, Ilene Cooper, review of *Martha Blah Blah,* p. 248; June 1, 2000, Ilene Cooper, review of *Martha and Skits,* p. 1910.
Bulletin of the Center for Children's Books, June, 1982, p. 192; March, 1990, Zena Sutherland, review of *Tree of Birds,* p. 170; September, 1991, p. 16; September, 1994, Deborah Stevenson, review of *Martha Calling,* p. 19.
Five Owls, November-December, 1992, Mary Lou Burket, review of *Martha Speaks,* p. 33.
Horn Book, September-October, 1990, Mary M. Burns, review of *Tree of Birds,* p. 595; November, 1996, Roger Sutton, review of *Martha Blah Blah,* p. 727; September, 1997, Ann A. Flowers, review of *Cinderella's Rat,* p. 560; November, 1998, Ann A. Flowers, review of *Martha Walks the Dog,* p. 716.
Kirkus Reviews, October 1, 1978, p. 1070; March 15, 1980, p. 361; August 15, 1991, review of *The Witches' Supermarket,* p. 1091; July 15, 1997, review of *Cinderella's Rat,* p. 1113.
New York Times Book Review, November 8, 1992, Benjamin Cheever, "What the Dog Said," p. 32.
Parents' Choice, Vol. 18, no. 4, 1994, review of *Martha Calling.*
Publishers Weekly, July 31, 1978, review of *Too Short Fred,* p. 98; February 22, 1980, review of *Maude and Claude Go Abroad,* p. 108; February 20, 1981, review of *Beast,* p. 94; March 5, 1982, review of *Too Many Monsters,* p. 70; March 16, 1990, review of *Tree of Birds,* p. 69; August 15, 1994, review of *Martha Calling,* p. 95; July 6, 1998, review of *Martha Walks the Dog,* p. 60; November 2, 1998, review of *Hog-Eye,* p. 86; October 11, 1999, review of *The Best Place,* p. 75; April 10, 2000, review of *Five Little Piggies,* p. 101; August 7, 2000, review of *Martha and Skits,* p. 94; September 25, 2000, Nathalie op de Beeck, "A Talk with Susan Meddaugh," p. 39.
School Library Journal, May, 1981, p. 58; April, 1982, pp. 59-60; November, 1991, Liza Bliss, review of *The Witches' Supermarket,* p. 103; September, 1999, Tom S. Hurlburt, review of *The Best Place,* p. 197; August, 2000, Laura Scott, review of *Martha and Skits,* p. 159.
Tribune Books (Chicago, IL), November 12, 1995, Mary Harris Veeder, review of *Hog-Eye,* p. 6; January 12, 1997, Mary Harris Veeder, review of *Martha Blah Blah,* p. 5.
Washington Post Book World, May 8, 1994, Michael J. Rosen, review of *Martha Speaks,* p. 18; December, 1994, Linda Perkins, review of *Martha Calling,* p. 32.

—Sketch by J. Sydney Jones

*   *   *

MURRAY, Martine 1965-

Personal

Born December 31, 1965, in Melbourne, Australia; daughter of Ian (a lawyer) and Julie (a homemaker; maiden name, McLaren) Murray. *Education:* University of Melbourne, B.A. and graduate diploma of movement and dance; Victorian College of the Arts, B.F.A.

Addresses

Home—2 Orari Ave., East Brunswick 3057, Australia. *E-mail*—Whirlingbean@hotmail.com.

Career

Writer.

Writings

A Dog Called Bear, Random House Australia (Milsons Point, Australia), 2000.
A Moose Called Mouse, Allen and Unwin (Melbourne, Australia), 2001.
Because of Stinky, Allen and Unwin (Melbourne, Australia), 2002.

Sidelights

Martine Murray told *SATA:* "I was at art school because I like making pictures. I don't really like illustrating; I like making something up, bringing an idea or sense into some kind of being. It doesn't have to be in paint. After art school, I wanted to make images with a moving body in theater, because there are more colors and dimensions, more elements to play with. An embodied image can try to speak more directly, less symbolically.... But then, you can get exhausted by the size of all that. What I would like is to go back and forth between working with other people and movement and the huge scape it provides, and then working with the small quiet of just myself and a page to write on. I like writing because I can do it on my own. Also, I like the way it nourishes my thinking bits. I draw or paint or dance because it gets me out of my thinking bits. I like to put them together because it surprises me the way they can meet up. I'm excited by meeting places.

"I was attracted to the idea of making books, even when I was at art school. I wasn't interested in the big, clever system that art leans on. Books are so much friendlier. You can touch them or throw them around or love them. I make lots of unpublishable books: encyclopedias and books about common places or things I saw on the tram or books of lists. I started writing children's books because I saw it as an area where you could still be a little bit playful, yet also write a publishable book that someone other than my friends could read. I think children are great and funny, so I like to try and find a way of entering their world.

"I remember when I was first painting pictures how precious and intimidating a new blank canvas was, and how once you had messed it up and made mistakes and found bits of beauty within the mistakes, you became more playful and adventurous and willing to trust that playfulness. I think my natural process is very messy. I feel like a blind person charging through a forest. I have no idea of where I am going or what I'm likely to bump into, but I know as long as I keep going, I'll find something there. Something will whack me in the head. I don't make plans. Often I just start with one sentence or notion that appeals to me, and then I build on it. So I don't have very good architecture in my writing. It is more like a rambling path which digresses a bit. With *A Moose Called Mouse,* I started with the idea of a moose because I thought the antlers were great.

"When I'm working on a project, even if it is in dance, I get very involved in it. I am thinking about it all the time, especially when I am walking the dog or trying to sleep at night. I think and think, and then when I'm doing something else an idea just arrives. It comes from all the thinking, but it only arrives when I'm not looking for it, when there is a good space for it to slide into. Usually anything that I see or hear is potentially raw material. Last night, for example, there was a rat scratching in the bedroom wall, and it was keeping me awake, so I was throwing shoes at the wall to scare it off. The next day that dark little episode got woven into something I was writing.

"I am very easily inspired, but I am also very hard to please. As far as art and books and theater are concerned, I like to be moved, or startled, or excited by an image. I'm generally not interested in very stylish technical things. I like the way of animals and children; they usually inspire me. Some favorite books that come to mind are *Oh the Places You'll Go* by Dr. Seuss, *Alice in Wonderland* by Lewis Carroll, *Drawings and Observations* by Louise Bourgeois, *Journal of an Understanding Heart* by Opal Whitely, *To the Lighthouse* by Virginia Woolf, *Catcher in the Rye* by J. D. Salinger, *Chicken, Soup, Boots* by Maira Kalman, and poems by Mary Oliver, William Stafford, Charles Simic, and Rilke. Artists I like include Alfred Wallis, Colin Macahon, Mark Rothco, Whistler, Morandi, and all children.

"Without planning it, my [first two] children's books have been about children who make friends with an animal. I expect this is because I feel strongly about people needing to have a connection to the natural world. What I love about both animals and children is their naturalness. What I hope to encourage in children through stories is their natural playfulness and sense of wonder."

Biographical and Critical Sources

PERIODICALS

Australian Book Review, July, 2001, Margaret Dunkle, "Creatures of Fantasy," p. 61.

Sunday Age, June 17, 2001, review of *A Moose Called Mouse.*

N–O

NATTI, Susanna 1948-

Personal

Born October 19, 1948, in Gloucester, MA; daughter of Robert Henrik (a teacher and principal) and Lee (an author; maiden name, Kingman) Natti; married Alan S. Willsky (an associate professor of electrical engineering), May 25, 1980; children: two daughters. *Education:* Smith College, B.A., 1970; attended Montserrat School of Visual Design, 1972-73, and Rhode Island School of Design, 1973-75. *Hobbies and other interests:* Gardening, playing the piano, crafts such as hooking, knitting, and sewing.

Addresses

Home—Bedford, MA. *Office*—c/o Author Mail, Viking/Penguin Putnam, 375 Hudson St., New York, NY 10014.

Career

Illustrator, 1977—. Worked as a secretary/technical typist at Massachusetts Institute of Technology, part-and full-time, 1970-78. Volunteer work in high school classes, working with learning disabled students. *Exhibitions:* Biennale of Illustrations, Bratislava, Czechoslovakia, 1981; Master Eagle Gallery, New York, NY, 1981, 1982. *Member:* Society of Children's Book Writers and Illustrators.

Awards, Honors

Christopher Award, 1979, for *Frederick's Alligator;* International Reading Association's Children's Choices list, 1980, for *Today Was a Terrible Day.*

Illustrator

Charlotte Pomerantz, *The Downtown Fairy Godmother,* Addison-Wesley (Reading, MA), 1978.

Esther Allen Peterson, *Frederick's Alligator,* Crown (New York, NY), 1979.

William Cole, editor, *Dinosaurs and Beasts of Yore,* Collins (Cleveland, OH), 1979.

Clyde Watson, *Midnight Moon,* Collins (Cleveland, OH), 1979.

Jim Murphy, *Harold Thinks Big,* Crown (New York, NY), 1980.

William Hooks, *The Mystery on Bleeker Street,* Knopf (New York, NY), 1980.

Jane Yolen, *The Acorn Quest,* Crowell (New York, NY), 1981.

Louise Fitzhugh, *I Am Three,* Delacorte (New York, NY), 1982.

Esther Allen Peterson, *Penelope Gets Wheels,* Crown (New York, NY), 1982.

Janet Quinn-Harkin, *Helpful Hattie,* Harcourt Brace (San Diego, CA), 1984.

Lee Kingman, *Catch the Baby!,* Viking (New York, NY), 1993.

Ann Banks, *It's My Money: A Kid's Guide to the Green Stuff,* Viking (New York, NY), 1993.

Louis Phillips, *School Daze: Jokes Your Teacher Will Hate,* Viking (New York, NY), 1994.

"CAM JANSEN" SERIES; WRITTEN BY DAVID A. ADLER

Cam Jansen and the Mystery of the Stolen Diamonds, Viking (New York, NY), 1980.

Cam Jansen and the Mystery of the U.F.O., Viking (New York, NY), 1980.

Cam Jansen and the Mystery of the Dinosaur Bones, Viking (New York, NY), 1981.

Cam Jansen and the Mystery of the Television Dog, Viking (New York, NY), 1981.

Cam Jansen and the Mystery of the Gold Coins, Viking (New York, NY), 1982.

Cam Jansen and the Mystery of the Babe Ruth Baseball, Viking (New York, NY), 1982.

Cam Jansen and the Mystery of the Circus Clown, Viking (New York, NY), 1983.

Cam Jansen and the Mystery of the Monster Movie, Viking (New York, NY), 1984.

Cam Jansen and the Mystery of the Carnival Prize, Viking (New York, NY), 1984.

Cam Jansen and the Mystery at the Monkey House, Viking (New York, NY), 1985.

Cam Jansen and the Mystery of the Stolen Corn Popper, Viking (New York, NY), 1986.

Cam Jansen and the Mystery of Flight 54, Viking (New York, NY), 1989.

Cam Jansen and the Mystery at the Haunted House, Viking (New York, NY), 1992.

Cam Jansen and the Chocolate Fudge Mystery, Viking (New York, NY), 1993.

Cam Jansen and the Triceratops Pops Mystery, Viking (New York, NY), 1995.

Cam Jansen and the Ghostly Mystery, Viking (New York, NY), 1996.

Cam Jansen and the Scary Snake Mystery, Viking (New York, NY), 1997.

Cam Jansen and the Catnapping Mystery, Viking (New York, NY), 1999.

Cam Jansen and the Barking Treasure Mystery, Viking (New York, NY), 1999.

Cam Jansen and the Birthday Mystery, Viking (New York, NY), 2000.

The Cam Jansen Fun Book, Viking (New York, NY), 2000.

Cam Jansen and the School Play Mystery, Viking (New York, NY), 2001.

"YOUNG CAM JANSEN" SERIES; WRITTEN BY DAVID A. ADLER

Young Cam Jansen and the Missing Cookie, Viking (New York, NY), 1996.

Young Cam Jansen and the Dinosaur Game, Viking (New York, NY), 1996.

Young Cam Jansen and the Lost Tooth, Viking (New York, NY), 1997.

Young Cam Jansen and the Ice Skate Mystery, Viking (New York, NY), 1998.

Young Cam Jansen and the Baseball Mystery, Viking (New York, NY), 1999.

Young Cam Jansen and the Pizza Shop Mystery, Viking (New York, NY), 2000.

Young Cam Jansen and the Library Mystery, Viking (New York, NY), 2000.

"PET PATROL" SERIES; WRITTEN BY BETSY DUFFEY

Puppy Love, Viking (New York, NY), 1992.
Wild Things, Viking (New York, NY), 1993.
Throw-Away Pets, Viking (New York, NY), 1993.

"RONALD MORGAN" SERIES; WRITTEN BY PATRICIA REILLY GIFF

Today Was a Terrible Day, Viking (New York, NY), 1980.
The Almost Awful Play, Viking (New York, NY), 1984.
Watch Out, Ronald Morgan!, Viking (New York, NY), 1985.
Happy Birthday, Ronald Morgan!, Viking (New York, NY), 1986.
Ronald Morgan Goes to Bat, Viking (New York, NY), 1990.
Ronald Morgan Goes to Camp, Viking (New York, NY), 1995.

Susanna Natti's pen-and-ink illustrations for Susan Wojciechowski's Beany and the Dreaded Wedding _bring a sense of fun to a young girl's plight of being forced into flower-girl duties at a family member's nuptials._

Good Luck, Ronald Morgan!, Viking (New York, NY), 1996.

"LIONEL" SERIES; WRITTEN BY STEPHEN KRENSKY

Lionel at Large, Dial (New York, NY), 1986.
Lionel in the Fall, Dial (New York, NY), 1987.
Lionel in the Spring, Dial (New York, NY), 1990.
Lionel and Louise, Dial (New York, NY), 1992.
Lionel in the Winter, Dial (New York, NY), 1994.
Lionel and His Friends, Dial (New York, NY), 1996.
Lionel in the Summer, Dial (New York, NY), 1998.
Lionel at School, Dial (New York, NY), 2000.

"LOUISE" SERIES; WRITTEN BY STEPHEN KRENSKY

Louise Takes Charge, Viking (New York, NY), 1998.
Louise Goes Wild, Viking (New York, NY), 1999.
Louise, Soccer Star?, Viking (New York, NY), 2000.

"BEANY" SERIES; WRITTEN BY SUSAN WOJCIECHOWSKI

Don't Call Me Beanhead!, Candlewick Press (Cambridge, MA), 1994.

Beany (Not Beanhead) and the Magic Crystal, Candlewick Press (Cambridge, MA), 1997.

Beany and the Dreaded Wedding, Candlewick Press (Cambridge, MA), 2000.

Beany Goes to Camp, Candlewick Press (Cambridge, MA), 2002.

OTHER

A portion of Natti's papers are housed in the de Grummond Collection, University of Southern Mississippi.

Sidelights

Susanna Natti is an illustrator of children's books whose collaborations have included works with authors David A. Adler, Patricia Reilly Giff, and Stephen Krensky, among others. Her award-winning artwork has graced the pages of over sixty books for young readers since her debut illustration title in 1978, when she provided the pictures for Charlotte Pomerantz's *The Downtown Fairy Godmother.* Perhaps best known for her illustrations of the over twenty books in Adler's series for young readers, the "Cam Jansen" mysteries, as well as its spin-off series, the "Young Cam Jansen," Natti is noted for her distinctive pen-and-ink style as well as for her wry sense of humor and gift for capturing facial expressions.

Born in 1948 in Gloucester, Massachusetts, Natti grew up in a household sure to encourage the artistic proclivities of a youngster. Her mother, Lee Kingman Natti, is a well-known children's author, and the making of books was absorbed by Natti at an early age. "By the time I was eight I knew I was going to be an illustrator," Natti once told *SATA.* "I'm not sure if it ever occurred to me that I might do something else. I always liked to draw and at the age of five was making crude copies of paintings from one of my parents' large art books. My favorite cousin and I used to devise contests in which we'd pick a subject and both illustrate it. I don't think we ever compared our drawings—it was just the fun of drawing that we were after."

Growing up in Gloucester, Natti was surrounded by artists outside her home, as well. "Among the children's book authors and author/illustrators living on Cape Ann when I was growing up," Natti recalled for *SATA,* "were Virginia Lee Burton, Ruth Holberg, Hetty Beaty, and Lee Kingman, who happens to be my mother. The business of making books seemed at once very normal and very special. Besides the many authors on Cape Ann, there were other accomplished people in the arts who lived there. There were sculptors, painters, and craftsmen. A number of my relatives were and are artists. These many people influenced me in some important ways. The two most important principles I gleaned from them were these: that good art involves integrity and a solid knowledge of basic skills and that the history of art and illustration is a resource to be treasured.

"I started studying figure drawing when I was ten with George Demetrios (Virginia Lee Burton's husband). He taught me how to express motion and spontaneity in my drawings. I use the basic method he taught me every time I lay out a drawing, lightly and quickly sketching the whole shape with the pencil barely leaving the paper until all the proportions are laid out satisfactorily—and only then going back and laying in the detail. He gave me a solid foundation and, of all my teachers, I owe him the greatest debt. I studied with him for five summers, but then it was another nine years before I began to prepare seriously for a career in illustration, when I attended art school for three years."

Graduating from Smith College in 1970, Natti went on to attend both the Montserrat School of Visual Art and the prestigious Rhode Island School of Design. However, she needed to work part-time and sometimes full-time as a typist during these years before her illustration career got off the ground. The first book contract came Natti's way in 1978, to do the artwork for Pomerantz's *The Downtown Fairy Godmother,* the story of young Olivia who is assigned a rather fumbling novice in the fairy-godmother department. Disappointed initially at the woman's lack of talent and experience, Olivia soon gets the benefit of this fairy-godmother's extreme devotion to her job. A *Publishers Weekly* critic called the book "airy fun, adorned by Natti's ink drawings." Natti's illustrations for her second title, Esther Allen Peterson's *Frederick's Alligator,* won her a Christopher Award in 1979, and her career was well and truly underway. She was soon receiving further illustration jobs, enough for her to leave her typing behind.

Another early title, Jane Yolen's *The Acorn Quest,* provided Natti the opportunity to let her fanciful side show. The book relates the tale of King Earthor of Woodland who, when his kingdom is threatened with hunger, must choose four of his faithful knights to go in quest of the Golden Acorn which will insure plentiful harvests. The four include Sir Runsalot, a mouse, Sir Belliful, a groundhog, Sir Tarryhere, a turtle, and Sir Gimmemore, a rabbit. Dudley B. Carlson, reviewing the title in *Horn Book,* commented that the illustrations "in black and white and soft grays are nicely placed and serve as a lively accompaniment to the text."

Other popular early titles include Clyde Watson's *Midnight Moon,* and *Dinosaurs and Beasts of Yore,* edited by William Cole. "I generally use black-and-white line drawings with a technical pen," Natti explained to *SATA.* "When I get a chance to do full-color illustrations I use watercolor as I did for *Midnight Moon* which was a wonderful opportunity to do a series of tiny watercolor paintings." Natti has also had the opportunity of collaborating with her mother, Lee Kingman, on the title *Catch the Baby!* in which a toddler makes a break for the backyard and is able to explore most of its reaches before mom and siblings can catch up. "In both words and pictures," noted Susan H. Patron in a *School Library Journal* review, "the joy of an unfettered, dirty-kneed romp outdoors is sweetly conveyed."

One of Natti's more enduring collaborations is with the writer David A. Adler. Beginning in 1980 with the first of a series, *Cam Jansen and the Mystery of the Stolen Diamonds,* Natti has worked with Adler on a score of chapter-book mysteries for young readers. Each book features plucky fifth-grader Cam (short for Camera) and her intrepid friend Eric, who together solve knotty mysteries in their everyday lives. Of no little help in such investigations is Cam's unique ability—her photographic memory that comes into play in each mystery. Together Cam and Eric, and Natti and Adler, deal with adventures from U.F.O.s and gold coins, to missing circus clowns and stolen corn poppers. Reviewing *Cam Jansen and the Mystery at the Monkey House,* Janie Schomberg remarked in *School Library Journal* that Natti's "twenty black-and-white illustrations will increase the visual appeal of this catchy story." Cheryl Cufari, also writing in *School Library Journal,* noted that Natti's "humorous black-and-white drawings appear on every other page" of *Cam Jansen and the Mystery at the Haunted House,* while Sharon R. Pearce observed in a *School Library Journal* review of *Cam Jansen and the Ghostly Mystery* that Natti's "frequent pen-and-ink drawings capture the action and the characters' personalities." In the 1997 addition to the series, *Cam Jansen and the Scary Snake Mystery,* Cam and Eric are at the

city museum when a woman lets a pet snake out of her bag and Mrs. Jansen records the ensuing panic with her camcorder. But when the camera goes missing and the video suddenly appears on television, Cam knows she has a mission—to track down the thief. "Fans of the series will not be disappointed with this new title," wrote Janet M. Blair in *School Library Journal,* further commenting that Natti's black-and-white line drawings "enliven the text." Over twenty books strong and growing, the "Cam Jansen" titles, claim critics, have lost none of their appeal for readers or their originality in creation. Reviewing *Cam Jansen and the Birthday Mystery,* published in the year 2000, Wendy S. Carroll commented in *School Library Journal,* "This is an exciting mystery book with great black-and-white illustrations."

Spinning off from this successful series, Natti and Adler have also created mysteries for younger readers, featuring Cam at age eight in beginning-to-read books instead of chapter books. Cam and Eric are, in these prequels, friends as they are later, and again Cam's unique gift of

Natti and Wojciechowski teamed up again in the award-winning Beany (Not Beanhead) and the Magic Crystal, *as the likeable young protagonist finds a crystal that she believes must possess magical powers.*

photographic memory comes to her aid in solving mysteries. Writing in *School Library Journal*, Mary Ann Bursk felt that the first two entries in the series, *Young Cam Jansen and the Dinosaur Game* and *Young Cam Jansen and the Missing Cookie,* would make excellent additions to books for beginning readers. "Natti's illustrations in both books will win the approval and attention of young readers," Bursk wrote. "The sharp, detailed strokes and bright colors complement Adler's simple texts." *Booklist*'s Hazel Rochman, in a review of *Young Cam Jansen and the Lost Tooth,* noted that "Natti's cheerful line-and-watercolor illustrations help set the scene." Lisa Smith, reviewing *Young Cam Jansen and the Ice Skate Mystery* in *School Library Journal,* felt that the "bright, full-color drawings that illustrate every page will have readers searching for details they may have missed." "With its simple vocabulary, large type, and brightly colored line-and-wash illustrations, this will appeal to beginning readers," commented Carolyn Phelan in a *Booklist* review of *Young Cam Jansen and the Baseball Mystery.* "Natti's illustrations underscore Cam's visual memories and provide perceptive readers with helpful clues," commented Pat Leach in a review of the same title in *School Library Journal.* Also writing in *School Library Journal,* DeAnn Tabuchi noted that Natti's "bright cartoonlike watercolors" in *Young Cam Jansen and the Pizza Shop Mystery* "reflect the action and illustrate the pictures in the young detective's head."

Natti has had other fruitful collaborative efforts, most notably with Patricia Reilly Giff on the "Ronald Morgan" books, and Stephen Krensky on the "Lionel" series and also the "Louise" books, all for beginning readers. The illustrations for Giff's *Today Was a Terrible Day* in 1980 inaugurated the first of a half dozen titles about the trials and tribulations of second-grader Ronald Morgan. Ronald's misadventures continue in *The Almost Awful Play,* a book which is "saved by the occasional bits of whimsy in the illustrations which are bright and colorful," according to Sarah L. Connelly writing in *School Library Journal.* Elaine Lesh Morgan also called attention to Natti's illustrations for *Happy Birthday, Ronald Morgan!,* "bright and colorful with a touch of humor," in *School Library Journal.* And according to Pamela K. Bomboy, also writing in *School Library Journal,* Natti's "brightly colored" illustrations for *Ronald Morgan Goes to Camp* "are a perfect complement to the story."

Working with Stephen Krensky, Natti has helped produce many easy-to-read volumes about young Lionel and his older sister Louise. These chapter books feature several short stories with limited vocabulary and bright, often humorous, descriptive illustrations. In the debut volume, for example, *Lionel at Large,* "Natti's natty illustrations hook into Lionel's world as he envisions an escaped snake ... or as he sneaks a phone call to his mother," according to a *Publishers Weekly* critic. Adventures continue in *Lionel in the Fall* when the youngster returns to school. "Krensky's stories and dialogue are realistic and humorous," noted a contributor to *Publishers Weekly,* "perfectly matched by Natti's upbeat color drawings." Sharron McElmeel, writing in

School Library Journal, felt "Natti's sprightly illustrations bring color and visual interest to the text" in *Lionel in the Spring,* while she also called attention to Natti's "softly expressive watercolors" combining "just the right blend of realism and humorous whimsy" in *Lionel in the Winter.* Writing in *Booklist,* Susan Dove Lempke praised Natti's "lively illustrations" in *Lionel and His Friends,* which "show an ethnically diverse group of kids." Reviewing the same title in *School Library Journal,* Morgan felt "Krensky and Natti have once again created a wonderfully humorous book with lively illustrations done in pencil, colored pencils, and watercolors." Lionel celebrates the solstice and Fourth of July in *Lionel in the Summer,* and "Natti's expressive colored-pencil drawings with watercolor washes look as bright as a summer day," according to *Booklist*'s Phelan.

Lionel's older sister, Louise, takes center stage in other books in the series. In *Lionel and Louise,* for example, Lionel rescues Louise from a fly, and then the older sister helps him build a sandcastle. McElmeel wrote in *School Library Journal* that Natti's "warm, colored-pencil and watercolor-washed illustrations" for this book "are energetic and capture the happenings." *Horn Book*'s Ellen Fader, reviewing the same title, thought Natti's illustrations "make this book an inviting and entertaining choice." Reviewing the year 2000 title, *Louise, Soccer Star?,* in *School Library Journal,* Blair Christolon found Natti's illustrations "[a]ttractive."

Additional successful collaborative efforts include works with Betsy Duffey in the "Pet Patrol" series, and with Susan Wojciechowski in the "Beany" books. Reviewing Wojciechowski's *Don't Call Me Beanhead!,* the humorous debut to the short novels about young Bernice, Jacqueline Rose of *School Library Journal* called Natti's black-and-white illustrations "a perfect complement to the text." Also writing in *School Library Journal* about *Beany (Not Beanhead) and the Magic Crystal,* Christina Dorr concluded, "The black-ink sketches and page-turning text give a delightful view of the world through a child's eyes."

Such collaborative efforts have made Natti a high-demand illustrator. Working with myriad authors, Natti manages to be true to the text of each. As Marilyn Courtot noted in an interview with Natti in *Meet Authors and Illustrators,* the illustrator is able to maintain such textual and illustrative integrity by not having contact with the author. Even in the case of Krensky, who is something of a neighbor, Natti maintains "fences" between the two sides of the picture book creation: text and illustration. "Since the author and illustrator normally do not find each other, they are dependent upon the publisher who in essence plays the role of matchmaker," Courtot wrote, paraphrasing Natti. "All parties hope that the 'marriage' will work, and often the author does not see the illustrations until they are complete." However, this is not an absolute rule on Natti's part. As Courtot commented, "[T]he fences should have gates and these gates need to be opened on occasion."

Biographical and Critical Sources

PERIODICALS

Booklist, April 1, 1992, p. 1445; October 1, 1992, p. 326; March 1, 1993, p. 1229; July, 1993, p. 1966; October 15, 1993, p. 440; April 1, 1994, p. 1466; July, 1995, p. 1878; November 1, 1995, p. 469; September 15, 1996, Susan Dove Lempke, review of *Lionel and His Friends,* p. 253; May 1, 1997, Hazel Rochman, review of *Young Cam Jansen and the Lost Tooth,* p. 1502; May 1, 1998, p. 1524; July, 1998, Carolyn Phelan, review of *Lionel in the Summer,* p. 1890; October 1, 1999, Carolyn Phelan, review of *Young Cam Jansen and the Baseball Mystery,* p. 364; April 15, 2000, p. 1555.

Horn Book, January-February, 1982, Dudley B. Carlson, review of *Acorn Quest,* pp. 48-49; July-August, 1990, p. 477; March-April, 1992, Ellen Fader, review of *Lionel and Louise,* pp. 219-220; March-April, 1994, p. 195.

Publishers Weekly, February 11, 1983, review of *Downtown Fairy Godmother,* p. 71; June 27, 1986, review of *Lionel at Large,* p. 88; October 9, 1987, review of *Lionel in the Fall,* p. 86; July 13, 1992, p. 56.

School Library Journal, December, 1982, p. 78; May, 1983, p. 90; May, 1984, pp. 70, 100; August, 1984, Sarah L. Connelly, review of *The Almost Awful Play,* p. 59; December, 1984, p. 98; March, 1985, p. 138; December, 1985, Janie Schomberg, review of *Cam Jansen and the Mystery at the Monkey House,* p. 64; May, 1986, p. 113; January, 1987, p. 70; April, 1987, Elaine Lesh Morgan, review of *Happy Birthday, Ronald Morgan!,* p. 82; March, 1990, Sharron McElmeel, review of *Lionel in the Spring,* pp. 195, 198; April, 1991, Susan H. Patron, review of *Catch the Baby!,* p. 97; April, 1992, Cheryl Cufari, review of *Cam Jansen and the Mystery at the Haunted House,* p. 86; April, 1992, Sharron McElmeel, review of *Lionel and Louise,* p. 95; September, 1992, p. 202; April, 1993, p. 96; September, 1993, pp. 206, 228; March, 1994, Sharron McElmeel, review of *Lionel in the Winter,* p. 202; October, 1994, Jacqueline Rose, review of *Don't Call Me Beanhead!,* p. 106; October, 1994, pp. 136-137; June, 1995, Pamela K. Bomboy, review of *Ronald Morgan Goes to Camp,* p. 80; December, 1995, p. 72; July, 1996, Mary Ann Bursk, review of *Young Cam Jansen and the Dinosaur Game* and *Young Can Jansen and the Missing Cookie,* p. 56; September, 1996, p. 178; December, 1996, Sharon R. Pearce, review of *Cam Jansen and the Ghostly Mystery,* p. 84; December, 1996, Elaine Lesh Morgan, review of *Lionel and His Friends,* p. 98; July, 1997, Christina Dorr, review of *Beany (Not Beanhead) and the Magic Crystal,* p. 79; December, 1997, Janet M. Blair, review of *Cam Jansen and the Scary Snake Mystery,* p. 81; August, 1998, Lisa Smith, review of *Young Cam Jansen and the Ice Skate Mystery,* p. 132; September, 1998, p. 175; January, 1999, p. 79; June, 1999, Pat Leach, review of *Young Cam Jansen and the Baseball Mystery,* p. 85; July, 1999, p. 75; December, 1999, p. 87; May, 2000, DeAnn Tabuchi, review of *Young Cam Jansen and the Pizza Shop Mystery,* p. 126; September, 2000, p. 202; October, 2000, p. 142; January, 2001, Wendy S. Carroll, review of *Cam Jansen and the Birthday Mystery,* p. 91; January, 2001, Blair Christolon, review of *Louise, Soccer Star?,* p. 102.

ON-LINE

Meet Authors and Illustrators, http://www.childrenslit.com/ (June 11, 2001).*

—*Sketch by J. Sydney Jones*

* * *

NOBLE, Marty 1947-
(Ellen Harper)

Personal

Born March 19, 1947, in Berkeley, CA; daughter of Morton (a tile setter and teacher) and Helen Bonner (an artist and homemaker; maiden name, Harper) Noble; children: Eric John Gottesman. *Education:* "Self-taught." *Religion:* Unitarian. *Hobbies and other interests:* Gardening, hiking, yoga, travel.

Marty Noble

Addresses

Home and office—480 Canyon Springs Circle, Royal, AR 71968. *E-mail*—martyenoble@prodigy.net.

Career

Artist and illustrator. Teacher of marketing art and silk painting. Owner of a silk screen business, 1974-76; product designer and advertising artist, 1974—; children's art teacher at a school in Ojai, CA, 1978; designer and manufacturer of dolls, 1979-81; owner of Angel Light Creations (candle manufacturer). Teaches weekend workshops in silk painting. *Exhibitions:* Work has been exhibited at Cespedes Gallery, Palm Springs, CA; Prima Vera Gallery, Santa Barbara, CA; Artist and Outlaw Gallery, Ojai, CA; Riggs Gallery, La Jolla, CA; Studio Gallery, Channel Islands, CA; Hobar Gallery, Montecito, CA; and Crisani Gallery, Del Mar, CA. Work also represented in private collections.

Illustrator

Karen Pandell, *By Day and by Night* (poems), H. J. Kramer/Starseed Press (Tiburon, CA), 1991.

Terry Lynn Taylor, and others, *Guardians of Hope: The Angels' Guide to Personal Growth,* H. J. Kramer (Tiburon, CA), 1993.

Andrew Lang, editor, *Cinderella and Other Stories from "The Blue Fairy Book,"* Dover Publications (Mineola, NY), 1996.

Rapunzel: Full-Color Sturdy Book, Dover Publications (Mineola, NY), 1996.

John Robbins, and others, *In Search of Balance,* also published as *The Awakened Heart: Finding Harmony in a Changing World,* edited by Ann Mortifee, revised edition, H. J. Kramer (Tiburon, CA), 1997.

Peter C. Asbjørnsen, George Webbe Dasent, and others, *East o' the Sun and West o' the Moon and Other Fairy Tales,* Dover Publications (Mineola, NY), 1997.

Mythical Creatures, Dover Publications (Mineola, NY), 1997.

Ready-to-Use Angel Illustrations, Dover Publications (Mineola, NY), 1997.

Margery W. Bianco, *Velveteen Rabbit: Full-Color Sturdy Book,* Dover Publications (Mineola, NY), 1997.

(With Krista Brauckmann-Towns) Mary Rowitz, adaptor, *The Tortoise and the Hare,* Publications International (Lincolnwood, IL), 1997.

(With Krista Brauckmann-Towns) Sarah Toast, adaptor, *The Lion and the Mouse,* Publications International (Lincolnwood, IL), 1997.

(With Linda Dockey Graves) Jennifer Boudart, adaptor, *The Little Red Hen: A Tale of Hard Work,* Publications International (Lincolnwood, IL), 1997.

My First Book of Christmas Songs: Twenty Favorite Songs in Easy Piano Arrangements, Dover Publications (Mineola, NY), 1997.

My First Book of Irish Songs and Celtic Dances: Twenty-one Favorite Pieces in Easy Piano Arrangements, Dover Publications (Mineola, NY), 1998.

Lewis Carroll, *Alice in Wonderland,* adapted by Bob Blaisdell, Dover Publications (Mineola, NY), 1998.

Noble's detailed pen-and-ink drawings bring a sense of history to the traditional Norse tales in George Webbe Dasent's **East o' the Sun and West o' the Moon.**

Fairies and Elves, Dover Publications (Mineola, NY), 1998.

Clara Stroebe, editor, *The Magic Hat and Other Danish Fairy Tales,* Dover Publications (Mineola, NY), 1999.

Ancient Greek Designs, Dover Publications (Mineola, NY), 2000.

Merry Christmas, Dover Publications (Mineola, NY), 2000.

Melanie from the Old South, Dover Publications (Mineola, NY), 2000.

Knights, Dover Publications (Mineola, NY), 2000.

African, Dover Publications (Mineola, NY), 2000.

(With others) *Fantasy Fashions,* Grosset & Dunlap (New York, NY), 2000.

Happy Chanukah, Dover Publications (Mineola, NY), 2000.

(With son, Eric Gottesman) *Snowflake Designs,* Dover Publications (Mineola, NY), 2001.

Costume Ball, Dover Publications (Mineola, NY), 2001.

Real-Life Princesses, Grosset & Dunlap (New York, NY), 2001.

Stories from the Old Testament, Dover Publications (Mineola, NY), 2001.

OTHER

Creator of numerous activity books for children, including stencil, sticker, and coloring books. Also creator of illustrations for greeting cards, calendars, posters, limited edition prints on plates and paper, puzzles, and other products.

Contributor of articles and cover illustrations to magazines, including *Ventura County, Surface Design Journal, American Artist, Monthly Aspectarian, Connecting Link,* and *Creative Crafts.*

Work in Progress

Various book projects for Dover Publications, including *Book of Kells* coloring book, and collaborative art projects with artist son Eric. Research on ancient historical costumes of various cultures.

Sidelights

"Born in 1947 in Berkeley, California, and raised in Santa Barbara, I was fortunate to come into a family of artists," Marty Noble told *SATA*. "All four of my grandparents attended art school together in Chicago in the 1920s. My paternal grandfather, George Harper, went on to become known as a very fine commercial artist and my mother continued in the tradition with her own artistic pursuits. It seemed a natural thing for me to consider myself an artist from a young age. It was always my main interest, always encouraged and continues to challenge and excite me. In the early 1960s, when street fairs were becoming all the rage, I had just begun experimenting with batik (the application of dyes and wax to fabric). My first pieces were primitive and simple yet proved quite popular at the street fairs in San Francisco. I sold out my week's creations every weekend over a period of months.

My favorite subject matter and a passion from an early age was, and still is, the depiction of ethnic peoples from around the world. My fascination with other cultures grew as I began traveling in my early twenties. Living in southern California at that point, with my former partner and our toddler Eric, we made many trips to Mexico and lived in a few places for several months at a time. The beauty of the area and of the indigenous people inspired a whole series of paintings.

As my technique and detail grew I moved to Ojai, California, and into the gallery scene. The community was most supportive of my art, and I was nurtured there for many years and encouraged to pursue illustration. I began that avenue by submitting designs to greeting card companies. Sunrise Publications was the first company to publish my work and over time my focus has shifted completely to illustration. I really love the continuing variety of projects that come my way and the pleasure of seeing the work in so many formats, from book illustration to plate designs to calendars. I appreciate that most publishers give me assignments that call for the type of subject matter that is close to my heart.

Five years ago I moved to Arkansas where I purchased six acres and built a lovely little country home with a bright airy studio, overlooking a pond and meadow in a beautiful rural area, much like what I have always envisioned. The illustration work continues to keep me at the drawing board, with occasional breaks for gardening, soaking up the stillness, and romping around with my dogs, Sam and Zollie."

Biographical and Critical Sources

PERIODICALS

American Artist, February, 1988, p. 40.

* * *

NUWER, Hank
See NUWER, Henry J.

* * *

NUWER, Henry J. 1946-
(Hank Nuwer)

Personal

Born August 19, 1946, in Buffalo, NY; son of Henry Robert (a truck driver) and Teresa (a maid; maiden name, Lysiak) Nuwer; married Alice M. Cerniglia, December 28, 1968 (divorced, 1980); married N. Jenine Howard (an editor), April 9, 1982; children: (first marriage) Henry Christian; (second marriage) Adam Robert Drew. *Education:* Buffalo State College, B.S., 1968; New Mexico Highlands University, M.A., 1971. *Politics:* Democrat. *Religion:* Roman Catholic. *Hobbies and other interests:* Collecting stamps and tropical fish, quarter horses, playing baseball.

Addresses

Home—3220 West 39th St., Indianapolis, IN 46268. *E-mail*—nuwer@attglobal.net.

Career

Freelance writer, 1969—. Professor at Clemson University, 1982-83, Ball State University, and University of Richmond, 1995-97; editor-in-chief of *Arts Indiana Magazine,* 1985-89. Consultant, NBC television movie *Moment of Truth: Broken Pledges,* 1994. *Member:* Society of Professional Journalists, Investigative Reporters and Editors.

Awards, Honors

Distinguished alumnus, 1999, Buffalo State College.

Writings

UNDER NAME HANK NUWER

(With William Boyles) *The Deadliest Profession* (novel), Playboy Press, 1980.
(With William Boyles) *A Killing Trade* (novel), Playboy Press, 1981.
(With William Boyles) *The Wild Ride* (novel), Playboy Press, 1981.
(With William Boyles) *Blood Mountain* (novel), Playboy Press, 1982.
(With Carole Shaw) *Come Out, Come Out, Wherever You Are* (nonfiction), R & R Press, 1982.

Hank Nuwer explores the psychology of teen groups—from cheerleading squads to street gangs—and the rituals that membership entails in **High School Hazing: When Rites Become Wrongs.** *(Photograph courtesy of Liaison Agency, Inc.)*

(Editor, with Robert G. Waite) *Rendezvous at the Ezra Pound Centennial Conference,* 1986.

Strategies of the Great Football Coaches, Franklin Watts (New York, NY), 1987.

Strategies of the Great Baseball Managers, Franklin Watts (New York, NY), 1988.

Rendezvousing with Contemporary Authors, Idaho State University Press, 1988.

Recruiting in Sports, Franklin Watts (New York, NY), 1989.

Steroids, Franklin Watts (New York, NY), 1990.

Broken Pledges: The Deadly Rite of Hazing, Longstreet Press (Atlanta, GA), 1990.

Sports Scandals, Franklin Watts (New York, NY), 1994.

How to Write Like an Expert about Anything, Writers Digest (Cincinnati, OH), 1995.

The Legend of Jesse Owens, Franklin Watts (New York, NY), 1998.

Wrongs of Passage: Fraternities, Sororities, Hazing, and Binge Drinking, Indiana University Press (Bloomington, IN), 1999.

High School Hazing: When Rites Become Wrongs, Franklin Watts (New York, NY), 2000.

To the Young Writer, Franklin Watts (New York, NY), 2001.

Contributor to periodicals, including *Saturday Review, Harper's, Inside Sports, Nation, Outside, Success,* and *Sport.*

Work in Progress

To the Young Athlete and *To the Young Musician;* a novel with an Australian shepherd dog as hero.

Sidelights

Henry J. Nuwer, who writes under the name Hank Nuwer, began his writing career as a journalist, mainly writing sports-related articles. He once wrote, "My first books and magazine articles were humorous, frivolous, satirical, and adventurous pieces that reflected both the times in the seventies and early eighties and my own thrill-seeking tendencies. ... From 1983 to 1990, I began thinking of myself more as a journalist and less and less as an entertainer, writing mainly about health, fitness, and sports. My work after 1990 tends to be serious and spiritual: personal essays, a book examining deaths resulting from fraternity initiations, a history of women's education, and investigative journalism." More recently, Nuwer has turned his attention to young adults, writing several books about subjects such as hazing, sports, recruiting, and most recently a book offering advice to young writers.

Nuwer drew upon his own knowledge as a sports journalist to write *Recruiting in Sports,* a book intended for high school athletes who are aspiring to participate in athletics at the college level. Including an index, bibliography, and a list of schools that have been cited for rules violations, Nuwer offers practical advice to young athletes such as choosing the right school, the importance of academics, and recruiting tactics employed by both schools and recruiters. Reviewing this book for *Voice of Youth Advocates,* Mary Kinne lauded Nuwer's thorough research and noted that *Recruiting in Sports* can serve both as a "reference work as well as a guide." Similarly, *Steroids,* Nuwer's next sports-related book for young adults, contains a collection of stories about young athletes who have either used steroids or have been adversely affected by the use of drugs by other athletes. Including quotes from such famed sports figures as Olympic runner Ben Johnson and football player Brian Bosworth, both of whom were found guilty of taking performance-enhancing drugs, as well as several quotes from drug-free athletes such as Edwin Moses, Carl Lewis, and Florence Griffith-Joyner, the book views the issue from several angles.

In 1994, Nuwer issued *Sports Scandals.* Accompanying the narrative with several anecdotes once again, the book, which is geared towards young adults, includes chapters on gambling, recruiting, drug use, and cheating. In this work, Nuwer presents a social history of sports that spans a long period of time, beginning with the 1919 Red Sox gambling scandal. The stories in the book, such as Rosie Ruiz's Boston Marathon win and Mike Tyson's conviction for rape, help Nuwer cover issues related to recruiting violations, racial prejudice, and other problems. In a review of this work for the *Bulletin of the Center for Children's Books,* Roger Sutton praised Nuwer for not sensationalizing the scandals related in the book and for providing "plenty of stimulus for discussion of ethics."

Next, Nuwer wrote *The Legend of Jessie Owens,* a biography of the famous Olympian. In this detailed work about the legendary African-American athlete, Nuwer "offers readers a clear and inspiring picture" of how someone can overcome extreme adversity and prejudice, noted Roger Leslie in *Booklist.* Writing for the *School Library Journal,* Tom S. Hurlburt also lauded Nuwer for the "well-balanced" biography on Owens, noting that in addition to Owens' inspiring story, the work provides fascinating social history of African Americans during the time, including such topics as their migration to the North, segregation, and the racial issues surrounding World War II.

Nuwer's *Broken Pledges: The Deadly Rite of Hazing* deals with a difficult issue faced by many young adults entering college. In this work, the author recounts the alcohol and hazing-related death of twenty-one-year old Alfred University student Chuck Stenzel. According to Nuwer's book, Stenzel was a popular student who died of acute alcohol poisoning while participating in the "initiation" ceremony of a fraternity in early 1978. Following Stenzel's death at the fraternity house, his parents, especially his mother, helped found an organization that eventually helped pass a stiff anti-hazing law in the state of New York. Writing about *Broken Pledges* in *Booklist,* Sue-Ellen Beauregard noted that the book is a "compelling" look at this tragedy, threading together Stenzel's story with several other accounts of hazing in settings such as colleges, high schools, the armed forces, and even sports teams. Nuwer himself once said that he viewed *Broken Pledges* as a "major career satisfaction" because it has helped to "illuminate the problem of hazing."

In 1999, Nuwer again addressed the problem of hazing with his *Wrongs of Passage: Fraternities, Sororities, Hazing, and Binge Drinking.* Tracing the origins of hazing back to ancient Greece, Nuwer offers an overview of customs and practices connected with hazing, including a brief summary of hazing in the early-nineteenth century and the 1960s, contrasting the relatively innocuous stunts of these years to the current level of violence, which often includes death and injury. The lack of responsibility on the part of upper-classmen as well as the educational institutions where these incidents occur are also discussed in the book. Calling the work "extremely well researched," *Library Journal* contributor Danna C. Bell-Russel commended Nuwer for con-

tinuing the work he began with *Broken Pledges,* noting that in addition to relating stories about hazing, Nuwer also offers suggestions for removing hazing from college campuses.

Biographical and Critical Sources

PERIODICALS

Booklist, November 1, 1990, Sue-Ellen Beauregard, review of *Broken Pledges: The Deadly Rite of Hazing,* p. 487; July, 1992, Ellen R. Paterson, review of *Steroids,* p. 1932; January 1, 1999, Roger Leslie, review of *The Legend of Jesse Owens,* p. 851.

Boston Globe, October 2, 1990.

Bulletin of the Center for Children's Books, July-August, 1994, Roger Sutton, review of *Sports Scandals,* p. 369.

Chicago Tribune, March 22, 1994.

Kirkus Reviews, August 15, 1999, review of *Wrongs of Passage: Fraternities, Sororities, Hazing, and Binge Drinking,* p. 1290.

In **The Legend of Jesse Owens** *Nuwer describes the life of one of the greatest athletes of the twentieth century.* (*Photograph courtesy of Corbis-Bettmann.*)

Library Journal, November 15, 1990, Danna C. Bell, review of *Broken Pledges: The Deadly Rite of Hazing,* p. 78; September 1, 1999, Danna C. Bell-Russel, review of *Wrongs of Passage: Fraternities, Sororities, Hazing, and Binge Drinking,* p. 219.

Los Angeles Times Book Review, April 16, 1981.

New York Times, January 27, 1993; December 21, 1994.

School Library Journal, January, 1999, Tom S. Hurlburt, review of *The Legend of Jesse Owens,* p. 150.

Voice of Youth Advocates, April, 1990, Mary Kinne, review of *Recruiting in Sports,* p. 54; February, 1991, Penny Blubaugh, review of *Steroids,* pp. 379-380; December, 1994, Sally Kotarsky, review of *Sports Scandals,* pp. 302-303.

ON-LINE

Hank Nuwer Web site, http://www.hanknewer.com/ (August 27, 2001).*

*   *   *

OSTENDORF, (Arthur) Lloyd (Jr.) 1921-2000

OBITUARY NOTICE—See index for *SATA* sketch: Born June 23, 1921, in Dayton, OH; died October 27, 2000, in Oakwood, OH. Historian, artist, illustrator, and author. Ostendorf was an artist and historian who dedicated his life to studying and drawing the former president Abraham Lincoln. An avid collector of original Lincoln photographs, as well as other relics associated with the former president, Ostendorf's interest in Lincoln began at about age twelve. He went on to write and publish several books on Lincoln, such as his 1962 *Picture Story of Abe Lincoln,* intended for a younger audience. His classic 1963 *Lincoln in Photographs,* which earned him the Benjamin Barondess Award from the Civil War Round Table of New York in 1964, was co-written with Charles Hamilton. Ostendorf also illustrated a number of books for children, including *The Quiet Flame: Mother Marianne of Molokai,* by Eva Betz, and *No Luck for Linclon ...,* by Helen B. Walters.

OBITUARIES AND OTHER SOURCES:

PERIODICALS

Chicago Tribune, November 4, 2000, section 1, p. 22.

Dayton Daily News, November 5, 2000, p. 3C.

P

PATSCHKE, Steve 1955-

Personal

Surname is pronounced "*Patch*-key"; born December 25, 1955, in Morocco; son of Charles (a naval commander) and Jean (an executive secretary) Patschke; married Grace (an art teacher), September 27, 1986; children: Katie, Zoe. *Education:* State University of New York College at New Paltz, B.A.; University of Long Island, M.L.S.

Addresses

Home—41 Hanzel Lane, Shokan, NY 12481. *Agent*—Andrea Brown, P.O. Box 429, El Granada, CA 94018. *E-mail*—patch-key1@prodigy.net.

Career

Phoenicia Elementary School, Phoenicia, NY, worked as library media specialist; freelance writer. *Member:* Society of Children's Book Writers and Illustrators, American Library Association.

Writings

Don't Look at It, Don't Touch It, Troll (Mahwah, NJ), 1997.
The Spooky Book, Walker (New York, NY), 1999.

Adaptations

The Spooky Book has been recorded on audiocassette and made into a videotape for Listening Library, Inc.

Work in Progress

Children's picture books; a children's chapter book of humorous tall tales.

Sidelights

Steve Patschke told *SATA:* "I began writing poetry in high school. After I became an elementary school librarian, I realized many children's picture books were similar to poetry in their format. One day I became mesmerized when I heard someone use the chance phrase, 'Don't look at it, don't touch it.' From this title I created my first Halloween book. In the story, the characters find a spooky black box with the words 'don't look at it, don't touch it, don't open it' painted across the top. So what do you think the children do? From there, similar messages lead the children to a haunted house and a surprise Halloween party. It took me twenty minutes to write the majority of that story, I was so fascinated by the idea.

"My second book took two years to write. It was a bit more complicated in concept. *The Spooky Book* is the story of a boy reading about a girl alone in a spooky house. In the story the girl is also reading a spooky book. Whatever frightens the girl also frightens the boy. The girl ends up running out of the house. The boy hears a knock on his door. Guess who's there? *The Spooky Book* has been adapted as an audio book set and as a thirty-minute videotape, released by Listening Library, Inc."

Biographical and Critical Sources

PERIODICALS

Booklist, October 15, 1999, Lauren Peterson, review of *The Spooky Book,* p. 456.
Publishers Weekly, September 27, 1999, review of *The Spooky Book,* p. 48.

*   *   *

PETERS, Emma
See PRICE, Karen

PHILLIPS, Irv(ing W.) 1905-2000

OBITUARY NOTICE—See index for *SATA* sketch: Born October 29, 1905, in Wilton, WI; died October 28, 2000, in Santee, CA. Cartoonist and writer. Phillips was the cartoonist responsible for the comic strip "The Strange World of Mr. Mum," which ran from 1958 to 1970. His other syndicated strips included "Scuffy" and "Barnaby Bungle." Books featuring his cartoons and several screenplays number among his published works. His books, intended for children, include his 1965 *Strange World of Mr. Mum* and his 1971 *No Comment by Mr. Mum.* Phillips was also a playwright; his play *Caricature* was first staged in 1948, and his *Rumple* followed in 1956.

OBITUARIES AND OTHER SOURCES:

PERIODICALS

Los Angeles Times, November 1, 2000, p. B6.

*　　*　　*

POWER, Margaret (M.) 1945-

Personal

Born October 29, 1945, in Melbourne, Australia; daughter of Richard and Sylvia (an artist and potter; maiden name, McPherson) Power; divorced. *Education:* Royal Melbourne Institute of Technology Art School, diploma of illustration, 1964. *Politics:* "Green."

Addresses

Home and office—6/6 Sidwell Ave. E, St. Kilda, Victoria 3183, Australia.

Career

Children's book illustrator, 1986—. Has worked as a fashion illustrator for stores in London and Australia and as freelance illustrator for magazines and newspapers. *Member:* Society of Children's Book Writers and Illustrators, Australian Society of Book Illustrators.

Awards, Honors

Children's Book of the Year picture book honor prize, Children's Book Council of Australia, 1988, for *The Long Red Scarf.*

Illustrator

Roger Vaughan Carr, *Running Away,* Macmillan (South Melbourne, Australia), 1977.
Barbara Mitchelhill, *A Mirror for Midnight,* Longman Cheshire/Ginn (Melbourne, Australia), 1985.
Margaret Wild, *Creatures in the Beard,* Omnibus Books (Adelaide, Australia), 1986.
Nette Hilton, *The Long Red Scarf,* Carolrhoda Books (Minneapolis, MN), 1987.

Carolyn Marrone, *With a Mum Like Mine,* Rigby Education (Melbourne, Australia), 1987.
Keith Pigdon and Marilyn Woolley, *Senka's New Coat,* Macmillan (South Melbourne, Australia), 1987.
Edel Wignell, *Spider in the Toilet,* Lothian (Melbourne, Australia), 1988.
Robert Klein, *The Ghost in Abigail Terrace,* Omnibus Books (Adelaide, Australia), 1989.
Lorraine Wilson, *Kim,* Little Mammoth (Port Melbourne, Australia), 1992.
Lorraine Wilson, *Paul,* Little Mammoth (Port Melbourne, Australia), 1992.
Lorraine Wilson, *Poss,* Little Mammoth (Port Melbourne, Australia), 1992.
Lorraine Wilson, *Max,* Little Mammoth (Port Melbourne, Australia), 1992.
Christina Dwyer, *Jimmie Jean and the Turtles,* Walter McVitty Books (Montville, Australia), 1992.
Jean Chapman, *Grey Cat Magic,* Omnibus Dipper (Norwood, Australia), 1993.
Michael Dugan, *Daisy Drew an Elephant,* Moondrake Australia (Carlton, Australia), 1994.
Penny Hall, *Cat-Face,* Omnibus Books (Norwood, Australia), 1994.
Jonathan Harlen, *Mango,* Omnibus Books (Norwood, Australia), 1994.
Elizabeth Hutchins, *Brat Cat,* Omnibus Books (Norwood, Australia), 1994.
Jutta Goetze, *Penguin Island,* Mammoth (Port Melbourne, Australia), 1994.
Joanne Horniman, *Jasmine,* Omnibus Books (Norwood, Australia), 1995.
Diana Noonan, *Hercules,* Omnibus Books (Norwood, Australia), 1996.
Kerri Lane, *The Ghost of Barton Beach,* Rigby Heinemann (Port Melbourne, Australia), 1996.
Lucy Sussex, *The Penguin Friend,* Omnibus Books (Norwood, Australia), 1997.
Christobel Mattingley, *Ginger,* Penguin Australia (Ringwood, Australia), 1997.
Eleanor Nilsson, *The Eighty-ninth Kitten,* Omnibus Books (Norwood, Australia), 1998.
Liliana Stafford, *Just Dragon,* Cygnet Books (Redlands, Australia), 2000.
Jackie French, *How the Finnegans Saved the Ship,* HarperCollins (Pymble, Australia), 2001.

Also illustrator of *Dad's Camel* and *Anna Pavlova.* Illustrated covers for *Anne of Green Gables* paperback series.

ILLUSTRATOR; "VOYAGES" SERIES

Yvonne Winer, *Ssh, Don't Wake the Baby!,* SRA School Group/McGraw-Hill (Santa Rosa, CA), 1994.
David Drew, *When I Turned Six,* SRA School Group/McGraw-Hill (Santa Rosa, CA), 1994.
June Epstein, *The Name,* SRA School Group/McGraw-Hill (Santa Rosa, CA), 1994.
John Fitzgerald, *The Baby Brother,* SRA School Group/McGraw-Hill (Santa Rosa, CA), 1994.
Val Marshall,—*And Grandpa Sat on Friday,* SRA School Group/McGraw-Hill (Santa Rosa, CA), 1994.

Gwenda Smyth, *Horrie the Hoarder*, SRA School Group/ McGraw-Hill (Santa Rosa, CA), 1994.

Sidelights

Margaret Power once told *SATA:* "All I ever wanted to do was draw—and this even before I began school. It must have been written on the slate when I was born!

"My first children's book was called *Dad's Camel* and was part of the Heinemann 'Red Apple' series. *Dad's Camel* was done in pen and ink, and it was printed in two colors with a three-color overlay. I was clearly at the height of my pen-and-ink period! In those early days I worked with Janet Ahlberg in a studio in London; she illustrated *The Jolly Postman* and is one of my favorite illustrators.

"I love watercolors, but strangely enough I haven't used them in any of my picture books so far, though *Spider in the Toilet* and the covers I did for the *Anne of Green Gables* paperback series are a combination of pantoue markers, watercolor, and pencil. My other picture books are all in pastels, so clearly *this* is my pastel period! I am often asked if I draw in other styles, and I do use a more cartoonish style for some of the reading scheme books I'm involved in. I love the freedom this gives me. But I try to bring a sense of fun and fantasy even to my realistic works.

"With all my books, I do a tremendous amount of research to get the details right. Before I began *Jimmie Jean and the Turtles,* for example, I read and studied books about turtles and vegetation and landscape particular to those areas of Queensland where the turtle rookeries are located. I also asked my brother, who is one of the scientists in the story, to take photographs of beachscapes and vegetation around turtle rookeries near where he was vacationing—just to add to the mountain of references I already had. I really feast on this part of the creative process, drenching my brain with all the appropriate data. Then the really fun part begins— deciding what the characters in the story will look like. I do working drawings and take photographs of different people; the granddaughter of some friends was the model for Jimmie Jean.

"For *The Long Red Scarf,* I didn't use models at all. I had a strong idea already as to how I wanted the characters to look—particularly Grandpa. When I had completed the artwork for the book and sent it off to the publishers, the very next day I was crossing the street near my home and the very 'character' of Grandpa, complete with woolly cap, peddled by on a battered old bike. I was so astonished! I stared after him and wanted to call out, 'You're in my book!' Though I have no recollection of it, I must have seen him somewhere before and filed him away in my mind as a wonderful character to draw."

Biographical and Critical Sources

PERIODICALS

School Library Journal, March, 1991, Liza Bliss, review of *The Long Red Scarf,* p. 173; January, 2001, Meghan R. Malone, review of *Just Dragon,* p. 108.*

* * *

PRICE, Karen 1957-
(Karen Price Hossell; Emma Peters)

Personal

Born March 5, 1957, in Chester, PA; daughter of George A. (in business) and Shirley E. (in business) Price; married David C. Hossell (a technology trainer), 1991. *Education:* Cedarville College, B.A.; Long Island University, M.A.

Addresses

Home—401 Jo-Al-Ca Ave., Winter Park, FL 32789. *E-mail*—Human Voices@aol.com.

Career

Editor, writer, and part-time college instructor. Avery Publishing Group, book editor, 1988-90; Pace Products, managing editor, 1997-2000.

Writings

(Under pseudonym Emma Peters) *Alien Chemistry,* Troll Communications (Mahwah, NJ), 1998.
The Birthstone Book, Pace Products, 1998.
Amazing Magic Tricks, Pace Products, 1998.
Batty Science, Pace Products, 1999.
Micro Science: Flight, Pace Products, 1999.
Geography Mapping Kit, Pace Products, 1999.
Scrapbooking for Kids, Scholastic, 1999.
Super IQ Challenge, Scholastic, 1999.
Scent Science, Pace Products, 1999.
50 States Quarters, Scholastic, 1999, hardcover edition, 2000.
(With others) *Smithsonian Institution: Gemstones,* Pace Products, 2000.
Smithsonian Institution: Ancient Egypt, Pace Products, 2000.
(As Karen Price Hossell) *Virginia* ("Thirteen Colonies" series), Lucent Books, 2001.

Also creator of *Around the Town Stencil Kit,* Scholastic, 1999; and the games *Bonehead Mania,* 1999, *Truth or Dare: True Blue Friends,* 2000, *Quiz Me Presidents,* 2000, and *Quiz Show Mania,* Scholastic, 2000. Contributor of articles and short stories to periodicals, including *Ink Literary Review* and *Orlando Sentinel.* Editor, *Florida Police Chief,* 1994-99; assistant editor, *Fund Concept,* 1996-97.

Sidelights

Karen Price told *SATA:* "The first book I wrote was called *Cowboy Joe.* I was six years old and wrote and illustrated using crayon on notebook paper. I trimmed the edges, then sewed the binding with a needle and thread. I'd written short stories before, but never an entire book!

"I always knew I'd have something to do with books. I've tried other jobs but always ended up going back to anything to do with the written word. I've edited physics journals, children's educational materials, a newsletter for real estate attorneys, a book on management, books on macrobiotics and child care, a law enforcement magazine, and children's books.

"Now I am concentrating on writing. So far I've written fourteen children's books and created—or helped to create—and developed/written four children's games. My next goal is to make history accessible to children, and I am working on one or two children's history books that I hope will do just that."*

R

ROBINSON, Eve
See TANSELLE, Eve

* * *

RODRIGUEZ, Luis J. 1954-

Personal

Born July 9, 1954, in El Paso, TX; son of Alfonso (a laboratory custodian) and Maria Estela (a seamstress and homemaker; maiden name, Jimenez) Rodriguez; married Camila Martinez, August, 1974 (divorced, November, 1979); married Paulette Theresa Donalson, November, 1982 (divorced, February, 1984); married Maria Trinidad Cardenas (an editor and interpreter), March 28, 1988; children: (first marriage) Ramiro Daniel, Andrea Victoria; (third marriage) Ruben Joaquin, Luis Jacinto. *Education:* Attended California State University, 1972-73, Rio Hondo Community College, California Trade-Technical Institute, Watts Skills Center, Mexican-American Skills Center, East Los Angeles College, 1978-79, University of California at Berkeley, 1980, and University of California at Los Angeles. *Politics:* "Revolutionary." *Religion:* "Catholic/Indigenous Spirituality."

Addresses

Home and Office—716 Orange Grove Ave., San Fernando, CA 91340.

Career

Worked variously as a school bus driver, lamp factory worker, truck driver, paper mill utility worker, millwright apprentice, steel mill worker, foundry worker, carpenter, and chemical refinery worker, 1972-79; Eastern Group Publications, Los Angeles, CA, photographer and reporter for seven East Los Angeles weekly newspapers, 1980; reporter in San Bernadino, CA, 1980-82; *People's Tribune,* Chicago, IL, editor, 1985-88; computer typesetter for various firms in the Chicago area, including the Archdiocese of Chicago, 1987-89; writer, lecturer, and critic, 1988—; part-time news writer for WMAQ-AM in Chicago, 1989-92.

Director of the mural project for the Bienvenidos Community Center, 1972; public affairs associate for the American Federation of State, County, and Municipal Employees, AFL-CIO, 1982-85; publisher and editor of *Chismearte,* 1982-85; facilitator of the Barrio Writers Workshops, Los Angeles, 1982-85; board member of KPFK-FM, Pacifica Station in Los Angeles, 1983-85; founder and director of Tia Chucha Press, 1989—; writer in residency, Shakespeare and Company, Paris, France, 1991; writer in residence, North Carolina's

Luis J. Rodriguez

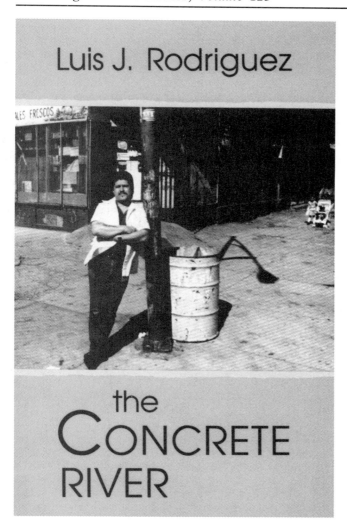

As with most of Rodriguez's writing, his 1996 poetry collection expresses his thoughts on barrio life. (Cover photograph by Chuck Kramer.)

"Word Wide," 2000; founder of the following organizations: Rock a Mole (rhymes with guacamole) Productions, League of Revolutionaries for a New America, the Guild Complex, Youth Struggling for Survival, and Tia Chucha's Café Cultural. Conductor of talks, readings, and workshops in prisons, juvenile facilities, public and private schools, migrant camps, churches, universities, community centers, and homeless shelters throughout the United States, Canada, Mexico, Puerto Rico, Central America, and Europe, 1980—. *Member:* PEN USA West, Poets and Writers, American Poetry Society, National Writers Union, Los Angeles Latino Writers Association (director/publisher, 1982-85).

Awards, Honors

Honorable mention for the Quinto Sol Chicano Literary Award, 1973; second place for the best freelance story, from the Twin Counties Press Club, 1982; honorable mention for the Chicano Literary Award, University of California at Irvine, Department of Portuguese and Spanish; second place for the Corazon de Aztlan

Literary Award, 1984; best of the *Los Angeles Weekly,* 1985; honorable mention for the Patterson Poetry Prize and PEN West/Josephine Miles Award for Literary Excellence, both for *The Concrete River;* Poetry Center Book Award, San Francisco State University, for *Poems across the Pavement,* 1989; Illinois Arts Council Poetry Fellowship, 1992, 2000; Lannan Fellowship in Poetry, 1992; Dorothea Lange/Paul Taylor Prize, Center for Documentary Studies, Duke University, 1993; Carl Sandburg Literary Award for nonfiction, *New York Times Book Review* Notable Book, both 1993, and *Chicago Sun-Times* Book Award for nonfiction, 1994, all for *Always Running: La Vida Loca, Gang Days in L.A.;* Lila Wallace-*Reader's Digest* Writers' Award, 1996; National Association for Poetry Therapy Public Service Award, 1997; Hispanic Heritage Award for literature, 1998; Paterson Prize for Books for Young Adults, 1999; "Skipping Stones" Magazine Honor Award, 1999 and 2000; *Foreword Magazine*'s Silver Book Award, 1999; Parent's Choice Books for Children Award, 1999; Illinois Author of the Year Award, 2000; Americas Award for Children's and Young Adult Literature Commended Title, 2000; Premio Fronterizo of the Border Book Festival, Las Cruces, New Mexico, 2001; "Unsung Heroes of Compassion" Award, 2001.

Writings

Poems across the Pavement, Tia Chucha Press, 1989.
The Concrete River (poems), Curbstone Press, 1991.
Always Running: La Vida Loca: Gang Days in L.A. (memoir), Curbstone Press, 1993, Touchstone Books, 1994.
America Is Her Name, illustrated by Carlos Vazquez, Curbstone Press, 1998.
Trochemoche: Poems, Curbstone Press, 1998.
It Doesn't Have to Be This Way: A Barrio Story, illustrated by Daniel Galvez, Children's Book Press, 1999.
Hearts and Hands: Making Peace in a Violent Time, Seven Stories Press, 2001.

Contributor of articles, reviews, and poems to periodicals, including *Los Angeles Times, Nation, U.S. News and World Report, Utne Reader, Philadelphia Inquirer Magazine, Chicago Reporter, Poets and Writers, Chicago Tribune, American Poetry Review, TriQuarterly, Bloomsbury Review, Rattle Magazine,* and *Latina Magazine.* Also contributor to anthologies, including *The Outlaw Bible of American Poetry, Letters of a Nation: A Collection of Extraordinary American Letters, Las Christmas: Favorite Latino Authors Share Their Holiday Memories, Inside the L.A. Riots: What Happened and Why It Will Happen Again, Mirrors beneath the Earth: Short Fiction by Chicano Writers, After Aztlan: Latino Writers in the '90s, Fifty Ways to Fight Censorship, With the Wind at My Back and Ink in My Blood: A Collection of Poems by Chicago's Homeless, Unsettling America: An Anthology of Contemporary Multicultural Poetry, Power Lines: A Decade of Poetry at Chicago's Guild Complex,* and *Voices: Readings from El Grito.* Rodriguez's work has been translated into German, French, Arabic, and Spanish.

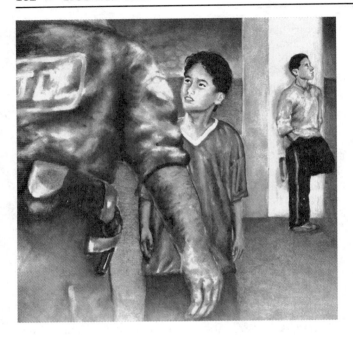

The challenges faced by a young man growing to adulthood in a Hispanic neighborhood becomes Rodriguez's focus in **It Doesn't Have to Be This Way: A Barrio Story.** *(Illustration by Daniel Galvez.)*

Work in Progress

Sometimes You Dance with a Watermelon and Other Stories, a short story collection to be published by HarperCollins/Rayo Books in early 2002; *My Nature Is Hunger: New & Selected Poems,* to be published by Curbstone Press; "Nations," an original treatment for a possible TV pilot and series for Shore Media Productions, registered with the Writers Guild.

Sidelights

In his 1993 memoir, poet-author-journalist Luis J. Rodriguez encapsulates the trapped feeling of the Latino in East Los Angeles: "It never stopped this running. We were constant prey, and the hunters soon became big blurs: The police, the gangs, the junkies, the dudes on Garvey Boulevard who took our money, all smudge into one." But the enemy was not always on the street for young Mexican Americans like Rodriguez: "Sometimes they were teachers who jumped on us Mexicans as if we were born with a hideous stain. We were always afraid, always running." It was this feeling of persecution, of being the target of others, that led young men like Rodriguez into gang membership.

Always Running: La Vida Loca: Gang Days in L.A. was Rodriguez's personal statement, his *mea culpa,* both a cautionary tale and gut-wrenching personal document. Written two decades after his own gang activity, the book was partly inspired by his own son, Ramiro, who was himself becoming involved in gangs at the time Rodriguez was writing his book. In the event, the memoir was not enough of a deterrent to keep Ramiro out of trouble: Rodriguez's son was sent to prison in

1998 for attempted murder. However, despite school bans on the book and a mini-controversy over its content, Rodriguez still believes his book is essential reading for many. "I actually hope my book will lose its validity some day," he told Patrick Sullivan in an interview for the *Sonoma County Independent,* "that there isn't a need for a book like *Always Running. . . .* But right now that's not the case. The book is very relevant, and as long as that's the case, then we should make sure that people can get access to it."

Rodriguez has written three books of poetry and two children's books in addition to this partly fictionalized memoir, and has also contributed journalistic articles to national publications such as the *Los Angeles Times, Nation,* and *U.S. News and World Report,* chronicling the Mexican-American experience and speaking out articulately for social justice and equity in the country. But he continues to view himself primarily as a poet. As he told Aaron Cohen in an interview for *Poets and Writers,* "Poetry is the foundation of everything I do. It's poetry with a sense of social engagement. The written, powerful expressive language of poetry is the springboard for everything I want to write."

Rodriguez is no stranger to the mean streets he depicts in all his work. Born in El Paso, Texas, on July 9, 1954, he spent two years in Ciudad Juarez, Mexico, before his family immigrated to the United States in 1956. His father, Alfonso Rodriguez, a school principal in Mexico, brought his family north because the pay was so poor in his native country that he could not support his children. But once settled in the Watts community of south central Los Angeles, Alfonso and his family were presented with the cruel reality of low-status work and constant racism. The father held a number of jobs, ultimately working as a laboratory custodian, while Rodriguez's mother, Maria Estela Jimenez, worked as a seamstress. Rodriguez grew up with three siblings and three nieces, the daughters of his half-sister, and in 1962 the family moved to the East Los Angeles community of South San Gabriel. Rodriguez's teenage years were spent in the barrio there.

These were turbulent years for the young Rodriguez, who felt always on the outside, harassed by both Anglo children and the police. To find a sense of solidarity and belonging, Rodriguez joined the gangs of East Los Angeles. Dropping out of school at fifteen, he led a life during the 1960s and 1970s characterized by ever-escalating violence and mayhem. Jailed for attempted murder, he was released only to take part in a fire bombing of a home and in store robberies. Sex and drugs formed a continual base line to his life. "Everything lost its value for me," Rodriguez wrote in *Always Running,* describing the nihilism of those days. "Death seemed the only door worth opening, the only road toward a future."

But Rodriguez was one of the fortunate ones. From his early youth he had tried to find a safe haven in books, in an interior life. Even as a very young child, as he told Cohen, "I found refuge in books because I was a shy, broken-down little kid. They were fairytale books, Walt

Disney books, whatever. I would go inside and hide myself in books and not have to worry about the yelling and screaming and bullets flying." Even as a gang member, he was composing verses based on his experiences on the streets. This propensity for self-reflection came in handy when, at the height of the Chicano Movement, Rodriguez was pulled from the gangs by the lure of education and political activism. A recreational leader at a local youth center introduced Rodriguez to Mexican history and a new way of looking at himself, while a counselor at school, when he returned to graduate in 1970, also helped to make the young man into a student leader instead of a gang dupe, taking pride in his culture, in his race, in his heritage. Slowly Rodriguez turned away from violence to the world of words.

Graduating from high school in 1970, Rodriguez won his first literary award two years later, the Quinto Sol Literary Award, which earned him $250 and a trip to Berkeley. Throughout the 1970s, Rodriguez continued writing while holding down blue collar jobs. He also married for the first time and became the father of two children. Then in 1980 he became a full-time writer, working as a journalist and photographer for several Los Angeles newspapers.

Rodriguez became heavily involved in the east Los Angeles political and literary scene, serving as director of the Los Angeles Latino Writers Association and publishing the literary magazine *Chismearte,* in whose pages some of the bright and rising stars of Latino literature were first introduced to a wider public. By the mid 1980s, divorced, remarried, and divorced again, Rodriguez had resettled in Chicago, where he worked as an editor on the *People's Tribune,* a weekly leftist journal. He also became deeply involved in not only literary matters, giving poetry workshops and crafting his journalism, but also in social issues, working with gang members, the homeless, convicts, and migrants. During this time he also established Tia Chucha Press, the publishing house of the Guild Complex, an arts center in Chicago focusing on multicultural issues. In 1988, he married for a third time and has two children by this marriage in addition to the two from his first.

In 1989, his Tia Chucha Press published his first collection of poetry, *Poems across the Pavement,* verses that focus on "life in America," according to Dina G. Castillo, writing in *Dictionary of Literary Biography,* "but his America is one that relatively few people want to acknowledge." Castillo described the America Rodriguez portrays as "an environment fraught with economic oppression, racism, cultural alienation, class battles, industrial displacement, strained human relations, and street turmoil in Los Angeles and Chicago." Rodriguez depicts this situation in poems in the collection such as "'Race' Politics," "No Work Today," "Tombstone Poets," and "Alabama," which take the reader on "an emotional roller coaster," according to Castillo. Some of the poems were written when Rodriguez was still a teenager, and all display the influence of his own favorite writers, poets from Walt Whitman to Pablo

Neruda, and Latino and African-American authors such as Claude Brown and Piri Thomas, whose work portrayed the hard lives of society's outcasts and downtrodden.

A second collection, *The Concrete River,* appeared in 1991, confirming Rodriguez's early promise and delving more deeply into the themes of urban violence, race relations, gender conflicts, and drug addiction which he explored in his first volume of poetry. An interesting development in *The Concrete River* was the use of both poetry and prose in longer pieces, ones that tie together to provide a witnessing of his own past, from Mexico to Watts to East Los Angeles to Chicago. In the first of five sections, with the poem "Prelude to a Heartbeat," Rodriguez talks of his youth in Watts "Where fear is a deep river. / Where hate is an overgrown weed." His dangerous gang years are dealt with in the second section while his failed first marriage comes to center stage in the third, "Always Running": "When all was gone, / the concrete river / was always there / and me, always running." Other sections deal with his life as a blue-collar worker and with his new life in Chicago,

In the 1998 collection Trochemoche, *Rodriguez experiments with a variety of poetic forms.*

away from the city that spawned him and nearly destroyed him.

Castillo noted that Rodriguez uses the "motifs of concrete and pavement to represent all that has limited him in the past but that nevertheless became the source of his literary creativity." For Rodriguez there is some value, some resiliency to be gained from such a hard life. "He views poetry as the water that runs through the concrete river," Castillo observed, "cleansing and restoring life." A reviewer for *Publishers Weekly* felt that Rodriguez "writes eloquently of ... a populace locked out of privilege and prosperity." The same writer concluded, "This poetry is of the barrio yet stubbornly refuses to be confined in it—Rodriguez's perceptive gaze and storyteller's gift transport his world across neighborhood boundaries." Audrey Rodriguez, writing in *Bilingual Review,* noted that *The Concrete River* "involves a return to and recovery of the past ... and a recognition of chaos, death, and the reality of a place that locks in or jeopardizes the thinking-feeling self." Rodriguez, the critic, concluded that Luis J. Rodriguez "is one of Chicano literature's most gifted and committed artists today.... His is a refreshing voice—of rebellion and beauty—in an increasingly narrow age of literature's disengagement from the ground of great art and true history." *The Concrete River* won an honorable mention for the Patterson Poetry Prize and the PEN West/Josephine Miles Award for Literary Excellence. In 1992, Rodriguez received both an Illinois Arts Council Poetry Fellowship and a Lannan Fellowship in Poetry.

For his next work, Rodriguez moved away from poetry, but not from the lyrical inspiration, to tell in prose form the story of his own years in the Los Angeles gangs. He dedicated his book to twenty-five childhood friends who died, victims of gang violence before the author reached the age of eighteen. In *Always Running: La Vida Loca: Gang Days in L.A.,* Rodriguez also explains the needs out of which the Hispanic gang culture springs. As Dale Eastman reported of the book in *New City* magazine: "Socially ostracized and economically segregated from their white counterparts, the young children of mostly migrant workers who had come north to earn a living, first formed clicas, or clubs, to create some sense of belonging." These Mexican youths were denied, for the most part, membership in other organizations, be it the Boy Scouts or even athletic teams. These alternate, ad hoc youth clubs slowly evolved into the gangs of today, many of them simply another way to hang out with friends. Eastman further noted: "As increasing numbers of Mexicans moved into the barrio areas, the clubs adopted a more dangerous profile, offering much-needed protection from rival groups and a sense of power in an increasingly powerless world."

As Rodriguez grew older, he became increasingly involved in drugs and gang violence. Gary Soto, critiquing *Always Running* in the *New York Times Book Review,* noted that "the body count rises page by page. The incidents become increasingly bizarre and perversely engaging. Mr. Rodriguez is jailed for attempted murder, then let go. He participates in the firebombing

of a home. He robs stores. He experiments with heroin. He wounds a biker with a shotgun blast, is arrested, then let go. When police officers beat him to the ground, his 'foot inadvertently came up and brushed one of them in the chest,' and he is booked for assault and eventually tried and jailed." But Rodriguez also tells how he escaped the gang life, and he brings *Always Running* up to date by discussing the role of gangs in the 1992 riots in Los Angeles, and his own son's gang involvement in Chicago. Soto concluded that *Always Running* "is a chilling portrait of gang life during the 1960s, a gang life that haunts us even now.... The book is fierce and fearless."

Castillo noted that while some critics call the book "a memoir, others have qualified it as a novel of redemption because of its fictional/poetic qualities." As Rodriguez noted to Cohen, the book is a little of both, for he "synthesized events and reorganized the material so that it would work as literature [fiction] but still maintain the truth and reality of the situation." Castillo further observed: "Often poetic, the narration is nevertheless a straight presentation of life as it was for Rodriguez. Readers witness a childhood and adult behavior that is surprising for its violence." Ultimately, Rodriguez was saved from the violence by two mentors who showed him a different path; such a path was not open to Chava, a former gang leader whom Rodriguez meets at the end of the book, outside a party. Battered and wounded—

When nine-year-old America learns to write poetry, she finds her place in the world in **America Is Her Name.**

Chava carries a colostomy bag as a result of a stabbing—this once feared enemy is "a fragment of the race, drunk, agonized, crushed, and I can't hate him anymore; I can't see him as the manifestation of craziness and power he once possessed; he's a carica-ture, an apparition, but also more like me, capable of so much ache beneath the exterior of so much strength . . . ."

Other reviewers lauded Rodriguez's gritty tale, while a storm of controversy began to brew over its use in the schools. Suzanne Ruta called the book "beautifully written and politically astute" in an *Entertainment Weekly* review, while Floyd Salas, writing in the *Los Angeles Times,* felt it was "a pilgrim's progress, a classic tale of the new immigrant in the land of the melting pot." Salas went on to describe *Always Running* as "a tome of the torturous, faltering, sometimes progressing, sometimes repressing journey of a gifted migrant. With this memorable, often tragic story, Rodriguez has fulfilled that journey by achieving the American dream of success in art and life." Fred Whitehead, reviewing the book in *National Catholic Reporter,* concluded, "By expressing the pain of those most destroyed, Rodriguez never lets us forget where we need to go together. He thinks it is possible for us all to deal with these problems, not by way of patching here and there, but through fundamental change." Echoing these sentiments, a reviewer for *The Progressive* wrote that this "beauti-fully written insider's account of what it's like to live in the desolation of America's urban ghettoes" tells "how our society leaves minorities and the poor no viable alternatives . . . . The problem, Rodriguez makes clear, is not with the gangs but with the society that creates gangs."

In artistic content, Rodriguez was perhaps too successful in his reproduction of the climate of violence in which he grew up. Several school boards around the country banned the book from its library shelves, criticizing it for promoting violence. But Rodriguez is steadfast. The book neither glorifies nor demonizes gang involvement, for as Rodriguez told Sullivan, "[b]oth views distort reality." The book contains, according to its many supporters, a message that will reach kids in gangs, that touches their lives directly and that may lead them—as a similar approach did for Rodriguez himself—out of the violence and into the light. Ilan Stavans, reviewing the book in *The Nation,* posed this very desire: "Although gang life may be impossible to eradicate fully, one hopes that *Always Running* (a fortunate title) will be read where it most counts, and widely, and have an impact."

Rodriguez has maintained a busy schedule of writing and speaking in schools since the publication of *Always Running,* becoming a spokesman for Latino causes, as well as for youth and the dispossessed. Deeply involved in social causes, Rodriguez has also continued to publish distinguished and innovative verse and prose. In 1998, he added to his poetry publications with *Trochemoche,* or "helter-skelter" in Spanish. These verses are once again highly autobiographical in nature and explore the phases of Rodriguez's life from gang member to "his

more sedate role as a Chicago publisher," as Lawrence Olszewski noted in a *Library Journal* review of the collection. In the poem "Notes of a Bad Cricket," Rodriguez assays his inner worlds: "There is a mixology of brews within me; I've tasted them all, still fermenting / as grass-high anxieties. I am rebel's pen, rebel's son, father of revolution in verse." Olszewski went on to observe the "head-on, no-holds barred style" which "smacks more of newspaper accounts than lyricism without succumbing to sensationalism." Susan Smith Nash described the collection as "raw, honest, hard-hitting" in *World Literature Today,* with voices that "are dissident, angry, raised in protest." Nash further com-mented that these voices "are truly unforgettable."

Additionally, Rodriguez has branched out into new territory with his children's books, *America Is Her Name* and *It Doesn't Have to Be This Way.* Castillo called the former book "a sensitive story for young children" in *Dictionary of Literary Biography.* The story of nine-year-old America Soliz, an illegal Mexican immigrant living in a Chicago barrio, the book takes young readers inside the head and heart of this young girl whose greatest wish is simply to return to her native Oaxaca. But when a Puerto Rican poet visits her English as a second language (ESL) class one day, she is inspired to become a citizen of the world through poetry.

Writing in *School Library Journal,* Denise E. Agosto felt that the "story is generally well told, and its message is an important one." Agosto concluded that *America Is Her Name* is a "solid choice for bilingual and ESL collections." Though a reviewer for *Publishers Weekly* thought the book "ponderous" and "wordy," *Skipping Stones*' Beth Erfurth called the book a "story about hopes, memories, and dreams amid a reality of discrimi-nation and despair," and found it to be an "inspiration to readers of all ages."

In a second picture book, *It Doesn't Have to Be This Way,* Rodriguez tells another cautionary tale about gangs. Ten-year-old Monchi relates his own near miss with joining a gang—saved by the shooting of his older girl cousin who has advised him to avoid the gangs. Dreamer, the older cousin, is left in a wheelchair as a result of the shooting, but Monchi refuses to be drawn into the cycle of retribution that others demand. "The message is spelled out," wrote Hazel Rochman in a *Booklist* review, "but Rodriguez's personal experience, as a teenage gang member and now as an adult counselor, gives the story immediacy." *School Library Journal*'s Reina Huerta felt the book could be "a springboard for discussion."

Rodriguez once commented: "Despite great odds, today I'm a poet and writer of note, driven by the great social upheavals of our day. I say to any young person—especially one linked to a great cause such as the fundamental progress of humanity—never give up. We all have the capabilities of great art and poetry. It's a matter of tapping into that creative reservoir we contain as human beings. Once tapped, this reservoir is inex-haustible. Skills and technique can always be learned.

Opening up to our innate powers as communicators and artists is a strong foundation for obtaining such skills."

And the poet also once noted in an autobiographical essay that after a life lived through cultural and economic hardships, his "resolve has only strengthened" and his "vision has only sharpened." Sober, reconciled with family members and the world at large, Rodriguez faces the future with optimism. He concluded his essay: "There are difficult roads ahead; if anything, I'm more prepared for them than I have ever been. According to the ancient Mexican people, we are living under the Fifth Sun. Nahui Ollin. A time of change. Of movement, from the heart of a person to the heart of the universe."

Biographical and Critical Sources

BOOKS

Dictionary of Literary Biography, Volume 209: *Chicano Writers, Third Series,* Gale (Detroit, MI), 1999.
Contemporary Authors Autobiography Series, Volume 29, Gale (Detroit, MI), 1998.
Rodriguez, Joseph, "La Vida Loca: Joseph Rodriguez and Luis J. Rodriguez on 'The Crazy Life,'" *East Side Stories: Gang Life in East LA,* Powerhouse Books, 1998.
Rodriguez, Luis J., *Always Running: La Vida Loca: Gang Days in L.A.,* Curbstone Press, 1993, Touchstone Books, 1994.
Rodriguez, Luis J., *Trochemoche: Poems,* Curbstone Press, 1998.
Schwartz, Michael, *Luis J. Rodriguez,* Raintree/Steck-Vaughn, 1997.

PERIODICALS

Bilingual Review, September-December, 1996, Audrey Rodriguez, "Contemporary Chicano Poetry," pp. 203-207.
Booklist, August, 1999, Hazel Rochman, review of *It Doesn't Have to Be This Way,* p. 2059.
Chicago Tribune, February 25, 1993.
Entertainment Weekly, February 12, 1993, Suzanne Ruta, review of *Always Running,* p. 51.
Hartford Courant, March 5, 1993, pp. C1, C8.
Hispanic, June, 1993, p. 72.
Hungry Mind Review, summer, 1993.
Library Journal, June 15, 1998, Lawrence Olszewski, review of *Trochemoche,* p. 82.
Los Angeles Times, March 7, 1993, Floyd Salas, "Leaving the Gang Behind," p. 2; March 31, 1993; June 18, 1998.
Nation, April 12, 1993, Ilan Stavans, review of *Always Running,* pp. 494-498.
National Catholic Reporter, January 8, 1993, Fred Whitehead, review of *Always Running,* p. 61.
New City, February 8, 1993, Dale Eastman, review of *Always Running,* pp. 10, 12.
New York Times Book Review, February 14, 1993, Gary Soto, "The Body Count in the Barrio," p. 26.
Poets and Writers, January-February, 1995, Aaron Cohen, "An Interview with Luis J. Rodriguez," pp. 50-55.
Progressive, September, 1993, review of *Always Running,* p. 43.

Publishers Weekly, May 17, 1991, review of *The Concrete River,* p. 58; February 1, 1993, p. 86; September 23, 1996, p. 12; April 13, 1998, review of *American Is Her Name,* p. 75; August 16, 1999; p. 85.
Rattle, winter, 1999, interview with Luis Rodriguez.
School Library Journal, September, 1998, Denise E. Agosto, review of *America Is Her Name,* p. 180; October, 1999, Reina Huerta, review of *It Doesn't Have to Be This Way,* p. 124.
Skipping Stones, May-August, 1999, Beth Erfurth, review of *America Is Her Name,* p. 6.
Sojourners, March, 1999, p. 57.
Sonoma County Independent, February 4-10, 1999, Patrick Sullivan, "Class War: Luis J. Rodriguez Casts a Skeptical Eye on Attempts to Ban His Autobiography," pp. 21-22.
Sun, April, 2000, Derrick Jensen, interview with Luis Rodriguez.
World Literature Today, winter, 1999, Susan Smith Nash, review of *Trochemoche,* p. 156.

ON-LINE

Academy of American Poets, http://www.poets.org/ (September 2, 2001), biography of Luis Rodriguez.
Luis Rodriguez Home Page, http://www.wordsculptures.com/luis/ (September 2, 2001).

OTHER

The Choice of a Lifetime: Returning from the Brink of Suicide (video), New Day Films, 1996.
In Their Own Voices: A Century of Recorded Poetry (audio cassette), Rhino/Word Beat Records, 1996.
Luis Rodriguez (video), Lannan Foundation, 1992.
Making Peace: Youth Struggling for Survival (video), Moira Productions, 1997.
A Snake in the Heart: Poems and Music by Chicago's Spoken Word Performers (audio cassette), Tia Chucha Press, 1994.
La Vida Loca: El Testimonio de un Pandillero en Los Angeles (audio cassette), AudioLibros del Mundo, 1998.

—*Sketch by J. Sydney Jones*

*   *   *

RUFFINS, Reynold 1930-

Personal

Born August 15, 1930, in New York, NY; son of John (a salesman) and Juanita (Dash) Ruffins; married Joan Young (an artist), May 29, 1954; children: Todd, Lynn, Beth, Seth. *Education:* Graduated from Cooper Union, 1951. *Hobbies and other interests:* Sailing, listening to classical and jazz music.

Addresses

Home—112-38 178th Pl., St. Albans, New York, NY 11434. *Office*—c/o Harcourt, 15 East 26th St., New York, NY 10010.

Career

Push Pin Studios, New York, NY, designer and illustrator, beginning in 1950s; assistant art director of advertising agency, c. 1954; graphic designer for International Business Machines (IBM), Time-Life, Pfizer, Children's Book Council, McDonald's, CBS-TV, New York Times, and Family Circle magazine; illustrator and author of children's books, 1970—. Instructor, School of Visual Arts, 1967-70, and Parsons School of Design; visiting adjunct professor, Syracuse University, College of Visual and Performing Arts, Department of Visual Communications, 1973. *Exhibitions:* Work featured in exhibitions at Bologna Children's Book Fair, 1976, and "Two Hundred Years of American Illustration," New York Historical Society.

Awards, Honors

Professional Achievement Award, Cooper Union, 1972; *The Chess Book* selected for American Institute of Graphic Arts Children's Books Show, 1973-74; Bologna (Italy) Children's Book Fair Award, 1976; Children's Choice awards, Children's Book Council/International Reading Association, 1976, for *The Code and Cipher Book,* 1978, for *The Monster Riddle Book,* 1980, for *My Brother Never Feeds the Cat,* and 1983, for *Words?! A Book about the Origins of Everyday Words and Phrases;*

Reynold Ruffins enhances Verna Aardema's Misoso: Once upon a Time Tales from Africa *with his paintings that provide a colorful feast for the eyes of young readers.*

American Library Association Notable Book citation for *Words?! A Book about the Origins of Everyday Words and Phrases;* Silver Medal, Society of Illustrators, for "Dragon" (a commercial illustration).

Writings

(And illustrator) *My Brother Never Feeds the Cat,* Scribner (New York, NY), 1979.

ILLUSTRATOR

(With Simms Taback) Harry Hartwick, *The Amazing Maze,* Dutton (New York, NY), 1970.

John F. Waters, *Camels: Ships of the Desert,* Crowell (New York, NY), 1974.

Franklyn M. Branley, *Light and Darkness,* Crowell (New York, NY), 1975.

Denise Burden-Patmon and Kathryn D. Jones, *Carnival,* Modern Curriculum Press (Cleveland, OH), 1992.

Brian Gleeson, *Koi and the Kola Nuts,* Picture Book Studio (Saxonville, MA), 1992.

Verna Aardema, reteller, *Misoso: Once upon a Time Tales from Africa,* Knopf (New York, NY), 1994.

Marcia K. Vaughn, *Riddle by the River,* Silver Burdett (Morristown, NJ), 1995.

Denize Lauture, *Running the Road to ABC,* Simon & Schuster (New York, NY), 1996.

James Berry, *Everywhere Faces Everywhere: Poems,* Simon & Schuster (New York, NY), 1997, published as *Plays a Dazzler,* Hamish Hamilton (London, England), 1997.

Teri Sloat, *There Was an Old Lady Who Swallowed a Trout,* Holt (New York, NY), 1998.

Sheron Williams, *Imani's Music,* Atheneum (New York, NY), 2000.

Judy Sierra, *The Gift of the Crocodile: A Cinderella Story,* Simon & Schuster (New York, NY), 2000.

Wesley Cartier, *Marco's Run,* Harcourt (San Diego, CA), 2001.

ILLUSTRATOR; WRITTEN BY JANE SARNOFF

A Great Bicycle Book, Scribner (New York, NY), 1973, revised edition, 1976.

The Chess Book, Scribner (New York, NY), 1973.

What? A Riddle Book, Scribner (New York, NY), 1974.

A Riddle Calendar: 1975, Scribner (New York, NY), 1974.

The Code and Cipher Book, Scribner (New York, NY), 1975.

The Monster Riddle Book, Scribner (New York, NY), 1975, revised edition, 1978.

I Know! A Riddle Book, Scribner (New York, NY), 1976.

The 1977 Beastly Riddle Calendar, Scribner (New York, NY), 1976.

A Great Aquarium Book: The Putting-It-Together Guide for Beginners, Scribner (New York, NY), 1977.

Giants! A Riddle Book [and] Mr. Bigperson's Side: A Storybook, Scribner (New York, NY), 1977.

Take Warning: A Book of Superstitions, Scribner (New York, NY), 1978.

Space: A Fact and Riddle Book, Scribner (New York, NY), 1978.

The 1979 Out-of-This-World Riddle Calendar, Scribner (New York, NY), 1979.

A young boy's love of running inspires him to imagine connections with a series of wild creatures known for their speed in Wesley Cartier's **Marco's Run.** *(Illustration by Ruffin.)*

Riddle Calendar, 1980, Scribner (New York, NY), 1979.

Light the Candles! Beat the Drums! A Book of Holidays, Occasions, Celebrations, Remembrances, Occurrences, Special Days, Weeks, and Months, Scribner (New York, NY), 1979.

If You Were Really Superstitious, Scribner (New York, NY), 1980.

That's Not Fair, Scribner (New York, NY), 1980.

Words?! A Book about the Origins of Everyday Words and Phrases, Scribner (New York, NY), 1981.

Adaptations

The Monster Riddle Book was adapted as a filmstrip with cassette, Random House, 1981.

Sidelights

A successful designer and commercial artist based in New York City since 1950, Reynold Ruffins has also produced illustrations for a number of children's books for such authors as Brian Gleeson, Verna Aardema, and Judy Sierra, as well for his solo picture book, *My Brother Never Feeds the Cat.* As a book illustrator, Ruffins is well known for his successful collaborations with author Jane Sarnoff, with whom he worked from the 1970s through the early 1980s. Ruffins and Sarnoff have produced over fifteen books together on such subjects as games and riddles, word origins, and superstitions; their collaborations include *The Code and Cipher Book, Take Warning: A Book of Superstitions,* and their last effort, 1981's *Words?! A Book about the Origins of Everyday Words and Phrases.*

Born in 1930, in New York City, Ruffins grew up in the borough of Queens, and from an early age knew that drawing would be his first love. His father, a salesman who broke the color barrier at New York utility company Con Edison by being the first African American employed there, encouraged Ruffins' efforts by keeping his son supplied with paper and pencils. Art supplies also appeared on birthdays and at Christmas. "I was often challenged in school by kids who wanted to see if I could draw Superman or Captain Marvel," Ruffins once recalled to *SATA*. "I didn't particularly like to do it; I hated the idea of copying, preferring instead to draw from my imagination. But there was the class bully who constantly challenged me, so I did it."

Ruffins' talent gained him entry into New York's High School of Music and Art, which staged an exhibition of his work during his senior year. He even had his first

sale when someone offered him fifty dollars for one of his paintings. After graduation, he enrolled at Cooper Union, where he continued his training in drawing, painting, illustration, and advertising. "I knew that people made a living at art," Ruffins explained to *SATA*, "but at that time I didn't exactly know how it was done. At Cooper Union, we thought of ourselves as fine artists and easel painters. We came to understand the buying and selling of art, and what we had to do to make money in commercial art, but the thought of leaving a place like Cooper Union and going door to door with our portfolios under our arms scared all of us to death. Of course we all had naïve hopes of impressing people and making a million dollars."

To avoid the door-to-door routine, Ruffins and several fellow students decided to found their own studio, and Push Pin Studios was the result, in operation even before Ruffins graduated from Cooper Union. Due to the fresh talent of its founders, Push Pin quickly gained a

Ruffins's acrylic paintings reflect the Indonesian love for color and pattern in **The Gift of the Crocodile: A Cinderella Story,** *written by Judy Sierra.*

reputation for innovation, and published a monthly periodical titled the *Monthly Graphic* (later the *Push Pin Almanac*). Among the artists at work at the studio during the 1950s and 1960s were Milton Glaser, Seymour Chwast, Paul Davis, Isadore Seltzer, and John Alcorn ... and, of course, Ruffins himself. They created everything from book jackets to ads for pharmaceutical companies to graphic projects for major television networks. In the late 1960s, Ruffins supplemented his twelve-hour workdays at Push Pin Studios with a job as an instructor at New York's School for Visual Arts, and went on to become a visiting professor at Syracuse University in the early 1970s. However, these teaching stints never drew him too far from the drawing board.

From his strong, successful base in commercial art, Ruffins branched out into children's books when he was asked to join Simms Taback in illustrating Harry Hartwick's 1970 book *The Amazing Maze*. Soon afterward, he was working alongside author Jane Sarnoff on *A Great Bicycle Book,* the picture book that would begin their eight-year collaboration. Sarnoff would provide Ruffins with a draft of the text; then "we'd meet and discuss it, we'd fight a bit, we'd talk things out—it was a very good arrangement," Ruffins recalled. "If I thought something would make a great visual, she would write around it. My only collaboration in the writing was in terms of discussion. Pen to paper to typewriter is *not* my thing. In fact, Ruffins' experience in creating the text for his one solo picture book, *My Brother Never Feeds the Cat,* more than convinced him that he would stick to illustration and leave the writing to someone else.

Among the books Ruffins enjoyed working on the most during his collaboration with Sarnoff were those that involved monsters and other fantasy characters, such as 1975's *The Monster Riddle Book* and 1977's *Giants! A Riddle Book [and] Mr. Bigperson's Side: A Storybook.* "What I like best about creating monsters is that they can't be drawn right or wrong. They just are what they are."

Ruffins has teamed up with other award-winning authors as well. In 2000, he provided the illustrations for Judy Sierra's *The Gift of the Crocodile: A Cinderella Story.* Essentially a retelling of the traditional tale with an Indonesian twist, *The Gift of the Crocodile* features a young girl who is helped by an unusual fairy godmother, Grandmother Crocodile, to endure the harsh treatment by her stepmother and stepsister, and eventually find a prince to marry. Praising the retelling, reviewers found Ruffins's illustrations a worthy accompaniment to the text. "Ruffins's brightly colored, patterned paintings, with their angular figures and wavy landscapes," noted a *Horn Book* critic, "express and evoke the story's island setting." A *Publishers Weekly* reviewer felt that the illustrator's "primitivist acrylic art ... captures the lush vegetation, sparkling multi-toned waters and the people's patterned clothing while retaining an essential calm and spareness."

Although Ruffins has continued to enjoy his success as a children's book illustrator, he maintains flexibility in his career as an artist. The majority of his illustration work has been in advertising, and he has provided illustrations and design work for such corporations as IBM and Pfizer. Both the demands of providing for his family— which includes wife and fellow artist Joan Young and their four children—and the changing needs of the illustration/graphic design market "made it necessary for me to develop an ability to work in different ways," as Ruffins explained to *SATA*. "An extension of that is learning how to apply these acquired skills to book illustration. Whether it's an advantage or a disadvantage, I've never been locked into one way of working. It sounds immodest, but I have versatility."

Ruffins has helpful advice for budding artists: "Draw all the time. Develop a keen sense of observation. In everything there is something to be learned and remembered. For example, if you study a brick, the brick will change as the sun moves across the sky, it will cast a shadow on one side or another. If you are really interested in art, you should keep your eyes and your mind open."

Biographical and Critical Sources

PERIODICALS

American Artist, September, 1958.

Graphis, no. 177, 1975.

Horn Book, January, 2001, review of *The Gift of the Crocodile: A Cinderella Story,* p. 104.

Publishers Weekly, January 11, 1993, review of *Carnival;* October 31, 1994, review of *Misoso: Once upon a Time Tales from Africa;* October 19, 1998, review of *There Was an Old Lady Who Swallowed a Trout;* December 20, 1999, review of *Running the Road to ABC;* November 13, 2000, review of *The Gift of the Crocodile: A Cinderella Story,* p. 104.

School Library Journal, November, 2000, Susan Hepler, review of *The Gift of the Crocodile: A Cinderella Story,* p. 148.*

S

SABBETH, Carol
See SABBETH, Carol Landstrom

* * *

SABBETH, Carol Landstrom 1957-
(Carol Sabbeth)

Personal

Born March 26, 1957, in Chicago, IL; daughter of Dave (a sheet metal worker) and Eileen (a homemaker) Landstrom; married Alex Sabbeth (a writer and musician), October 7, 1990. *Education:* Southern Illinois University, B.A., 1978. *Politics:* Democrat.

Addresses

Home—40 Garfield St., No. G, Denver, CO 80206. *E-mail*—Sabbeth@aol.com.

Career

Mount Hood Community College, Gresham, OR, instructor in computer graphics, 1992-97; writer. Instructor of teachers at public schools in and around Portland and Corvallis, OR, 1992-97; Saturday Academy, Portland, teacher, 1992-96; Marylhurst University, instructor, 1993-96. Portland Art Museum, visiting artist, 1995-99. *Member:* Computer Using Educators, Technology in Education.

Awards, Honors

Nappa Book Award, 1998, for *Crayons and Computers.*

Writings

AS CAROL SABBETH

Kids' Computer Creations, Williamson Publishing (Charlotte, VT), 1995.

Carol Landstrom Sabbeth

Crayons and Computers, Chicago Review Press (Chicago, IL), 1998.
Monet and the Impressionists for Kids, Chicago Review Press (Chicago, IL), in press.

Sidelights

Carol Landstrom Sabbeth told *SATA:* "I wrote my first book almost by accident. In 1992 I began teaching classes in the Portland area, classes which featured my

191

idea of using the computer to design crafts projects. I taught classes both in the public schools (for teachers) and through a children's after-school enrichment program. For these classes, I designed a collection of arts and crafts projects, all created on the computer. I found that students enjoyed combining their computer skills with their creativity. The projects got kids thinking about the computer in a new way. It wasn't just something for typing or playing computer games.

"I was so pleased with the results in class that I decided to publish a book including the projects, along with interesting information about the personal computer. That enabled me to reach many more children and teachers than I could in my classes. My first book, *Kids' Computer Creations,* was a hit with technology and art teachers, as well as parents and children.

"The success of the book inspired my husband to try it, too. He wrote a book about science and music, drawing on his background as a professional musician. It's called *Rubber Band Banjos and a Java Jive Bass.* We've had fun giving classes based on both books, as well as my second computer art book, which is about color and how it's used by famous artists like Vincent van Gogh, Walt Disney, and the very colorful Mother Nature.

"The purpose of these books is to publicize our approach to teaching. We employ projects to encourage children's imagination and dexterity. Building something really helps in understanding the ideas behind the project. I've also developed a Web site, *Crayons and Computers,* that includes art lessons and fun ways to use a computer as an art tool. Many schools and libraries are linked to this site and use it in their classrooms.

"Currently I'm working on a children's book about Monet and the impressionist painters. Over several months, I've read dozens of books about the artists. I've also visited many museums in the United States and Europe to see their work. As an author, I find that I spend much more time doing research than I do actually writing. My books have also enabled me to meet hundreds of interested parents, teachers, and children. I give classes through the Girl Scouts, Project Head Start, and the public schools.

"My advice to aspiring writers is to try hard to accomplish their dream of being published. It's important to know why their book is needed and who would benefit most from reading it. That way, the writer can find a publisher involved in a particular niche, a publisher who would be helpful in bringing the book to the public. It might take dozens of tries before a publisher is found, so don't give up!"

Biographical and Critical Sources

ON-LINE

Crayons and Computers Home Page, http://members.aol.com/Sabbeth/CrayonsandComputers.html/ (April 15, 2001).

MacHome Interactive, http://www.newerstore.com/ (November 1, 2000), review of *Kids' Computer Creations.*

Monet and the Impressionists for Kids Home Page, http://members.aol.com/sabbeth/monet.html/ (fall, 2001).

*   *   *

SCHULTZ, Betty K(epka) 1932-

Personal

Born December 11, 1932, in Reedsburg, WI; daughter of Edward Anthony and Caroline (Dvorak) Kepka; married Robert R. Schultz; children: Diana, Barbara, Robin, Robert, Jr., Robb. *Education:* High school graduate.

Addresses

Office—Raspberry Press, Ltd., P.O. Box 1, 1989 Grand Detour Rd., Dixon, IL 61021. *E-mail*—raspberrypress@essex1.com.

Career

Worked as a newspaper reporter between 1980 and 1982; Raspberry Press, Ltd., Dixon, IL, publisher and writer, 1988—. Also worked as an administrative secretary.

Writings

Chooch, illustrated by Lori Becicka, Raspberry Press (Dixon, IL), 1990.

Purple Patches, illustrated by Cindy Buffo, Raspberry Press (Dixon, IL), 1995.

The Stairway from Here to There, illustrated by Betty A. Kott, Raspberry Press (Dixon, IL), 1995.

Morn of Mystery, illustrated by Betty A. Kott, Raspberry Press (Dixon, IL), in press.

Work in Progress

A poetry book.

Sidelights

Betty K. Schultz told *SATA:* "My story may be quite different from that of other writers, and I write it to bring hope and encouragement to those people who are attempting to get a start in the business of writing.

"Writing was my hobby since I was eleven years of age. It was only after my fifth and youngest child went out to find his way in the world that serious consideration was given to making writing my career of choice so late in life. With only a high school education, I reached out to see if I would be able to walk in the halls of higher education, but fate had other plans. Cancer soon became my day-to-day instructor.

"At the time, my hopes and plans to obtain a degree in journalism were crushed. The world appeared to me as a gray sphere where all activity ceased. I stood at a precipice where one step could have taken me physically down to where despair chisels away at the dreams of those who give up hope. I prayed for an answer to my question, 'God, what should I do?' After five years of living in the drab uncertainty that cancer provides for its victims, the answer was given to me. I brushed away the fear that had consumed my reasoning and decided to move forward toward my dream of becoming a published writer.

"Time was now more important to me than it had ever been in the past. Did I have the time to go to college? Did I have the time to send my works to publishers for consideration? Perhaps there was not much time left for the usual mailing of correspondence between publisher and writer, so research became the higher education I desperately needed. As a cancer survivor, I took the disease by the horns and rode with it on a successful journey into the field of writing and publishing. Being uncertain about the future, I believed my first book, *Chooch,* might be the last to be completed, but time was on my side. *Chooch* was followed by *Purple Patches* and *The Stairway from Here to There. Morn of Mystery* is near completion. I have also published Barbara Templeton's poetry book, *Just Me, Barbara.* I speak to women's clubs, writer's groups, and at schools.

"My mother was a great inspiration to me, and during my teen years, she used to read my stories, giving me a 'great going' sort of compliment, even though the stories were horribly written. She encouraged me, saying 'Betty, you can do anything you really want to do. Never give up, and never give in.' Perhaps those words gave me the strength to carry on. So I wish to encourage those of you who are beginning your writing journey with the words of my mother, and for those who are writing while suffering from a serious health ailment, 'Never give up!' Your writing can be a great cathartic for you, and it can also give incentive and pleasure to others."

*   *   *

SINGER, Marilyn 1948-

Personal

Born October 3, 1948, in New York, NY; daughter of Abraham (a photoengraver) and Shirley (Lax) Singer; married Steven Aronson (a financial manager), July 31, 1971. *Education:* Attended University of Reading, 1967-68; Queens College of the City University of New York, B.A. (cum laude), 1969; New York University, M.A., 1979. *Hobbies and other interests:* Dog obedience and agility, hiking, theater, avant-garde and independent film, bird watching and caring for animals, tap dancing, singing, Japanese flower arranging, gardening, meditation, and computer adventure games.

Addresses

Home and office—42 Berkeley Pl., Brooklyn, NY 11217.

Marilyn Singer

Career

Daniel S. Mead Literary Agency, New York, NY, editor, 1967; *Where* (magazine), New York, NY, assistant editor, 1969; New York City Public High Schools, New York, NY, teacher of English and speech, 1969-74; writer, 1974—. *Member:* Society of Children's Book Writers and Illustrators, Authors Guild, American Library Association, Mystery Writers of America, Dog Writers Association of America, PEN American Center, Nature Conservancy, Staten Island Companion Dog Training Club, North American Dog Agility Council, Phi Beta Kappa, New York Zoological Society, Brooklyn Botanic Garden, American Museum of Natural History.

Awards, Honors

Children's Choice Award, International Reading Association, 1977, for *The Dog Who Insisted He Wasn't,* 1979, for *It Can't Hurt Forever,* 1988, for *Ghost Host,* and 1991, for *Nine O'Clock Lullaby;* Maud Hart Lovelace Award, Friends of the Minnesota Valley Regional Library (Mankato), 1983, for *It Can't Hurt Forever;* American Library Association (ALA) Best Books for Young Adults citation, 1983, for *The Course of True Love Never Did Run Smooth;* Parents' Choice Award, Parents' Choice Foundation, 1983, for *The Fido Frame-Up; New York Times* best illustrated children's book citation, and *Time* best children's book citation, both 1989, Notable Trade Book in the Language Arts, National Council of Teachers of English 1990, and Texas Bluebonnet Award nomination, 1992, all for *Turtle in July;* South Carolina Book Award nomination, 1992-93, for *Twenty Ways to Lose Your Best Friend;*

Iowa Teen Award nomination, 1993, for *Charmed;* Notable Children's Trade Book in the Field of Social Studies, National Council for the Social Studies and Children's Book Council, 1995, for *Family Reunion,* and 2000, for *On the Same Day in March;* Washington Children's Choice Picture Book Award nomination, 1996, for *Chester the Out-of-Work Dog;* Dorothy Canfield Fisher Award nomination, 1997-98, for *All We Needed to Say;* Society of School Librarians International Best Books, 1997-98, for *Deal with a Ghost,* and 1998-99, for *Bottom's Up!;* Best Books for the Teen Age selection, New York Public Library, 1998, for *Stay True: Short Stories for Strong Girls,* and 2001, for *I Believe in Water: Twelve Brushes with Religion;* Edgar Award nominee, 1998, for *Deal with a Ghost;* Tayshas List selection, 1998-99; for *Deal with a Ghost,* and 2001-02, for *I Believe in Water: Twelve Brushes with Religion;* Popular Paperbacks for Young Adults selection, Young Adult Library Services Association, 2000, for *Stay True: Short Stories for Strong Girls;* Top Ten Science Books for Children selection, *Booklist,* 2000, for *On the Same Day in March.*

Singer collects the work of authors such as Norma Fox Mazer, M. E. Kerr, and Andrea Davis Pinkney in her anthology of stories for young women seeking their own path through life. (Cover illustration by Lisa Desimini.)

Writings

PICTURE BOOKS

The Dog Who Insisted He Wasn't, illustrated by Kelly Oechsli, Dutton, 1976.

The Pickle Plan, illustrated by Steven Kellogg, Dutton, 1978.

Will You Take Me to Town on Strawberry Day?, illustrated by Trinka Hakes Noble, Harper, 1981.

Archer Armadillo's Secret Room, illustrated by Beth Lee Weiner, Macmillan, 1985.

Minnie's Yom Kippur Birthday, illustrated by Ruth Rosner, Harper, 1989.

Nine O'Clock Lullaby, illustrated by Frané Lessac, Harper-Collins, 1991.

The Golden Heart of Winter, illustrated by Robert Rayevsky, Morrow, 1991.

Chester the Out-of-Work Dog, illustrated by Cat Bowman Smith, Holt, 1992.

The Painted Fan, illustrated by Wenhai Ma, Morrow, 1994.

The Maiden on the Moor, illustrated by Troy Howell, Morrow, 1995.

In the Palace of the Ocean King, illustrated by Ted Rand, Atheneum, 1995.

Good Day, Good Night, illustrated by Ponder Goembel, Marshall Cavendish, 1998.

Solomon Sneezes, illustrated by Brian Floca, HarperFestival, 1999.

On the Same Day in March: A Tour of the World's Weather, illustrated by Frané Lessac, HarperCollins, 2000.

The One and Only Me, illustrated by Nicole Rubel, HarperFestival, 2000.

Fred's Bed, illustrated by JoAnn Adinolfi, HarperFestival, 2001.

Didi and Daddy on the Promenade, illustrated by Marie-Louise Gay, Clarion, 2001.

Boo-Hoo, Boo-Boo!, illustrated by Elivia Savadier, Harper-Festival, 2002.

Quiet Night, illustrated by John Manders, Clarion, 2002.

CHILDREN'S FICTION

It Can't Hurt Forever, illustrated by Leigh Grant, Harper, 1978.

Tarantulas on the Brain, illustrated by Leigh Grant, Harper, 1982.

Lizzie Silver of Sherwood Forest (sequel to *Tarantulas on the Brain*), illustrated by Miriam Nerlove, Harper, 1986.

The Lightey Club, illustrated by Kathryn Brown, Four Winds, 1987.

Mitzi Meyer, Fearless Warrior Queen, Scholastic, 1987.

Charmed (fantasy), Atheneum, 1990.

Twenty Ways to Lose Your Best Friend, illustrated by Jeffrey Lindberg, Harper, 1990.

California Demon, Hyperion, 1992.

Big Wheel, Hyperion, 1993.

Josie to the Rescue, illustrated by S. D. Schindler, Scholastic, 1999.

The Circus Lunicus, Holt, 2000.

CHILDREN'S POETRY

Turtle in July, illustrated by Jerry Pinkney, Macmillan, 1989.

In My Tent, illustrated by Emily Arnold McCully, Macmillan, 1992.

It's Hard to Read a Map with a Beagle on Your Lap, illustrated by Clement Oubrerie, Holt, 1993.

Sky Words, illustrated by Deborah K. Ray, Macmillan, 1994.

Family Reunion, illustrated by R. W. Alley, Macmillan, 1994.

Please Don't Squeeze Your Boa, Noah!, illustrated by Clement Oubrerie, Holt, 1995.

The Morgans Dream, illustrated by Gary Drake, Holt, 1995.

All We Needed to Say: Poems about School from Tanya and Sophie, photographs by Lorna Clark, Atheneum, 1996.

Monster Museum, illustrated by Gris Grimly, Hyperion, 2001.

Footprints on the Roof: Poems about the Earth, illustrated by Meilo So, Random House, 2002.

The Company of Crows, illustrated by Linda Saport, Clarion, 2002.

Fireflies at Midnight, illustrated by Ken Robbins, Atheneum, in press.

"SAM AND DAVE" MYSTERY SERIES

Leroy Is Missing, illustrated by Judy Glasser, Harper, 1984.

The Case of the Sabotaged School Play, illustrated by Judy Glasser, Harper, 1984.

A Clue in Code, illustrated by Judy Glasser, Harper, 1985.

The Case of the Cackling Car, illustrated by Judy Glasser, Harper, 1985.

The Case of the Fixed Election, illustrated by Richard Williams, Harper, 1989.

The Hoax on You, illustrated by Richard Williams, Harper, 1989.

"SAMANTHA SPAYED" MYSTERY SERIES

The Fido Frame-Up, illustrated by Andrew Glass, Warne, 1983.

A Nose for Trouble, illustrated by Andrew Glass, Holt, 1985.

Where There's a Will, There's a Wag, illustrated by Andrew Glass, Holt, 1986.

YOUNG ADULT FICTION

No Applause, Please, Dutton, 1977.

The First Few Friends, Harper, 1981.

The Course of True Love Never Did Run Smooth, Harper, 1983.

Horsemaster (fantasy), Atheneum, 1985.

Ghost Host, Harper, 1987.

Several Kinds of Silence, Harper, 1988.

Storm Rising, Scholastic, 1989.

Deal with a Ghost, Holt, 1997.

(Editor) *Stay True: Short Stories for Strong Girls,* Scholastic, 1998.

(Editor) *I Believe in Water: Twelve Brushes with Religion* (short stories), HarperCollins, 2000.

NONFICTION

(Editor and author of introduction) *A History of Avant-Garde Cinema,* American Federation of Arts, 1976.

(Editor and contributor) *New American Filmmakers,* American Federation of Arts, 1976.

The Fanatic's Ecstatic, Aromatic Guide to Onions, Garlic, Shallots and Leeks, illustrated by Marian Perry, Prentice-Hall, 1981.

Exotic Birds (for children), illustrated by James Needham, Doubleday, 1990.

A Wasp Is Not a Bee (for children), illustrated by Patrick O'Brien, Holt, 1995.

Bottoms Up! (for children), illustrated by Patrick O'Brien, Holt, 1998.

Prairie Dogs Kiss and Lobsters Wave (for children) illustrated by Normand Chartier, Holt, 1998.

A Dog's Gotta Do What a Dog's Gotta Do: Dogs at Work (for children), Holt, 2000.

A Pair of Wings (for children), illustrated by Anne Wertheim, Holiday House, 2001.

Tough Beginnings: How Baby Animals Survive (for children), illustrated by Anna Vojtech, Holt, 2001.

OTHER

Also author of several teacher's guides, catalogs, and program notes on films and filmstrips, including Jacob Bronowski's *The Ascent of Man* and David Attenborough's *The Tribal Eye.* Past curator of *SuperFilmShow!,* a series of avant-garde films selected for children. Writer of scripts for the children's television show *The Electric Company.* Contributor of short stories to books, including *Shattered,* edited by Jennifer Armstrong, Knopf. Contributor of poetry to books, including *Food Fight,* edited by Michael J. Rosen, Harcourt Brace, and to periodicals, including *Yes, Archer, Encore, Corduroy, Tamesis,* and *Gyre.* Writer of articles for magazines, including *Click* and *American Kennel Club Gazette.*

Sidelights

Marilyn Singer is an award-winning author of children's books in a wide variety of genres, including fiction and nonfiction picture books, juvenile novels and mysteries, young adult fantasies, and poetry. Among her many characters are a dog who insists he is not a dog, an armadillo, a young heart surgery patient, obsessive Lizzie Silver, Stryker the poltergeist, twin detectives named Sam and Dave—even a dog detective. "People often ask me why I write so many different kinds of things," Singer commented in an essay for the *Something about the Author Autobiography Series* (*SAAS*). "I tell them it's because I have so many different parts to my personality, and each part has a different way of expressing itself. I tell them too that I like to challenge myself so that I'll never be bored."

Singer was born in Manhattan in 1948, but she grew up in North Massapequa, Long Island. As a young girl Singer began writing, partly influenced by her grandmother, with whom she had a close relationship. Poems were and still are her favorite form, but she also experimented with plays, and this early love of the theater eventually carried over into many of her books.

"It seemed in those years that my childhood would remain pretty carefree," Singer once commented.

In 1956 Singer had to undergo heart surgery, but the fact that her parents and doctor kept the truth of her illness from her was more traumatic than the actual surgery. Years later, Singer dealt with her emotional wounds in her 1978 novel, *It Can't Hurt Forever*. As a high school student, she felt unpopular and on the outside of the cliques. In 1965 she began attending Queens College—a branch of the City University of New York—as an English major and education student. College was a more rewarding experience for Singer and a Junior Year Abroad program to England's Reading University would also be a formative experience for the budding writer.

Returning to Queens College, Singer finished her last year there and then moved to an apartment in New York City. She began teaching and became very committed to her job. "I wanted to inspire my students, to make literature come alive for them, to make school a pleasure and not a chore," Singer once recalled. In 1970 she met her future husband, Steve Aronson, who had come to New York from Wisconsin to become an actor, and a year and a half later they were visiting some of Singer's friends in England when they decided to get married.

Singer began her writing career doing teaching guides on film and filmstrips, and, although she enjoyed the work for a while, she was not entirely satisfied. She also began looking into magazine writing. Her article proposals were not very successful, but she did manage to have some of her poetry published. The following year brought a major turning point in Singer's life. She was sitting in the Brooklyn Botanic Garden with a pad of paper and a pen in case she wanted to write a new poem, when she suddenly found herself writing a story instead. Upon seeing this first story, her husband encouraged her to write more, so Singer wrote a number of children's stories featuring animals and mailed them off to publishers. In the meantime, she joined a workshop for unpublished children's authors at Bank Street College and continued writing. Then one day she received a letter from Dutton, telling her that they wanted to publish one of her books—*The Dog Who Insisted He Wasn't*. "I barely got through reading the letter before I let out a scream," Singer once wrote. "A book! A published book! I was about to become an author! A children's author! How extraordinary! How fine! I had a new career."

In *The Dog Who Insisted He Wasn't* Singer tells the story of Konrad the dog, who is absolutely positive that he is not a dog but a person instead. He is lucky enough to find Abigail, who convinces her family to go along with Konrad and treat him as a human. Konrad sits at the table to eat, takes baths, and even goes to school. When the other dogs in the neighborhood decide that they too want to be treated like people, all chaos breaks loose. They are eventually convinced to go back to their carefree lives as dogs, and Konrad compromises by agreeing to pretend he's a dog. A reviewer for the *Bulletin of the Center for Children's Books* praised Singer's portrayal of conversations between animals and humans and further observed that "the adult-child relationships are exemplary."

Singer often features dogs in her work, including the non-fiction book *A Dog's Gotta Do What a Dog's Gotta Do: Dogs at Work* and the poetry collection *It's Hard to Read a Map with a Beagle on Your Lap. Chester the Out-of-Work Dog*, one of Singer's most popular books, features a border collie who loses his job when he and his family move from their farm to the city. Writing in *Booklist*, Ilene Cooper claimed, "This picture book has it all—slapstick comedy, a touch of pathos, and an actual story with a beginning, a middle, and an end."

Singer's writing for younger children has also addressed a variety of people and places in the world. In the 1991 picture book *Nine O'Clock Lullaby*, Singer's text explores what children around the world are doing at the time a child in Brooklyn is going to sleep. Complemented by the illustrations of Frané Lessac, the book provides a simple introduction to time zones and children of other cultures as well as serving as a "rhythmic, pleasing lullaby," according to a *Publishers Weekly* critic. Patricia Dooley, writing in *School Library Journal*, praised the way *Nine O'Clock Lullaby* demonstrates "the connectedness of the inhabitants of our global village." Singer and Lessac again teamed up for *On the Same Day in March*, a picture book look at weather in seventeen locations around the world. For each location, "Singer provides a few lines of lyrical text that vividly create the climate," noted *Booklist*'s Michael Cart, who concluded that the book "doubles as a delightfully agreeable introduction to both climatology and geography." Jody McCoy, writing in *School Library Journal*, called the same title a "useful and engaging addition."

Dramatically different picture books take young readers into the land of myth in *The Golden Heart of Winter*, an original folktale about three sons sent off to bring back a prize to their aging father. "The rich prose and haunting illustrations of this original story give it the texture of a folktale," wrote Miriam Martinez in *Language Arts*. In *The Painted Fan* readers are transported to ancient China where a cruel ruler destroys all the fans in the kingdom after a soothsayer tells him a painted fan will be his undoing. This is a story told with "simplicity and dignity," according to Carolyn Phelan in *Booklist*. Medieval England and verse prove the inspiration for *Maiden on the Moor*, a story about two shepherd brothers who find a young maiden on a snowy moor. Donna L. Scanlon, reviewing the picture book in *School Library Journal*, felt the tale "is sure to spark imaginations as it transcends ordinary fairy-tale conventions." Scanlon also noted that Singer "knows how to distill words into images, and she conveys the bleak beauty of the setting with clarity and precision." Singer presents another original fairy tale in *In the Palace of the Ocean King*, in which traditional roles are reversed: it is the maiden who must save the imprisoned young prince.

Young readers are also taken onto the bustling streets of multi-cultural Brooklyn in *Didi and Daddy on the Promenade,* which is about an eager preschooler and her father on a Sunday morning outing. The two view such sights as the Brooklyn Bridge and Statue of Liberty. Shelle Rosenfeld, writing in *Booklist,* commented that both young and adult readers will "recognize and enjoy Didi's humorous enthusiasm (and Daddy's good-natured participation) as the walk brings anticipated joys and unexpected surprises."

In addition to this rich collection of fiction picture books, Singer has also produced a wide array of nonfiction works for young readers as well as numerous poetry volumes in picture book format. In *Exotic Birds,* Singer presents a "fact-filled but readable introduction" to the subject, according to *Booklist* contributor Leone McDermott. Ellen Dibner, reviewing the same title in *School Library Journal,* concluded that *Exotic Birds* is a "most satisfying book for browsing, general information, and exotic bird watching." Other flying creatures are dealt with in *A Wasp Is Not a Bee* and *A Pair of Wings.* Animal anatomy is the subject of the engaging and often humorous *Bottoms Up!,* a "cheerful book about behinds and their uses," according to *Booklist*'s Ilene Cooper. In *Prairie Dogs Kiss and Lobsters Wave,* Singer shows how animals greet one another. The book, according to *Booklist*'s Hazel Rochman, is noteworthy for its "friendly, immediate text and active, colorful pictures." Of her several poetry books for young readers, Singer's personal favorite is the award-winning *Turtle in July,* "a lovely picture book of poetry that moves through the seasons," according to Janet Hickman in *Language Arts.* Nancy Vasilakis, reviewing *Turtle in July* in *Horn Book,* felt that Singer and illustrator Jerry Pinkney created a "vivid picture book that is visually as well as auditorily pleasing," and that Singer, by using the first person, "captures the essence of each animal."

Singer's first middle grade novel, *It Can't Hurt Forever,* recounts the trauma Singer had herself experienced as a child undergoing surgery. In this fictionalized version of her experience, Singer presents Ellie Simon, who is to enter the hospital for the same corrective heart surgery Singer had. Unlike Singer, however, Ellie is told what is going to happen to her, with the exception of the catheterization she must undergo. When she learns about it, she argues with the doctors and her parents, just as Singer wished she had done. Singer "provides an honest and thorough look at pre- and post-operative care and at the concerns of a girl facing a major trauma," pointed out Karen Harris in *School Library Journal.* A *Kirkus Reviews* contributor concluded that *It Can't Hurt Forever* is "sharp, fast, funny, genuinely serious, and helpfully informative."

Among her other early works for middle grade children are two novels about the obsessions of a young girl named Lizzie Silver. *Tarantulas on the Brain* has ten-year-old Lizzie doing everything she can to earn enough money to buy a pet tarantula. She tries having a junk sale and even works as a magician's assistant to get the necessary money, lying to her mother about what she is doing. In the end, her secret desire and activities are discovered and everyone is much more sympathetic than Lizzie imagined they would be. The pace of *Tarantulas on the Brain* "is fast and exciting; the characters are sufficiently quirky to keep the readers engrossed and narrator Lizzie Silver, 10, wins their affections," asserted a *Publishers Weekly* reviewer. In the sequel to *Tarantulas on the Brain, Lizzie Silver of Sherwood Forest,* Lizzie's new preoccupations include her desires to be one of Robin Hood's merry followers and to learn how to play the harp so she can attend the same music school as her best friend. *Lizzie Silver of Sherwood Forest* is a "funny, touching sequel," stated another *Publishers Weekly* contributor, adding: "This is an adroitly balanced and enjoyable tale about a naive and eager girl."

Singer has also produced a fantasy novel for younger readers, *Charmed.* Miranda, a twelve-year-old with an active imagination, travels to worlds around the galaxy in a quest to collect the "Correct Combination"—a group of characters who must unite to destroy an evil being known as the Charmer. Besides Miranda and the humanoid named Iron Dog, the group includes Bastable, Miranda's invisible feline friend, Rattus, a clever rodent, and the wise cobra-goddess, Naja the Ever-Changing. The fact that the characters manage to work together even though some of them represent animals that are natural enemies was appreciated by *Voice of Youth Advocates* contributor Jennifer Langlois, who stated that the book's plot is "a good way to show young people that just because someone is different doesn't mean they are bad." Sally Estes declared in *Booklist* that in *Charmed* "the various worlds created by Singer are fascinating," and *School Library Journal* reviewer Susan L. Rogers lauded the fantasy's "somewhat surprising and quite satisfying conclusion."

Other middle-grade and juvenile novels by Singer include *Twenty Ways to Lose Your Best Friend, California Demon, Big Wheel, Josie to the Rescue,* and *The Circus Lunicus.* Rosie Rivera opens up the wrong bottle in her mother's magic shop and unleashes a genie in *California Demon,* a book in which "humor keeps the story buoyant, magic gives it sparkle," according to Kathryn Jennings in *Bulletin of the Center for Children's Books.* Wheel Wiggins, a leader of a gang, is trying to organize a Fourth of July Carnival, but is running into problems from a rival in *Big Wheel,* a "surefire story from a popular author," as a writer for *Kirkus Reviews* noted. More magic and fantasy is served up in *The Circus Lunicus* when young Solly's toy lizard turns into a fairy godmother and helps him to learn some home truths about himself, his supposedly dead mother, and his evil stepmother and siblings. "This loony, fast-paced mystery-fantasy . . . is full of surprises and clever plot twists," observed Cart in *Booklist,* "and it's as much fun as a three-ring circus." A *Kirkus Reviews* critic described *The Circus Lunicus* as "luminous and humorous."

Mysteries and young adult fantasy novels are also among Singer's writings. The "Sam and Dave" series stars a pair of twins who solve mysteries, some set in school, some further afield. *A Clue in Code* has the detectives in search of the thief who stole the class trip money. There is an obvious suspect who insists he is innocent, so Sam and Dave embark on an investigation. "Singer's ability to subtly incorporate the necessary facts of the case into the narrative demonstrates her respect for young readers eager for satisfying mysteries they can solve on their own," pointed out a *Booklist* reviewer.

Elements of the supernatural are introduced into Singer's young adult novel *Ghost Host*. Bart Hawkins seems to have an ideal life—he is the quarterback of the high school football team and dates Lisa, the captain of the cheerleading squad. He secretly loves to read, though, and fears that if this gets out he will be labeled a nerd. When he discovers that his new house is haunted by Stryker, a nasty poltergeist, his life is thrown into chaos and he must enlist the help of a friendly ghost and the class brain to pacify Stryker. "*Ghost Host* is above all else fun to read," maintained Randy Brough in *Voice of Youth Advocates*. "Singer's deft introduction of the supernatural into the world of a high school junior, his family, and friends creates headaches for everyone, ghosts included." Ghosts are also at the center of the 1997 title *Deal with a Ghost* in which fifteen-year-old Deal, or Delia, thinks she is terribly sophisticated until she comes face to face with a ghost who knows her name. *Booklist* critic Chris Sherman described this novel as "fast-paced" and "engrossing."

Singer has written several other books for young adult readers, including *The Course of True Love Never Did Run Smooth*, which deals with the difficulties encountered by Becky and Nemi, a girl and boy who, during the production of a high school presentation of *A Midsummer Night's Dream*, find that their friendship is changing from one of childhood buddies to something more sexually charged. "Singer neatly uses Shakespeare's comedic mix-up as a foil for the tangled web woven by her teenage protagonists," noted Estes in a *Booklist* review of the novel. Highlighting Singer's writing style, *Bulletin of the Center for Children's Book* reviewer Zena Sutherland found much merit in *The Course of True Love Never Did Run Smooth*, noting that "the minor characters are sharply defined [and] the familial relations are strongly drawn, with perceptive treatment of the dynamics of the acting group and especially of its gay members." In *Several Kinds of Silence* Singer tackles the theme of prejudice when young Franny falls in love with a Japanese boy, and in *Storm Rising* the author tells an inter-generational tale of lonely Storm, who finds comfort with an older woman who possesses unusual powers. Additionally, Singer has edited volumes of short stories for young adult readers, including *Stay True: Short Stories for Strong Girls* and *I Believe in Water: Twelve Brushes with Religion*.

Singer once mentioned that people often ask her why she writes books for children and young adults instead of for a more mature audience. "I've given them a lot of answers such as 1) Kids are interesting to write about and for; 2) If you understand the child in yourself, you can understand the grown-up better. I want to understand myself better; 3) There's nothing else I know how to do. All of these answers are basically true. But now I think the truest, most honest answer I can give is that I write books for children and young adults because I like to."

Biographical and Critical Sources

BOOKS

Authors of Books for Young People, 3rd edition, edited by Martha E. Ward, Scarecrow Press, 1990.

Children's Literature Review, Volume 48, Gale (Detroit, MI), 1998.

St. James Guide to Young Adult Writers, 2nd edition, edited by Tom Pendergast and Sara Pendergast, St. James (Detroit, MI), 1999.

Something about the Author Autobiography Series, Volume 13, Gale (Detroit, MI).

PERIODICALS

Booklist, May 15, 1983, Sally Estes, review of *The Course of True Love Never Did Run Smooth,* p. 1197; September 15, 1985, review of *A Clue in Code,* p. 140; January 1, 1991, Sally Estes, review of *Charmed,* p. 922; February 1, 1991, Leone McDermott, review of *Exotic Birds,* pp. 1126-1127; May 15, 1991, p. 1806; September 15, 1991, p. 166; October 15, 1992, Ilene Cooper, review of *Chester the Out-of-Work Dog,* p. 425; December 1, 1992, p. 671; May 1, 1994, Carolyn Phelan, review of *The Painted Fan,* p. 1609; June 1, 1997, Chris Sherman, review of *Deal with a Ghost,* pp. 1686-1687; March 15, 1998, Ilene Cooper, review of *Bottoms Up!,* pp. 1242-1243; April 1, 1998, p. 1313; December 1, 1998, Hazel Rochman, review of *Prairie Dogs Kiss and Lobsters Wave,* p. 681; May 1, 1999, p. 1596; February 15, 2000, Michael Cart, review of *On the Same Day in March,* p. 1116; November 15, 2000, p. 640; December 1, 2000, Michael Cart, review of *The Circus Lunicus,* p. 708; April 1, 2001, Shelle Rosenfeld, review of *Didi and Daddy on the Promenade,* p. 1480; May 15, 2001, p. 1755.

Bulletin of the Center for Children's Books, January, 1977, review of *The Dog Who Insisted He Wasn't,* p. 82; May, 1983, Zena Sutherland, review of *The Course of True Love Never Did Run Smooth,* p. 179; February, 1993, Kathryn Jennings, review of *California Demon,* p. 191.

Horn Book, July-August, 1989, p. 478; January-February, 1990, Nancy Vasilakis, review of *Turtle in July,* pp. 82-83; March-April, 1998, p. 223.

Kirkus Reviews, October 15, 1978, review of *It Can't Hurt Forever,* p. 1140; December 1, 1993, review of *Big Wheel,* p. 1529; August 1, 1999, p. 1231; December 1, 1999, p. 1890; September 15, 2000, review of *The Circus Lunicus.*

Language Arts, April, 1990, Janet Hickman, review of *Turtle in July,* pp. 430-431; January, 1992, Miriam Martinez, review of *The Golden Heart of Winter,* p. 67.

Library Journal, November, 1992, p. 78.

Publishers Weekly, July 9, 1982, review of *Tarantulas on the Brain,* p. 49; June 1, 1984, p. 65; February 22,

1985, p. 158; June 27, 1986, review of *Lizzie Silver of Sherwood Forest,* pp. 91-92; April 24, 1987, p. 71; May 12, 1989, p. 291; April 13, 1990, p. 64; March 1, 1991, review of *Nine O'Clock Lullaby,* p. 72; July 12, 1991, p. 66; October 12, 1992, p. 78; June 14, 1993, p. 70; April 18, 1994, p. 62; August 29, 1994, p. 78; January 25, 1999, p. 96; January 24, 2000, review of *On the Same Day in March,* p. 311; October 23, 2000, p. 76; February 12, 2001, p. 210.

School Library Journal, September, 1978, Karen Harris, review of *It Can't Hurt Forever,* p. 149; December, 1982, pp. 68-69; August, 1983, Joan McGrath, review of *The Course of True Love Never Did Run Smooth,* p. 80; May, 1984, p. 102; May, 1985, p. 110; September, 1985, p. 149; December, 1985, pp. 82-83; October, 1986, p. 83; May, 1987, p. 104; September, 1987, pp. 182-183; August, 1989, p. 132; November, 1989, p. 99; June, 1990, p. 126; December, 1990, Susan L. Rogers, review of *Charmed,* p. 111; June, 1991, Ellen Dibner, review of *Exotic Birds,* p. 120; July, 1991, Patricia Dooley, review of *Nine O'Clock Lullaby,* p. 64; December, 1991, p. 102; January, 1993, p. 84; July, 1993, p. 95; April, 1995, Donna L. Scanlon, review of *The Maiden on the Moor,* p. 146; June, 1997, p. 128; June, 1998, p. 122; July, 1998, p. 91; September, 1999, p. 206; April, 2000, Jody McCoy, review of *On the Same Day in March,* p. 126; July, 2000, p. 87; November, 2000, p. 162; December, 2000, p. 148; February, 2001, p. 115; May, 2001, p. 135.

Voice of Youth Advocates, August, 1985, p. 164; June, 1986, p. 83; June, 1987, Randy Brough, review of *Ghost Host,* p. 83; December, 1990, Jennifer Langlois, review of *Charmed,* p. 32.

ON-LINE

Commitment, http://www.commitment.com/ (June 22, 2001).

Marilyn Singer, Children's Writer, http://www.users.aol.com/writerbabe/singer/ (June 22, 2001).

—*Sketch by J. Sydney Jones*

*   *   *

SNYDER, Anne 1922-2001

OBITUARY NOTICE—See index for *SATA* sketch: Born October 3, 1922, in Boston, MA; died February 2, 2001, in San Juan Capistrano, CA. Author. Snyder was the author of several books for children and young adults. Also a writer for such television shows as *I Love Lucy Show* and *Hollywood Squares,* she focused her other writings on serious issues faced by her young audiences. Snyder's books include *50,000 Names for Jeff, Nobody's Family, Old Man and the Mule, Goodbye, Paper Doll,* and *You Want to Be What?* In 1969 her *50,000 Names for Jeff* was named one of the ten best children's books by the Child Study Association of America.

OBITUARIES AND OTHER SOURCES:

PERIODICALS

Los Angeles Times, February 13, 2001, p. B6.
Washington Post, February 16, 2001, p. B7.

*   *   *

SNYDER, Paul A. 1946-

Personal

Born January 19, 1946, in New Enterprise, PA; son of Jacob J. (a dairy farmer) and Jenny D. (a homemaker; maiden name, Stone) Snyder; married Janet K. Whitfield (an office worker), November 5, 1964; children: Robin D. (son), Tracy S. Snyder Keith. *Religion:* Protestant.

Addresses

Home—317 Snyder Creek Rd., New Enterprise, PA 16664.

Career

Writer.

Writings

Courageous Journey, Royal Fireworks Publishing (Unionville, NY), 2000.
The Trail of the North Star, Royal Fireworks Publishing (Unionville, NY), in press.

Work in Progress

Wrestling the Wind, "a young adult novel about a girl growing up during the Great Depression, 1933-41."

Sidelights

Paul A. Snyder told *SATA:* "My first professional writing involved term papers for upperclassmen in high school. Although she did not mention it at the time, apparently our senior English teacher knew a lot more about personal style than we did. Several years after graduation she told me that the moment I entered her class she knew where those papers had been coming from. She then strongly encouraged me to keep writing. Although I didn't get started again until thirty years later, her words never left me. In 1994 I completed a correspondence course for writers. Less than a year later I signed a contract for my first book with only the second publisher to read it.

"In my writing I try to give my lead characters a strong set of moral values, something that is sadly missing in much of the printed material available to young people. I have always enjoyed history and adventure, so it has been natural for me to combine these in novels for young adults. As a young daydreamer, I practically wore out North American maps plotting the courses of lakes and rivers that would take me by canoe to the great wilderness adventure.

"Among my many hobbies woodworking tops the list. It should come as no surprise, then, that designing, building, and paddling cedar-strip canoes and kayaks takes up much of my spare time. When possible I spend two days a week paddling one of my wooden kayaks on nearby Lake Raystown. The rest of my spare time is spent reading.

"Writers who have inspired me greatly include Wilson Rawls in *Where the Red Fern Grows* and *Summer of the Monkeys,* Charles Portias in *True Grit,* Jean Craighead George in *My Side of the Mountain,* almost anything written by James Michener or Mark Twain, and everything written by Patrick McManus."*

T

TANSELLE, Eve 1933-
(Eve Robinson)

Personal

Born October 3, 1933, in Louisville, KY; daughter of John Thomas (a railway clerk) and Georgia (a homemaker; maiden name, Armstrong) Frederick; married David Teager Robinson, Jr., May 19, 1956 (divorced, December 7, 1971); married Robert E. Tanselle (an advertizing executive), June 12, 1993; children: (first marriage) Douglas Lee, Glenn Thomas, Mark David. *Education:* Attended University of Louisville Art Center. *Politics:* Republican. *Religion:* Presbyterian.

Addresses

Home—421 Glen Abbey Lane, Debary, FL 32713. *E-mail*—bobeve@webtv.net.

Career

L. M. Berry, Louisville, KY, illustrator, 1952-58; Neltors, Fort Lauderdale, FL, art director, 1972-90; American Media Group, Boca Raton, FL, graphic artist, 1990-93; Sutherland & Rand, Boca Raton, graphic artist, 1993-95. Creations of Eve, graphic artist. Presbyterian Women, president, 1998-2001. Executive board artist, du Pont Manual. *Member:* Debary Art League (vice-president).

Awards, Honors

Wilberding Art Award; good citizenship pilgrimage award, Daughters of the American Revolution.

Illustrator

Margriet Ruurs, *Virtual Maniac,* Maupin House (Gainesville, FL), 2000.

Illustrator of *Fun with Feelings,* by Jane Land, 2000. Also illustrator of book covers. Some work appears under the name Eve Robinson.

Work in Progress

Research on illustrating wild animals.

Sidelights

Eve Tanselle told *SATA:* "I have always enjoyed doing illustrations, especially for children's books. When asked to do the cover of Maity Schrecengost's book *Panther Girl,* I used my nine-year-old granddaughter Amy as my model. Her age and coloring fit the description of the heroine Mariah, right down to the freckles on her nose!"

*　　*　　*

TCHANA, Katrin Hyman 1963-

Personal

Born May 2, 1963, in Malden, MA; daughter of Harris (an engineer) and Trina (an illustrator; maiden name, Schart) Hyman; married Eugene Tchana (a computer systems administrator), 1988; children: Michou Tchana Hyman, Xavier Tchana Tchatchoua. *Education:* Attended Bennington College, 1979-81; College of the Atlantic, B.A., 1983; Columbia University, M.A., 1990. *Politics:* "Ecofeminist." *Hobbies and other interests:* Tai chi, gardening.

Addresses

Home—4711 Route 113, Thetford Center, VT 05075. *E-mail*—ke.tchana@valley.net.

Career

U.S. Peace Corps, Washington, DC, volunteer teacher in Cameroon, 1985-88; teacher of English as a second language, 1988-98; Headrest (substance abuse treatment center), Lebanon, NH, hotline counselor, 1998-2000; Clara Martin Center (community mental health center), Randolph, VT, emergency worker, 2000—. Open Fields School, member of board of directors; volunteer for a domestic violence hotline.

Writings

Anastasia Reading, Golden Books (New York, NY), 1997.
(With Louise Tchana Pami) *Oh No, Toto!,* illustrated by Colin Bootman, Scholastic (New York, NY), 1998.
(Reteller) *The Serpent Slayer: and Other Stories of Strong Women,* illustrated by Trina Schart Hyman, Little, Brown (Boston, MA), 2000.
Sense Pass King, illustrated by Trina Schart Hyman, Holiday House (New York, NY), 2001.

Work in Progress

A Girl's Book of Goddesses (tentative title), publication expected in 2003; research on how to have "out of body" experiences.

*　　*　　*

THIELE, Colin (Milton) 1920-

Personal

Surname pronounced "TEE-lee"; born November 16, 1920, in Eudunda, South Australia; son of Carl Wilhelm (a farmer) and Anna (Wittwer) Thiele; married Rhonda Gill (a teacher and artist), March 17, 1945; children: Janne Louise, Sandra Gwenyth. *Education:* University of Adelaide, B.A., 1941, Dip. Ed., 1947; Adelaide Teachers College, diploma, 1942.

Addresses

Home—Endeavour Ln., Dayboro, Queensland 4521, Australia.

Career

Writer. South Australian Education Department, English teacher and senior master at high school in Port Lincoln, 1946-55, senior master at high school in Brighton, 1956; Wattle Park Teachers College, Wattle Park, South Australia, lecturer, 1957-61, senior lecturer in English, 1962-63, vice principal, 1964, principal, 1965-72; Murray Park College of Advanced Education, director, 1973; Wattle Park Teachers Centre, Wattle Park, director, 1973-80. Commonwealth Literary Fund lecturer on Australian literature; speaker at conferences on literature and education in Australia and the United States. *Military service*—Royal Australian Air Force, 1942-45. *Member:* Australian College of Education (fellow), Australian Society of Authors (council member, 1965—; president, 1987-90), English Teachers Association (president, 1957), South Australian Fellowship of Writers (president, 1961).

Awards, Honors

W. J. Miles Poetry Prize, 1944, for *Progress to Denial;* Commonwealth Jubilee literary competitions, first prize in radio play section, for "Edge of Ice," and first prize in radio feature section, both 1951; World Short Story Quest, South Australian winner, 1952; Fulbright scholar in United States and Canada, 1959-60; Grace Leven Poetry Prize, 1961, for *Man in a Landscape;* Silver Pencil Award (the Netherlands), for *Storm Boy;* Commonwealth Literary Fund fellowship, 1967-68; Honours List, Hans Anderson Award, 1972, Certificate of Honour, International Board on Books for Young People, and Highly Commended citation, Children's Book Council of Australia (CBCA), all for *Blue Fin;* Mystery Writers of America citation, for *The Fire in the Stone;* Visual Arts Board award, 1975, for *Magpie Island;* Austrian State Prize for Children's Books, 1979, for *The SKNUKS,* and 1986, for *Pinquo;* Book of the Year award, CBCA, 1982, for *The Valley Between;* Book of the Year, Blind Mission International, for *The Seeds Inheritance;* Australian Family Award for Children's Books, for *Jodie's Journey;* Book of the Year, Australian Christian Literature Society, for *Martin's Mountain;* Wilderness Society Award, for contributions to environmental writing in Australia; Special Award, New South Wales Premier's Literary Awards; Dromkeen Medal; numerous awards commendations from Australian Children's Book Council, American Library Association, Mystery Writers of America, and the Miles Franklin Award (Australia). Companion of the Order of Australia, 1977, for services to literature and education.

Writings

FOR CHILDREN

The State of Our State (textbook), Rigby (Adelaide, Australia), 1952.
The Sun on the Stubble (novel), Rigby (Adelaide, Australia), 1961.
Gloop the Gloomy Bunyip, illustrations by John Baily, Jacaranda, 1962, expanded as *Gloop the Bunyip,* illustrations by Helen Sallis, Rigby (Adelaide, Australia), 1970.
Storm Boy, illustrations by John Baily, Rigby (Adelaide, Australia), 1963, Rand McNally (Chicago, IL), 1966, new edition with illustrations by Robert Ingpen, Rigby (Adelaide, Australia), 1974, film edition with photographs by David Kynoch, Rigby, 1976, original edition reprinted, Harper (New York, NY), 1978.
February Dragon (novel), Rigby (Adelaide, Australia), 1965, Harper (New York, NY), 1976.
The Rim of the Morning Six Stories, Rigby (Adelaide, Australia), 1966, published as *Storm Boy and Other Stories,* Rigby (Adelaide, Australia), 1986.
Mrs. Munch and Puffing Billy, illustrations by Nyorie Bungey, Rigby (Adelaide, Australia), 1967, Tri-Ocean, 1968.
Yellow-Jacket Jock, illustrations by Clifton Pugh, F. W. Cheshire (Melbourne, Australia), 1969.
Blue Fin (novel), illustrations by Roger Haldane, Rigby (Adelaide, Australia), 1969, Harper (New York, NY), 1974.

Flash Flood, illustrations by Jean Elder, Rigby (Adelaide, Australia), 1970.

Flip Flop and Tiger Snake, illustrations by Jean Elder, Rigby (Adelaide, Australia), 1970.

The Fire in the Stone, Rigby (Adelaide, Australia) 1973, Harper (New York, NY), 1974, film edition, Puffin (New York, NY), 1983.

Albatross Two, Rigby (Adelaide, Australia), 1974, published as *Fight against Albatross Two,* Harper (New York, NY), 1976.

Uncle Gustav's Ghosts, Rigby (Adelaide, Australia), 1974.

Magpie Island, illustrations by Roger Haldane, Rigby (Adelaide, Australia), 1974, Puffin (New York, NY), 1981.

The Hammerhead Light, Rigby (Adelaide, Australia), 1976, Harper (New York, NY), 1977.

Storm Boy Picture Book, photographs by David Kynoch, Rigby (Adelaide, Australia), 1976.

The Shadow on the Hills, Rigby (Adelaide, Australia), 1977, Harper (New York, NY), 1978.

The SKNUKS, illustrations by Mary Milton, Rigby (Adelaide, Australia), 1977.

River Murray Mary, illustrations by Robert Ingpen, Rigby (Adelaide, Australia), 1979.

Ballander Boy, photographs by David Simpson, Rigby (Adelaide, Australia), 1979.

Chadwick's Chimney, illustrations by Robert Ingpen, Methuen (Australia), 1980.

The Best of Colin Thiele, Rigby (Adelaide, Australia), 1980.

Tanya and Trixie, photographs by David Simpson, Rigby (Adelaide, Australia), 1980.

Thiele Tales, Rigby (Adelaide, Australia), 1980.

The Valley Between, Rigby (Adelaide, Australia), 1981.

Little Tom Little, photographs by David Simpson, Rigby (Adelaide, Australia), 1981.

Songs for My Thongs, Rigby (Adelaide, Australia), 1982.

The Undercover Secret, Rigby (Adelaide, Australia), 1982.

Pinquo, Rigby (Adelaide, Australia), 1983.

Coorong Captive, Rigby (Adelaide, Australia), 1985.

Seashores and Shadows, Walter McVitty (Montville, Australia), 1985, published as *Shadow Shark,* Harper (New York, NY), 1988.

Farmer Schulz's Ducks, Walter McVitty (Montville, Australia), 1986, Harper (New York, NY), 1988.

Shatterbelt, Walter McVitty (Montville, Australia), 1987.

Klontarf, Weldon (Chatswood, New South Wales, Australia), 1988.

The Ab-Diver, Horwitz, Grahame (Melbourne, Australia), 1988.

Jodie's Journey, Walter McVitty (Montville, Australia), 1988, Harper (New York, NY), 1990.

Stories Short and Tall, Weldon (Chicago, IL), 1989.

Poems in My Luggage, Omnibus, 1989.

Danny's Egg (novelization of a television feature) Angus & Robertson (Sydney, Australia), 1989, published as *Rotten Egg Paterson to the Rescue,* Harper (New York, NY), 1991.

Farmer Pelz's Pumpkins, illustrated by Lucinda Hunnam, Walter McVitty (Montville, Australia), 1990.

Emma Keppler: Two Months in Her Life, illustrated by Lyn Liebelt, Walter McVitty (Montville, Australia), 1991.

Speedy, Omnibus, 1991.

The Australian ABC, illustrated by Wendy DePaauw, Weldon Kids (Australia), 1992.

The Australian Mother Goose, illustrated by Wendy DePaauw, Weldon Kids (Australia), 1992.

Aftershock: The Sequel to Shatterbelt, Walter McVitty (Montville, Australia), 1992.

Charlie Vet's Pet, illustrated by Michael Wright, Macmillan Australia, 1992.

Timmy, Walter McVitty (Montville, Australia), 1993.

Martin's Mountain, Lutheran Publishing, 1993.

The March of Mother Duck, Walter McVitty (Montville, Australia), 1993.

Gemma's Christmas Eve, Open Book, 1994.

Reckless Rhymes, Walter McVitty (Montville, Australia), 1994.

(With Max Fatchen and Craig Smith) *Tea for Three,* Moondrake, 1994.

The Australian Mother Goose II, Weldon Kids (Australia), 1994.

Brahminy: The Story of a Boy and a Sea Eagle, Walter McVitty (Montville, Australia), 1995.

High Valley, Walter McVitty (Montville, Australia), 1996.

The Mystery of the Black Pyramid, Walter McVitty (Montville, Australia), 1996.

Dangerous Secret, Walter McVitty (Montville, Australia), 1997.

Landslide, Lothian (Melbourne, Australia), 1997.

The Monster Fish, illustrated by Craig Smith, Omnibus, 1999.

Wendy's Whale, Lothian (Melbourne, Australia), 1999.

Pannikin and Pinta, Lothian (Melbourne, Australia), 2000.

The Sea Caves, Lothian (Melbourne, Australia), 2000.

Swan Song, Lothian (Melbourne, Australia), 2001.

Thiele's children's books have been translated into numerous languages, including German, Russian, French, Italian, Chinese, Japanese, Spanish, Afrikaans, Swedish, Finnish, Danish, Dutch, and Czechoslovakian.

FOR CHILDREN; "PITCH, POTCH, AND PATCH" SERIES

Patch Comes Home, Reading Rigby (Adelaide, Australia), 1982.

Potch Goes down the Drain, Reading Rigby (Adelaide, Australia), 1984.

Pitch the Pony, Reading Rigby (Adelaide, Australia), 1984.

POETRY; FOR ADULTS

Progress to Denial, Jindyworobak, 1945.

Splinters and Shards, Jindyworobak, 1945.

The Golden Lightning, Jindyworobak, 1951.

Man in a Landscape, Rigby (Adelaide, Australia), 1960.

In Charcoal and Conte, Rigby (Adelaide, Australia), 1966.

Selected Verse (1940-1970), Rigby (Adelaide, Australia), 1970.

EDITOR

Jindyworobak Anthology (verse), Jindyworobak, 1953.

(And annotator) *Looking at Poetry* (textbook), Longmans, Green, 1960.

(With Ian Mudie) *Australian Poets Speak,* Rigby (Adelaide, Australia), 1961.

(With Greg Branson) *One-Act Plays for Secondary Schools,* Rigby (Adelaide, Australia), Books 1-2, 1962, one volume edition of Books 1-2, 1963, Book 3, 1964, revised edition of Book 1 published as *Setting the Stage,* 1969, revised edition of Book 2 published as *The Living Stage,* 1970.

Favourite Australian Stories, Rigby (Adelaide, Australia), 1963.

(And author of commentary and notes) *Handbook to Favourite Australian Stories,* Rigby (Adelaide, Australia), 1964.

(With Greg Branson) *Beginners, Please* (anthology), Rigby (Adelaide, Australia), 1964.

(With Greg Branson) *Plays for Young Players* (for primary schools), Rigby (Adelaide, Australia), 1970.

FOR ADULTS

Heysen of Hahndorf (biography), Rigby (Adelaide, Australia), 1968, Tri-Ocean, 1969.

Barossa Valley Sketchbook, illustrations by Jeanette McLeod, Tri-Ocean, 1968.

Labourers in the Vineyard (novel), Rigby (Adelaide, Australia), 1970.

Coorong, photographs by Mike McKelvey, Rigby (Adelaide, Australia), 1972, illustrated by Barbara Leslie, Wakefield Press, 1986.

Range without Man: The North Flinders, photographs by Mike McKelvey, Rigby (Adelaide, Australia), 1974.

The Little Desert, photographs by Jocelyn Burt, Rigby (Adelaide, Australia), 1975.

Grains of Mustard Seed, South Australia Education Department, 1975.

Heysen's Early Hahndorf, Rigby (Adelaide, Australia), 1976.

The Bight, photographs by Mike McKelvey, Rigby (Adelaide, Australia), 1976.

Lincoln's Place, illustrations by Robert Ingpen, Rigby (Adelaide, Australia), 1978.

Maneater Man: Alf Dean, the World's Greatest Shark Hunter, Rigby (Adelaide, Australia), 1979.

The Seeds Inheritance, Lutheran Publishing, 1986.

South Australia Revisited, illustrations by Charlotte Balfour, Rigby (Adelaide, Australia), 1986.

Something to Crow About, illustrations by Rex Milstead, Commonwealth Bank, 1986.

A Welcome to Water, photographs by David Simpson and Ted James, Wakefield Press, 1986.

Ranger's Territory: The Story of Frank Woerle, Angus & Robertson (Sydney, Australia), 1987.

With Dew on My Boots: A Childhood Revisited, Walter McVitty (Montville, Australia), 1997.

Thiele's poetry and short stories have appeared in many anthologies and journals; also contributor of articles and reviews to periodicals. National book reviewer for Australian Broadcasting Commission.

PLAYS

Burke and Wills (verse; produced at Adelaide Radio Drama Festival, 1949), published in *On the Air,* edited by P. R. Smith, Angus & Robertson (London, England), 1959.

Edge of Ice (verse), produced on radio, 1952.

The Shark Fishers, produced, 1954.

Edward John Eyre (verse), produced at Adelaide Radio Drama Festival, 1962.

Author of other verse plays for radio, and radio and television features, documentaries, children's serials, and schools broadcast programs.

Adaptations

Storm Boy and *Blue Fin* were adapted as feature films by the South Australian Film Corporation, 1976 and 1978, respectively; *The Fire in the Stone* was adapted as a television feature, South Australian Film Corporation, 1983; *The Sun on the Stubble, The Shadow on the Hills, The Valley Between,* and *Uncle Gustav's Ghosts* were adapted as a six-hour television mini-series by an Australian-German consortium, 1996.

Sidelights

A poet, novelist, biographer, and playwright, the prolific Australian author Colin Thiele is responsible for an impressive array of award-winning books for young people that includes *Storm Boy, Jodie's Journey,* and *The Fire in the Stone.* While holding down a succession of positions in teaching and educational administration from the time he left the Royal Australian Air Force at the end of World War II, Thiele has become an active force in all areas of children's publishing, from textbooks to plays to poetry anthologies to picture books to young adult novels. As an essayist commented of his more recent work in *St. James Guide to Young Adult Writers,* "Thiele's clarity and vigor as a skillful storyteller for the young has not diminished. His work continues to reflect a belief in the human spirit and in the peaceable coexistence of people and nature."

Thiele has always taken to heart the writer's dictum, "Write what you know." As a result, most of his books are set in South Australia, "on the coastline, the River Murray, the opal fields, the desert, and in the German communities where my ancestors settled," as he once explained in an essay for *Fifth Book of Junior Authors and Illustrators.* The son of first-generation Australians of German parentage, he was born in 1920 in the town of Eudunda, near South Australia's Barossa Valley. Raised within that region's strong German culture, Thiele and his three sisters and brother grew up with the hymns of the Lutheran church, sausages drying in the cellar, and a regular schedule of farm chores. As he noted in an essay for *Something about the Author Autobiography Series* (SAAS), his early life was "basically rural—farm and township, fallow and stubble, week-day and Sunday ... yabby creek and red-gum hillock, candlelight and oven bread, mealtime grace and family Bible, Christening font and graveside coffin." Thiele ranged far and wide about the countryside in his leisure time, a factor to which he attributes his lifelong interest in the environment. Much of his children's fiction deals with environmentalist or conservationist themes.

Thiele began primary school in the town of Julia at the age of four, and he once recalled that the educational experience affected him "profoundly." By the time he was ten he had read all twenty-five books in the local library, and by eleven he had written what he termed "a massive pirate novel called 'Blackbeard.'" After graduating from high school in the town of Kapunda, he enrolled at the University of Adelaide in 1936. There he met and worked with other writers, read voraciously, and in 1939, worked as a junior teacher in the education department. He also began to publish poetry, which was published by a local Adelaide press. In 1940, he went on to teachers' college and earned his certification as a high school teacher.

World War II disrupted Thiele's writing career; putting down the pen, he joined the war effort as a member of the Royal Australian Air Force and served in New Guinea and other islands north of Australia. In 1945, he married and took a job as a high school English teacher. During the next several decades he advanced in his education career and in 1973 took a position as director of Wattle Park Teachers' Centre, retiring in 1981 due to the advance of rheumatoid arthritis that had plagued him for many years. Since leaving full-time employment, Thiele has had to battle his condition in order to continue writing and working with young people by speaking at schools, colleges, and other groups, and has also done numerous radio broadcasts in his native Australia. A life-sized sculpture of Thiele has been placed in the civic gardens of his birthplace, Eudunda. It shows him seated with a notebook and pencil, and with a pelican sitting at his side.

In 1961, with four volumes of poetry already under his belt, Thiele published his first children's novel, the classic *The Sun on the Stubble,* which has remained in continuous publication since. Written while its author was a Fulbright fellow in the United States, the novel focuses on the German-Australian culture of his childhood. Calling it "episodic in form—a series of related pictures and incidents held together by a simple plot with a boy in the centre," in his *SAAS* essay, *The Sun on the Stubble* is "partly a book of boyhood, partly of adulthood." Other books that would focus on Thiele's cultural origins include *Uncle Gustav's Ghosts, The Shadow on the Hills, The Valley Between,* and *Emma Keppler,* a 1991 historical novel about a young woman's coming of age. Reviewing *Emma Keppler* in *Magpies,* Jenni Connor praised Thiele's ability to "vividly convey . . . the hardships and rhythms of rural existence and the humorous and sometimes dramatic social interactions of a small community."

Storm Boy, Thiele's next book for young readers, is the story of a boy raised in an isolated region in South Australia. The story focuses on Storm Boy, who lives with his father, Hide-away Tom, in a hut in the wilderness, their only friend an aborigine. The boy tends to three orphaned pelicans, one of which becomes his constant companion, until one day it is shot by hunters. In the opinion of a *Bulletin of the Center for Children's Books* contributor, *Storm Boy* carries the "perennial

appeal of a tender, if sad, pet story," with an "appeal to young conservationists." Made into a feature film in 1976 by the South Australian Film Corporation, the story helped typecast its author as an environmental writer. His 1974 novel *Albatross Two* would continue this tradition in its portrayal of the dangers inherent in offshore oil drilling, while 1993's *Timmy,* intended for younger readers, is about an orphaned boy named Denny who discovers compassion while taking care of a tiny wild hare who has lost his family. Praising the novel for its realistic characters and its depiction of the natural world as full of both beauty and tragedy, *Magpies* reviewer Virginia Lowe noted that "There are few good animal stories written today and this one is true and horrifying and warm."

More humorous but equally affecting is *Rotten Egg Paterson to the Rescue,* released in Australia as *Danny's Egg.* Eleven-year-old Danny earns a new nickname when he finds an emu egg and attempts to get it to hatch by wearing it to school inside his shirt. In a review for *School Library Journal,* contributor Yvonne A. Frey praised the story for offering "a glimpse of life at home and at school in another part of the world," and for couching within it "a gentle message on the importance and beauty of nature." Equally enthusiastic, Carolyn Phelan noted in *Booklist* that "Animal lovers will warm to Thiele's tale."

February Dragon, published in Australia in 1965, is the story of the destruction of a farm family's home and miles of surrounding bush country by fire. *Blue Fin,* also made into a feature film, introduces readers to a boy who seems hopelessly untalented until he discovers his niche as a deep-sea tuna fisherman. *The Fire in the Stone* is about the struggles of a boy living a harsh life among the Australian opal fields at Cooper Pedy, where, Thiele once recalled, "the countryside looked like a moon landscape—dusty, waterless, and pockmarked with mines and mullock heaps." And in *Jodie's Journey,* which Thiele published in 1988, a pre-teen equestrian is forced from the saddle by juvenile rheumatoid arthritis, feeling she has lost everything important in her life until a threat to her horse's life changes everything. As Betsy Hearne noted in her *Bulletin of the Center for Children's Books* review of *Jodie's Journey,* the compelling story informs readers "about the disease that keeps the author in a hospital while he writes his novels."

The Hammerhead Light deals with the relationship between a young girl and an elderly seaman, while the historical novel *River Murray Mary* focuses on the establishment of irrigation settlements by Australian soldiers returning home after World War I, as seen through the eyes of a resourceful young girl living with her father in their small farm on the banks of the Murray River. Another historical work, 1997's *Landslide,* finds Trudi and Peter Swan thrown from the saddle during a peaceful Sunday morning ride; the car that spooked their horses is carrying land developers who intend to dam a local creek and change the Swan's sleepy rural community's landscape for the worse. Noting that "to read a Colin Thiele novel is to see a practiced professional in action," *Magpies* contributor John Murray noted that in *Landslide* the author "keep[s] the narrative moving [by] foreshadowing events, offering false scents to lead readers into wrong guesses, and using every detail of the story to drive the plot. Frequent moments of fun ... give the narrative a lift; short chapters and plenty of action will keep reluctant readers interested too."

Ballander Boy, Tanya and Trixie, and *The SKNUKS* are intended for very young readers, as is *The March of Mother Duck,* a true tale about a duck family whose trip through the streets of Adelaide, Australia, was supervised by the local police force. Dubbing it a "captivating story," Mandy Cheetham praised Thiele in her *Magpies* review, noting the "deft turn of phrase" and "light touch of humor" used in relating this tale of wildlife adaptation.

Thiele once commented on his responsibilities as a writer for children. "I have often argued that all writers for children are teachers whether they are aware of it or not.... But if I teach when I write I sincerely hope that I don't also preach." He also commented on writing in general: "One of the tasks of the writer is ... to 'hold the mirror up to Nature, to reveal humanity to humanity, to comment on the variousness of the human condition.' And although society and the environment in which people live have changed beyond recognition, and will continue to do so, human beings are still human beings. They still show human strengths and human weaknesses—kindness, cruelty, love, malice, wisdom, stupidity, and all the rest. They still suffer loneliness and rejection, still respond to love and compassion, still rise to heights of altruism and nobility, still stoop to depths of pettiness, perfidy, and meanness. In exploring these themes, it doesn't much matter whether the writer uses settings in Sleepy Hollow or at the Crossroads of the World—wherever they are. The universal verities of life can be revealed anywhere because they reside in the hearts of human beings, not in facades of city streets or ephemeral houses. It is to reflect these convictions that I hold up my particular mirror—unpolished and inadequate as it may be."

Biographical and Critical Sources

BOOKS

Contemporary Literary Criticism, Volume 17, Gale (Detroit, MI), 1981.

Contemporary Poets, 2nd edition, St. Martin's Press (New York, NY), 1976.

Holtze, Sally Holmes, editor, *Fifth Book of Junior Authors and Illustrators,* H. W. Wilson (New York, NY), 1983.

McVitty, Walter, *Innocence and Experience,* Nelson (London, England), 1981.

Oxford Companion to Australian Literature, Oxford University Press (Melbourne, Australia), 1985.

Prentice, Jeffrey, and Bettina Bird, *Dromkeen: A Journey into Children's Literature,* J. M. Dent (London, England), 1987.

St. James Guide to Young Adult Writers, 2nd edition, St. James Press (Detroit, MI), 1999.

Something about the Author Autobiography Series, Volume 2, Gale (Detroit, MI), 1986.

Twentieth-Century Children's Writers, 3rd edition, St. James Press (Detroit, MI), 1989.

PERIODICALS

Australian Book Review, Children's Supplement, 1964, 1967, 1969.

Booklist, May 1, 1991, Carolyn Phelan, review of *Rotten Egg Patterson to the Rescue,* p. 1716.

Books & Bookmen, July, 1968.

Bulletin of the Center for Children's Books, November, 1966; April, 1979; January, 1991, Betsy Hearne, review of *Jodie's Journey,* p. 130.

Childhood Education, December, 1966; April, 1967.

Children's Book Review Service, January, 1991, Barbara Baker, review of *Jodie's Journey.*

Five Owls, May, 1996, review of *Storm Boy,* p. 104.

Kirkus Reviews, January 1, 1966.

Magpies, September, 1991, Maurice Saxby, review of *Farmer Pelz's Pumpkins,* pp. 29-30; July, 1992, Jenni Connor, review of *Emma Keppler,* p. 31; September, 1992, Anne Hanzl, review of *Speedy,* p. 29; May, 1993, Don Pemberton, review of *The Australian ABC,* p. 25; July, 1994, Mandy Cheetham, review of *The March of Mother Duck,* p. 30; July, 1994, Virginia Lowe, review of *Timmy,* p. 29; July, 1995, Glenn Jones, review of *Brahminy,* p. 28; July, 1996, Mandy Cheetham, review of *High Valley,* p. 32; May, 1998, John Murray, review of *Landslide,* p. 35; May, 1999, Russ Merrin, review of *The Monster Fish,* p. 28.

New York Times Book Review, May 1, 1966; February 23, 1975.

Publishers Weekly, March 24, 1989.

School Library Journal, August, 1991, Yvonne A. Frey, review of *Rotten Egg Patterson to the Rescue,* p. 169.

Young Readers Review, September, 1966.

V–Y

VIZZINI, Ned 1981-

Personal

Born April 4, 1981, in New York, NY; son of James D. (an executive vice president) and Emma (a chief executive officer) Vizzini. *Education:* Attends Hunter College, 2000—. *Religion:* Lutheran.

Addresses

Home—New York, NY. *Office*—c/o Author Mail, Free Spirit Publishing, 217 Fifth Ave. N., Ste. 200, Minneapolis, MN, 55401-1299. *E-mail*—nvizzini@yahoo.com.

Career

Freelance writer, 1996-2000; *New York Press,* New York, NY, contributing writer, 2001—. Former computer programmer at New York Cityscape, Edison Price Lighting.

Writings

Teen Angst? Naaah ...: A Quasi-Autobiography, Free Spirit Publishing (Minneapolis, MN), 2000.

Contributor of articles to newspapers and magazines, including *New York Press, Teen,* and *New York Times Magazine.*

Work in Progress

"Since When?," a weekly column for *New York Press.*

Sidelights

Ned Vizzini has been writing from a very early age. In high school, he sent off an essay about winning a school literary prize to the *New York Press,* a free newspaper he often read on his way to class. He eventually became a columnist for the paper, and the essays he wrote on family vacations, the prom, playing Nintendo as an antidote to the boredom of being a teenager, and so

"Zany, tender, and hysterically funny. . . ."

Teen Angst? Naaah...

free spirit PUBLISHING

A Quasi-Autobiography by **Ned Vizzini**

With good humor and intelligence, nineteen-year-old Ned Vizzini writes about his junior and senior high school experiences in **Teen Angst? Naaah—A Quasi-Autobiography.**

forth, earned him an invitation to contribute an article of advice for teenagers to the *New York Times.* These columns also became the core of his first book, *Teen Angst? Nah ...: A Quasi-Autobiography,* published when the author was nineteen years old. In the essays, Vizzini comes across as geeky, intelligent, and funny, critics noted. Ironic sidebars written by the more mature author as the book went into print comment on the original essays, and the book concludes with an index that stands alone as a piece of comic writing. Through it all, Vizzini's observations have a ring of truth to them, according to reviewers, that seems vindicated since the author was between the ages of fifteen and seventeen when he wrote them.

The critical response to *Teen Angst?* was generally positive. "[Vizzini's] wonderfully sardonic voice, like Daniel Pinkwater's in *The Education of Robert Nifkin,* suggests a wisdom beyond his years," remarked Laura Glaser in *School Library Journal.* Other reviewers emphasized the humorous aspect of Vizzini's unglamorous tales of high school life. "He's gifted but gawky, adventurous yet filled with anxiety. Most of all, he shows a real talent for self-deprecating humor," wrote a reviewer for *Publishers Weekly.* Although *Booklist* contributor Todd Morning claimed that Vizzini's humor "occasionally . . . seems forced," he also concluded that both teenagers and adults would find much they could agree with in *Teen Angst?.*

Vizzini has the following advice for aspiring authors: "Write what you know, and kill your darlings, which means get rid of the stuff that sounds good to you and you alone," Vizzini told Lauren Beckham Falcone in the *Boston Herald.* "That's the hard part. The easy part is submitting. Prepare to be rejected, but, really, just have the guts to do it."

Biographical and Critical Sources

PERIODICALS

Booklist, October 15, 2000, Todd Morning, review of *Teen Angst?,* pp. 428, 431.

Boston Herald, June 12, 2000, Lauren Beckham Falcone, "Write-Minded."

Publishers Weekly, July 31, 2000, review of *Teen Angst?,* p. 97.

School Library Journal, November, 2000, Laura Glaser, review of *Teen Angst?,* p. 177.

*   *   *

WEAVER, Robyn
See CONLEY-WEAVER, Robyn

*   *   *

WEAVER, Robyn M.
See CONLEY-WEAVER, Robyn

*   *   *

WHITMORE, Arvella 1922-

Personal

Born March 14, 1922; daughter of Horace Crandell (a surgeon) and Marguerite Krier (a homemaker) Embry; married Page G. Whitmore (an electrical engineer), October 3, 1953; children: Bruce, Clark, Laura Ranum, Diane Whitmore-Hagger. *Education:* Christian College (now Columbia College), A.A., 1942; Washburn University, A.B., L.L.B., 1944; University of Iowa, M.A., 1947. *Religion:* Episcopalian.

Addresses

Home and office—5228 W. Lake Nokomis Parkway, Minneapolis, MN 55417. *E-mail*—arvellawhitmore@aol.com.

Career

Author. Head of Speech and Drama Department, Marymount College, Salina, KS; former director, Twig Theater (a theater troupe performing in Minneapolis schools). *Member:* Society of Children's Book Writers and Illustrators, American Association of University Women (chair, Writers' Workshop).

Awards, Honors

Notable Children's Trade Book in Social Studies, National Council for the Social Studies/Children's Book Council, 1990, for *The Bread Winner;* Best Book for Young Adults, American Library Association, and Young Adult Award, Society of Midland Authors, both 2000, both for *Trapped between the Lash and the Gun;*

Arvella Whitmore

nominated for the Minnesota Book Award, young adult category, 2000; nominated for young adult choice awards in Minnesota, Pennsylvania, and Nevada, all 2002.

Writings

You're a Real Hero, Amanda, Houghton Mifflin (Boston, MA), 1985.
The Bread Winner, Houghton Mifflin (Boston, MA), 1990.
Trapped between the Lash and the Gun: A Boy's Journey, Dial (New York, NY), 1999.

Work in Progress

Research on early Kansas history.

Sidelights

Arvella Whitmore told *SATA:* "I hold a master's degree in speech and theater from the University of Iowa. Before starting my career as a children's author, I taught speech and theater, married and raised four children, and wrote and directed plays which were performed in the Minneapolis Public Schools."

Whitmore has written three novels for young adults, each an unusual coming-of-age story in which a young person finds within him or herself the courage to face down adversity. In her first book, *You're a Real Hero, Amanda,* fifth-grader Amanda's small-town Midwestern life in 1931 revolves around her pet rooster, Mazda. Given to Amanda as a chick by her dying grandmother the year before, Mazda is especially dear to the young girl. But Amanda's troubles begin when an ordinance forbidding chickens within city limits is passed and suddenly her pet is an outlaw. She tries to hide him from everyone, especially from the stranger who offers to train him to be a fighting cock, but he eventually goes missing. Amanda's troubles are compounded by her discovery that a local beauty has been seduced by the same man she suspects of stealing Mazda, becoming pregnant. Barbara Lynn, who reviewed *You're a Real Hero, Amanda* for *Voice of Youth Advocates,* praised the accuracy of Whitmore's depiction of small-town life in the early days of the Depression, saying, "the attitudes and morals of the times are clearly brought to life through the unwanted pregnancy of Virginia Thornhill, a very confusing situation to a ten-year-old girl in 1931," Lynn remarked. Amanda's sometimes humorous travails with her chicken teach her a few things about growing up, but it is the weightier subplot of Virginia's plight that forces Whitmore's heroine into some serious thinking about important issues. The result is "a highly readable yet complex coming-of-age story that takes young people to some unexpected places," claimed Ilene Cooper in *Booklist.*

Whitmore's second young adult novel, *The Bread Winner,* features another young girl of heroic proportions struggling with big problems during the Depression. "Twelve-year-olds often dream of being the hero or heroine, of saving someone from the brink of disaster," remarked Pat Costello in *Voice of Youth Advocates.* In *The Bread Winner,* readers find a plucky girl who saves her family from financial ruin by baking and selling her prize-winning bread. "The engaging characters, the well-developed plot, as well as the believable dialogue make this a sure-fire winner with the middle school reader," predicted Costello. Sarah overcomes a series of obstacles on her way to saving her family, including confronting a bully at her new school and standing up to a hobo who tries to steal the cash box in her new storefront. While a reviewer for *Publishers Weekly* found her unrelenting high spirits in the face of adversity a little less than believable, the critic did add, "Sarah's reactions to her parents' despair are both convincing and moving, and it's impossible not to admire her never-say-die attitude."

Whitmore took a step back from her own experience growing up during the Depression in the American Midwest with the publication of *Trapped between the Lash and the Gun: A Boy's Journey.* Here she creates an African-American male protagonist in a contemporary urban setting, where the lure of gang membership is stronger than bonds to family members, and then transports him back in time to the antebellum South. There Jordan not only experiences firsthand what it is like to be a slave, but he also learns to respect the other slaves and discovers the courage it takes to stand up for what is right. "Whitmore smoothly weaves the strands of history with the quest for personal identity into a story that powerfully illustrates the horrors of slave life," wrote Cindy Lombardo in *Voice of Youth Advocates.* Although *Booklist* reviewer Hazel Rochman faulted Whitmore's writing style in this work, she also noted that "The time travel will draw readers in and so will the well-researched detail of what is was like to be a slave."

Biographical and Critical Sources

PERIODICALS

Booklist, December 15, 1985, Ilene Cooper, review of *You're a Real Hero, Amanda,* p. 632; November 15, 1998, Hazel Rochman, review of *Trapped between the Lash and the Gun: A Boy's Journey,* p. 591.
Bulletin of the Center for Children's Books, February, 1986, review of *You're a Real Hero, Amanda,* p. 119.
Publishers Weekly, September 14, 1990, review of *The Bread Winner,* p. 126; December 21, 1998, review of *Trapped between the Lash and the Gun: A Boy's Journey,* p. 68.
Voice of Youth Advocates, February, 1986, Barbara Lynn, review of *You're a Real Hero, Amanda,* p. 387; October, 1990, Pat Costello, review of *The Bread Winner,* p. 222; April, 1999, Cindy Lombardo, review of *Trapped between the Lash and the Gun: A Boy's Journey,* p. 52.

WOOG, Adam 1953-

Personal

Born August 17, 1953, in Seattle, WA; son of Alan H. (an environmental forester) and Ronnie Baumgarten (an artist; maiden name, Friedman) Woog; married Karen L. Kent (a geriatric psychotherapist), April 10, 1988; children: Leah Marie. *Education:* Fairhaven College and Simon Fraser University, B.A., 1975; Antioch University, M.A., 1980. *Hobbies and other interests:* Reading, hiking, beer-making, bread-making.

Addresses

Home and office—8016 Meridian Ave. N., Seattle, WA 98103.

Career

Freelance writer, 1982—. *Kansai Time Out,* Kobe, Japan, music editor, 1982-84; International Christian University, Tokyo, Japan, writing instructor, 1984-86; Kodansha International, Tokyo, copy editor, 1984-86; *Seattle Times,* Seattle, WA, book reviewer, author, and interviewer, 1986—, jazz critic, 1986-90, staff reporter, 1987; *Seattle Home and Garden,* Seattle, contributing editor, 1989-91.

Awards, Honors

Writing Scholarship, Seattle Music and Art Foundation, 1970; Second Place, Lifestyles, Sigma Delta Chi Awards, 1983, for "Let's Japan"; First Place, Columns, Sigma Delta Chi Awards, 1987, for "The Floating Life"; First Place, History, Washington Press Association Annual Communicator Competition, 1991, for *Sexless Oysters and Self-Tipping Hats; Harry Houdini* and *Louis Armstrong* were named to the New York Public Library Books for the Teen Age list, 1995.

Writings

Sexless Oysters and Self-Tipping Hats: 100 Years of Invention in the Pacific Northwest, Sasquatch (Seattle, WA), 1991.

(With Harriet Baskas) *Atomic Marbles and Branding Irons: A Guide to Museums, Collections, and Roadside Curiosities in Washington and Oregon,* Sasquatch (Seattle, WA), 1993.

Poltergeists: Opposing Viewpoints ("Great Mysteries" series), second edition, Lucent (San Diego, CA), 1994.

The United Nations ("Overview" series), Lucent (San Diego, CA), 1994.

Suicide ("Overview" series), Lucent (San Diego, CA), 1997.

Amelia Earhart ("Mysterious Deaths" series), Lucent (San Diego, CA), 1997.

Marilyn Monroe ("Mysterious Deaths" series), Lucent (San Diego, CA), 1997.

The Shark ("Endangered Animals and Habitats" series), Lucent (San Diego, CA), 1998.

Roosevelt and the New Deal ("World History" series), Lucent (San Diego, CA), 1998.

The History of Rock and Roll ("World History" series), Lucent (San Diego, CA), 1999.

The 1900s ("A Cultural History of the United States through the Decades" series), Lucent (San Diego, CA), 1999.

(With Rick Marino) *Be Elvis! A Guide to Impersonating the King,* Sourcebooks (Naperville, IL), 2000.

Crossroads: The Collection of the Experience Music Project, Marquand Books, 2000.

Killer Whales ("Nature's Predators" series), Kidhaven Press, 2002.

"THE IMPORTANCE OF . . ." SERIES

Harry Houdini, Lucent (San Diego, CA), 1995.
Louis Armstrong, Lucent (San Diego, CA), 1995.
Duke Ellington, Lucent (San Diego, CA), 1996.
Elvis Presley, Lucent (San Diego, CA), 1997.
The Beatles, Lucent (San Diego, CA), 1998.
Frank Sinatra, Lucent (San Diego, CA), 2001.

"PEOPLE IN THE NEWS" SERIES

Bill Gates, Lucent (San Diego, CA), 1999.
Steven Spielberg, Lucent (San Diego, CA), 1999.
George Lucas, Lucent (San Diego, CA), 2000.

"HISTORY MAKERS" SERIES

Gangsters, Lucent (San Diego, CA), 2000.
Magicians and Illusionists, Lucent (San Diego, CA), 2000.
Rock and Roll Legends, Lucent (San Diego, CA), 2001.

OTHER

Also contributor to books, including *Handbook of Acoustic Ecology,* World Soundscape Project (Vancouver, Canada), 1974; *Japan,* Gaimusho (Tokyo, Japan), 1984; *1992 Fodor's Pacific North Coast Guide,* Random

In Roosevelt and the New Deal, *Adam Woog examines former U.S. President Franklin Roosevelt's policies and programs that led the country out of the Great Depression. (Photograph from the Library of Congress.)*

House (New York, NY); and *1993 Seattle Access,* HarperCollins (New York, NY). Contributor to inflight magazines for airlines including Aer Lingus, All Nippon, American, Cathay Pacific, Northwest, TWA, United, and USAir; contributor to periodicals, including *Chicago Tribune, San Francisco Chronicle, USA Today, Seattle Rocket,* and *Village Voice;* contributor to overseas publications, including *Hikari, Japan Times, Tokyo Journal, Asia 2000,* and *The Emigrant;* contributor to CD-ROM publications, including *Encarta* (encyclopedia), Microsoft, 1993, and *The Magic School Bus Inside the Human Body* and *The Magic School Bus in Outer Space,* Microsoft/Scholastic, 1994.

Sidelights

Adam Woog writes informative biographies for teenagers on personalities ranging from jazz great Louis Armstrong to software billionaire Bill Gates. He has also tackled endangered animals and political matters for Lucent, a San Diego-based publishing house. Woog was born in the Seattle area and graduated from Simon Fraser University in 1975. He went on to earn a master's degree before moving to Japan. As he recalled, "I became a writer by default. My background and previous work experience had been in radio when, in 1980, I moved overseas. The interviewing skills I'd learned were then put to use as I began to freelance magazine and newspaper pieces, which I did full-time beginning in 1982." In Japan, Woog worked as the music editor for a local English-language paper for two years, taught writing at the university level, then became a copy editor in Tokyo.

"By the time I returned to my home town of Seattle in 1986," Woog continued, "I had developed a specialty: writing for airline inflight magazines. I continued in this vein until my schedule and work habits received a rude shock: in December, 1990, my daughter, Leah, was born, and I became a full-time father (my wife, Karen, has a 'real' job—she's a geriatric psychotherapist).

"During my daughter's first year, I wrote my first book. Leah is now in school, which means that (although I'm still the primary parent and full-time cook in our household) I get something like a twenty-hour work week. I now spend my work time on book projects—all nonfiction, some for students and some for grown-ups. The subject matter has ranged from inventions to unusual museums, from Harry Houdini to Louis Armstrong. I love writing biography, and I find myself irresistibly drawn, over and over, to unusual topics."

Woog has extensive experience as a music writer—he served as jazz critic for the *Seattle Times* for four years—and this led him into his first books for Lucent: *Louis Armstrong,* published in 1995, and *Duke Ellington,* which appeared the following year. The latter biography sketches the American-born jazz pianist who began playing in Harlem and went on to achieve international fame in the 1920s. Ilene Cooper, writing in *Booklist,* noted that though much of Woog's text was

The difficult subject of suicide, its causes, and possible prevention is covered in great detail by Woog in **Suicide.** *(Photograph from UPI/Bettman.)*

culled from lengthier biographies on Ellington, "this still has a readable style of its own."

Woog has also written about Elvis Presley, the Beatles, and Frank Sinatra. He penned an overview of one genre in *The History of Rock and Roll,* published in 1999. Woog begins by providing a definition of the genre, then moving forward to chronicle the leading innovators and how their work found its audience. Tim Wadham, writing in *School Library Journal,* commended initial sections that, he asserted, give readers "a pretty good sense of how [rock and roll] evolved, as well as with an appreciation for African influences."

Woog has written two 1997 titles about Amelia Earhart and Marilyn Monroe for Lucent's "Mysterious Deaths" series. In the first book, Woog recounts the fascinating story of the first aviatrix to attempt to circumnavigate the globe—a 1937 journey on which she vanished while over the South Pacific. Much of the work is given over to discussion of the various theories regarding her disappearance. Some of these scenarios involve a foreign enemy or spy work, for relations between Japan and the United States were somewhat hostile at the time. "All of the speculations make for engrossing reading," declared Susan F. Marcus in *School Library Journal,* reviewing the Earhart book. In Woog's chronicle of the death of film star Marilyn Monroe, a huge celebrity in her day, he presents the unusual circumstances of her death, the investigation into it, and the wildly speculative guesses about possible foul play. "The theories put forward range from the ludicrous to the truly distasteful," remarked Wadham in *School Library Journal.*

For Lucent's "Overview" series, Woog penned *Suicide,* which discusses the various theories about why people take their own lives. Some of the explanations involve brain chemistry or sociological matters, but as one reviewer noted, Woog makes no particular case for any of the reasons. Because the book is aimed at middle-school readers, it offers a special chapter on teen suicide and contains extensive information at the end about warning signs of suicide and where to go for help. Other sections discuss the impact that suicide has on those left behind. Joyce Adams Burner, writing in *School Library Journal,* commended the "clear and impartial manner" in which Woog writes about a difficult subject.

In *Magicians and Illusionists,* published in 2000, Woog writes about Harry Houdini, whose life he had previously chronicled, and seven other entertainers from the nineteenth and twentieth centuries. They range from forgotten illusionists, once famous in their day, to contemporary favorites, including David Copperfield and Penn and Teller. Ann G. Brouse, writing in *School Library Journal,* called Woog's profiles of Hermann the Great and Jasper Maskeldyne "especially valuable." Woog wrote *Poltergeists* for middle-school readers, delving into the phenomenon of spirits who disturb objects and people. He presents several case stories of homes whose owners believed a poltergeist was present, and then writes extensively about several investigators who devoted their lives to tracking—and in some cases, solving—such supernatural phenomena. The chapters also note the ways in which investigative techniques have improved over generations. Brouse, writing in *School Library Journal,* compared *Poltergeists* to another work on the subject for younger readers, but lauded Woog's book for "providing a deeper look into this puzzling subject."

Woog has also written titles for Lucent's "People in the News" series, beginning with *Bill Gates* in 1999. Here, he details the life and achievements of the Microsoft Corporation founder. Gates, as Woog's chapters reveal, revolutionized the personal-computer industry but became a controversial figure in the process. Debbie Feulner, reviewing *Bill Gates* for *School Library Journal,* compared it to another biography of Gates for teens and found Woog's version "more detailed and better balanced."

Biographical and Critical Sources

PERIODICALS

Booklist, February 15, 1996, Ilene Cooper, review of *Duke Ellington,* p. 1004.

Children's Book Review Service, February, 1999, John E. Boyd, review of *The 1900s,* p. 80.

Horn Book Guide, spring, 1994, p. 101; spring, 1997, Barbara Barstow, review of *Suicide,* p. 95; spring, 1997, Peter D. Sieruta, review of *Marilyn Monroe,* p. 96, and review of *Elvis Presley,* p. 157; fall, 1997, Sheryl Lee Saunders, review of *Amelia Earhart,* p. 381.

Library Journal, March 1, 1993, p. 50.

Los Angeles Times Book Review, December 29, 1991, p. 10.

School Library Journal, March, 1994, p. 245; January, 1995, Sandra L. Doggett, review of *Harry Houdini,* p. 142; March, 1995, Ann G. Brouse, review of *Poltergeists,* p. 234; February, 1996, Robin Works Davis, review of *Duke Ellington,* p. 122; March, 1997, Susan F. Marcus, review of *Amelia Earhart,* p. 203; March, 1997, Tim Wadham, review of *Marilyn Monroe,* p. 212; April, 1997, Joyce Adams Burner, review of *Suicide,* p. 164; December, 1997, Tim Wadham, review of *The Beatles,* p. 150; August, 1998, Linda Beck, review of *Roosevelt and the New Deal,* p. 186; April, 1999, Debbie Feulner, review of *The 1900s,* p. 157, and review of *Bill Gates,* p. 160; November, 1999, Tim Wadham, review of *The History of Rock and Roll,* p. 178; March, 2000, Ann G. Brouse, review of *Magicians and Illusionists,* p. 263.

*   *   *

YORK, Rebecca
See GLICK, Ruth (Burtnick)

Cumulative Indexes

Illustrations Index

(In the following index, the number of the *volume* in which an illustrator's work appears is given *before* the colon, and the *page number* on which it appears is given *after* the colon. For example, a drawing by Adams, Adrienne appears in Volume 2 on page 6, another drawing by her appears in Volume 3 on page 80, another drawing in Volume 8 on page 1, and so on and so on . . . .)

YABC

Index references to *YABC* refer to listings appearing in the two-volume *Yesterday's Authors of Books for Children,* also published by The Gale Group. *YABC* covers prominent authors and illustrators who died prior to 1960.

Illustrations Index

Author Index

The following index gives the number of the volume in which an author's biographical sketch, Autobiography Feature, Brief Entry, or Obituary appears.

This index includes references to all entries in the following series, which are also published by The Gale Group.

YABC—*Yesterday's Authors of Books for Children: Facts and Pictures about Authors and Illustrators of Books for Young People from Early Times to 1960*

CLR—*Children's Literature Review: Excerpts from Reviews, Criticism, and Commentary on Books for Children*

SAAS—*Something about the Author Autobiography Series*

C

Author Index